WHEN KIDS CAN'T READ

JAW

WHEN KIDS CAN'T READ

WHAT TEACHERS CAN DO

A Guide for Teachers 6–12

Kylene Beers

HEINEMANN
PORTSMOUTH, NH

Heinemann

361 Hanover Street
Portsmouth, NH 03801–3912
www.heinemann.com

Offices and agents throughout the world

The author and publisher wish to thank those who have generously given permission to reprint borrowed material:

Excerpts from *Reading Strategies Handbook for High School: A Guide to Teaching Reading in the Literature Classroom* by Kylene Beers. Copyright © 2000 by Holt, Rinehart and Winston. Reprinted by permission of the publisher.

"Grandmother Grace" from *Tunes for Bears To Dance To* by Ronald Wallace. Copyright © 1983 by Ronald Wallace. Reprinted by permission of the University of Pittsburgh Press.

"old age sticks" from *Complete Poems 1904–1962* by E. E. Cummings, edited by George J. Firmage. Copyright © 1958, 1986, 1991 by the Trustees for the E. E. Cummings Trust. Used by permission of Liveright Publishing Corporation.

Excerpt from "Taking the Guesswork Out of Spelling" by Jay Richards in *Voices from the Middle,* March 2002. Reprinted by permission of the National Council of Teachers of English.

Photo credits and thanks are due to Sandy Hayes, Mary Ings, Shirley Lyons, Romy Cassack, Meredith Hulen, and Meredith Beers who took pictures of students or the author working with students and/or teachers in Texas, Florida, and Minnesota.

Library of Congress Cataloging-in-Publication Data
Beers, G. Kylene, 1957–
    When kids can't read, what teachers can do : a guide for teachers,
6–12 / Kylene Beers.
      p. cm.
    Includes bibliographical references and index.
    ISBN 0-86709-519-9 (pbk. : alk. paper)
    1. Reading—Remedial teaching.   2. Reading (Middle school).   3. Reading
(Secondary).   I. Title.
LB1050.5 .B45 2003
428.4'071'2—dc21

                                    2002011670

EDITOR: *Lisa Luedeke*
PRODUCTION: *Lynne Reed*
COVER DESIGN: *Judy Arisman*
TEXT DESIGN: *Jenny Jensen Greenleaf*
TYPESETTER: *TechBooks*
MANUFACTURING: *Steve Bernier*

Printed in the United States of America on acid-free paper
    09 10 11 12   ML   15 16 17

This book is dedicated to

Bonnie Singer, my mom, for being a lighthouse in my life;
Ed Farrell for remaining my teacher long after the semester ended;
and George for showing me what happens when kids can't read.

Contents

A Defining Moment

I approach writing this book with fear and conviction. The fear comes from worrying that, though I bring to this task twenty-three years of teaching experience and about twelve years of direct work with struggling readers, somehow I'll get it all wrong. I worry that I'll write something inaccurately, leave out the single most important strategy we should all know, misrepresent a student, mislabel someone's comments, or be so boring that you'll set the book aside. Putting those fears into words, actually confronting them, doesn't make them less daunting and certainly doesn't make them go away. So I summarized them onto an index card that I taped to my desk beside my computer when I began writing. It said simply, "Get it right."

The conviction comes from my absolute certainty that, first, teachers want to help the struggling readers who sit in their classrooms; second, those students want to be helped; and, third, the right instruction can make a difference. Many of us who are secondary teachers (I'll use that term throughout this book to describe teachers in either middle or high school) never anticipated needing to help students learn to read when we first entered this profession. Many of us with secondary certificates had nothing more than a content area reading course (if that) in our teacher-preparation courses. So, for some of us, recognizing that we can help those students requires time; understanding how to do that takes even more.

Those kids who struggle with texts were not the children I'd planned on teaching. My goal as I finished my degree at the University of Texas in 1979 was to be a twelfth-grade AP literature teacher. I'd expected to walk down polished hallways of a well-ordered high school to arrive in a small, cozy classroom that held well-read volumes of the great works of literature, thus giving the room that slightly musty smell of a small-town library or a used bookstore. I anticipated moving down the school halls (holding my steaming cup of coffee in one hand and a stack of brilliantly written essays in the other) only to be constantly stopped by students wanting to know if they could drop by after school to continue our discussion of *The Great Gatsby* or *Native Son* or *My Antonia.* I thought I'd be the sponsor of the grammar club, where we'd celebrate the triumph of traditional grammar over transformational grammar, and debate the finer points of *that* and *which* and the serial comma. It never entered my mind that some of my students would not know how to read; I presumed they would embrace books with the same passion I did. They would mourn the moment when our class would end and they would have to leave the world of Dickens or Ellison, Poe or Hughes to reenter the corridors of our school.

And then I got my first teaching job.

During the last semester of my senior year at UT, I began to search for a teaching position. It appeared I was not alone in my desire to teach twelfth-grade AP literature. Furthermore, I soon discovered that once that position was secured, that teacher never left. In other words, the inn was full. Finally, I had an interview with the Alief School District. I didn't know what an Alief was, or where it was, but I did have a postcard saying they would be happy to meet with me. As I walked into my interview, I heard the two men who would be talking with me say, "All these women, they all want to teach high school English." The other agreed and said, "Sure wish someone, anyone, wanted to teach middle school."

Now, it's important to note that I didn't know what a middle school was in the spring of 1979. I grew up in a small town in east Texas in the days of the junior high, and although I had done my student-teaching in a junior high, I had never even heard the term *middle school.* It's also important to know that as I walked into that interview, I was carrying in my purse a letter from my dad. It said, "My darling daughter—get a job."

So, with those tender words of advice, I walked into that meeting. The men didn't even look up. One said, "What's your name?" I told him.

The other said, "And what do you want to teach?"

I paused, took a breath, and boldly proclaimed, "I want to teach—middle school!"

Both men looked up simultaneously and then asked in unison what is perhaps the single most important question I've ever been asked in my career: "Why?"

I muttered something about it being a challenge. Little did I know how right that was! I left that interview a short time later with a teaching job at a middle school in Alief.

My first goal was to find Alief (it's a large school district with 42,000+ students located in the southwest part of the Greater Houston Area Metroplex). My second goal was to figure out what a middle school was. I quickly discovered that it was sort of like a junior high, only with sixth grade added. My assignment was to teach seventh-grade language arts, which didn't daunt me at all. My plan was still to teach twelfth-grade AP literature, just to do it with seventh graders. Needless to say, that plan didn't last long.

That first year of teaching is etched in my mind with a clarity that I sometimes wish would fade. If not for my two teammates, I doubt I would have returned for year two. These women, veteran teachers, took this "rookie" (as they loved to call me) under their tutelage and began to teach me how to be a teacher. Our school was an open-concept school, so the social studies teacher, the math teacher, and I shared a huge open space—along with the 153 students we saw throughout the day. We taught six periods of the seven-period day. I had fourth period off so I could serve as lunch monitor.

Within the first few days of school, I made some important discoveries, the most important being that my vision of how schools run was some sort of warped blend of *Room 222* (some of you reading this won't have a clue what that references and thus we learn the first lesson in the importance of background knowledge), the classroom Opie attended in that idyllic town of Mayberry, and personal memories of my own twelfth-grade English classroom, which really *was* filled with wonderful musty-smelling books and essays that at least my classmates and I thought were brilliant.

I should have been thinking *Welcome Back, Kotter.*

My students, precious though they were, overwhelmed me. There were *so* many of them. Student-teaching one class of twenty-eight students with the cooperating teacher sitting at the back of the classroom was so much easier, so much more manageable. Plus, the assistant principal at our school, a woman named Anne Black, whom I respected and admired, had given me all the wrong students. I explained to her after a few weeks of teaching that I had wanted the *literary* ones. Instead, she had given me students who didn't like to read. Well, that's not entirely true. Some were inveterate readers, and I latched onto them like a drowning swimmer clutches a buoy. But as many as half of my students didn't like to read, and half of those *couldn't* read. These were most certainly not the students I had in mind while studying literature, composition, and grammar in the English department at the University of Texas.

> But as many as half of my students didn't like to read, and half of those couldn't read. These were most certainly not the students I had in mind while studying literature, composition, and grammar in the English department at the University of Texas.

As I patiently explained all this to Anne, she merely nodded her head, peered at me over the tops of her half-rimmed glasses, and then replied simply, "I'll make a note." She didn't change one thing.

If I was confused by students who *didn't like* to read, then I was absolutely confounded by those who *couldn't* read. I had no idea why they couldn't read. I also had no way (or perhaps "no interest" is a more honest statement) to systematically uncover what their reading difficulties were. In all my years of study at UT, I did not have one class in reading. If I had wanted to teach reading, then I would have pursued an elementary degree and looked for a first-grade teaching position. So, I began a chant that I repeated to all who would listen: "These kids can't read." With that simple phrase, I relegated my students who couldn't decode to the same position as students who could say the words but couldn't make sense of what they had read. Equally frustrated by both groups, I took care of the problem by placing the blame squarely on my students' shoulders: these kids can't read. With this refrain, I removed myself from responsibility.

Then, in October of that first year, something happened that has guided my path as a teacher ever since. Anne called me into her office one afternoon and asked me to come in early the next morning. It seemed that George's parents had requested a conference with me.

George was a student in one of my classes. Though he tried hard, George couldn't read. By that, I mean there were many multisyllabic words George couldn't decode and plenty of single-syllable words that caused him to stumble. When he did manage to get through a story, he'd stare blankly at the page as I asked questions. His favorite response to any comprehension question was, "I dunno," said with a shrug of the shoulders and a raise of the eyebrows that said, "Stop asking me questions." I thought of George's slumped posture, messy notebook, stubbled pencil, and hooded eyes as Anne repeated that his parents wanted to meet with me.

"Whatever for?" I asked, suddenly fearing my first parent-teacher conference.

"You're his language arts teacher. They want to know why he can't read and what you're going to do to help him."

"But Anne," I pleaded, "I don't know why he can't read. He can't read. That's it. He just can't read." Anne peered again over those half-rimmed glasses and told me I had the night to figure it out.

I spent that evening going through the one book I had from my college days that I thought would come closest to helping me understand George's reading problems: *The Norton Anthology of Short Stories.* But no, nothing in those hundreds of onion-thin pages gave me any insight into

George's difficulties. So, the next morning I walked into the school for what was not only my first parent-teacher conference but a conference in which I had nothing to say. George's father, mother, and Anne sat there, waiting.

George's father began: "We are here today to discuss with you George's reading problems." I nodded. He continued. "What we want is for you, his teacher, to tell us what those problems are." I kept nodding. Slowly, reluctantly, I began to speak.

"Well, George's problems, which are problems in reading, are therefore identified as *reading* problems." I paused. "These problems, reading problems to be specific, are problems in . . . " and suddenly, I knew the answer. Like it was delivered to me on a platter, I knew what to say. "They are problems in comprehension." Surely that was the answer. *Comprehension* is a somewhat technical term most often linked to discussions about reading. And the answer seemed to work. George's father began to nod his head. George's mother nodded her head. Anne nodded her head. I most certainly nodded mine.

Then suddenly George's father announced, "We know that." All heads stopped nodding.

"What does that mean?" he asked, none too happy.

I was undaunted. I could answer this question, for surely he just needed a synonym for comprehension. "That would mean," I responded, "that George has a problem with understanding." I stopped. Not a single head nodded.

I have no recollection of what happened next. I don't know what Anne or George's parents said. I don't know how we concluded the conference or how we exited the room. That memory is a blessed blank. What isn't a blank, though, is the absolute humiliation I felt sitting there in that room with those parents. It was apparent to all there that I had been hired to do a job—teach their son—and I didn't have a clue how to do that. I have carried that humiliation with me all these years, to every time I tell George's story, to this moment as I write these words.

The year moved on toward May. George continued to show up every day, to sit in that front desk behind the overhead projector, to sleep more than not, to draw intricate pictures on the margins of every paper, to occasionally attempt whatever task I put before him, only to be more sullen when that little effort resulted in yet again another low grade. So, at the end of the school year, I failed him. I don't mean I retained George; I wasn't smart enough to contemplate such a move or wonder what retention might or might not accomplish. I mean I failed him in the truest way a teacher can fail a child: I never taught him anything he needed to acquire the literacy skills necessary for success in school, or in the world. I failed that child.

But George didn't fail me. George did what I have come to believe is one of the most powerful things an adolescent who struggles with literacy can do: George just showed up. Every day that year, George came to class. Yes, he certainly seemed disengaged from most of what we did, and it's true that he seldom brought his book to class or did anything that would prepare him for class, but he showed up. And occasionally he'd look at me with a look that asked if today would be the day that I'd get it right, if today would be the day that I'd say something that would help him make sense of text.

I've come to see that gesture of just showing up as a strength of character that continually amazes me. These students who struggle with reading know they struggle with reading; they know that they lack the single most important tool for success in school—the ability to read and make sense of texts—and they know that in not having that ability, they are open to ridicule from peers and from teachers. They do what I think is a last gesture at self-esteem: They choose to act as if reading doesn't matter. They sit slumped, heads on desk, or leaning back—far back—with arms crossed, sweatshirt hoods over their heads, sweatshirt sleeves stretched down over their hands, a look of disdain on their faces. They do anything they can to distance themselves from the place and the people who will remind them once again that they can't read. I don't blame them.

I can think of nothing that I do 186 days out of the year, in front of my peers, that I know I will consistently do poorly. Be honest. Can you think of anything *you* do that qualifies? I gave up tennis because it was too embarrassing to constantly run to that adjacent court and retrieve my errant ball. I stopped aerobics class, for I never could understand that grapevine-turn-around-dip thing, and I got tired of the instructor standing directly in front of me, shouting, "Cross-over *now.*" Yes, I certainly understand that if I had perhaps put in more effort, I'd have become a better tennis player, better aerobics student. But the embarrassment I'd have suffered while getting better outweighed my expectation for improvement, so I gave up.

Students who can't read also give up. At first, they give up trying. Eventually, many of them give up on school. They sit in our classrooms disengaged, disinterested, and sometimes defiant. These students would prefer to get in trouble with us for not doing their work rather than be embarrassed in front of their peers for doing it wrong. They give us the most they can: they show up. I believe we must celebrate the courage required to walk through the doors day after day of a place that is designed to reward those who can read when you know you are one of the ones who can't. Make no mistake. These students do not reach middle school or high school unaware that reading is a problem for them. They *know* they can't read; they've known it for years.

I don't know what happened to George. In that first year of teaching, I was more concerned about finishing the year than I was about tracking students over time. I can only hope that somewhere in his remaining years of school, some other teacher did what I failed to do and helped George become a member of the literacy community. Maybe that teacher already understood what I now understand—that when kids give up and drop out, they perpetuate the vicious cycle in which their offspring grow up in an aliterate environment and become the next generation of struggling readers whose teachers might chant: "These kids can't read."

> *Maybe that teacher already understood what I now understand—that when kids give up and drop out, they perpetuate the vicious cycle in which their offspring grow up in an aliterate environment and become the next generation of struggling readers whose teachers might chant: "These kids can't read."*

Now, more than two decades later, I find myself ready to answer George's parents, to discuss what can be done when kids can't read. I do not claim to know all the answers, but over the years some have emerged. I'll share two critical ones here. First, there is no one answer to understanding why an adolescent struggles with reading. For there to be only one answer, there would have to be only one cause, and for there to be one cause, all students would have to be alike, learn alike, have had the same experiences. Instead, there is no single template for the struggling reader. Second, while there is no *single* answer, there *are* answers. My chant of "These kids can't read," wasn't the wrong chant—they *couldn't* read. What *was* wrong was using that as an excuse for not teaching them. Once I was willing to add the question, "They can't read, so what am I to do?" then answers—not one, but many—began to emerge.

When Kids Can't Read explores those answers, offers direction for those of us who stand before students like George, who sit in small rooms with parents who wonder how we'll help their son or daughter, who know the consequences of failing a child. The fear I face in writing this book pales in comparison to the conviction I hold that we can make a difference. Guided by both, let's begin.

CHAPTER TWO

Creating Independent Readers

Dear George,

On yet another day you put your book on my desk and said, "I don't get it." I had heard this line from you before and, frankly, was frustrated to be hearing it again. I tried to be patient. "Did you read it?" I asked. You nodded. "Are you sure, George?" You nodded again. "Well, go read it again. You can get it."

Beginning to Listen

I think back to any one of many days that I encouraged George to "just reread it" and acknowledge that there's wisdom in that comment, but more important, I recognize the assumption that guided me for a long time: if they read it (the text), it (the meaning) will come. "Did you read it?" I asked. "Well, go read it again. You can get it." Meaning was obviously something in the text that George could surely grasp if he just read it often enough.

That same year that I taught George, I had a wonderful time spending Saturday afternoons with my friend's five-year-old daughter, Leah. One Saturday, I took Leah to the Houston Rodeo to see livestock up close and enjoy the excitement of the adjacent carnival. Leah was precocious, inquisitive, and generally willing to try any new adventure. At the Livestock Show, we marveled at Hereford, laughed at pigs rooting around sawdust-filled pens, watched sheep stand still as they were combed. At the carnival, we rode on an elephant, tossed rings over bowling pins, won a cake at the cakewalk, and then, for a final moment of fun, jumped on the carousel, a beautiful reproduction complete with ornately painted horses and the classic brass ring. Leah chose a blue horse near the outside edge, and I stood next to her, ready to catch her if this ride proved too much.

The first time by the brass ring, she asked what it was. "It's the brass ring," I explained.

We circled again. Again she asked, "What is that?"

Again I replied, "It's a ring made out of brass; it's called a brass ring. You're supposed to lean over and grab it."

On the third pass, Leah's hands clutched around the pole, the brass ring untouched. "So what it is?" she asked yet again over the calliope music.

"It's a thing; you're supposed to get it," I said. The ride slowed, then stopped. As we got off, she walked up to the brass ring and stood there, hands on nonexistent hips, a look of complete confusion on her face.

"So *what is it?*" she tried a fourth time.

I tried, too: "It's like a prize. See, you're on your horse and as the horse goes past it, you grab it. It's made out of a metal called brass so it's called a brass ring." She shook her head slowly as her frustration began to erupt.

"Are you listening to me at *all*? *How* do you grab it? And what do you grab it *for* and what do you do with it once you have it, and do you have to give it back? And why is it made out of brass? And is that like what our candlestick holders are made out of because they both are that shiny yellow? Is it heavy and if you drop it, then how do you get it without getting off your horse because the man said don't get off your horse until we come to a complete standstill and if you get it but don't drop it, then what do the other kids on their horses get to get?" Then, thankfully, she spotted the cotton candy and headed for that.

Look carefully at our exchange, and you'll see what was and wasn't being said in that conversation. The biggest problem was that four times her question remained the same: "What is it?" I, not understanding any of the subtext of her question—or perhaps not even recognizing there was a subtext—kept answering the question essentially the same way, though I believe I did move from not very helpful to not helpful at all:

First response: "It's the brass ring." Here, I offer her a straightforward definition.

Second response: "It's a ring made out of brass; it's called a brass ring. You're supposed to lean over and grab it." Now, I elaborate the definition a bit and add an explanation of what she's supposed to do.

Third response: "It's a thing; you're supposed to get it." I'm as confused as she is by this point, so I offer a simpler definition by substituting *thing* for *brass*. Brilliant.

Fourth response: "It's like a prize." Moving toward definition by analogy. "See, you're on your horse and as the horse goes past it, you grab it." Note that I can't seem to let go of what she's supposed to do with it. "It's made out of a metal called brass so it's called a brass ring." I obviously believe that if she understands the label "brass ring," all will be fine.

Finally, Leah asks if I'm listening at all. This is an interesting comment, as it shows that in her mind, she was asking all the questions that followed; I was simply not answering them. Look at what she heard embedded in "What is it?":

1. How do you grab it?
2. What do you grab it for?
3. What do you do with it once you have it?
4. Do you have to give it back?
5. Why is it made out of brass?
6. Is that like what our candlestick holders are made out of because they both are that shiny yellow?
7. Is it heavy?
8. If you drop it, then how do you get it without getting off your horse because the man said don't get off your horse until we come to a complete standstill?
9. If you get it but don't drop it, then what do the other kids on their horses get to get?

Once home from our day out, and after Leah's mom, Paula, and I had finished laughing over my obvious inability to communicate with a five-year-old, I thought a long time about all her embedded questions and about the nature and extent of George's embedded questions when he stated, "I don't get it." He must, I decided, have many more questions he's expecting me to answer. So now when George would approach my desk and say he didn't get it, we'd have a conversation like this:

GEORGE: I don't get it.
ME: Don't get what, George?
GEORGE: It.
ME: It what?
GEORGE: *It*. I don't get *it*.

Now I was the confused one. Why could a five-year-old identify all the things she still wanted to know about a brass ring when a twelve-year-old couldn't explain what he needed to know about a book?

ME: But, George, *it* has to stand for something. What is it that you don't understand?

GEORGE: The story.

ME: Great, George. This is good. What about the story?

GEORGE: I don't get it, the story. I don't get the story.

ME: What about it don't you get?

GEORGE: It. All of it.

I had written Leah's conversation with me on a card and looked at it often. It served as a tangible reminder that when George said, "I don't get it," there were probably lots of underlying questions in his mind. But unlike Leah, George lacked the ability to verbalize those questions. For him, the complexities of comprehension had been reduced to a single phrase: getting it.

That year with George was a lesson in patience. It was also a year that I sometimes found myself more interested in what kids were saying *about* what we were studying than what we *were* actually studying. Their conversations gave me a glimpse into what they were thinking, and often those glimpses were far more interesting than whatever conclusions they reached. I was beginning to learn that studying the *process* is far different than grading the product. That year, I found myself scribbling comments that students made on whatever sheet of paper I had handy—from the back of my grade-book to someone's spelling test. I loved capturing their words to read and reread later, not at all sure of what I was looking for, but positive that their thinking aloud was an indication of something important. I felt like an eavesdropper, and years later, was relieved to discover I could call these notes "anecdotal records."

Some of those early notes from conversations with George stayed in a file labeled "Year One" at the bottom of a box, almost forgotten until my family and I moved into our second house in the early 1990s. By then, I had finished my doctorate and written a dissertation on aliterate students. I knew then that though I was very interested in what causes a dislike of reading, I was more interested in working with students who couldn't read.

I pulled out that Year One file. My discoveries included my journal from that year, which is not worth sharing anywhere, and my notes on conversations with George and several other students. My interpretations or analyses of those conversations lacked, shall we say, depth. Here's an example:

GEORGE: Mrs. Beers?

ME: Yes, George?

Aliterate students are those students who can read, but choose not to read. These reluctant readers range from students who will read if we find them that one good book to students who claim to have never read a book in their lives. Read more about aliteracy in Chapter 13.

GEORGE: What's this word?

    [Pointing to *concerned*.]

ME: Did you sound it out, George?

GEORGE: [Long pause.] No.

ME: Well, there you go. You need to sound it out.

GEORGE: Sound out what?

ME: The word. Sound out the word.

GEORGE: Huh?

Notes: George needs help sounding out words.

Next day:

ME: George, come here.

GEORGE: Yes?

ME: George, let's work on sounding out this word.

    [Pointing to *concerned* written on a piece of paper].

GEORGE: Okay.

ME: Okay, so sound it out.

GEORGE: [Long pause.] Well, how do I sound it out if I can't read it?

ME: No, you can sound it out so you can read it.

GEORGE: Huh?

ME: Like this: /k-uh-n-s-r-n-d/.

GEORGE: Huh?

When letters appear between diagonal lines, don't read the word, but read the sounds that those letters make. So, /c-a-t/ isn't decoded as the word that means the animal that says meow, but instead as the sound that the letters *c*, *a*, and *t* make.

Notes: George needs *a lot* of help sounding out words.

Though I sometimes laugh and other times shudder at the notes I took that first year, I do recognize that those notes and the hundreds and hundreds that followed through the years are tangible proof of how my thinking about and understanding of reading have evolved.

Toward an Understanding of Reading

Initially, I thought that if I made sure kids could sound out all the words (something I remembered from my own days in elementary school) and made sure we practiced skills like finding the main idea (jump ahead to Chapter 4 right now if you want to see how well that went), then students would become readers—meaning they'd not only be able to understand whatever I put in front of them, they would also *like* to read. Originally, then, my model for helping students become skilled readers might have looked like what you see in Figure 2.1.

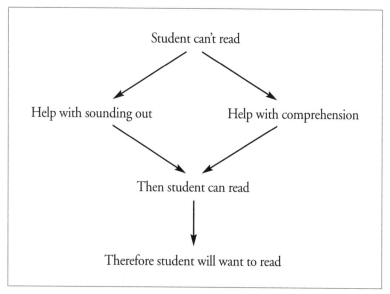

FIGURE 2.1 *Early model for working with struggling readers*

You'll note that even early on I didn't believe that decoding (sounding out) led to comprehension, though I did believe it was important. Also, I believed that if students could comprehend and decode, then they not only *could* read but *would* read. By that I assumed that they'd be willing to do all those things I envisioned happening in my classes: they would be willing participants in conversations discussing a range of texts; they'd linger over poignant passages and mull over thoughtful or controversial ideas. Put simply, they would think and talk passionately about what they had read. They would be independent readers—those readers who are skilled at the cognitive and affective demands of reading and see benefit in and derive pleasure from this skill.

Over the years, continued observation of students' reading behaviors and careful listening to their comments and conversations about this complicated act have helped me revise my understanding of how we assist students in becoming lifelong, independent readers. That knowledge has been refined most dramatically by my awareness that simply improving the cognitive aspects of reading (comprehension, vocabulary, decoding, and word recognition) does not ensure that the affective aspects of reading (motivation, enjoyment, engagement) will automatically improve. Now, I recognize that there are multiple aspects that must be addressed when working with struggling readers—beginning with defining *struggling reader*.

So Who Is a Struggling Reader?

For a moment, I want you to conjure up an image of a struggling reader in your class. Now, sit like that reader would sit in your room. Did you slump down into your seat? Did you put your head down on the table in front of you? Did you cross your arms, extend your legs, maybe turn around to doodle on the paper of the person behind you? (Okay, maybe you didn't do that—but some students would!) Everywhere I go throughout this nation to talk with teachers about struggling readers, I always ask them to do just that, to sit like a struggling reader would sit. And everywhere people do the same thing. Whether in Los Angeles, Spokane, Minneapolis, St. Louis, Palm Beach, Phoenix, Columbia, Fairfax, or Dallas—when asked to sit like a struggling reader, teachers choose one of three positions: slumped down, heads down, or bodies turned around.

I believe that when we can find that type of universal body language, we've got to pay attention to it. It means something. I'll return to the bigger implications of that language in Chapter 13, but for now I want to consider what it suggests when we all visualize that same type of student, this stereotypical posture of the struggling reader. I believe it suggests a stereotype that excludes more readers than it includes, that doesn't allow for diversity—something critical when studying adolescents who can't read. Remember in Chapter 1 I wrote, "There is no single template for the struggling reader"? I meant that. We cannot make the struggling reader fit one mold or expect one pattern to suffice for all students. Not all struggling readers sit at the back of the room, head down, sweatshirt hood pulled low, notebook crammed with papers that are filled with half-completed assignments, a bored expression, though that often is the image that springs to mind when we hear the term *struggling reader.*

Not all struggling readers sit at the back of the room, head down, sweatshirt hood pulled low, notebook crammed with papers that are filled with half-completed assignments, a bored expression, though that often is the image that springs to mind when we hear the term struggling reader.

Now think for a moment about the girl who sits about three seats back, usually over toward the side of the room. She's quiet, neat, and offers quick smiles right before she sticks a strand of hair into her mouth. She's the one who, after class is over, you're not sure was even in class. If you call on her, she'll answer, sometimes, in a soft voice that you strain to hear. She's got two or three best friends and hangs with them all the time. Not unhappy, just invisible. And sometimes she's a struggling reader.

Or think about the boy who always keeps the class laughing. He's cute, well-dressed, well-liked, and willing to run any errand for you (sure—it gets him out of class). If you call on him, he sometimes knows the answer, but most often he says something witty that gets the class laughing and, for a moment, even you forget he hasn't answered the question. He's popular, his parents are involved, and he can be a struggling reader.

Picture that new girl from Vietnam or Cambodia or Russia or Mexico who barely speaks English. She's confused in her new surroundings, goes home to where no English is spoken, and misses her previous school and friends. Or, perhaps she's been in your school for a while, but the transition to English is slow for her. You don't speak much Vietnamese and therefore can't communicate in her first language, and she doesn't say much to you in your language. You aren't sure if she can't read at all or just can't read English. She's supposed to read *To Kill a Mockingbird* in class this year, and she can't, just like she can't read her social studies or science books. She is certainly a struggling reader.

And then think about that student who is your gifted reader. This student is bound for AP English, if not already there. He's a good writer, a thoughtful reader, a willing debater, and you want to keep him in your class forever, for he's one of those students you dream of teaching. Give him the right text (which I guess from his point of view would be the wrong text) and he can stumble over ideas, worry over words, get lost in the sequence of events, become confused over who is the narrator. Another struggling reader.

So, as we struggle to define *struggling reader,* remember that that term may call to mind just one of those types of students—the sleeping, slumping, eye-rolling one—and ignore the rest.

Additionally, remember that *anyone* can struggle given the right text. The struggle isn't the issue; the issue is what the reader does when the text gets tough.

Independent and Dependent Readers

I think about reading my VCR programming manual. With that text, I'm a struggling reader. I remember when I read *Beloved*; I certainly struggled my way through that text. I pick up the IRS tax booklet and I am not only a struggling reader but also a reluctant one. What separates me from many students who struggle is that if I really must get through the text, I can. That's because I struggle as an *independent* reader. I know how, on my own, to make the text make sense. I have strategies I can rely on to help me recognize the author's purpose, see biases, note an unreliable narrator, find the antecedents needed to navigate a maze of confusing characters, or make connections to my own life. I know how to use the context as a clue to help me define unknown words; I can analyze dense expository text so that little by little, that text makes sense.

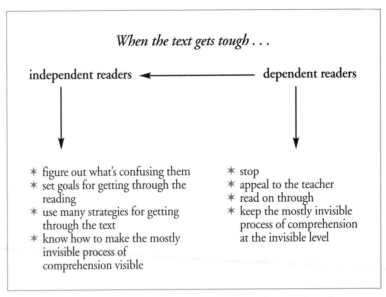

FIGURE 2.2 *How independent readers and dependent readers struggle with a text*

Some readers, by contrast, can't do those things. I call them *dependent* readers, for they depend on an outside-of-themselves source not only to tell them what to do but in many cases, to do it for them. They have strategies for moving through a difficult text, but those strategies look very different from the ones an independent reader would use (see Figure 2.2).

My goal is to move dependent readers—whether that slumping sleepy one who sits at the back of the room or the quiet one who sits toward the middle or the class clown who enjoys the front row—toward independence. I'm not about to tell students they will never again struggle through a text. In fact, what I want to do is to teach them *how to struggle* with a text, how to develop the patience and stamina to stick with a text, how to figure out on their own what is separating them from success with the text, and what they should do to fix it. In short, I want to teach students how to struggle *successfully* with a text. That success is possible if we address not just the cognitive demands of reading but the other demands as well.

Moving Dependent Readers Toward Independent Reading

MARK (a sixth grader): I can't read that book.

ME: Why not?

MARK: It's way too hard.

ME: How do you know it's too hard?

MARK: Well, it's so thick. And the words, you know the print, it's so little. And there're no pictures [turning through the book]; hey, there are *no* pictures. Yeah, this book is hard.

ME: You want to try reading a few pages to see if it really is a hard book?

MARK: No need. It's too hard. I can't read it [handing the book back to me].

The night I looked over this transcript, I thought that what Mark really lacked as a reader was confidence. He was convinced that the book was too difficult for him, and he couldn't get past that perception to discover if it really was. This notion of confidence, or lack of confidence, stayed with me over the next several years as I continued to explore what readers did and didn't do when they read. Over time, I saw that students' reading problems could be grouped into three areas.

♦ First, dependent readers might lack the cognitive abilities to read independently. Without this cognitive confidence, they might struggle with comprehension, vocabulary, word recognition, or fluency and automaticity.

♦ Second, these readers might have negative attitudes toward reading. They might claim that reading is "boring" or a "do-nothing." They have had so many moments of failure with reading that they not only dislike it but have come to believe that they cannot do it. They are disengaged from the reading process so that whether or not they have the cognitive abilities to read independently does not matter. Their attitudes toward reading keep them distanced from reading. These students lack social and emotional reading confidence.

♦ Third, dependent readers don't know what types of books they might enjoy, which authors might excite them, or what range of genres exists for them to read. Our suggestions to "find a good book" are not helpful because, as one student said, "and just where would those books be?" Furthermore, they read their social studies textbook like their science book like the novel they read in their language arts class. Additionally, these readers lack the ability to stick with a difficult text. They lack the stamina to find a text or complete a text.

Figure 2.3 offers a more detailed explanation of each area. What's critical to note is that as one area improves, others do, too.

While it is possible to address each area in this book separately, the reality is that when we are working with students, the areas comingle, creating a ricochet effect—attending to one issue creates a momentum that ricochets to another confidence.

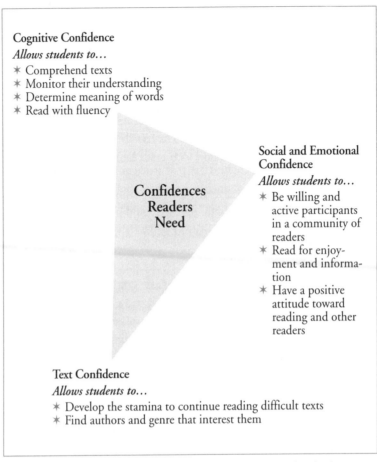

Cognitive Confidence
Allows students to...
* Comprehend texts
* Monitor their understanding
* Determine meaning of words
* Read with fluency

Confidences Readers Need

Social and Emotional Confidence
Allows students to...
* Be willing and active participants in a community of readers
* Read for enjoyment and information
* Have a positive attitude toward reading and other readers

Text Confidence
Allows students to...
* Develop the stamina to continue reading difficult texts
* Find authors and genre that interest them

FIGURE 2.3 *An overview of the confidences dependent readers need to develop*

Step Inside a Classroom

To illustrate this ricochet effect, let's look at Haley, an eighth grader. In seventh grade, Haley scored in the twenty-eighth percentile for reading comprehension on the Iowa Test of Basic Skills. Her oral reading lacked fluency as she struggled through texts word-by-word. Her writing was equally hesitant, so that her written assignments lacked elaboration and were filled with misspelled words. While she could recall specific information from a text that was read to her, she rarely connected the text to her own life and often had difficulty answering questions that required inferences. With that profile in mind, read the following transcript. In it, you'll see me trying to help Haley figure out how to correctly add the suffix *-ing* to words by using a word-sort activity. (You can find out more about word sorts and spelling

Kylene helps a teacher learn to do a word sort

strategies in Chapter 12.) Notice Haley's affective attitude as her cognitive confidence improves:

ME: So look at all the words you put in this list (see Figure 2.4), and now look at all the ones that you put into this second list. Okay, let's look at the ones in this last group. [Pause.] Why did you group the words this way?

HALEY: I put them like this, like this into these groups, because. Well, I put these words here [pointing to the first group] because they had, like each of them had two letters, you know, two letters that were the same before the end, like *nn* or *mm* or *tt*.

ME: Okay.

HALEY: And here, in this group, okay, this group it had, well, it's like a word, you know, like you just have the word and you just add it, just add the *-ing*. And this last group, you have to, in this, in these words, well they, I think they had an *e* like you spell *hike h-i-k-e* but you don't spell *hiking h-i-k-e-i-n-g* because you have to take off the *e*.

ME: That's great. So, you've shown me how all the words in each group are similar.

HALEY: Yeah.

ME: I wonder why the words in group one have a doubled consonant before the suffix *-ing*, but the words in groups two and three don't.

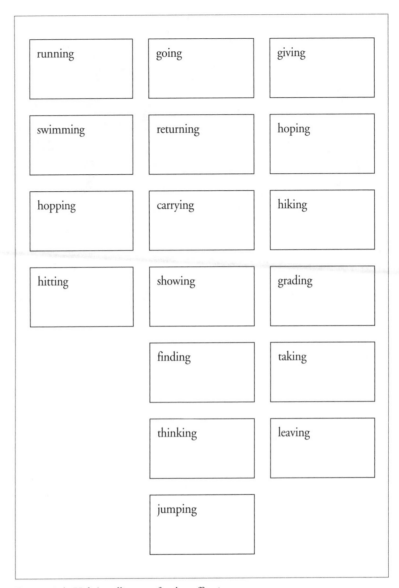

FIGURE 2.4 *Haley's spelling sort for the suffix -ing*

HALEY: I don't know. I mean, they just do. [Pause.] I don't know.

ME: Let's just look at *hop* and *hope.*

HALEY: Okay.

ME: How do these words sound different?

HALEY: In one, in *hop,* the sound, uh, the vowel sound, it's like not the *o* sound, it's the short sound, like *ah.* But in *hope,* well, the sound is *o* just like you would say the letter *o. O.* So they are different.

ME: That's right. Now, what's the cue when you are looking at those two words that will show you in one the *o* will make its short sound and in the other it will make its long sound?

HALEY: The *e*. The *e* on *hope*. The *e*, it doesn't make a sound, but it makes the long sound, or it makes the *o* make its long sound. But *hop* doesn't have it so you know it is short. /h-o-p/ /h-op/ hop.
[Pause.]

ME: Do you remember what pattern that word is? Remember we talked about the consonants and vowels and using those words to describe the pattern in the word?

HALEY: Yeah. So this, *hop*, it is a consonant-vowel-consonant pattern. Yeah, we talked about those. [I nod.] Okay. That pattern means it is a short sound, but if you have consonant-vowel-consonant-silent *e*, then it is long. [Long sigh. Haley studies the words and picks up individual slips of paper from the different groups. Then she begins to grin.] Well, I get it but can't say it. [Pause.] It's that *i* in *-ing*, the *i*, it becomes like the *e* so, so look on *hop*, if you just added *-ing* then it would be *h-o-p-i-n-g* and that would be consonant-vowel-consonant-vowel and then it would have to be long. Get it? [Smiling broadly.] I mean I get it. Look here at like *running*. Okay that word is really *run* and that's just *r-u-n* so you have to make it *nn* before you add the *-ing* or the pattern would be wrong. [Pause.] And then it would sound wrong. It would be *r-oo-n-ing*. [Pause.] That's it, isn't it? I figured it out. I mean, like it's just right there and I got it. This is like hard stuff, isn't it? And I got it.
[Big smile.]

ME: You think you could explain this to one of our groups tomorrow?

HALEY: This. Oh sure. I got it.

In this very focused lesson, the purpose was to attend to some spelling problems that weren't correcting themselves. We were certainly paying attention to the cognitive processes that surround encoding (writing) and decoding (reading). Yet, by the end of the lesson, her emotional confidence had improved, and she was willing to share her new knowledge with a small group. While we were attending to one confidence, another confidence benefited. That ricochet effect proved to be the case more often than not.

Reflections

My daughter, Meredith, a junior in high school while I was writing this book, played in a lacrosse tournament at Texas A & M University one cold

Lest you think all interviews were as productive and helpful as this one with Haley, let me share one of the hundreds that was more typical of what came out of a guided reading lesson. Here's Justin, a ninth grader. We're working on a spelling sort similar to the one I had done with Haley.

ME: So, Justin, how would you sort these words?

JUSTIN: I don't know.

ME: Go ahead and look at each one. Begin moving them around to see what you notice.

[Justin plays with the words, moves a few around, sits back into his chair, and shrugs.]

ME: What did you notice?

JUSTIN: About what?

ME: About the words.

JUSTIN: There was only one word on each piece of paper. I noticed that.

Justin and I got to the same point that Haley got to, eventually, but it took patience on my part and stamina on his. I think the Justins are what frustrate us. Haleys we can handle, but Justins can do us in. The only advice I can offer is to remember that he's showing up. Justin, and all the kids like him, have had years of practice at failure. Their willingness to try, even halfheartedly, one more time is a fragile gift they hand to us.

January day. While she was there, I sat home, in my study, writing this chapter, experiencing her game vicariously as Baker, my ten-year-old, or Brad, my husband, called in reports every hour or so. During the third call (I probably should have just gone to the game), Brad said that Meredith had made a great goal, doing something called a shovel shot, a move she had tried repeatedly the day before and missed. And repeatedly, the day before, the coach had told her how to correct her mistake. When she finally got it right, the coach yelled from the sideline, "See, when you do it like I tell you to, it works." Brad said that later Meredith hugged the coach and said, "Yeah, but if I hadn't messed it up all those times yesterday, you wouldn't have had all those chances to tell me how to get it right."

Meredith's right. Making mistakes is a part of the learning process. And Coach Straup is right, too: giving the correct information (sometimes repeatedly) to kids is critical. As a teacher, I've made mistakes and from those mistakes I've learned a lot. And I've sometimes given the right information, and that's made all the difference. Teaching reading to adolescents is both rewarding and frustrating; it's a science and an art. It's making mistakes and growing from them. It's the most important thing I do as a teacher.

Dear George,

Now I get it. Your repeated comment "I don't get it" was your signal to me that you were a dependent reader who lacked strategies to make sense of the text on your own. I think of the many times that you stood at my desk and waited for me to get it for you—and I did. I explained what was happening, gave you my interpretations, told you my thoughts on the text so that you could return to your desk ever more dependent on me to get you through difficult texts. I was almost on the right track the day I asked you to define what "it" was. I just didn't understand what to do when you lacked the language to identify what was going wrong in your reading. I wonder if you ever found those words.

CHAPTER THREE

Assessing Dependent Readers' Needs

Dear George,

   Much too late in the year, I asked you what you needed me to do to help you be a better reader.

   "You could just do it all for me," you said, hiding behind what I was coming to recognize as truth hidden behind flip responses.

   "I'm afraid I can't do that. What's your next choice?" I said.

   You stared for a moment and said, "What makes you think there's anything you could do? I can't read. That's it."

Defining "This Kid Can't Read"

"I don't know what you mean by 'glory,'" Alice said.

   Humpty Dumpty smiled contemptuously. "Of course you don't—till I tell you. . . . When I use a word," Humpty Dumpty said in a rather scornful tone, "it means just what I choose it to mean—neither more nor less."

   "The question is," said Alice, "whether you can make words mean so many different things." (Carroll, 1865/1961, p. 213)

I fear that when I began teaching, I wasn't as smart as Alice or as bold as Mr. Dumpty. Humpty wants to define words as he sees fit; Alice doubts whether he can, upon any whim, define words whatever way he chooses. I seemed to be the person in the middle—using words without any idea of meaning, mine or anyone else's. In particular, I failed to define what I meant when I said, "These kids can't read." My principal repeatedly pushed me toward definition, clarity, and specificity as she asked what I meant. I gave her ambiguity: "It means they can't read."

Her question haunted me through that first year and for several years that followed, as it not only forced me to acknowledge what I didn't know but also helped me understand how critical it is that we, as teachers, learn to be precise in our language. Even now I work to focus indefinite language:

"You're a good writer," I said recently to an undergraduate student.

"Why?" she said, pleased.

"Why what?" I asked.

"Why am I a good writer?"

I said nothing for a moment, thinking through my answer, so she continued: "No, I mean, thank you for saying that, but people have always told me that and I need to know what I'm doing that's good. For one of my other classes, I'm tutoring a kid, and I have to help him with his writing. If you could tell me exactly what I'm doing that's good, then maybe I could show him how to do the same thing."

She was correct, of course. Once we can define what's working and what isn't working, then we know how instruction should proceed.

Dependent Reading Behaviors

While I still catch myself saying, "This kid can't read," I now clarify what that means. Not being able to read can mean a range of things, depending on the student's strengths and weaknesses. Take a moment and think of two or three students you've taught who had problems reading. Once you have those students in mind, read through the following list and decide which descriptors fit which student.

When we say a student can't read, that might mean he or she

◆ cannot easily and quickly recognize single-syllable words
◆ cannot easily and quickly recognize multisyllable words
◆ has few or no strategies for recognizing unknown words
◆ has a limited sight word vocabulary
◆ does not know how to use the context as a clue to help with word recognition or word meaning
◆ does not have or use knowledge of word parts to help with word recognition or word meaning

- reads haltingly, one word at a time
- reads aloud or whisper-reads when silent reading would be more appropriate
- reads very slowly, paying no attention to punctuation
- reads aloud with little or no expression
- reads too fast, blurring words, rushing through punctuation
- does not visualize the text
- does not "hear" the text when reading silently
- reads all material at the same rate
- does not reread to clarify meaning
- reads to finish rather than to understand
- cannot keep events of text in correct order
- does not recognize cause and effect relationships
- has trouble comparing and contrasting events, settings, and characters
- does not predict without prompting
- cannot answer literal-level questions about the text
- does not easily make inferences, draw conclusions, or make generalizations from texts
- cannot state the main idea of a text
- has difficulty summarizing the important points in a text
- does not recognize how point of view impacts a text
- does not set a purpose for reading other than to complete the assignment
- cannot identify literary elements in a text or discuss how those elements affect the text
- cannot discuss how one genre differs from another
- does not connect events in the text to other texts or to events in personal experience
- does not try to relate what is being presented in text to what is already known
- has trouble recalling information from a text
- does not recognize when comprehension is not taking place
- knows when comprehension is not occurring but does not know how to adjust reading to help
- has a difficult time creating questions about a text
- has a difficult time expressing thoughts or ideas about a text in small- or large-group settings
- has a difficult time organizing thoughts about a text in writing
- has difficulty spelling
- sees no difference in reading for information and reading for pleasure

- does not know how to use or does not use features of a text to aid in comprehension (like charts, graphs, indexes, italicized words, boldfacing, headings and subheadings, chapter titles, cover information)
- stops reading at first sign of difficulty
- continues reading through the assignment knowing that nothing is making sense
- expects you to explain what text means instead of working to explain text to self
- thinks "good" readers understand a text with little or no effort
- is frustrated easily by a text
- says that reading is "boring" and "dumb"
- avoids reading at all costs

Looking through this list, I would give anything to meet with George's parents again. I'd tell them that George can't recognize some single-syllable words and is overwhelmed with most multisyllable words. I would say that though he understands what I read to him, he reads so slowly on his own that meaning gets lost. He can't recall specific information from a text, can't make inferences or generalizations about a text, and doesn't relate what he's reading to other texts or to his own life. Then I'd give them a chart (see Figure 3.1) that would show them my plan for helping George overcome these problems. All of the items on this plan will be covered in later chapters.

A teacher listens and takes notes as a student reads aloud

Instructional Plan for George

What George Can't Do	What I Will Do
Can't decode some single-syllable words	Teach onset-rime patterns; teach high-frequency words
Has a lot of trouble decoding multisyllable words	Teach chunking, recognition of word parts; prefixes and suffixes, syllabification
Reads slowly, one word at a time, without expression	Work on automaticity of high-frequency words; have him follow along while listening to books on tape; model good phrasing and expression; give George opportunities to read aloud various types of texts, including plays
Can't recall specific information from a text	Teach George to use retelling rubrics; show George how to stop while reading to identify and clarify important information; have George read shorter chunks of texts as he builds recall abilities; make sure George recognizes and understands time-order words and words that show causal relationships
Can't make inferences or generalizations	Model for George thinking aloud so he can hear how inferences and generalizations are formed; have George practice making different types of inferences and generalizations; help George learn to monitor where his understanding breaks down so he can determine if he needs to be making an inference; assess if George is having trouble with pronoun referents, connectors such as *therefore* or *however*, making elaboration, or other types of inferences
Doesn't connect what he's reading to other texts or to his own life	Use K-W-L charts; spend more time helping George to access prior knowledge before reading a selection; find high-interest reading material that George enjoys

FIGURE 3.1 *Instructional plans help teachers move from assessment to instruction*

And I'd have left that conference with the support of two parents who saw that their son's teacher recognized specific areas of weakness and had specific plans for strengthening those areas. I'd have left with a plan that would have given George a chance for becoming a better reader.

This book is designed to be a handbook, so reading through it from beginning to end isn't necessary. In fact, you might use the chart found in Figure 3.2 to help you assess students' needs. This chart lists some behaviors you might see in your dependent readers and then suggests a focus for instruction and directs you to appropriate chapters.

If a student	If a student	If a student	If a student
* can call all the words * reads at an appropriate rate *but* * consistently has difficulty answering questions * creating questions * discussing the text, or * repeatedly says that reading is boring or that he doesn't "see" anything in his mind while reading * thinking beyond literal level questions * understanding unknown words	* stumbles through many words * tries to sound out a lot of words (either correctly or incorrectly) * confuses what we'd call simple words such as *were* and *where* * decodes the first few letters or first syllable of a multisyllable word and then makes up the rest of it (or gives up) * reads very slowly, a word at a time * says he doesn't "hear" words in his mind while reading silently * has trouble recognizing high-frequency sight words * misspells a lot of words	* does not participate in small- or large-group discussions * does not offer opinions or questions about what was read * is not willing to take risks in discussions (so you hear a lot of "I agrees" or "I guess sos" or "I don't knows") * does not believe he is a good reader * thinks that good readers are "just smarter" or "just better students" than he is * makes fun of good readers * is disengaged not just from reading activities but from many or most learning activities * does not appear to put much if any effort into reading assignments	* has good word recognition skills * appears to understand written selections, *but* * resists reading * says he can't find any books that are interesting * repeatedly claims that reading is boring * reads all types of texts the same way (probably all too fast) * cannot name any favorite authors * cannot describe a favorite genre * cannot list a favorite book * does not understand how different parts or features of a textbook offer different types of information
then this student needs help with * vocabulary * making predictions * seeing causal relationships * comparing and contrasting * drawing conclusions * questioning the text * recognizing authors' purpose/point of view * summarizing * finding the main idea * monitoring own understanding * making connections * sequencing * visualizing	*then* this student needs help with * word recognition * spelling * fluency	*then* this student needs help * gaining confidence about his ability to comment on or question a text * learning how to be an active participant in a community of readers * becoming comfortable with sharing ideas * learning the academic language that facilitates literary discussions * learning to believe that he can be a part of the community of readers	*then* this student needs help * learning how to find texts that interest him * finding authors he enjoys * understanding how parts of a textbook can assist understanding * recognizing how formatting issues can aid in comprehension * learning to navigate a library * discovering resources that can help him find reading material
See Chapters 4, 5, 6, 7, 8, 9	See Chapters 10, 11, 12	See Chapter 13	See Chapter 14

FIGURE 3.2 *If–Then Chart*

Step Inside a Classroom

Though most dependent readers need help in all areas—cognitive confidence, text confidence, social and emotional confidence—there are students who need help in one area more than another. Furthermore, knowing that a student needs help with cognitive confidence doesn't pinpoint exactly what type of help is needed. Some need help with decoding, others with vocabulary, still others with comprehension. As you read the following profiles of students, ask yourself where you think the main instructional focus for each student should be.

MIKE

When I met Mike, he was in ninth grade. He was shorter than most boys, didn't play any organized sports but loved skateboarding, and when given the choice, sat at the back of the room, hunched down into his seat. He was retained in third grade and made barely passing grades throughout middle school. He was tested for resource classes in sixth grade and did not qualify since there was no significant difference between his achievement level and his IQ. He was a quiet young man who appeared to have mastered the art of being invisible. He rarely brought his books to class and used his notebook as a place to cram papers that he seldom looked at again. He resisted any reading aloud and generally refused to do so by just putting his head down on his desk or saying that he forgot his book. When he did read aloud just for me, it was slow, halting, and revealed an overreliance on sounding out words and little attention to comprehension.

Here is a transcript of his oral reading of the first four sentences of "The Gift of the Magi" by O. Henry, a story in his ninth-grade literature anthology. Mike's words appear in italics above the actual words from the text:

On-one d-d-do-l-l-ar and, and eight-eighty-sev-eighty-seven c-e-nts.
One   dollar   and   eighty-   seven cents.

Th-that w-was all.
That   was   all.

And eight-six and six cents off it was in pen-pens pens   saved
And   sixty   cents of it was in pennies. Pennies saved

one and two   at a
one, one twi-two   at a

time. By b-b-bull, bulldozers, by the bulldozers the gro-groc-er and the
time by bulldozing   the grocer   and the

veg-vegetar-veternarian man and the but-cher, butcher, man
vegetable   man and the butcher

until one, one check, one check got burned, burned up,
until one's   cheeks   burned

with the si-slice, im-impo-impossible . . . of par-parts-pars-i-my.
with the silent imputation   of parsimony.

When asked what these four sentences were about, he responded:

> I don't know. [Pause.] I guess, somebody, [pause] there was like a
> bulldozer, and somebody's check, the check it got burned up, into
> parts. [Pause.] I don't know. [Long pause.] You know I can't read
> this stuff.

Mike needs help with both cognitive and emotional confidence. But
specifically what cognitive help does he need? First, Mike does have problems
with word recognition. He's trying to sound out words a letter at a time and
sometimes a syllable at a time. With multisyllabic words, he often makes up
what the final syllables would be, perhaps to create a word he knows, or
drops the final syllable entirely. He is reading through punctuation, not pausing at periods or, conversely, pausing where there is no end punctuation. He
does know some sight words and does recognize some high-frequency words,
but that gets lost in the slow reading rate and the misspoken words.

Second, there is some indication that while reading this text, he does
try to make it make sense. That's most apparent in the words he inserts
while reading, words that are not a part of the original text. For example,
where the text reads, "by bulldozing," he decides the word is "bulldozer"
and then inserts the article *the*, so he reads it, "by the bulldozer." The inser-
tion shows that he is attempting to make what he's reading make sense at
some level. Later, he reads, "one check got burned, burned up," for "one's
cheeks burned." Substituting "check" for "cheek," he then inserts "got" and
"up" to create the phrase "one check got burned up," a phrase that makes
good sense. When he had finished reading and I asked him to tell me what
the passage was about, he continued to rely on that phrase and even tried
to extend the meaning—"the check it got burned up, into parts"—by
changing "parsimony" into "parts." He then says, "I don't know," in an

admission that the text really didn't make sense to him. These slim indicators tell me that he does know that texts are supposed to make sense and he's working—at least to some degree—to make that happen.

Finally, his comment, "You know I can't read this stuff," reminds me that Mike is no novice when it comes to facing difficult texts. He expects that he can't do it, expects that I *know* he can't do it, and doesn't expect anything to change.

So, where do we start with a student like Mike? His most obvious problem was that decoding wasn't automatic; therefore, he was a slow, disfluent reader. Helping him with word recognition was a priority. As his ability to quickly recognize words improved, his fluency and reading rate improved. As that happened, he had more cognitive energy to spend on comprehension. Then we began to see that Mike also had a very limited vocabulary. Spending time building that vocabulary became a priority. As his cognitive confidence began to improve, his emotional confidence began to grow.

Sharamee

Sharamee was a seventh grader who was facing retention for that grade. She was energetic, funny, and loved to talk. She willingly read aloud and always volunteered for any sort of oral reading: reading directions, reading poems, reading the morning announcements, reading minutes from the student council meetings, reading selections from her literature book. Her oral reading was very fast, sometimes so fast that her words slurred together. When asked to slow down, she would vary her rate for a few words, then speed back up. Though a fast reader who could pronounce almost any word in almost any text, she did not have a lot of expression in her reading.

Though she enjoyed reading aloud, she rarely read silently. During sustained silent reading time, she would find many excuses to not read—everything from needing to go see the school nurse to saying she forgot her book. If she did get her book opened in front of her, it wasn't long before she was writing notes or turning around to whisper to the person behind her. When asked why she didn't like to read silently, she responded, "I just like to read aloud, you know, to say the words." I asked her if, when she read silently, she heard the words in her mind. She said, "I don't know. What do you mean hear them in my mind? If you want to hear it, you have to read it aloud." If *you* aren't sure what I mean by "hearing the words in your mind," then reread this sentence and try not to hear the words. Can you do it? Probably not. Most skilled readers "hear" the words of a text as easily (sometimes more easily) than they visualize a text. Many disabled readers, however, like Sharamee, claim they don't hear anything when they read.

When her class read aloud the play "The Diary of Anne Frank," Sharamee read the part of Anne. The teacher spent several days discussing the Holocaust, World War II, Hitler, and how some people helped Jews by hiding them. She talked at length about Anne and the diary she wrote. The class then spent several more days reading the play aloud. When they finished, I had the opportunity to interview Sharamee:

ME: What did you think about the play?

SHARAMEE: It was good.

ME: Yeah? What was good about it?

SHARAMEE: Uh, you know, just the play, it was good.

ME: What did you think about Anne?

SHARAMEE: About Anne?

ME: Yeah, you know, about what she went through?

SHARAMEE: I'm not sure. Like when?

ME: Do you remember what happened to Anne?

SHARAMEE: She got this diary. And there's a play. And they hid, you know they hid, in the play. She had a sister.

ME: Remember how your teacher told you that Anne's diary was published as a book, and how part of it was turned into the play you just read?

SHARAMEE: Uh-huh.

ME: Why do you think what she put in her diary was important enough to turn into a book or make into a play?

SHARAMEE: Because, uh, well it's a play, you know, and she wrote this diary, because of the war, and then wrote a play. It was the war. She didn't want there to be a war.

Later, I asked Sharamee if she was a good reader. "Oh, yeah, I'm real good," she quickly replied.

"Why?" I asked.

"I just am. I can read real fast. The teachers always call on me to read."

"So how well do you comprehend what you read?" I asked.

No reply.

"You know, when you've finished reading," I explained, "do you understand what you were reading?"

"Well, sometimes that part's a little hard. [Pause.] But the reading part I do real good," she said.

For Sharamee, reading was decoding. She came from an elementary setting that used a scripted phonics program (see page 44 for a description of scripted phonics instruction). She learned many phonics rules and developed the ability to sound out words easily. What she didn't learn to do, though, was know when a text was making sense, when it wasn't, and what to do when meaning was unclear. I didn't need to spend any time working on word recognition skills; this child needed help with comprehension. She needed to learn to hear the text she was reading, to slow down and focus on the meaning of the text, to ask herself what was going on in the text.

AMY

Amy, an eighth grader, hated to read. On a reading interest survey she wrote, "Reading is my worst thing to do. I hate it." When asked why, she repeatedly said, "It's boring," and "It's a do-nothing." Amy made Cs and some Bs in her classes. She generally did her homework, though often didn't complete it, but rarely entered into class discussions. When assigned a story or novel to read, she would read some of it and, once it was explained, would declare, "If it's a really good story, I'll read all of it." When asked what would have to be in it to make it good, she said she didn't know: "It just has to be good." She also said that she never could find any good books to read and didn't know what types of books interested her. When asked questions about a text, she could answer questions about characters' names or the setting and could recall the correct order of events in the story; however, she had trouble answering anything other than literal-level questions. When asked what she did as soon as she realized the text was confusing her, she said, "Do? I don't know. I mean, what can you do? If you get confused, I guess you wait for the teacher."

She saw herself as "an okay reader" but admitted, "I don't try real hard with it because sometimes I just don't get it and sometimes, it's like, what's the point? Most of it just seems boring and then some of it, sometimes it's just too hard."

Like Sharamee, Amy doesn't need help with word recognition. Unlike Sharamee, she doesn't need help with recalling information from a text. She does need help with making inferences, with reading beyond what the text offers at a literal level. Her repeated comments that reading is boring may be an indication that she has trouble visualizing the action. Her inability to define what makes a "good story" may show us she has little experience with a range of texts and needs help defining just what she likes to read.

As her teacher and I helped Amy with making inferences and visualizing, we also helped her clarify what types of stories she enjoyed. Three months later when asked what she liked to read, she quickly responded, "I really like books, like a love story, where someone has a problem, they make you sad but then you just love how they end." She even could point out her favorite author: "I love Lurlene McDaniel. I've read five of her books since Christmas and they, they are the best." Amy's inability to find any type of book that interested her had kept her from reading during sustained silent reading time and supported her notion that she couldn't find any good books. As we developed her text confidence and worked on inferencing and visualizing, Amy began to enjoy reading and at the end of the year said that "reading can be okay, sometimes, with the right book."

With each of these students, moving beyond "These kids can't read" to defining what they could and couldn't do helped focus instruction. Another factor that helped focus instruction was the constant awareness of what good readers do when they read.

What Good Readers Do

I asked a class of juniors in high school what good readers do when they read. Raymond's answer floated up from the back row: "Do you mean you think they are good because they are *doin'* somethin'? You mean there's somethin' you *do* to be a good reader? [Laughter from class.] I just thought they were good readers because they just are. You know. Just good readers. Man, they don't do nothin' other than maybe suck up to the teacher."

Part sarcasm, part intimidation, part let's-shock-the-teacher, and part let's-keep-the-class-laughing, Raymond's answer was also a suggestion of what many students who struggle with reading think: Good readers just *are*. There's nothing they particularly do before, after, or during reading the text. It's just the way they read.

But we know that isn't right. Good readers, while not always able to articulate what they do, do more than simply read the words. These skilled readers do the following:

◆ They recognize that the purpose for reading is to get meaning—whether when reading for enjoyment, to complete a school assignment, or to find information to help with a personal question. Reading is a meaning-making process that requires active participation from the reader.

◆ They use a variety of comprehension strategies that include, but are not limited to, predicting, summarizing, questioning the text, and visualizing the text.

- They make a range of inferences about the text—from providing their own examples of a concept presented in the text to figuring out the meaning of a word from the context to understanding pronoun-antecedent relationships.

- They use their prior knowledge to inform their inferences, to relate ideas in the text to ideas in the world and their own beliefs, to place what they are reading within a relevant context of their lives.

- They monitor their understanding of the text. As a part of this, they recognize when what they are reading is difficult; they know when they've stopped paying attention; they can identify when vocabulary is a problem; they can identify the parts of a text that confuse them. This level of monitoring then leads to actions or fix-up strategies such as rereading, changing their reading rate, or using a dictionary. In other words, once they recognize something is wrong, they work to correct it.

- They question the author's purpose and point of view.

- They are aware of text features—headings, boldfaced terms, italicized terms, charts, graphs, indexes—and use those features to aid in comprehension.

- They evaluate their engagement and enjoyment with a text so they know if they liked it, why or why not it appealed to them, and whether or not they would recommend it to anyone else.

- They know the meaning of many words and, when they don't automatically recognize the meaning, know how to use the context as a clue or word parts such as root words and affixes to discern the meaning.

- They recognize most words automatically, read fluently, vary their reading rate to match the purpose and level of difficulty, and "hear" the text as they read the words.

Raymond's answer, when viewed as a question—"You mean there's somethin' you *do* to be a good reader?"—helped me understand just how confused some struggling readers are about reading. As we teach necessary skills, we must also convince disabled readers that reading is an active process, one that requires their engagement, their active construction of meaning. I kept working with Raymond, trying to get him to be an active participant in the reading process. During one of our meetings I asked, "So what do you think is important for me to know while helping you with reading?" He responded:

> I don't have a clue. [Pause.] But, hey, isn't it more important that you know what you think is important about helping me with readin'? I mean, after all, you are the teacher-lady. You're the one gettin' paid to be here. Not me. If you don't know what you think is important and if you're expectin' me to be tellin' you what's important, then lady, we're in big trouble.

Underlying Beliefs

I don't know if Raymond was being profound or simply trying to get out of answering another question, but he was right: I better know what my beliefs are about reading instruction or "we're in big trouble." I made a list that day, and in the years that followed I revisited that list, making adjustments as I learned more. My beliefs about teaching reading to struggling readers include the following:

1. Students can be taught to use a range of comprehension strategies so that these strategies influence how they make meaning from a text (Wilhelm, 2001; Pressley, 2000; Keene and Zimmerman, 1997; Collins, 1991; Brown et al., 1996; Brown and Coy-Ogan, 1993).

2. There are multiple ways to help students improve their comprehending abilities. Some of these ways are less explicit; others more explicit. Teachers must be prepared to switch to more direct, explicit models of instruction if that is what any particular student needs. Holding tight to only one methodology not only limits what a teacher can do but limits who can be successful. Believing that one single method can make (or not make) the difference in any given student's chance of success negates the importance of the teacher. In fact, though, the teacher's skill in assessing students' abilities, effectively responding to students' needs, and successfully analyzing and monitoring students' improvement makes the difference (Duffy, 1991, 1992; Collins and Pressley, 2002). This means, in short, we can't fix the reading problem by buying a particular program; instead, as teachers, we must learn how to teach students to comprehend texts. The less we depend on programs and the more we depend on our own knowledge—informed by practice and research—the less likely we are to be controlled by politically driven mandates, expensive programs that appear and disappear from our

classrooms without rhyme or reason, and federally funded (or not funded) programs.

3. Some students do benefit from direct, explicit instruction in comprehension strategies. While some will argue that comprehension strategies cannot be taught directly, others find that struggling readers do benefit from direct instruction (Beers, 2001; Dole, Brown, and Trathen, 1996; Duffy, 2002; Pressley et al., 1992; Tierney and Cunningham, 1984; Vygotsky 1934, 1986).

   These strategies can be taught directly and explicitly following a process in which the teacher models and explains the strategy, then students apply the strategy by practicing it with a range of texts under the coaching of the teacher or a more skilled reader (scaffolded practice). The teacher's role is to

   ◆ monitor the use of the strategy
   ◆ offer less coaching as less is called for (removing the scaffold)
   ◆ ask students what strategy they are using and why (therefore bringing the use of the strategy to the student's awareness)
   ◆ give students continued opportunity to observe more modeling
   ◆ provide multiple and ongoing opportunities for students to transact with other students with a range of texts

4. In addition to direct and explicit comprehension strategy instruction, some students will also need and benefit from direct vocabulary study. While we recognize that most words are not learned via direct instruction, but in a more indirect manner (you hear someone say, "This is a great buffet," while standing before a buffet and you infer the meaning of the word *buffet*), we know that vocabulary knowledge affects comprehension (Beck, Perfetti, and McKeown, 1982; McKeown et al., 1983, 1985; Blachowicz, 1987; Blachowicz and Fisher, 2000). Methods that encourage students to actively construct meanings (as opposed to merely copying definitions from a dictionary) help students learn and retain word meanings longer (Allen, 1999; Anderson and Freebody, 1981; Bannon et al., 1990; Becker, Dixon, and Inman-Anderson, 1980; Blachowicz, 1986; Blachowicz and Fisher, 2000; Hill, 1998).

5. Some readers struggle through a text because they lack fluent word recognition. Let me say now that I believe that strong word recognition skills are a major component of comprehending a text; however, they alone don't ensure comprehension. If you aren't sure of that, pick up a medical textbook. You might be able to decode all the words, but once finished,

might not have any idea what the text is saying. On the other hand, if you can't decode the words, getting to that meaning is difficult at best. When students stumble through words on a consistent basis, they need help with word recognition skills that will allow fluent decoding of a text (Adams, 1990; Metsala and Ehri, 1998; Juel, 1988; Gough and Tunmer, 1986; Langenberg et al., 2000; Snow, Burns, and Griffin, 1998).

The less cognitive energy students must spend figuring out the words on the page, the more energy they can spend figuring out what the text means. Think of it this way: If an adolescent will give us ten units of energy comprehending a text and nine of those units go to just figuring out what the words are, then she only has one unit left for the most critical part of reading—comprehension. Therefore, automaticity and fluency are critical to comprehension. This, of course, has been the focus of much attention recently as reading researchers, politicians, publishers, and parents debate the role of phonics and the best way to help students learn to decode texts. What's not debated, though, is that the point of reading is to get meaning and you can't get to the meaning if you can't get through the words.

6. Teachers who encourage a wide range of reading, who give their students plenty of opportunity for sustained, silent reading, who read aloud to their students on a regular basis, who provide ongoing opportunities for students to discuss—in small- and large-group settings—their understanding of a text, who encourage extensive rather than intensive reading, who encourage self-selection of some texts, and who recognize that students become better readers by reading, not merely practicing reading skills, increase students' opportunity for developing a positive attitude toward reading, for improving fluency, for improving vocabulary, and for improving comprehension.

7. Reading is a social process, an interactive activity, one in which readers create meaning through transactions—interactions—with the text, their prior knowledge, the context, and other readers (Weaver, 1994; Rosenblatt, 1978; Durkin, 1993).

These beliefs provide the direction for strategies outlined in this book. They are based on three premises:

◆ Teachers—not programs—are the critical element in a student's success.
◆ The goal of reading is comprehension.
◆ Comprehension is a complex, abstract activity.

It's not enough knowing what good readers can do or struggling readers can't do. We must also know what we believe about teaching, about learning, and about our role in both. Once that's determined, we can make intelligent choices about the instruction that best suits the needs of our students.

Dear George,

Looking back, I'd have to say that the only things that guided my instructional decisions that first year were our literature book and grammar book. Had I only known then what I know now, I'd have plotted a much different course for you. I'd have known how to assess your strengths and weaknesses as a reader. That assessment, rather than textbooks, would have guided instruction. Then perhaps I would have been a teacher who made a difference in your life.

4

Explicit Instruction in Comprehension

◆ ◆ ◆

Dear George,

I thought if I just explained the story to you, you'd understand it. And, I suppose you did. We had an interesting pattern—you'd try to read something, or I'd read it aloud to the class, and then I'd tell you to answer the questions at the end of the story. You'd come and stand at my desk and point to any, or all, of the questions and ask for help and I would tell you the answers. You'd nod and go and write something down and then come back. Never once did I explain how I got the answers; I just explained the answers. Now I see the difference—sort of like "if you give a man a fish, you feed him for one day; if you teach him how to fish, you feed him for a lifetime." I fed you a day at a time.

◆ ◆ ◆

Teaching Comprehension

Though we spend much time testing comprehension—using everything from teacher-made quizzes over literary selections to chapter tests in content area classes to standardized exams such as the Iowa Test of Basic Skills to state-mandated skill exams—we actually spend little time *teaching* comprehension strategies. We sometimes confuse explaining to students what is happening in a text with teaching students how to comprehend a text.

It is important to remember that we can teach students *how* to comprehend texts. We shouldn't assume that if we simply explain what something means, students will automatically know how to comprehend other texts. To help dependent readers become independent readers, we must teach them what many of us, as independent readers, do with seemingly little effort. We must teach them strategies that will help them understand texts. These strategies include

- clarifying
- comparing and contrasting
- connecting to prior experiences
- inferencing (including generalizing and drawing conclusions)
- predicting
- questioning the text
- recognizing the author's purpose
- seeing causal relationships
- summarizing
- visualizing

"And Just How Do I Teach Any of Those Strategies?"

While teachers almost always agree that the strategies in the previous list are important, they often resist teaching them directly; instead, they hope that awareness of and competency with these strategies are by-products of class discussions. However, if we really want to affect students' comprehension abilities—as opposed to affecting their understanding of one particular text—then we must realize that for at least some of our struggling readers, we need to teach comprehension strategies explicitly and directly. This is more difficult than it appears. As one teacher asked me, "Just how could I ever teach someone to actually predict something?"

She's asking an excellent question: Can we really teach someone to recognize or predict causal relationships? I don't know that we can force that level of understanding. But we *can* model how we, the more expert readers in the classroom, use those strategies to understand texts. The key lies in the words *explicitly* and *directly*.

We don't help dependent readers when our instruction is limited to, "Don't forget to predict," or "It will help if you visualize," or "Look for the causal relationships." Instead, we've got to show these students how we use strategies to enhance our understanding of a text as we "think aloud" a text for them. (Read more about think-alouds on page 119). I constantly remind my undergraduate teacher-education students that education is not a Nike commercial: you can't say, "Just do it." Instead, we must show students *how* to do it. That means we've got to be very direct and explicit in strategy instruction. It doesn't mean following a script that someone else has prepared. In fact, you shouldn't rely on scripted lessons, for part of successful strategy instruction hinges on your ability to respond to students' questions and comments, not your ability to read what comes next in the teacher's manual.

So, what does it mean to teach comprehension strategies explicitly and directly? It means that you'll take the guesswork out of what you want students to learn. In other words, it means embracing instructional practices like the following:

1. *First, decide what specific strategies you want to model and what text to use.* Though some people suggest doing "cold" readings with students—where you bring in a text you haven't studied and read it for the first time in front of students so that your think-aloud is authentic—I find it more helpful to carefully select which text I'll use and to plan where I'll model the strategy. Occasional use of a cold reading activity is certainly appropriate, of course, but when I'm trying to teach something explicitly, the more I've planned, the better.

2. *Next, tell your students exactly what strategy you'll be practicing while reading this passage.* Begin with a direct statement such as, "While I read this, I'm going to practice visualizing the action. Listen to how I try to create the picture in my mind as I read. In particular, listen for what types of words help me visualize the text." Remember, you are doing this to help dependent readers, those students who in many years of schooling have not intuited or deduced how to think strategically about a text.

   In other words, when working with dependent readers, modeling without some clear information as to what you are modeling is often "cool" (as one eighth grader described his teacher's think-aloud) but not much more. When this young man was asked, "Why do you think your teacher just did that [i.e., the modeling]?" he replied, "I don't know. Something for the lesson, maybe?" However, when the teacher began making sure students understood that she was modeling specific strategies, we saw some difference in the students' understanding of what she was doing. Prior to one think-aloud she said, "Today, I'm going to read aloud a bit of the story for you. As I read, I'll be stopping to think aloud so you'll hear how I'm trying to make sense of this story. In particular I want you to listen to how I try to predict what will happen next, try to visualize what's happening in the scene, and try to clarify anything that's confusing me. Okay? Predicting, visualizing, clarifying." Afterward, she asked students what thinking strategies they

Kylene listens to a student think-aloud a passage

heard her using. They named the ones she had targeted and several others. Our "cool" respondent noted, "Man, this reading stuff is hard work." He got that one right!

3. *Then, read the passage to students, modeling the strategy or strategies you are using.* This "thinking aloud" gives your students the chance to hear how a skilled reader uses strategies to comprehend a text. This is the time when your thinking (which is normally invisible) becomes visible for them. When possible, I like for students to have a copy of the text I'm reading. Then they have the bonus of reading along while I'm reading to them. When it isn't possible for them to follow along, I must be very clear about when I'm thinking through the text and when I'm reading from the text. When I'm thinking aloud, I'll put the text down, or even shift my body in a different direction. If you think that sounds too exaggerated, just think about some of your most dependent readers; I think you'll agree that they are confused easily and need all the cues we can provide.

4. *Next, during real reading situations, give your students multiple chances to practice the strategies you've demonstrated.* These readers need time to practice strategic reading with peers—some more skilled, some at their level, and some even less skilled—while you listen in and coach them as needed. Without that time to listen, you miss observing students develop as strategic readers and therefore miss assisting them at critical points.

5. *Continue modeling as students' needs indicate or when the genre changes.* You can't assume that students who have watched you model how to predict using a short story will be able to transfer that skill to their study of a poem or expository text. As the genre changes, you must model again.

6. *Finally, give students opportunities to try the strategy without your coaching or support.* This shift from you doing and students watching to students doing and you watching is critical.

Distinguishing Between Direct Instruction and Scripted Instruction

Some of you have heard the term *direct instruction* associated with phonics instruction. In that situation, the term is almost always used interchangeably with the term *scripted instruction.* The two, however, are very different. Scripted instruction provides a script, giving teachers a detailed plan of what to say and when to say it. Such programs suggest, first, that teachers cannot make instructional decisions and, second, that all learners need the same instruction at the same level, at the same time, and in the same order. I've rarely, if ever, found that to be the case. Duffy (2002) reminds us that we must not confuse the direct instruction found to be so critical in improving comprehension with the scripted programs that some advocate using to teach decoding. Figure 4.1 compares the two.

I point out this comparison because some use these terms interchangeably when discussing phonics programs. Direct instruction, as described in this chapter, has nothing to do with the scripted phonics instruction put forth by some textbook programs such as Reading Mastery or Open Court.

Step Inside a Classroom

Perhaps the best way to understand what it means to teach comprehension strategies explicitly is to take a look at some very inexplicit teaching I did. This was during my third year of teaching. All was going great—or so I thought. During the summer before that third year, I had found an old reading textbook and had made myself a list of reading *skills* that the book mentioned. The list included things like finding the main idea, identifying cause and effect relationships, and making comparisons.

Note that then the term was *skill.* Now the term is *strategy.* If that distinction confuses you, don't worry, you aren't alone. Think of the difference

If you've not seen a scripted phonics program, you might be surprised at how scripted they are. Teachers are told what to say, when to say it, and even what gestures to use. Here's a portion of a scripted lesson from program called Reading Mastery. Everything shown here in italics is printed in red in the teacher's manual. The red print (or in this case, italicized print) indicates what the teacher says to the students. "Task 1 Children say mmm as in mat. A. *Let's say some sounds. Listen to the sound: mmm. When I hold up my finger, we're going to say* (pause) *mmm. Get ready.* Hold up one finger and say mmm with the children. *mmm.* B. *Again. Get ready.* Hold up one finger and say *mmm* with the children. *mmm.* C. *Your turn. Get ready.* Hold up finger. *mmm.* D. *Again. Your turn. Get ready.* Hold up one finger. *mmm.* E. Call on different children to do C."

—from *Reading Mastery I, Presentation Book A* by Engelmann and Bruner, 1995, page 1

Direct Instruction	Scripted Instruction
Teacher evaluates student's needs to determine what needs to be taught	Program decides what should be taught
Teacher determines order of instruction	Program determines order of instruction
Teacher listens critically to student's responses to know how to proceed and at what pace to proceed	Program determines pacing
Teacher decides on amount of reteaching	Program dictates amount of reteaching
Teacher responds to needs of students	Program doesn't recognize student needs
Teacher encourages analysis and synthesis	Program focuses on recall
Teacher embeds explanations into authentic learning experiences	Program sequences lessons in an artificial learning experience

FIGURE 4.1 *Distinguishing between direct instruction and scripted instruction*

between a skill and a strategy by thinking about riding a bicycle. Remember learning to ride with no hands? That's a skill; it's the end product of a lot of practice. Getting to that skill, you might need a strategy such as learning to balance the bike by shifting your weight, not by maneuvering the handlebars. The strategy takes you to the skill. Another way of thinking about that is that the reading skill is the product (identifying the main idea, for example) while the strategy is the process (think-aloud, for example). For many years in reading education, the emphasis was on the product (i.e., the skill) because comprehension was thought of as a product—the meaning of the text. The move to the word *strategy*, however, highlights a shift in our understanding about comprehension. Now we view comprehension as a dynamic process, a transaction between the reader, the text, and the context (Rosenblatt, 1978). Comprehension is both a product and a process, something that requires purposeful, strategic effort on the reader's part—anticipating the direction of the text (predicting), seeing the action of the text (visualizing), contemplating and then correcting whatever confusions we encounter (clarifying), connecting what's in the text to what's

Comprehension is both a product and a process, something that requires purposeful, strategic effort on the reader's part.

in our mind to make an educated guess about what's going on (inferencing). But in that book I found, the emphasis was on the skill we wanted students to exhibit, not the thinking we wanted the students to use.

Back to the point: that skill list made sense to me mostly because I remembered having to find the main idea on worksheet passages when I was in school. So, I visited a teachers supply store and bought several reading workbooks. I spent the summer pulling out the worksheet pages and putting them all together into one large three-ring binder. I returned to school in August with my reading notebook in hand and worksheets ready to be duplicated on the mimeograph machine. I had decided that I was going to march my students through each of those worksheets as we read our literature book, and then they would be better readers.

On this particular day, I had written the daily objective on the board ("The learner will find the main idea in a text.") and had told the students that this week we'd be reading a story in our literature books and then discussing the main idea. Obviously, a captivating class. To get them ready, I announced that we'd begin by completing one of the main idea worksheets. (If you've been teaching long enough, then you may remember the Madeline Hunter lesson design and might recognize my attempt at "guided practice.") I then distributed the freshly mimeographed pages (remember purple ditto?). All the kids sniffed the sheets (now surely you remember that!), took one, passed the others back, wrote names in the required blanks, and then listened as I read the instructions aloud: *Read each of the following paragraphs. After each paragraph, read options A, B, C, and D and circle the one that is the main idea of the paragraph.*

"Okay?" I said. "Remember to read carefully so you can find the main idea." That was the extent of my instruction on finding the main idea.

Twenty-seven heads bent down as students began reading. I returned to my desk to catch up on some grading. Then Al, the new student who had been listening intently, appeared at my desk.

"Yes, Al?" I said.

"What do I do?" he asked, pointing to the worksheet.

"Did you read the directions?" I responded.

He nodded.

"Okay. Well, did you read the first paragraph?" I asked.

He nodded again.

"Okay. So, now you read these options and circle the one that is the main idea," I said.

"Which one is that?" he asked.

"Is what?"

"Is the main idea?" he said.

"You know, it's the most important one, the main one," I said.

"Yeah, but *which* one is that?" he asked again.

"It would be the really main one, the biggest idea, the one that really captures what the paragraph is about," I said, not liking where this conversation seemed to be heading.

"Yeah, but which one *is* that?" he asked one more time.

I looked him square in the eyes. "What are you asking me, Al?"

He waited a moment, looked at his paper again, glanced around the room, took a deep breath, and then tried explaining his question one more time: "How does your telling me to find the main idea help me to know which one is the main idea unless I already know which one is the main idea? How do I know unless I already know?"

He stood there waiting for an answer. I, too, looked at his paper, glanced around the room, took a deep breath, and then said, "Al, sit down."

How do I know unless I already know? I thought about Al's words for weeks after he had returned to his seat to guess at answers. I stared at that worksheet; I studied other worksheets. The ones on cause and effect all basically said the same thing: *Read the following sentences. Underline the cause and draw an arrow to the effect.* I kept thinking about Al's question. How did telling someone to do that help him know how to do that unless he already could do that? And if he could do that, why in the world would he want to do that? *How do I know unless I already know?* I finally had to admit that twenty or so students in the class easily completed any worksheet I distributed. They made good grades, and therefore I thought I was doing a good job. But for the rest, the ones who didn't already know how to do whatever the worksheet directed them to do, those worksheets didn't help at all. More important, neither did I.

By the end of the year, I realized that I had confused two important words: instruction and instructions. I was great at giving instructions—directions—but not so great at offering instruction. I had to admit that I had no idea how to teach students how to understand what they read. No one had ever taught me how to teach comprehension, and I was only beginning to grasp that instead of focusing on skills, we needed to focus on strategies.

"Does Teaching Strategies Mean I Have Less Time to Teach Content?"

The honest answer to that question is *yes*; however, if we don't teach these strategies, students will not become better readers and we'll all continue to chant, "These kids can't read." The extra time we have to spend early in the

Listen carefully as students try strategies on their own

school year working on these strategies pays off later in the school year when students *are* more strategic readers. Actually, I have to wonder how we can afford *not* to spend the time teaching strategic reading. Let's think about this: We know the result of not teaching comprehension strategies, for we see kids in our classes every day who don't know how to make sense of a text. So, let's try teaching the strategies and see if that doesn't make a long-term difference.

Step Inside a Classroom

My example with Al gives us a wonderful negative example: what *not* to do. Starting there is important because I think that my previous approach to comprehension instruction might look familiar to many of you. The difference in my comprehension instruction between that third year and this, my twenty-third year, is my awareness that telling isn't showing and my conviction that, though I embrace a constructivist model, there is nothing wrong with being explicit and direct when modeling certain strategies. Because I believe that learning begins with observing, I want to share four transcripts with you that illustrate better than I could ever explain what it means to explicitly teach comprehension strategies. These transcripts emerged from a yearlong study I did in a middle school. While there, I spent some time with a sixth-grade teacher who, for part of the school year, supervised a student teacher, a young woman I'll call Kate. Kate understood that I was not there to "officially" observe her student-teaching as a part of her university course requirements; she wasn't even a student at my university. Instead, I was there to observe how teachers help students make sense of texts. However, since I was there on a daily basis, Kate and I struck up a friendship, and she often asked me for feedback on what she was doing. After conferring with her university supervisor, we decided that while I still was not responsible for assigning her student-teaching course grade, I would, upon her request, offer critical comments and guidance on what she was doing.

Kate and all the students had signed permission forms for me to audio-record everything that went on in the class. Consequently, Kate and I didn't have to rely on our memories or my handwritten notes when discussing her lessons. The first transcript is of a lesson Kate taught to a class of sixth graders. She had just finished reading aloud "Eleven" by Sandra Cisneros, a short story in which a young girl is humiliated when her teacher forces her to wear a tattered, smelly sweater that had been left in the lost-and-found box even though the girl denied that it was hers. After completing the story, Kate began what she later labeled a "class discussion" over the text. Next, you'll read a transcript of a debriefing session Kate and I had about the "Eleven" discussion. The third transcript shows Kate teaching the same literary selection in a different class while trying to do some of the things she and I had discussed extensively after the first lesson. Finally, you'll read the transcript of our debriefing of the second lesson. My thanks to Kate for allowing me to use her lessons with the students and our conversations as an example. I think Kate will be an excellent teacher, and I'm most pleased to have met her at the beginning of her journey.

TRANSCRIPT 1: A DISCUSSION OF "ELEVEN"

KATE: Okay. Today we're going to read a story by a woman named Sandra Cisneros. It's called "Eleven" and you can find it in your book on page 139. Let's go ahead and get those opened. Sandra Cisneros is a famous author who is still alive. You'll probably read one of her books, it's called *A House on Mango Street,* when you are in high school. In this story, you meet a character on her birthday, the day she turns eleven. Okay. It's pretty short, so if you'll follow along, I'll read it to you.

Note: Kate read the story aloud. Most students did follow along. Kate read aloud well, with good expression and good eye contact with the students. After reading, she began asking students questions about the story. As you read the next portion, you'll see that she called on many students. Each student Kate called on had raised his or her hand to respond. Also, there was generally a pause of one to three seconds between when she asked the question and when she called on someone.

KATE: Okay. That was a good story. How many of you liked the story? [More than half the students raise their hands.] Good. Okay. Let's answer some questions over the story. Why didn't the girl want the sweater to be on her desk? Amanda?

AMANDA: It smelled and had germs.

KATE: Good. Ben?

BEN: It embarrassed the girl, you know, having people thinking it was hers.

KATE: That's right. Hallie?

HALLIE: It wasn't hers.

KATE: That's right; it was smelly and that embarrassed her and she didn't want anyone to think it was hers. Good. So, what did getting the sweater have to do with turning eleven? [No response.] Um, turning eleven must be important because it's the title. So why is it important that on the day she turns eleven she has this encounter with having to put on the sweater? [Pause.] Laura?

LAURA: It was like, it was her birthday.

KATE: Good. It was happening on the day it was her birthday. Good. [Pause.] So what did the author say about turning eleven on that day? William?

WILLIAM: It was . . . it didn't matter.

KATE: What do you mean it didn't matter?

WILLIAM: It's because she was also all those other ages. Ten and nine and eight and so on.

KATE: Okay. Very good. Do you all agree that it didn't matter that it was her birthday? [Several students nod; more do nothing.] Did it make it worse that this was her birthday? [Students look down at their text.] Amanda, what do you think?

AMANDA: I guess it was worse.

KATE: That's right. Good. Why was it worse? Amanda?

AMANDA: I guess because like on your birthday, you know, it's like your birthday and nothing bad was supposed to happen.

KATE: Okay. Also since it's her birthday, she's supposed to be more mature, but see what she's really saying is that she can't just be more mature because she's all those ages, those other ages, and those other ages sometimes come out—that's why she started crying. Okay? See, she's showing that you stay all those other ages even when you turn another year older. Okay?

STUDENTS: [Most nod.]

TRANSCRIPT 2: DEBRIEFING THE FIRST LESSON

ME: What did you think about how that lesson went?

KATE: It was good. Yeah, I thought it was a good class discussion.

ME: Yeah? Why's that?

KATE: I was, it was, the story was a little complicated for them, so I was helping them to understand it.

ME: Okay. How were you helping them understand it?

KATE: You know, by like, I was explaining it to them.

ME: So, you were helping them with comprehension?

KATE: Yeah. That's it. I was helping them with comprehension.

ME: How'd you do that? You know, help them with comprehension?

KATE: Well, by asking them questions.

ME: Anything else?

KATE: Well, part of it, when they didn't know the answers, then I just had to explain it to them. You know, just explain it.

ME: So, what did you show them that they could use with another story?

KATE: I'm . . . what did I show them? [Pause.] I'm not sure I know what you mean.

ME: Well, if you were helping them with comprehension, what were you showing them that they could do when they read another text that was hard to comprehend?

KATE: I . . . I'm not real sure. I mean, I was just helping them with comprehension in this story.

ME: Helping them by doing what?

KATE: You know, by telling them what was going on when they didn't understand.

After this debriefing session, Kate and I met six times for about two hours each over the next six weeks. During those meetings, we discussed comprehension strategies and watched several of her lessons that had been videotaped. Additionally, she watched me teach three lessons in another school where I was working with seventh graders. The point of those lessons was to model for the language arts faculty how to explicitly teach comprehension strategies. Kate and I spent some time revisiting the "Eleven" lesson. We analyzed the "class discussion" technique she used—one used by many teachers—called IRE: initiate, respond, evaluate (Cazden, 1986).

With this, the teacher initiates the discussion by asking a question. A student then provides a response. The teacher evaluates the response and then starts the pattern again by asking another question. This keeps the conversation controlled by the teacher.

I asked Kate to code the "Eleven" lesson by marking her initiating comments with an *I*, students' responses with an *R*, and her evaluative responses with an *E* (see Appendix A for her coding of this lesson). When she completed the coding, she remarked, "I could be the poster child for IRE." Then she asked, "But how did I know to do that? I mean, I don't remember anyone ever teaching me to do it that way. And it's so boring. Why would I want to do it that way? No wonder it didn't feel like much of a discussion. It wasn't a discussion. It was me asking questions and kids responding." She eventually concluded that she "naturally" ran her class discussions in this pattern because it was familiar from her own middle school and high school days.

TRANSCRIPT 3: "ELEVEN" REVISITED

About six weeks later, Kate taught "Eleven" to a different class of sixth graders. This group, like the first one, had about twenty-seven students, most of whom, again like the first group, struggled with either decoding, comprehension, or both. Here are her introductory remarks:

KATE: Okay, today we are going to read a short story called "Eleven." It's on page 139 in your book. Go ahead and get to that page. [Pauses while students get to that point.] Okay, look at that first page and the pictures. Does anyone have an idea, a prediction, about what, about why this is called "Eleven"? [Three or four students note the birthday cake with eleven candles and say it must be her birthday.] That's good. When we see the cake and candles that makes us think about a birthday. You know, that's what good readers do, they look at things—even like pictures—and use all the information they can to make a prediction. We'll keep that prediction in mind, that it's this girl's birthday, and think about that as we read the story to see if it's an accurate prediction. Today I'm going to read this story aloud to you and as I do, I'm going to stop some and think aloud what I'm wondering about as I read the story. In particular, I'm going to try to visualize, you know, see what's happening in my mind. And I'm going to try to clarify any part that's confusing. And I'm going to try to predict what might happen next. Okay. Follow along.

Note: Students followed along as Kate read aloud. She stopped several times and thought aloud about what was happening at that point in the text. (A transcript of her think-aloud can be found in Appendix B.) When she finished she initiated a discussion of the story. That discussion follows:

KATE: Who can tell me what this story is about, give us a summary? [Several students raised their hands.] Mark?

MARK: It's about a girl, and it's her birthday, and the teacher finds a red sweater and makes her say it is hers and it isn't and that . . . that makes her mad.

KATE: Good, Mark. You just gave a good summary of the story. Who can add to that summary? Hal?

HAL: She started crying at the end because she was so angry and the teacher, she wasn't even sorry, like she wasn't sorry, when someone else remembered that the sweater didn't belong to her.

KATE: That's right. Now, I wonder, does it matter that it's her birthday when this is happening? Patty?

PATTY: I think so, yeah. Because since it was her birthday, it made her angrier, you know.

KATE: I agree. But I wonder why it made her angrier. [No response from students.] I wonder if it's important that this happens on her birthday because she thinks that since she's older, she's supposed to be more mature now. Patty?

PATTY: No, I think it's just because it's her birthday and she doesn't want to feel sad on her birthday. You know, just because it's like her special day.

KATE: Okay. But look at this part of the story. [She directs students to a portion of the text.] When I read this, I thought, "Oh, she's comparing getting older to like the layers on an onion." How many of you have ever peeled an onion?

BRAD: Oh I did that. It makes your eyes cry . . .

JAN: . . . Yeah, and you take away that little filmy layer, it's like really thin.

TANISHA: I don't see an onion in the story [unintelligible]. Where'd you get the onion?

KATE: There's not really an onion; it's just what the story, this part here, what the story reminded me of. That's something good readers do when they read; they try to connect what's in the story to something they know. This time, I made a connection that was a comparison. It was like I was reading it and I thought, "Oh, the way she's describing how you are all those ages inside you even as you turn another year older, I thought about all the layers of an onion." So, I made a comparison. To the layers of an onion. And when you take off that layer, what's underneath? Jan?

JAN: More onion.

MARCUS: Oh, miss? Miss?

KATE: What is it, Marcus?

MARCUS: And it's like those dolls, like she said in the story, those little dolls, you open them up, you know them, those dolls? You open them up and there's another just like it . . .

BELINDA: . . . Oh—I have one of those except it's a Santa and you open it up and there [unintelligible] . . .

MARCUS: . . . Yeah, my sister, she has one, and inside it is another one only except it is littler . . .

BRAD: . . . So just like when she's these other ages inside her . . .

KATE: Let's raise our hands now. One at a time.

BELINDA: . . . So she's like those little dolls, with littler hers all inside her . . .

CATHY: . . . And with an onion, sometimes, it's a different color, like whiter, and like the outside part is cracklier and yellower but the inside layers, they are like wetter.

KATE: That's right. And when I read this part here [redirects students to the same part of the text], I visualized how turning another year older would be like adding another layer to your life, like adding another layer on an onion. Or, like Marcus was saying, having a littler one of you inside you now. Visualizing that, or trying to see it in my mind, that's good to do because then you can understand the story better.

BRAD: Yeah, I can see that, how she's like those dolls . . .

MARCUS: . . . Yeah, and one is yelling, "Let me out, let me out!"

KATE: Okay, so listen, Marcus. So, I was visualizing something in the text, and comparing it to something I already knew. Now, why was I doing that? [No response.] When you are reading, if you can visualize something in the story and if you can compare what you are reading to something you already know, sometimes you can understand it better. So, when I was thinking about her turning another year older and it was like adding a layer . . .

NICK: . . . Like with the onion.

KATE: Yes, that's right, like with an onion, then I thought when I got to this part here [directs students to a later passage], I thought, I get it, she's crying like she is because she's saying that even though today is her birthday and she's eleven, that underneath, there's another layer that's still there and at that layer, she's just two. See, I could figure out what was happening by remembering that image of the onion. Brad?

BRAD: So it's important that it is on her birthday because on her birthday is when like another layer of the onion comes up, or another outside layer of the doll gets added and [unintelligible].

JAN: . . . So the title, "Eleven," is important because it's like now she has these eleven layers . . .

MELANIE: . . . But I didn't get this part here where it says it goes up tiny, tiny, tiny.

KATE: So, Melanie, that's good, because there you are showing what was confusing. Mandy?

MANDY: She should have said like she was sorry or something. I wouldn't have put the sweater [unintelligible] . . .

TONYA: . . . Me neither. But except when the teacher tells you, you have to do something . . .

MANDY: . . . But it still doesn't matter. That was for why she had to do it, because the teacher told her.

KATE: Okay. Let's get back to Melanie's comment first . . .

TRANSCRIPT 4: DEBRIEFING THE SECOND LESSON

ME: So, what was different this time?

KATE: It was much longer. I mean this discussion, it went on and on. And sometimes it got harder to like . . . hard to keep them in control. You know, they like all just wanted to talk sometimes. Together. And I wasn't sure what they were going to say next, you know, like when they started talking about the dolls, that was a surprise because I didn't know anyone was going to do that. But I also did a much better job of showing them some strategies. And then I guess when Marcus started talking about the dolls, well, that was . . . Marcus was making his own, what do you call it, his own association. So, that was good. But it was hard. [Pause.] It's just easier to, you know, just tell them what the story is about. With this, I had to be thinking about what I was thinking, and listening to what they were thinking, and trying to put it all together. Hey, I guess it was like with the story—you know, it had layers.

ME: Yeah, I agree. Sometimes it would just be easier to tell the kids what the story means. But then what happens?

KATE: Well, I guess then they don't get any better at figuring out how to figure out a story. But you know, I don't remember any of my teachers ever showing me this stuff and I can figure out stories okay. I have good comprehension.

ME: Well, what kind of reader were you in school?

KATE: What do you mean?

ME: Were you a good reader?

KATE: Oh yeah. I was always a good reader.

ME: Did you like to read?

KATE: I love to read. I always have.

ME: But sometimes, when you didn't understand things, what do you think you did to help you understand them?

KATE: I don't know. I just . . . I don't know, like I guess I mostly would just reread them.

ME: And while you were rereading them, what were you trying to do?

KATE: I don't know, like, maybe, oh, like I'd be clarifying or connecting—those things we've been talking about. So, I'd just do those things, like do them, I'd just do those things naturally.

ME: Probably. I'm going to suggest that when you were reading, you were doing all those things at a subconscious or invisible level and when something didn't make sense, then you'd think about what you needed to do, you'd do things at the conscious level or visible level. Now, think about these kids you've been teaching. Would you say that's how they read?

KATE: Well, I guess some of the time they do that, but then when they get confused, they don't seem to know how to do it at, like what you were saying, at the conscious level. But some of them can.

ME: So, do you need to be that explicit on how to make meaning for all the kids?

KATE: Oh, well, no, probably not. But, oh, I get it, for kids that don't just do this, you know, like make predictions, then you've got to show them.

Kate was beginning to understand what it means to teach comprehension strategies explicitly. Her lessons weren't perfect (whose are?), and she did some things as a novice teacher that more experienced teachers wouldn't do. But, she came a long way in a very short period of time toward the practice of teaching strategies explicitly. She continued combining comprehension instruction with discussions about literary selections to such an extent that by the end of the year, her students commented if she didn't model her thinking.

KATE'S FIRST YEAR

I continued meeting with Kate during the next year, her first year as a seventh-grade teacher. During that year, she worked on presenting comprehension lessons where the focus was the strategy and not the literary selection. At one point, she commented on the need to teach comprehension strategies separately from the literary selection:

> Some of my students have such poor comprehension strategies that if I combine talking about what we've read with a specific strategy, they get confused. So, now, like on Monday, I'll introduce a strategy I really want them working on while they read. I'll introduce it by just telling them something like, "Good readers make predictions when they read. Making a prediction means thinking about what has happened already to let that help you think about what will happen next. Listen while I read this passage aloud and the predictions I make." See? Then they are focused on the strategy and not the story. Then, as we read a story, I still have to model making predictions, but this time they've already heard me talk about why it's important. Finally, I'll tell them when we're discussing the story, they have to make predictions, or whatever strategy we're working on. Sometimes I have to tell them to stop reading and do something—like predict or visualize or connect—like you do with a Say Something (read about Say Something on page 105)—but then eventually I stop coaching them on where to stop and let them do it all by themselves.

At the end of the first year, when Kate's students took the TAAS exam (Texas Assessment of Academic Skills), she expressed some concern over how her students in this large (2,800 students) low-achieving school might do. Her principal assured her that he had watched her closely and thought that her approach to teaching comprehension was very good. And, like all the other teachers in her school, she had spent three weeks prior to the test extensively reviewing test-taking skills. Unlike several of the teachers, though, she had not spent class time all year doing TAAS worksheets. At the end of the year, Kate was relieved to find that of her 115 students, 103 had passed the reading portion of the TAAS. Of that 103, it was the first time for 69 to pass. Her students' pass rate was among the top three in the school.

When she talked about her students' scores at a faculty meeting, she cited four factors for success:

1. the principal's continued support for her strategies approach
2. our ongoing dialogues
3. her willingness to continually examine what and how she was teaching
4. the explicit comprehension strategy instruction she modeled in her classroom on almost a daily basis

"But If I Teach Explicitly, Does That Mean I Have to Give Up a Workshop Approach?"

Absolutely not! Many of us who teach in middle school, and more and more of us who teach at high school, are turning our English/language arts classrooms into the reading/writing workshops Nancie Atwell talks about in her groundbreaking book, *In the Middle,* Second Edition (1998). A workshop classroom differs from a traditional classroom in many ways, including the amount of direct instruction the teacher offers. In a traditional classroom, you'll often find the teacher lecturing for the entire class period with the occasional departure as students

◆ participate in teacher-led discussions
◆ work in small groups to complete specific assignments
◆ work alone to complete written assignments
◆ make presentations to the entire class

For help in creating minilessons, see Nancie Atwell's newest book, *Lessons That Change Writers* (Heinemann, 2002).

You'll also see everyone reading the same text or writing to the same prompt. What you often don't see in the traditional classroom is big blocks of time almost every day for students to read, write, and respond to one another about their reading and writing—in other words, a workshop environment. In a workshop environment, students read different texts at different rates and respond to those texts in a multitude of ways. They write in response to what they've read so that the reading-writing connection is reciprocal—one informs the other.

One way to bring direct instruction into a workshop environment is via minilessons. Minilessons are short (as little as five minutes or as much as fifteen minutes), focused lessons that can be delivered to the entire class or a portion of the class. The purpose of the minilesson is to clarify something or to provide information about something that students need to be applying in that day's work. I find that some of the most effective minilessons are think-alouds from the teacher—direct modeling of a certain reading strategy that students should use that day as they are reading independently or meeting in literature circles (Daniels, 2002) or response groups. A workshop approach does not mean that teachers don't teach. It does mean that you provide specific information that students need to help them accomplish whatever they are working on at that time.

Reflections

At the beginning of the twentieth century, Huey outlined the complexity of the reading act:

> And so to completely analyze what we do when we read would almost be the acme of a psychologist's achievements, for it would be to describe very many of the most intricate workings of the human mind, as well as unravel the tangled story of the most remarkable specific performance that civilization has learned in all its history. (1908, p. 6)

Now, at the beginning of the twenty-first century, we continue to analyze and untangle the reading story. Research on reading has considered everything from eye movement to eye fixations, from silent reading to oral reading, from phonological mediation to visual decoding, from the text to the reader to both. It has looked at emergent literacy, illiteracy, and, most recently, aliteracy. Researchers have focused on early readers, avid readers, remedial readers, and disabled readers. They have studied cognitive aspects, social impacts, and linguistic facets as well as looked at instructional practices, textbook influences, motivational exercises, and social environments. But still, the story of reading is tangled.

I suspect that much of the reading story will always be tangled, in part because when one group decides that the best way to untangle the complexity is by pulling on one particular thread, another group will resist that solution and pull on a separate thread. The issues surrounding reading become more knotted, and the result is that the students, all the Georges of our classrooms, are caught, waiting for us to know what to do. What doesn't seem to ever be confused, though, is everyone's belief that the point of reading is comprehension. Though we might argue about how to teach phonics or when to teach phonics or for some even *if* to teach phonics, no one argues that the goal of reading is to make sense of

Though we might argue about how to teach phonics or when to teach phonics or for some even if to teach phonics, no one argues that the goal of reading is to make sense of the written word.

the written word. Consequently, let's make one part of this tangled story of reading less confusing for our students—the strategies they use to improve their comprehension.

Dear George,

Not only did I never teach you how to fish, I don't think I even showed you how to bait the hook. I guess I hoped the osmosis plan would work—that as you stood near me, how to think about a text would just magically move into you. But comprehension isn't sleight of hand; it's hard work that can be examined, modeled, practiced, and learned.

5

Learning to Make an Inference

Dear George,

I gave you after-school detention one day for mouthing off to me. I thought I had done such a good job of setting up the premise for the story we read—a great mountain-climbing adventure called "Top Man"—and then had read most of it aloud to the class. You, along with everyone else, were supposed to read the rest of it on your own and then, that night for homework, answer one question: Who was the top man? The next day, when I asked who you thought the top man was, you just shrugged. I asked what the shrug meant. "I don't know," you replied. "You don't know the answer to the question or you don't know why you shrugged?" I pressed. "The question. It didn't say who was the top man." "You're supposed to make an inference, George, you know, inferencing. That's how you answer the question. Make an inference." You stared at me for a moment, then said, "No, I guess I don't know. Don't you think if I did know, I'd just do it and get you off my back? Jeez."

Obviously, George, twenty-three years ago, it took much less for me to send a kid to detention. Honestly, though, I think I gave you detention because your answer was just too honest. I backed you into a corner and then punished you when you defended yourself. If I was so good at making inferences, I wonder why it took me so long to figure that one out?

Defining Inferences

We talk about inferences. We make inferences all the time. We tell kids to make inferences. When pushed, we can even define inferences: an inference is the ability to connect what is in the text with what is in the mind to create an educated guess.

Right.

I once thought that if my students could make an inference, any inference, then my teaching woes (and their comprehension worries) would end. And I wasn't alone with that thought. At school, at National Council of Teachers of English conventions, at local conferences, in my university classes, I heard dozens and dozens and dozens of other teachers say the same thing. The problem with comprehension, it appeared, was that kids couldn't make an inference.

I shared this frustration with Anne one day. In the five years since we'd first met, Anne had been promoted from assistant principal to principal. She continued to push me to be a better teacher than I ever thought I could be. On this particular day, I stood leaning against her office door, complaining that the kids she had given me that year could not make an inference. She quickly replied, "Well, teach them."

"Teach them what?"

"Inferencing. Teach them how to make an inference."

"You can't teach someone how to make an inference. It's inferential. It's just something you can or can't do," I said, beginning to mumble.

"Tell me you don't really believe that," she said.

"Well, it's just really, really hard," I said, now definitely mumbling.

She said nothing, just peered at me over those ever-present half-rimmed glasses.

I started talking. "Okay. How about this? You come in and teach the lesson on inferencing. I'll watch," I suggested.

"Nope. I'm the principal. You're the teacher. I'll principal. You teach," she said. We laughed, she sent me back to class, and I began to wonder just how I'd teach inferencing. It took years for me to get a handle on that one.

Types of Inferences

Read the following paragraph and then, in the margin, write what you think is happening in this text:

He put down $10.00 at the window. The woman behind the window gave $4.00. The person next to him gave him $3.00, but he gave it *back to her. So, when they went inside, she bought him a large bag of popcorn.*[1]

When I read that paragraph, I see a man and a woman who have gone on a date to the movies; I can figure out from the money he gave the lady behind the window and the amount that he got back that tickets are $3.00 per person, so they must be going to a matinee. Furthermore, the woman with the man doesn't want the man to buy her ticket. He won't accept her money because he's being nice. She doesn't want him to have to pay for everything, so she buys the popcorn when they get inside.

How did your interpretation of that text match mine? Even if yours differs, there is one thing we both did to make any sense of this text: we both made a lot of inferences. Take a look at Figure 5.1 on page 64 to see all the inferences I made.

You can see that I made several inferences—some from information that the author supplied in the text (text-based inferences) and others from knowledge that I have about the world (knowledge-based inferences) (Durkin, 1993). I used those inferences to create what Durkin calls an "internal text"—my personal thoughts about what is happening in this text. Readers construct internal texts as they connect the information in the "external text" (the printed information) with what they already know (p. 11). I created my internal text as I

- ◆ figured out to whom the pronouns referred   (1, 2, 3, 8)
- ◆ gave explanations for events   (5, 6)
- ◆ decided where this was taking place   (4, 6, 9)
- ◆ decided why the characters were doing what they were doing   (5, 7, 10)
- ◆ figured out what the relationship was between the characters   (10)
- ◆ used my own knowledge about the world to provide details   (6)

Numbers refer to numbers in boxes on Figure 5.1

1. Adapted from "Where Comprehension Comes From" in *Creating Support for Effective Literacy Education* by C. Weaver, L. Gillmeister-Krause, and G. Vento-Zogby. Copyright © 1996 by Constance Weaver, Lorraine Gillmeister-Krause, and Grace Vento-Zogby.

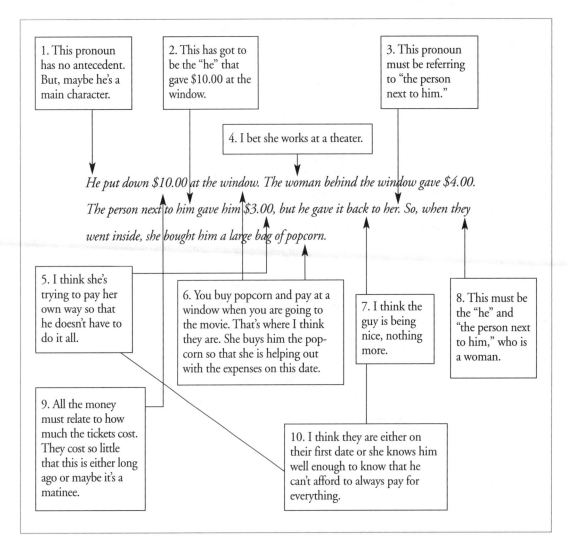

FIGURE 5.1 *Identifying types of inferences for one passage*

When we can analyze our own types of inferences, then we can begin to show students all the steps involved in making an inference. Figure 5.2 offers a longer list of types of inferences skilled readers make as they read.

I don't begin to suggest that this is a complete list. Instead, I encourage you to add to this list by noting the types of inferences you make and by listening to the types of inferences your students make. The purpose of such a list is to help make your modeling of inferencing more specific for students. Instead of telling students something vague like "make an inference," we can give students specific types of inferences to make by using comments like those shown in Figure 5.3.

Skilled readers . . .

1. recognize the antecedents for pronouns
2. figure out the meaning of unknown words from context clues
3. figure out the grammatical function of an unknown word
4. understand intonation of characters' words
5. identify characters' beliefs, personalities, and motivations
6. understand characters' relationships to one another
7. provide details about the setting
8. provide explanations for events or ideas that are presented in the text
9. offer details for events or their own explanations of the events presented in the text
10. understand the author's view of the world
11. recognize the author's biases
12. relate what is happening in the text to their own knowledge of the world
13. offer conclusions from facts presented in the text

FIGURE 5.2 *Types of inferences skilled readers make*

✓ "Look for pronouns and figure out what to connect them to."

✓ "Figure out explanations for these events."

✓ "Think about the setting and see what details you can add."

✓ "Think about something that you know about this (insert topic) and see how that fits with what's in the text."

✓ "After you read this section, see if you can explain why the character acted this way."

✓ "Look at how the character said (insert a specific quote). How would you have interpreted what that character said if he had said (change how it was said or stress different words)?"

✓ "Look for words you don't know and see if any of the other words in the sentence or surrounding sentences can give you an idea of what those unknown words mean."

✓ "As you read this section, look for clues that would tell you how the author might feel about (insert a topic or character's name)."

FIGURE 5.3 *Comments teachers can make to help students make certain types of inferences*

Students listen to a read-aloud and practice making inferences

Step Inside a Classroom

I was visiting an eleventh-grade honors English class. I put the popcorn pas-sage on the overhead and asked the students to read it; once they had figured out what was going on, they were to raise their hands. Soon, almost every hand was raised. Since I wasn't there long enough to learn students' names, I have transcribed their recorded conversation using S1 (for Student 1), S2, S3, and so on.

S1: There's a man, and he's on a date, and they've gone to the movies. It costs $3.00 to get in and he's paid her way, but she doesn't want him to do that, so she buys him popcorn.

ME: Why do you think they've gone to the movies?

S1: Because it says he paid her, and he paid her at a window . . .

S2: . . . And popcorn, he like bought popcorn and you do that at a movie . . .

S3: . . . Yeah but it was cheap or maybe like olden times because look, it was only like $3.00.

ME: What was $3.00?

S3: The movie.

ME: How do you know the movie cost $3.00?

S4: Well, look it was $10.00 and then he got $4.00, so that means it was $6.00 in two so that is $3.00. See?

S5: . . . Well, it could have been a matinee.

S6: . . . Nah, not even matinees are like that cheap. This was like really long ago.

S3: Or, maybe they're like old, you know like senior discount [unintelligible].

S1: . . . Oh, yeah, the over sixty card . . .

S3: . . . Okay so maybe like over sixty and a matinee.

S4: . . . But you don't get two discounts.

S7: . . . And if they were like old then why would they be on a date?

S8: Old people can date. My grandma started dating again when she was old. But I don't think if they date, the women want to pay their own way . . .

S9: . . . Yeah, I agree because I think they are into the chivalry and stuff and [unintelligible].

S3: . . . Okay well maybe, it's, okay maybe they aren't old, but they're like just, you know, like it's not really a date, but they're just hangin' and she doesn't want him to get the wrong idea . . .

S9: . . . Yeah, I think that she is like, "Man you ain't payin' my way and then thinking that later on this is goin' somewhere it ain't!" [Laughter.] [Unintelligible.]

S2: . . . Yeah I think that she had broken up with one boyfriend and this is, this is like a new one and she doesn't want him to think that they are, that she is, like not able to pull her own weight or that she owes him anything.

S7: . . . And so that's why she bought the popcorn.

ME: Is it important that it says she bought a large popcorn?

S5: Yeah, it, the popcorn, large popcorn must cost about $3.00 and that's what he paid, so now they are even.

ME: Who's the first "her" in the second sentence?

S1: That's, the first one, see, that's the woman. Behind the window. She's like the ticket taker.

S4: No it's not. Look. It said that "he gave it back to her" and the *her* is the person next to him. It's his date.

S1: Huh? [Rereads.] Oh, okay I thought he was giving the woman behind the window back some change, like maybe she had given him too much. But you're right. [Pause.]

ME: Is there anything else you can tell about this paragraph?

S4: You know, it could be a son. You know, like a little kid and his mom. And he wants to buy her ticket . . .

S6: . . . Oh that is so sweet . . .

S4: . . . But she says no because she doesn't want to use his money, like it's probably his allowance or something.

ME: You sure did come up with a lot of things for a text as short as this one.

S3: That is because we are the brilliant ones. [Laughter.]

S7: And it's not real. You know. We don't know that any of this stuff is right. We're just making it up.

ME: But you made it up based on something.

S7: Yeah, you know, you know you buy popcorn at a movie and you pay at the window . . .

S9: . . . Yeah, but all the girls I know, they all want you to pay. [Laughter.]

ME: So, you used some of the information that was in the text?

S2: Yeah, and some that you just know. You know, like before you read it. You just know.

ME: Yeah, that's called making an inference.

S4: Yeah, we studied that in English. It's on the TAAS [Texas Assessment of Academic Skills].

These students pulled a lot of information from a short passage. Look back at Figure 5.2 and see if you can figure out which types of inferences their statements represent.

Step Inside a Classroom

Now look at what another eleventh-grade class said about the same text. The difference is this group of students struggles with comprehension. None of them has ever passed the reading portion of the TAAS. They all make low Cs and Ds in their classes. They say they don't like to read and spend a lot of time trying to avoid reading. After they finished reading the same passage, we had this conversation:

ME: Well, what can you tell me about this passage? [Silence.] What do you think is happening in this paragraph?

S1: This doesn't make any sense.

S2: It sort of does, down here, with the popcorn, then you get the idea it's about going to a movie.

S3: It doesn't say anything about a movie.

S2: No, but they bought tickets and [cut off] . . .

S4: . . . Where do you get that they bought tickets?

S2: Here, where it says he gave her the money at the window.

S1: I don't get it.

S4: Me neither.

S5: What is this: "The person next to him gave him $3.00"?

S4: This is stupid.

These students don't understand that reading requires activity on their part; they fail to see the transactional nature of reading. Rosenblatt (1978) explains that readers interact—or to use her word, transact—with the text to create meaning. Readers don't just translate the text, don't merely decode the printed words into spoken words (even if spoken silently in the mind) and then suddenly have meaning. Instead, readers transact with the text, constructing meaning from the information that the author provides in the text and the information they bring to the text. This transactional nature of reading often escapes dependent readers who expect the text to provide everything. Their job, they believe, is at most to decode the print. After that, well, if the meaning isn't immediately apparent, they stop reading or ask us to explain.

Readers transact with the text, constructing meaning from the information that the author provides in the text and the information they bring to the text.

Helping Students Make Inferences

On page 165, you'll read about an activity called It Says—I Say. This structures the readers' thinking, helping them see the connection between what the text says and what that means to them. Some students, however, need additional help in making inferences. For those students you might try the following activities:

1. Put the list of types of inferences that independent readers make on a large poster or chart paper somewhere. Refer to this list often. The idea is to turn the word *infer* or *inference* into something more concrete, something students can point to on a list.

2. At least once a day, read aloud a short passage and think aloud your inferences. Have students decide what types of inferences you are making. Passages can be the first couple of paragraphs from a selection in your literature book, something from a magazine, a paragraph from a novel you are reading. I like to use *Two-Minute Mysteries* by Donald Sobol and *Five-Minute Mysteries* and *Even More Five-Minute Mysteries* by Ken Weber. These short texts offer lots of opportunities for inferencing. You can do this once a day because it's a short activity—seven minutes at the most.

3. Remind students that authors don't expect readers to create inferences out of nothing. Authors provide information (that's the external text); readers use that information in a variety of ways to create their internal text. When authors aren't providing literal information, then they are implying something. Tell students that readers *infer* and authors *imply*.

My mama, Love Ball Dotson, speech and drama teacher at Coal Station High

School and sister to the missing person, was plenty upset. In a Mountain Echo interview

she said it wasn't bad enough having your sister disappear like that without a trace, oh no,

people had to go running their mouths and making an already tragic situation worse. It

was just too much, she said, too much. Granny and Grandpa Ball, Mama's and Aunt

Belle's parents, wanted to take Woodrow to live with them, but Uncle Everett wouldn't

hear of it.

The days and weeks passed with nothing new coming to light. When the weeks

turned into months, the hill folks settled back into their humdrum lives and Belle Prater

became a kind of folk heroine, like Rose Conley in the song "Down in the Willow

Gardens." In fact, somebody did write a song about Aunt Belle, and it was sung in Coal

Station's main honky-tonk---the Busy Bee---accompanied by a bluegrass band, but

Mama double-dared anybody ever to sing it in her presence. There were insinuations in it,

she said.

married

where they live

?

FIGURE 5.4 *Syntax Surgery from* Belle Prater's Boy *by Ruth White (Syntax Surgery is explained on page 71.)*

For example, look at the following sentence: *Sam ate the food on her plate without slowing down between bites.* The literal information we have is that someone named Sam ate all the food that was on a plate. We also know, from the literal information, that Sam didn't slow down between bites. The author *implied* that Sam is a female by using the pronoun *her.* I *inferred* that she was very hungry since the author stated that she didn't slow down. After I read the next sentence, *Her bus would be arriving in about two more minutes,* I revised my inference of why she didn't slow down. Now, I'm not sure she was hungry, but instead think she was in a hurry. As I use the literal and implied information that the author supplies, I can begin to formulate and revise my inferences.

4. Read ahead in the text students will be reading and make notes of all the types of inferences you made to help the text make sense. Pull some

passages from your text and put them on an overhead transparency, then perform Syntax Surgery on them—in other words, as you think aloud the inferences you made, mark up the passage so students can see how pronouns related to nouns or how you used the context to define unknown words or how you added details to events described in the passage. Figure 5.4 shows you an eighth grader's Syntax Surgery on a paragraph from *Belle Prater's Boy*, by Ruth White. (Syntax Surgury is also discussed on page 135 in Chapter 7.)

5. Cut out some cartoons from the newspaper and put them onto a transparency. Put them on the overhead projector, read them aloud, and then think aloud the inferences you make that allow you to perceive the cartoon as funny. Then let kids cut out their favorites and bring them in. Eventually, I give extra credit for kids who bring in cartoons they *can't* figure out. These allow us to discuss how inferencing doesn't work if you don't have the right background knowledge. Most often, students bring in political cartoons for this.

6. Show students signs (or bumper stickers) and have them write the internal text that comes from the external text. Have students refer to the list of inferences and identify the types of inferences they made while writing their internal text. Figure 5.5 offers you some signs you could share.

A mom put this sign on her teenaged son's door:
Enter at your own risk.
An unknown bacteria is said to be growing in this room.

In the football team's locker room:
I am your coach, not your mother.

At the vet's office:
Puddles are for jumping over, not walking through!

Bumper sticker on a highway patrolman's car:
Don't slow down on my account.
But if you don't, it will probably hurt your account.

Bumper sticker on a teenager's car:
A floorboard? There's carpet on the floorboard?

At the library:
Check it out—really!

FIGURE 5.5 *Signs for writing internal text*

Dear George,

On the last day of class, you handed me a note. "Read it later," you said, then headed off for summer vacation. You had barely walked out our classroom door before I had unfolded your note. There, in your familiar pencil-smudged scrawl, you had written: "Sometimes what we show on the outside dosent realy match what's going on on the inside. Thank you for being my teacher."

My inferencing skills weren't too good, as I was never quite sure if the "we" meant students, in particular you, or the "we" meant teachers, in particular me. In either case, your words meant more than I ever had the chance to tell you. By the time I got into the hall, you were gone. I dreamed you a summer of basketball, skateboards, and fishing . . . I have hoped you a life of success.

6

Frontloading Meaning
Pre-Reading Strategies

◆ ◆ ◆

Dear George,

I'm quite sure that I introduced the short stories and novels we read that year in class by telling you all something about the author or something about the plot. Perhaps, for a little variation, I sometimes introduced some vocabulary words. I didn't understand how important it was for you to be thinking about the selection before you began reading the selection. Tapping into prior knowledge meant seeing if you had read another story by that same author. I was the only one doing something before we began reading— and I wonder why I was confused that you all were sometimes so passive. Reading is an active process and that activity starts long before you turn to the first page of the book.

◆ ◆ ◆

Activating Prior Knowledge

Several years ago, while speaking at the Texas Council of Teachers of English Annual Convention, I asked the 300+ teachers in my session to answer this question: "What do you do prior to reading to connect your students with that text?" As teachers filed out the room at the end of our session, they left their answers on a table. Later, as I read through the 238 responses, I saw that most teachers were introducing stories just like I had introduced them for so very long—by telling students something about the text.

While this practice could certainly be labeled as providing necessary background knowledge, I'm not sure it's the best way to help students become actively engaged with a text. Dependent readers are dependent in

How did these teachers introduce a new text? Sixty-eight percent said they tell students a little about the author, plot, and setting; 19 percent said they discuss vocabulary words; 8 percent said they introduce a story by asking students questions about topics or themes they will read about in the selection; 5 percent said they sometimes dress up as a character or bring in props such as clothing or food or photographs that help students understand the era or location.

part because of their passive reading. The challenge we face is to get them thinking about the selection and about how they will read the selection before they begin the text.

Dependent readers are dependent in part because of their passive reading.

In this chapter, you'll find several approaches that help students engage with texts prior to reading. Each strategy helps students

- access their prior knowledge
- interact with portions of the text prior to reading
- practice sequencing, find cause and effect relationships, draw comparisons, make inferences, and predict
- identify vocabulary that might be a problem
- construct meaning before they begin reading the text

Anticipation Guides

Little kids do it. They ask constantly what's going on and where they are being taken. Big kids do it. They ask repeatedly what the doctor is going to do before the doctor does it, and they plan what they'll say when they are approaching parents with special requests. Adults do it. We pick up travel brochures before we travel, study maps before we make a car trip, and consult the checkbook before we make a purchase. We all do it—we try to anticipate what's going to happen before it actually happens.

Skilled readers consciously try to anticipate what the text is about before they begin reading. They look at the cover, art, title, genre, author, headings, graphs, charts, length, print size, front flaps, and back covers. I've even seen kids reading the bibliographic information on the copyright page. They ask friends, "Is this any good?" They do anything to find out something before they begin reading. Dependent readers, on the other hand, often don't do that; they are told to read something, and once the text is in hand, they just begin. They often skip titles and background information, hardly ever read book jackets, and rarely look through the text for clues. The assignment is to read, so they'll read—maybe.

But they'd read better if they would bring to reading what they bring to the rest of life: that need to anticipate. To help these students learn to do that, use Anticipation Guides (Tierney, Readence, and Dishner, 1995). An Anticipation Guide is a set of generalizations related to the theme of a selection. Students decide whether they agree or disagree with each statement in the guide. These guides activate students' prior knowledge, encourage them to make a personal connection to what they will be reading, and give them a chance to become an active participant with the text before they begin reading.

Step Inside a Classroom

"This is hard," one student from the back row complained as he looked up from the paper he was working on.

"Yeah," another said.

The teacher just smiled and nodded. "Hmm," he responded.

"Aw, come on, Mr. Davidson. These questions are really hard," the student said again.

Another student in the middle of the room looked up and said, "Not really hard like 'What's the answer?' but hard like it's tough to make a choice."

"Hmm," Mr. Davidson said again, smiling.

The students kept reading, kept completing the worksheet, occasionally looked up, and said things like, "Impossible," or "This is tough," or "Well, it depends," but kept working.

As they finished, Mr. Davidson finally spoke: "So, do you want to talk about them [the questions on the worksheet] now or later?"

"Now," eighteen voices replied.

"Okay. Let's just get a count of how many agreed and how many disagreed and then we'll come back and discuss. How many of you agreed with number 1: 'If you are going to be a good citizen, then you should always do what your government expects.'" Some hands went up, others stayed down.

"It's that word *always*, Mr. Davidson. What if bad people start running the government?" a student said.

Mr. Davidson said, "Hmm." They all laughed. Then the teacher started a chart of agree/disagree responses on the board. "Number 2: 'Hiding people that the government says are criminals is wrong.'" More hands up, still some hands down. "All right. Number 3: 'If you have limited food and limited space and are trying hard to make sure your family survives, you shouldn't be expected to take in other people who will make your supplies disappear even faster.'"

Before hands could go up, a student spoke up. "That one was really hard, Mr. Davidson. I mean, you know that you should take in people that need help, but if you are trying to help your own family to survive, then you could like really hurt them if you say yes, but if you say no then you are one cold dude."

"Yeah," came a chorus of supporters.

"Hmm," Mr. Davidson said.

"Aw, come on," several said, smiling.

"Aren't you going to help us at all?" one asked.

"No," Mr. Davidson said, shaking his head.

"So we just have to decide?" another said.

"Yes," Mr. Davidson said. "Now, how many agree?" Hands went up. "Number 4 says," he said after counting, " 'People who do cruel things can still be good people.' " More moans, but students finally raised hands showing if they agreed or disagreed.

After getting a sense of what the class thought about each statement, Mr. Davidson then returned to each point and began a discussion. Several students made comments about the last item, "People who do cruel things can still be good people."

MR. DAVIDSON: So, what do you think?

ALBERT: I think that's wrong. How could you be good and cruel at the same time?

KII: Well, what if you didn't want to be cruel but had to do a bad thing to survive? Like my uncle when he was leaving Vietnam. He had to steal some things because the government wasn't letting any more people out, and they weren't even supposed to leave. My cousin, he got into a fight and hurt another guy real bad, he thinks, but my cousin had to or the guy would have told what they were doing. My cousin and my uncle are not bad people.

ISAAC: Well, maybe sometimes you got to do what you do. But when people are just doin' stuff, that's wrong.

DEE: I think sometimes if you're bad, you're bad. That's it. But sometimes you're bad 'cause that's the way society makes you. You're tryin' to do right, but you have to join with a crew just to survive. Bein' in a crew, sometimes you do cold stuff.

ISAAC: Yeah, you do what you got to do.

MR. DAVIDSON: Okay, interesting thoughts, guys. You think you guys are the first group to ever have to face making choices about what you will do or won't do? You think you are the first group to wonder how far you'll go to protect yourself or those you love? It's happened throughout time to all sorts of people. One group of people has often tried to control another group. Now we are going to read a play about one girl's attempt to survive against a group that doesn't want her to survive. As you read the play, find the parts that address the issues we've been talking about. Go ahead and jot down page numbers on your Anticipation Guide. You'll find parts of the play that make you think more about each of those statements. After you have finished reading, look at those parts again and think about your statements. If something you've read has changed whether or not you agree with the statement, make a note and then we'll talk about what you are thinking. Now this play is going to take several days to read. . . .

Debriefing the Strategy

These students were working through an Anticipation Guide for *The Diary of Anne Frank*. Mr. Davidson had purposely created statements that were "tough" to answer, as one student pointed out. The goal of the discussion wasn't to change students' minds, but to continue the process of bringing issues to their awareness.

Anticipation Guides first act as a prereading strategy and encourage students to connect to ideas and make predictions. Then, they allow students to look for cause and effect relationships as they read. Finally, they allow students to generalize, to discuss those generalizations, and to explore their own responses to a text.

Through the Anticipation Guide, these students had not only started thinking about issues they'd encounter in the play, they had also already explored their own thoughts about those issues. They were anticipating what they might find and were ready to meet those discoveries.

Putting the Strategy to Work

1. *First, write the Anticipation Guide.* I've found that if I look for the big ideas or themes that are presented as I read the text, I've got a start on what will make a good item to include in the guide. If one of the issues in the text is survival, then I begin jotting down generalizations about survival, keeping the most controversial ones. You don't need a lot of items; two items that encourage discussion are better than ten items that inspire little debate. Students should mark each statement as one with which they agree or disagree rather than as true or false. You don't want students considering the truth of the statement; instead, you want them exploring what they believe about the statement. Make sure you understand that there isn't a right or wrong answer; otherwise, you'll write ineffective guides like the following one, used by a history teacher to introduce a unit on the Holocaust:

   1. It is wrong to persecute people because of their religious beliefs.
   2. Hitler should not have ordered the extermination of the Jews.

Anticipation Guide

Directions: Read each statement and write Yes in the blank if you believe the statement and could support it or put No in the blank if you do not believe the statement and could not support it. After you finish reading the selection, revisit the statements. This time, decide how a character in the story would react to each statement.

Before Reading   **After Reading**

_____   1. Mean people eventually get what they deserve.   _____

_____   2. Good deeds are always rewarded.   _____

_____   3. People see what they want to see.   _____

_____   4. Ignorance is bliss.   _____

_____   5. Marriage should be based on love.   _____

_____   6. Children should be obedient to their parents
                    even if it means having to do something they
                    don't want to do.   _____

_____   7. If a sibling is continually mean to another
                    sibling, the hurt sibling should tell the parents
                    even if that means hurting the parents.   _____

_____   8. Political leaders should prove their worthiness
                    to lead rather than inherit the leadership
                    position due to family history.   _____

FIGURE 6.1 *Sample Anticipation Guide for* Mufaro's Beautiful Daughters

3. Keeping a diary is a good way to record your feelings.
4. We should study the Holocaust to understand our past mistakes.

Every student marked "agree" for each item, since each statement had an obvious conclusion. The guide was not meaningful to students because it did not build anticipation. Effective Anticipation Guides present students with pertinent issues that are worth discussing but that don't have clear-cut answers. Figure 6.1 offers an example of an effective Anticipation Guide for the picture storybook *Mufaro's Beautiful Daughters*, an African Cinderella tale retold and illustrated by John Steptoe. I've used this guide with students in eighth, ninth, and tenth grades. To use it with sixth or seventh graders, you might want to omit a few of the items.

Effective Anticipation Guides present students with pertinent issues that are worth discussing but that don't have clear-cut answers.

2. *Next, introduce the strategy to students.* I've found that the best way to teach students how to use an Anticipation Guide is simply to do one with them. Make sure students understand that they aren't guessing the correct answer but are exploring their thoughts. I usually make one for the fairy tale "Cinderella." In the past I've included statements such as the following:

   1. Sometimes life hands you cruel situations; when that happens, the best thing to do is just get through the situation. You'll eventually get a reward.
   2. You should always be willing to turn the other cheek; in other words, if someone treats you poorly, you shouldn't fight back, but just keep on doing what you know is right.

   These two brief statements elicit a discussion that encourages students to anticipate what they will read, to find how these statements play themselves out in the text, and to return to the statements after reading, ready to have some more wonderful discussions.

3. *Use Anticipation Guides before, during, and after reading.* Before reading, students should complete an Anticipation Guide that addresses issues in the selection. After students have completed the Anticipation Guide and you've talked about their responses, tell students to keep the guide close as they read so they can make notes about issues as they are revealed in the text. After students have finished reading, have them look at their original responses to see if they feel the same or see some detours in their thinking. The reading may have changed their responses by strengthening their original position or by making them doubt that position. Also, after reading, students revisit the guide to see how a particular character would have responded to the statements. This level of analysis encourages students to read critically, understanding issues from a character's point of view.

Questions and Answers

1. *Can an Anticipation Guide be used as a pre- and post-test?*
   I've seen teachers try to use it as that, but I don't find it to be very effective. Instead, the more effective way of using it is either as a before-, during-, and after-reading strategy or as a brainstorming activity for writing.

2. *Should you use an Anticipation Guide if the text is about a topic that is unfamiliar to students?*

That's exactly when you need to use one. Remember, a major reason for using an Anticipation Guide is to activate students' prior knowledge. If students are about to read something that is outside their experience (say, reading Shakespeare for the first time), then we must form some bridges between their experiences and the text; otherwise, the reading will be for naught. That's why Anticipation Guides aren't based on facts but on generalizations you can draw from the text.

3. *Should the class always discuss their responses to the Anticipation Guide before reading the text?*

Not necessarily. I've told students to read the guide, answer it, read the text, find things in the text that relate to what's in the guide, and then revisit the guide after reading, marking whether or not they still agree. At other times, I've simply had students discuss their responses, as Mr. Davidson did. Do what works for that particular piece. However, my experience with dependent readers tells me that delayed gratification isn't a strong character trait. Keeping the guide short and allowing them to discuss their responses prior to reading the text is important.

K-W-L

What I *K*now, What I *W*ant to Learn, What I *L*earned (Ogle, 1986) provides a framework that helps readers access their knowledge about a topic before they read, consider what they want to learn, and then record what they have learned once they finish reading. Though this strategy was originally designed to help students with expository texts, I find that with some minor adjustments, students can use this to help them with narrative fiction.

Step Inside a Classroom

In this transcript, you are going to see a novice language arts teacher working with a class of sixth graders. They are about to start a three-week cross-curricular unit. With the topic of "Oceans," there's something for students to do in science, social studies, and language arts class. These twenty-seven students all read between the thirty-fifth and forty-second percentiles on the reading comprehension portion of the Iowa Test of Basic Skills. Four are repeating sixth grade. The teacher (identified as T) begins the lesson and then turns it over to me.

T: Okay, let's begin to think about what we know about oceans. [She stands near a wall with a large sheet of chart paper on it. At the left end, near

A fifth-grade class's K-W-L chart on rain forests

the top, she has written the words "What We Know." Students begin offering ideas. I write down most of their comments.]

S1: There's the Galveston Ocean. It's near here.

S2: That's not an ocean. That's like, like a river to the ocean.

S3: It's the Gulf.

S1: So what's a gulf? Like a bird?

S3: No, you know, like a gulf. It's called, what's it called? [He looks at the teacher.]

T: I think you mean the Gulf of Mexico.

S4: Oh yeah, I've heard of that. It's like, like the part that goes into the ocean.

T: Okay, so one thing we know is the word *gulf.* [She writes the word *gulf* under the What We Know column.]

S5: And it's, there is four of them.

T: Four gulfs?

S5: No four oceans.

T: Okay. Can someone name them? [After several attempts by several people, they get them all listed.]

S6: And there's like pirates. You know there still are pirates. Really. They are like by Mexico. You have to be real careful.

S7: And fish. The ocean is filled with fish.

S8: Don't forget whales and dolphins.

S9: We saw this show, it was about how whales migrate. You know like birds?

S10: Oh, yeah, how they swim with the tides. So, put that, Miss, put tides and waves. There are waves.

S7: And there are other things too, you know like plants and seashells. Not just fish.

S11: And it's salty. You know, the ocean water, it's salty so you can't drink it.

Responses continued for another ten minutes or so. When students seemed finished, they reviewed all they had said. The teacher then took the chart paper down and told them they would look at it again the next day. The next day, they studied their responses as the teacher asked them to group items so that similar ideas were together. Then they came up with headings for their groupings. These groupings and headings were copied onto another sheet of chart paper so they could see all the areas. Then the teacher asked them the following question:

T: So, we've got everything really organized now. Now, let's make a second column and make a list of everything we want to know. Okay. What all else do you want to know? [Silence.] Keep thinking about oceans and tell me what else you want to know? [Silence.] Come on, who wants to know something about oceans?

S5: But Miss, we already told you everything we know. What else are we supposed to know?

This nonresponsive conversation continued for a few moments. Finally the teacher walked over to me and said, "This is why I hate K-W-L. They never have anything to say. It's like they've told you everything they know, so now what?" She was clearly upset. I told her that I often had the same trouble until I learned how to link their comments about what they already knew to questions about what they wanted to know. "Show me," she said, handing me the marker. So I began.

ME: Okay guys. It's my turn now. Remember me, Dr. Beers? I need some practice working on a K-W-L chart. That's what you guys are creating right now. This is a chart that shows what you know, what you want to learn, and what you have learned. You've already done the first column. Let's see what we can get in the second column. [Silence.] Let's look at this first category, life in the ocean. Somebody said there were lots of fish in the ocean. I wonder what we want to know about these fish? [Silence.] You know, I've always wondered about what makes some fish saltwater fish and others what they call a freshwater fish. [I write that on the chart directly across from the word *fish*.]

S3: Yeah, I heard my uncle say that he went freshwater fishing, and I didn't know what that was.

S5: And there are bass and trout, but are they fresh- or saltwater fish?

S6: Yeah, and what about those fish that lay down flat and they have an eye on just one side. I always wanted to know what they are.

S7: Yeah we saw one of those at an aquarium. And that makes me think, you know, do fish blink their eyes? You know? And if they don't, then do they go to sleep?

ME: These are great questions. What questions do you have about the other things in this category? (Figure 6.2 shows you a sampling of their categories and some of their related questions.)

We moved through each category. I repeatedly asked them to connect their questions to the topic. Some students had questions in some categories but not in others. Generally, one question would encourage others. I thought the most interesting question came from the Characteristics About the Ocean category.

ME: Okay. What questions do you have about the topics in this area? As you think about the temperature or the waves or the tides or the salt or how much space it takes up, what questions do you have?

S12: Miss, I have a question.

ME: Okay.

S12: For the salty part, I was wondering how come the salt in the ocean burns your eyes but the salt in your tears doesn't?

S13: Oh that's such a great question. We went to the ocean and went swimming and man, the water it just burned my eyes but like if you cry, like when you were little, then your tears they don't burn but that's got salt too. That is like such a good question.

The students continued generating questions for each category through the next day. At one point, because I knew what students would be reading in their language arts class, I asked how the oceans got their names. That led to a student asking, "Are these the same names that people anyplace would have for oceans or are these just the American names?"

Debriefing the Strategy

This teacher was using a K-W-L chart because she had read about them in her undergraduate content area reading class; however, every time she created one with students, she admitted, she was the one who generated the questions for the second column, as students had little to offer. The problem was

What We *Know*	What We *Want* to Know

Life in the Ocean

Fish	What makes some fish saltwater fish and others fresh-water fish? What kind of water do bass and trout live in? What's the name of the flat fish that just has one eye on the side of his head? Do fish have eyelids? How do fish sleep?
Sharks	What are the man-eating sharks? Could there ever really be a shark like Jaws?
Whales	Why is it called a blue whale? Why do whales live in the ocean but have to breathe air?

Names of the Ocean

Atlantic Pacific Indian Arctic	Are these the same names that people anyplace would have for oceans or are these just the American names?
	How did they get their names?
	How do you know where one begins and the other ends?

Characteristics About the Ocean

Some is cold and some is warm	What makes it different temperatures? Do different fish live in different oceans because of the temperature?
Has low tides and high tides	Where does the water go during low tide? Is it causing a flood someplace else?
It is salty	What makes it salty? Is it the same kind of salt that's in your salt shaker? How come the salt in the ocean burns your eyes but the salt in your tears doesn't?

Exciting Things About Oceans

Pirates	Who were some pirates?
Sunken ships	What are some sunken ships other than the Titanic? If you find one, can you keep the treasure?

Problems for the Oceans

Pollution	What is the pollution doing to the sea life?
Oil spills	Why do they spill oil on the ocean? How do people clean it up?
The pollution is killing the fish	Have any fish gone extinct from the pollution?

FIGURE 6.2 *K-W-L grouping of terms*

What We *Know*	What We *Want* to Know
Types of Boats on the Ocean	
Ships	What's the biggest ship ever built? What makes something a ship and not a boat?
Canoes	Why did Indians make canoes instead of sailboats? What did they make canoes out of?
Words Connected to Oceans	
gulf	Is the Gulf of Mexico the only gulf?

FIGURE 6.2 *continued*

that this teacher saw the chart as three distinct columns to be completed. She had forgotten that the purpose of the chart was to link what the kids knew to what they wanted to know. That's what comprehension really is: linking the unknown to the known. Once I showed her how to constantly tie the questions to the information students had already generated, she began to see how powerful this strategy could be.

Putting the Strategy to Work

1. *First, decide what topic you want discussed on the K-W-L chart.* This is primarily used with nonfiction informational texts where deciding the topic is easy; if you are using this with fiction, you'll need to think about the theme or topic in the novel or story and see how that would lend itself to a discussion prior to reading.

2. *Next, decide how you'll record that information*—on chart paper, a transparency, or a computer.

3. *Then, ask students what they know about that topic.* Be aware, sometimes they know nothing. Once I asked a seventh-grade science class what they knew about photosynthesis. Not much. Generating questions was difficult because they didn't know enough to ask questions beyond, "What is it and how does it work?"

4. *Make sure that, after completing the K column, students have a chance to group responses and label those groups.* This alone is a wonderful exercise in comparing and contrasting.

5. *Finally, remember that when you move from the K column to the W column, the point is to connect what they wonder about to what they've already told you.* Linking the unknown to the known is critical.

Questions and Answers

1. *How do I use this for fiction?*

   Think about the topic or theme of the book students will be reading. For instance, before we read *To Kill a Mockingbird* in a ninth-grade class, we began a K-W-L chart on the topic of discrimination in the United States. Not only had I decided on the topic that would guide our K-W-L discussion, but I had made a list of some of the topics or questions I hoped students would offer. With this list in mind, I listened for certain responses from students as we worked through the K column. If these responses didn't emerge, I offered them myself. For instance, at one point I said, "I know that not only were the laws for black people and white people different for a long time in this country, but black people often didn't receive fair trials." Then when we moved to the W column, students asked, "Could black people serve on juries? Could they be judges or lawyers? Did some white lawyers not want to represent black people? How could it be a jury of your peers if no one on the jury was black?" Be careful with your topics, however. I tried this once in a sixth-grade class prior to reading *Summer of the Swans*. Students brainstormed what they knew about sibling rivalry (a lot). But then, when it came time to generate questions about the topics they had mentioned, there wasn't much discussion. They knew so much about this topic that they didn't question what caused it or what could be done to stop it.

2. *What do we do after we've completed the first two columns?*

   Many teachers, at this point, move to reading the material or teaching the content. If that's the case, the K-W-L is a great way to access students' prior knowledge, help them organize their information, generate questions about that knowledge, and then read to answer those questions. However, if you want to use K-W-L in a slightly different fashion, insert another column between the W and the L columns labeled G for "Where do I need to *Go* to answer these questions?" Now, you've made this into a research plan. That's what we did with the sixth graders studying the ocean. The group interested in the salt in the ocean decided they needed to ask the school nurse about why the salt in your tears doesn't burn your eyes but the salt in the ocean does. She referred them to a pediatric ophthalmologist who happily answered their questions during a phone conference. For this G column, avoid the quick reply of "library"—that's much too broad. Encourage primary sources. You'll have already scouted the phone book and thought through local resources so you'll have some ideas about places students might turn to get answers you've anticipated. Talk with your librarian to see what specific sources you might recommend if a trip to the library is the best answer.

3. *What's the L column for?*
That's a great place for students to record information that other students or small groups share with the class as a result of their research. You can also use this as a review column. Once you finish the unit, chapter, or novel, revisit the information you recorded on the K and W columns and ask students if they now can answer the questions they generated. Oftentimes they can't, but instead have gained new knowledge that now leads to more questions.

Probable Passage

Dependent readers often struggle because they don't predict what the selection might be about, don't think about what they already know about a topic, and don't form images as they read. These students simply open a book, look at words, and begin turning pages. Probable Passage (Wood, 1984) helps stop those passive reading habits by encouraging students to make predictions, to activate their prior knowledge about a topic, to see causal relationships, to make inferences, and to form images about a text.

As originally developed, Probable Passage is a brief summary of a text from which key words have been omitted. The teacher chooses these key words and presents them to the students. After discussing what the words mean, students arrange them in categories according to their probable functions in the story (such as setting, characters, conflicts, solutions, or endings), then use them to fill in the blanks of the Probable Passage. As students work through this process, they use what they know about story structure, think about vocabulary, look for causal relationships, and predict what they think will happen. I've adapted this process so that students now complete a Probable Passage worksheet. Students place words into boxes that are labeled "Characters," "Setting," "Problem," and "Outcomes" and then, from the placement of those words, write a prediction statement that offers the gist of what this selection might be about.

Step Inside a Classroom

Mr. Robin put the following words on a transparency on the overhead projector: *guilt, bird, seashore, frostflower, jagged ivory bones, plover, boy, gun, quicksilver, sins, headlands*. He then distributed the Probable Passage worksheet (see Figure 6.3, reproducible image on page 323).

Mr. Robin chose those words after reading *Forgive My Guilt*, by Robert Tristram Coffin. He looked for words that gave insight into the characters, setting, conflict, and resolution. He also chose some words he thought students would not know.

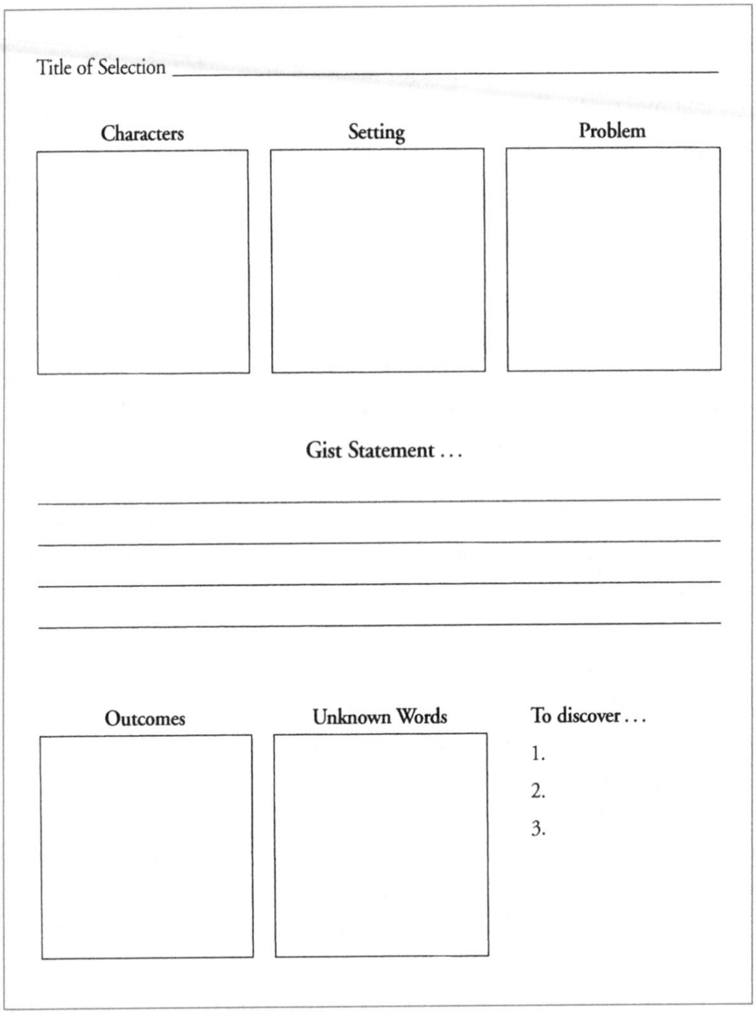

Title of Selection _____

Characters	Setting	Problem

Gist Statement . . .

_____

_____

_____

_____

Outcomes	Unknown Words	To discover . . .
		1.
		2.
		3.

FIGURE 6.3 *Probable Passage*

"Okay guys, get into groups of three and begin putting the words into the correct boxes. Who remembers what you can put into the Unknown Words box?"

"Only words that you don't know what they mean," one voice responded.

"That's right. You can't put a word there just because you can't decide where it goes," he explained. "And how many times can you put a word in a box?"

Another student replied, "Only once. Once you've put it into one box, you can't put it anyplace else."

"Good. Now get started. Once your group gets words into the boxes, then you can write your gist statement." (See Figure 6.4 on page 90 for a completed Probable Passage worksheet.)

The students in the room began discussing where they would put certain words.

Group 1

S1: Let's put *gun* under Problem. Because, you know, if you have a gun, then that could be a problem.

S2: Yeah, but it could be the solution, too. You know, like you don't feel safe so you get a gun.

S3: Yeah, but I think it's more like the problem. Having the gun is the problem and then whatever you did with it, that causes you to be guilty. So put *guilt* under Outcomes.

Group 2

S1: Anybody know what a plover is?

S2: Like a plumber? Plover. Plumber. They kind of sound alike.

S1: I don't think so. It's just the *pl* that sound alike. And anyway, read these words. There's nothing else like sink or anything that would make you think of plumber.

S3: Put it in Unknown Words.

Group 3

S1: So, like, what is *boy*? He could be the problem. Like he got the gun and then did something.

S2: Yeah, but if he's the one that got the gun, then he's the character. You know, like he's the one who did it.

S3: Put him in both.

S2: You can't, man, you gotta choose.

Title of Selection _____

Characters	Setting	Problem
boy birds	sea	gun sin

Gist Statement......

A boy goes ~~to the sea~~ ~~and is going~~ hunting but some birds fly up and they scare him so he shoots and someone else is there and he throws his jagged ivory bones into the sea and feels guilty.

Outcomes

guilt
jagged ivory bones

Unknown Words

plover
frostflower
quicksilver

To discover.....

1. Why did the boy have a gun?
2. Whose bones?
3. What is a plover?
4. Did the boy do the shooting or get shot?

FIGURE 6.4 *Completed Probable Passage*

S3: Then, put him in Character. You know, like characters are people and he must be a person.

Group 4

S1: *Jagged ivory bones.* Oh, that is so sad.

S2: It's a problem. Put it there.

S1: No, it's what happens. You know like maybe somebody kills the little boy and then just leaves him, here, at the sea—oh put that in Setting—and then, like you know, years later, somebody finds his body and all that's left is his jagged ivory bones. So, it's the outcome.

S3: What's the birds for?

S2: Like maybe they ate part of him.

S1: Oh, that is so gross. No. Like maybe somebody was out hunting birds and shot him instead. And then he felt guilty. So, put that in Outcomes.

Group 5

S1: So, what's our gist statement?

S2: I don't know.

S3: Like, well, like okay, we said the boy and the birds were characters. Okay, so the boy goes to the sea and is going hunting but the birds startle him and so he shoots somebody else instead and tosses his jagged ivory bones into the sea and then he feels guilty because that was a sin.

Group 6

S1: Read our gist statement.

S2: Okay. We said this is the story of the Native American Indians Quick-silver and Frostflower who go to the sea and think about the sins of the white men who came and shot their tribe, even the little boys, and tossed their jagged ivory bones into the sea.

S3: That is so good.

Debriefing the Strategy

Probable Passage forces students to think about the characters, setting, conflict, resolution, and vocabulary of the story before they read the story.

Mr. Robin was using Probable Passage as a pre-reading activity, not only to introduce students to terms and phrases they would encounter while reading the selection but also to get them to predict and anticipate what might happen in the text. As students categorized the words, they discussed what the words meant as well as what the category headings meant. They saw causal relationships ("Yeah, but if he used the gun to kill something, then he probably felt guilty."), made comparisons ("I like what we said about the boy being the character better than him being the problem."), made inferences about unknown words ("Don't you think a frostflower has to be some sort of flower? I mean, it has the word *flower* in it."), and reached conclusions ("I think the boy did the shooting rather than someone else shooting him. I mean, that's got to be it because no other characters are mentioned, except for birds, and they can't shoot anything.").

As students assign words to individual boxes, they make the invisible act of thinking visible. This strategy shows us that we don't need to spend time giving worksheets that direct students to underline the cause and draw an arrow to the effect or circle the response that states the main idea. Instead, when we give students strategies like Probable Passage, we give them the opportunity to bring those thinking skills to the visible level.

Putting the Strategy to Work

1. *First, choose eight to fourteen key words.* After reading a story, think about words that would fit in the boxes. I like to choose some words that have an obvious connection and other words that might encourage some disagreement. I also try to find some words that I know will be unknown. However, it's critical that these be words for which the students can grasp the meaning by reading the selection.

2. *Then, model the strategy a few times.* Students need to hear how you think through this strategy before they can do it well. Tell them that you are going to place words into particular categories based on what you know about the categories and what the words mean to you. As you begin putting words into the boxes, be sure to think aloud your reasoning. Model creating a gist statement. If it's important to you that students use all the words (except for those in the Unknown Words box) when they write the statement, then model that. If they don't need to use all the words, then don't use them all. Finally, move to the final part of the worksheet—the To Discover section. Aloud, think through all the things you want to discover as you read the selection. Be as specific as possible. Don't say, "What happened?" but do say, "What is a plover?" or "Whose jagged ivory bones are they?" You will probably have to complete your list of questions on the back of the worksheet.

Probable Passage forces students to think about the characters, setting, conflict, resolution, and vocabulary of the story before they read the story.

To be able to hear what types of causal relationships or inferences students are making, be sure to spend time walking from group to group. Take notes on what you hear the students saying. Later, you can use those notes to show students what types of thinking skills they used while working.

3. *After reading the story, return to the worksheet to see which of your To Discover questions you can answer.* Look to see if you now know the meaning of any words that are in the Unknown Words box. Then ask yourself, How would the author have arranged the words and how would that have changed the gist statement?

4. *After you've modeled this once with students, let them try it.* Once the groups have placed all their words in boxes and completed their gist statement, ask students where they placed the words. Record their answers on a blank transparency. I usually use two colors of markers to do this. One color of pen is used for the most common response and the other for the unusual response. That way, we have a quick visual cue about how the class responded. As students tell you what words they put into the Unknown Words box, don't spend time defining these words. The point is to make sure students see the word as one they don't know. Let students share their gist statements, and then, as a class, brainstorm what you want to discover when reading the selection. Finally, read the selection.

Questions and Answers

1. *Does everyone need to do a Probable Passage prior to reading a story?*
   Good readers often know how to use their prior experiences to help them understand the flow of the story, and they know how to predict what might happen next; therefore, they might not need this structured strategy.

2. *Why should students compare their Probable Passages to the story after reading?*
   Kids will make the comparison on their own. This comparison leads to interesting discussions. For instance, you can ask questions such as the following: Did your predictions make as much sense as what actually happened? How did your predictions differ from what happened in the story? Now that you've read the story, in what categories would the author place the key words? How did completing the Probable Passage help you better understand the story?

3. *Why is it important to ask students how the strategy helped them understand the story?*
   Struggling readers often say that good readers read fast, read with expression, and know all the words. They don't see skilled readers

making predictions, modifying their predictions as they read, monitoring for understanding, making connections between the text and what they already know, or rereading when they've got a problem. And because dependent readers don't see good readers doing those things, they don't believe or understand that good readers actually do them. So, a strategy like Probable Passage makes the invisible visible for them. The more students practice making predictions, the better the chance that this will eventually become a natural part of their reading process.

4. *Will students become frustrated if their predictions don't match the text at all?*
   If that happens, you might have put too much emphasis on "getting it right." Remind students throughout the process that what they are doing is considering some of the words or phrases they will soon be reading in the text to decide what they think about those terms. This isn't a guessing game; instead, this is a chance for students to see associations among and between words.

5. *Should students refer to their Probable Passages as they read?*
   Absolutely. Often that's exactly what they want to do. And that's great. If you see students referring to their Probable Passage as they read, then you know they are thinking about *what* they are reading *while* they are reading. That sort of metacognitive reflection is the big goal—getting kids to think while they read! You especially want to redirect them to their To Discover questions.

6. *How is this like Word Splash?*
   Word Splash, another pre-reading strategy, is very similar. You "splash" some words or phrases from a text on the board, transparency, or chart paper and have students write a prediction statement about what this text might be about based on these words. Again, use eight to fifteen words.

Tea Party

Like Probable Passage, Tea Party offers students a chance to consider parts of the text before they ever actually read it. It encourages active participation with the text and gives active adolescents a chance to get up and move around the classroom. This pre-reading strategy allows students to predict what they think will happen in the text as they make inferences, see causal

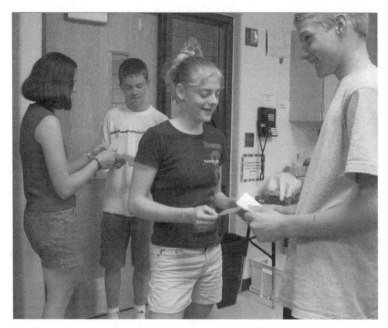

Students enjoy participating in Tea Party

relationships, compare and contrast, practice sequencing, and draw on their prior experiences. I first saw this strategy as I was working with teachers who were part of the South Coast Writing Project at the University of California Santa Barbara. It was developed by one of their very own teachers, Sue Perona. I've talked about this strategy all over the United States, mostly because it is one that students from all grade levels enjoy. Though I've made a few minor adjustments to Tea Party from what Sue first envisioned, the idea belongs to her.

Step Inside a Classroom

I was teaching an eighth-grade class. We were about to read a poem titled "Grandmother Grace" by Ronald Wallace. I distributed an index card to each of my thirty-three students. Each card had one phrase on it. I had chosen fifteen different phrases (see Figure 6.5), so nine were repeated two times and five repeated three times. After giving each student a card, I asked everyone to get up and move from student to student. They had four goals: (1) share their card with as many classmates as possible; (2) listen to others as they read their cards; (3) discuss how these cards might be related; and (4) speculate on what these cards, collectively, might be about.

I didn't give her a good-bye kiss

I remember going there every summer—

I remember . . . afternoons of spit-moistened hankies . . .

Cast off, abandoned, in Williamsburg, Iowa . . .

God wouldn't let the good person sink.

She always sealed it with a kiss . . .

. . . how could I know she would sink?

I was ten.

The idea of a kiss at that time made my young stomach sink.

Let it be summer.

The violet kiss . . . sealed some agreement we had for the next summer . . .

I sat in that angular house with summer dragging me onward . . .

I went off in the bus for the last time . . .

Grace

I could have done without the words of Jesus

FIGURE 6.5 *Lines and phrases from "Grandmother Grace" for Tea Party*

Try this Tea Party strategy on your own. Check your prediction by reading the poem found in Appendix N, on page 367.

ME: Does everybody have a card? All right, go ahead and begin. [As students begin reading their cards to one another, I circulate, listening.]

S1: Mine just says, "Grace."

S2: Okay, mine says, "I remember going there every summer."

S3: "God wouldn't let the good person sink."

S4: Huh?

S3: I know. "God wouldn't let the good person sink."

S4: So they must be on a boat?

S3: Maybe. What's yours say?

S4: "The kiss made my young stomach sink."

S5: Hey, mine says that, too.

S4: So, the kiss must be important.

S5: How come?

S4: Because we've both got it.

S6: Mine says, "I was ten."

S3: So somebody is ten and gets a kiss?

S6: Maybe when he was ten there was a girl and she wanted to kiss him but he didn't want to kiss her?

S3: Yeah, maybe.

I let students continue moving around the room, sharing cards, discussing ideas for a short amount of time—about ten to twelve minutes. I didn't want the conversation to drift to plans for Saturday night. I listened closely and sent them back to their chairs when they had either talked with everyone or the conversation began to lag.

ME: Now, get into groups of five or so and share your cards with everyone in the group. Discuss what you each heard and what the cards in front of you say; then write a "We think" statement that briefly describes what your group thinks this selection is about.

Students began to work in groups. Some occasionally got up and visited another group to refresh their memories about what was on other cards. Again, I circulated, listening to conversations.

One group:

S11: It's in Williamsburg. Did anyone else hear that card? "Cast off, abandoned, in Williamsburg, Iowa"?

S12: Yeah, and that "cast off," that made it sound like a boat, but I don't think there's an ocean in Iowa.

S13: Maybe a river?

S12: Yeah, maybe.

S14: So, somebody when he was ten went to Williamsburg?

S12: For like summer camp?

S13: Yeah, and he didn't want to go. I remember my brother when he went to camp. Oh my gosh, you'd have thought we were leaving him in a foreign country for a year. He certainly felt abandoned.

Another group:

S14: This one, this makes me think of my grandmother, see "spit-moistened hankies." That just sounds like a grandmother. And my grandmother, she's always trying to clean up my little sister's face by spitting on a napkin and cleaning her up. How gross.

S15: That is like so unhygienic. I mean spit. Gross.

S16: Yeah, but old people do it all the time. So maybe he's with his grandmother and she keeps trying to kiss him and clean him up and stuff?

S17: I think he's sad.

S15: Why?

S17: See here, see it says, "I didn't know this would be the last time." I think she died and now he misses her.

S18: So, like at first he didn't want to kiss her but then she died and now he feels really bad because he didn't kiss her. Yeah.

A third group:

S19: Don't you think they're on a ship?

S20: A ship?

S19: Or maybe a boat? You know it says about it sinking. And then there was something about her sinking and you call boats "her," you know, a girl's name.

S21: So maybe it is the Titanic. It sank.

S22: And that's why he didn't get to kiss her again because she drowned.

S23: But what's Iowa got to do with the Titanic? Wasn't that from England?

S21: Maybe he was from Iowa and he went to England and then was riding back on it or maybe like someone was coming over from England to go to Iowa?

S23: I don't know. How does this about "I could have done without the words of Jesus" fit with the Titanic? I don't think that's it.

Debriefing the Strategy

As these students studied the phrases on their cards, they began to identify possibilities for setting, characters, and problems in this text by connecting events to their prior experiences, sequencing events, considering causes of actions and the effects of those actions, and making inferences about characters and events. They were actively engaged with the meaning-making process long before they began reading the text. Eventually, they wrote brief statements that provided their predictions for this selection (see Figure 6.6).

Putting the Strategy to Work

1. *First, decide what phrases, sentences, or single words you want to place on index cards.* I try to select half as many phrases as I have students. Make sure you've chosen phrases that give insight into characters, setting, and conflicts. Choose some phrases that might be interpreted multiple ways.

2. *Don't paraphrase the text.* You can omit words if you need to shorten a phrase, but don't change the words.

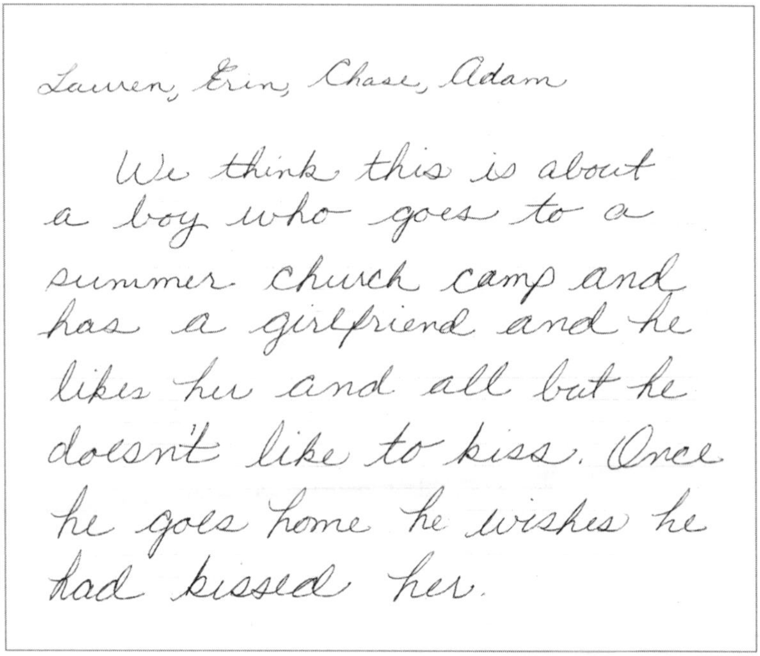

Lauren, Erin, Chase, Adam

We think this is about a boy who goes to a summer church camp and has a girlfriend and he likes her and all but he doesn't like to kiss. Once he goes home he wishes he had kissed her.

FIGURE 6.6 *"We think" statement*

3. *As students move from student to student, make sure they not only share their cards but also begin discussing what the text might be about.*

4. *Next, have students return to small groups (five is a good number for this activity) to discuss what they presume is happening in the text.*

5. *Ask students to record their predictions by writing a "We think" statement*—a paragraph that begins "We think that this selection is about. . . ."

6. *Finally, as students share their "We think" statements, make sure you ask them to explain how they reached that prediction.* While you might easily see the inferences they've made, others might not understand what they were thinking.

7. *Now, read the selection.* If you've done this to introduce a novel, I'd choose words from the first chapter so that they can revisit their predictions sooner rather than later.

Questions and Answers

1. *What if students don't get the "right" prediction?*
   This strategy, like Probable Passage, isn't about "right" and "wrong." It's about seeing relationships between words. This isn't a guessing game.

Instead, it's a time for students to combine their knowledge with the bits of information you've given them on the cards to practice making inferences, seeing causal relationships, sequencing, comparing and contrasting, drawing conclusions, and predicting.

2. *What do we do after we've read the selection?*
   Once students have completed the selection, or the part of the selection that was used for the Tea Party, let them discuss how their predictions differed from the text. What they are doing is comparing how the author created relationships between words and how they created relationships between those same words. Sometimes, we look again at the phrases I put onto cards (show them the entire list on a transparency), and we talk about which phrases led them astray or kept them on target. You can also have students skim the selection, looking for other key words or phrases, ones that, had they been included, might have triggered predictions either closer to or further from the actual text.

3. *Can you do this with expository texts?*
   Yes, though it takes more work. We did this in a class that was studying the Revolutionary War. Students shared their sentences and then, instead of writing a prediction statement, tried to group their cards by category: causes of the war, effects of the war, problems each side faced, and so on. Students placed their cards directly onto chart paper with tape and then, as they read the chapter, rearranged the cards as needed.

4. *What if some of my students are such disabled readers that they can't read the words on the cards?*
   This came up when I decided to use Tea Party with a portion of Thoreau's *Walden*. I was working with some high school students who read at about a third-grade level. This was a required text, so I didn't have a choice about whether or not to have students read it. I decided the best way to get them thinking about this difficult text was to start by working with small parts of it. Though I chose the sentences carefully, some cards still had very difficult vocabulary or confusing syntax. Consequently, when I prepared the cards, I color coded them so that all the red cards said the same, all the blue cards said the same, and so on. I told students to find other students with the same color card. Then, as I walked around helping with decoding and vocabulary, the groups practiced reading their sentences aloud to each other and discussed what their one sentence might mean. They wrote their comments about their sentence on the back of their cards. Some students rewrote

their sentences into their own words. Once students had rehearsed saying what was written on their cards and had discussed what their sentences might mean, they began the Tea Party.

5. *So, why's it called Tea Party?*

Think about what you do at a party. You walk around, visit with one person, then move on to the next. You pick up a bit of the conversation here, a bit more there. You share what you have to say and listen attentively (I hope) to the person you're visiting with at that moment. Tea Party simulates that talking-listening pattern. By calling it a Tea Party, you're making that association for students; setting the mood with some cookies for the students to munch can't hurt either!

Reflections

The more we frontload students' knowledge of a text and help them become actively involved in contructing meaning prior to reading, the more engaged they are likely to be as they read the text. Dependent readers must be reminded often that comprehension begins prior to reading and extends into the discussions they have after they've finished reading. Many dependent readers think of comprehension only as answering questions correctly after reading the text. That's too late. Pre-reading strategies that focus on active engagement with the text help struggling readers do what good readers do—think all throughout the reading process, not just at the conclusion.

> *The more we frontload students' knowledge of a text and help them become actively involved in contructing meaning prior to reading, the more engaged they are likely to be as they read the text.*

Dear George,

I was always so impressed at how well you listened to what I said about stories before we read them. Then, I heard you tell someone in the hall, "Yeah, if you listen to her before we read the story, then it's okay if you don't read it or don't get it. She's already told you all the important parts." So, while I was busy providing meaning for you, you were busy figuring out what you needed to remember so that you didn't actually have to comprehend anything on your own. We were quite a team, George. Quite a team.

CHAPTER SEVEN

Constructing Meaning
During-Reading Strategies

◆ ◆ ◆

Dear George,

Several days a week, people looking in our classroom would have seen students reading, or at least pretending to read. I thought I was very progressive by letting you all sit wherever you wanted to sit—sprawled on the floor, at the conference table, leaning against walls, or even in your seats. And I was so impressed with how quiet the room was while you were all reading. Except for an occasional cough or the crackle of a turning page, there was very little noise. I realize now that might have meant there was very little thinking as well.

◆ ◆ ◆

"You Mean You *Make* It Make Sense?"

Dependent readers often fail to see reading as an active process. As Gene, a twelfth grader, said, "What do you mean *active*? You sit. You stare. You turn pages. What's active about that?" I asked him what he thought good readers did while reading. He responded, "Do? I don't know. They just read it. And then they answer all the questions. That's what makes them good readers, because they can answer the questions."

"So why do you think they can answer the questions?" I asked.

"I don't know. Why do some people win the lottery? Why are some people always invited to the really popular parties? Why did Gore really lose the election? There are just some things we aren't supposed to know the answer to. It's just the way things are."

Gene's response, sadly, offers an explanation many dependent readers support: "It's just the way things are." In part, that attitude develops as struggling readers watch some students in class move easily (and apparently effortlessly) through a text. They only see the outward signs of comprehension—peers correctly answering questions. What they don't observe are all the times good readers reread a passage or a sentence, all the times they ask themselves, "What's going on here?" They don't hear that internal dialogue a good reader has with the text or with herself while reading.

Step Inside a Classroom

I gave three eleventh graders a difficult poem titled "Huswifery" (the full text of this poem appears on page 114 in Figure 7.3) and asked them to read it and then answer this question: "What did you do to make it make sense?"

KAREN: After I read it the first time, I thought, "Boy, I don't get it." I decided to read it again, and this time much more slowly. That second time, I found all these words I didn't know. I decided to look at the footnotes to see what they could tell me. They explained some of the terms, especially the terms about a spinning wheel. That helped a lot. Then, I decided to sketch a spinning wheel and see if I could label the parts. After I did that, I read it again. Some of it made more sense, but I still kept asking myself, "What is he really trying to say?" All the way through, I kept saying, "How is this part related to that part?" It was a hard poem.

AMA: This poem makes you think all the way through it. I started reading it and thought I'd better slow down. By the time I got to the end of the fourth line, I knew I was lost. At first, I went back and just started trying to reread each little part, each word, until I figured it out. But then I decided I needed a big picture of the whole thing, even if there was a lot I didn't understand. So, I just read all the way through it, just to get an idea of what it was about. Then I went back and started rereading. I could see right away that a big part of my problem was not knowing all the words. Some of the words were spinning wheel terms, and I saw that those were defined at the bottom of the page. But some of the words were just regular words but used in a different way—like *affection*. And I kept wondering why there were capital letters in the middle of sentences. That bothered me a lot because I never could figure it out. I finally made a list of what I didn't understand and then tried to figure out each part.

LAVERN: This poem was too hard. It made no sense. None at all. I read it, but it made no sense. I'm not sure what you want me to say because I don't know what you mean—"What did you do to make this make sense?" I read it. But it didn't make any sense. I hate it when they do that—give you poems and stories and stuff that don't make any sense. That is so boring.

The next day, I shared Karen's and Ama's responses with Lavern. He was amazed. "They did all that? I just read it. That's all you said to do. Just read it. You didn't say anything about doing that other stuff." Then Lavern talked with Ama and Karen about what they did to make this poem make sense.

LAVERN: I can't believe you did all that.
AMA: But that's what you do when you try to make something make sense, you know? You have to reread it and figure out definitions and figure out what you don't know. I like the way Karen said she drew a picture. I should have done that.
LAVERN: But she just said read it.
KAREN: But that's part of reading, you know. Figuring it out is reading.

Classroom Talk *During* Reading

It is more critical for dependent readers to talk about texts during *the reading experience than* after *it.*

Robert Probst and I wrote an article titled "Classroom Talk About Literature: The Social Dimensions of a Solitary Act" (1998). In that article, we make a case for encouraging students to talk about what they have read. Building on that premise that classroom talk about literature is important, I'd like to suggest that it is more critical for dependent readers to talk about texts *during* the reading experience than *after* it.

The issue is that Lavern and Gene are not alone in their misunderstanding of what it means to construct meaning. What we must do is show them how skilled readers build meaning. That means we must pull the invisible process of comprehension out to the visible level—and that suggests bringing conversation into the classroom *as* students are reading. That conversation needs to be about readers' responses to what they are reading *as well as* how they are making the reading make sense. Consequently, the conversation doesn't focus only on characters or setting or plot development but also on predictions, clarifications, questions, or connections that readers are making.

This chapter examines approaches that help students focus on constructing meaning while reading a text. These strategies encourage students to

♦ predict what will happen next
♦ question what they don't understand or what is confusing in the text
♦ monitor their understanding of the text
♦ identify ways to fix up what has confused them in the text
♦ clarify what has confused them
♦ comment on the text or their understanding of the text
♦ connect what they are reading to other texts or personal experiences
♦ visualize the text

To find out more about helping students construct meaning, take a look at *Mosaic of Thought* by Ellin Oliver Keene and Susan Zimmerman (1997), *Strategic Reading: Guiding Students to Lifelong Literacy* by Jeffrey Wilhelm, Tanya Baker, and Julie Dube (2001), and *Strategies That Work* by Stephanie Harvey and Anne Goudvis (2000).

Say Something

Often struggling readers struggle because while they read, their eyes move over the words but their minds move to thoughts of weekend plans, last night's phone conversations, or after-school sports events. They don't focus on what they are reading, confusing page turning with comprehending. To help those students break that habit, we need to help them attend to what they are reading. One such during-reading strategy is called Say Something.

Say Something (Harste, Short, and Burke, 1988) is a very simple strategy that interrupts a student's reading of a text, giving her a chance to think about what she is reading. Students get into groups of two or three and take turns reading a portion of a text aloud. As they read, they occasionally pause to "say something" about what was read. They make a prediction, ask a question, clarify a confusion, comment on what's happening, or connect what's in the text to something they know. The reading partners offer a response to what was said, then a different student continues the reading until the next time they pause to say something.

Step Inside a Classroom

Everyone in the fifth-period English class was reading. Really reading. No passing notes to a friend. No combing hair or filing nails. No trying to do math homework, digging through backpacks, or making trips to the pencil sharpener. Just reading. Suddenly, a student tapped another on the shoulder and whispered, "You there yet?" When the other said yes, their heads bent close and some whispering began.

JOSIE: I'll go first.
LUCI: Okay.

JOSIE: I didn't get it until this part here. [She points to the second paragraph of "The Tell-Tale Heart."] See this where he says, "You fancy me mad"? Well, then I thought, I get it—he is crazy. And then I decided at this part here that this is taking place a long time ago because see, he is using a lantern and I thought maybe this was like in western times.

LUCI: I don't think so. He doesn't sound like a rancher or anything. But I think he is crazy. Do you think that when he says "his evil eye," he means the man is evil? Like maybe that is his name. See how it's in capital letters?

JOSIE: Uh-uh. I don't think so. I think like you say, "Don't give me the evil eye," that the guy was giving him the evil eye, so he's like calling his eye that.

Josie and Luci went back to reading. At the same time they were having their conversation, two other students had also stopped reading.

BRUCE: I just don't get it.

ERIC: Get what?

BRUCE: Any of it. Like here—what does this mean? "Object there was none. Passion there was none."

ERIC: I guess I didn't see that part. [Eric starts to reread. Looks up.] Give me just a minute.

These quiet conversations continued throughout the room as students read, stopped, talked, and then continued reading. Occasionally, students like Eric could be seen turning back a few pages and rereading. Sometimes students jotted down notes on a piece of paper. Most conversations lasted three to four minutes. Seven students never stopped to talk; they just read.

Debriefing the Strategy

The students in this class were using a strategy called Say Something. The purpose of Say Something is to help students comprehend what they are reading as they predict, question, clarify, connect, or comment. Telling students to say something about the text, or, as I've found, giving them specific types of things they can say, keeps students interacting with the text, and from that interaction comes meaning.

Putting the Strategy to Work

1. *First, model the strategy.* If I've been able to recruit a colleague to help me, I demonstrate a Say Something to students. My colleague and I

Sidebar notes (left margin):

Josie is offering a clarification.

Next Josie tries to figure out something about the setting by connecting what the author says about lanterns to what she knows about lanterns.

Luci rejects Josie's connection and offers a clarification.
Now she's moved to questioning.

What's Josie doing at this point?

Bruce has recognized that he doesn't understand what he's read and is questioning a specific part of the text.

Eric is a read-on-through reader—one of those readers who just turns pages whether he gets it or not. Bruce's question has given Eric an opportunity to reread for understanding.

read a brief passage and then pause and say something about what we've read. We purposefully say a range of things—from asking very specific questions, such as how to say a certain word, to making connections as we discuss similar texts to clarifying something that confused us in the text. If I can't convince someone to join me for a moment or two, then I type out our dialogue instead, make a transparency of it, and put it on the overhead projector.

2. *Explain the procedure to students.* After I "show" a Say Something, we go over the rules (which I've put on a poster that hangs in the room) until students get the idea of how to do the strategy (see Figure 7.1). I tell students that when they stop to say something (after every three to four paragraphs or so), they must make a prediction, ask a question, clarify a misunderstanding, make a comment, or make a connection. These five general areas give them enough direction to begin the conversations with their partners, yet allow enough latitude for their own needs to emerge.

Rules for Say Something

1. With your partner, decide who will say something first.

2. When you say something, do one or more of the following:

   ◆ make a prediction

   ◆ ask a question

   ◆ clarify something you had misunderstood

   ◆ make a comment

   ◆ make a connection

3. If you can't do one of those five things, then you need to reread.

FIGURE 7.1 *Rules for Say Something*

Make a Prediction

* I predict that . . .
* I bet that . . .
* I think that . . .
* Since this happened (fill in detail), then I bet the next thing that is going to happen is . . .
* Reading this part makes me think that this (fill in detail) is about to happen . . .
* I wonder if . . .

Ask a question

* Why did . . .
* What's this part about . . .
* How is this (fill in detail) like this (fill in detail) . . .
* What would happen if . . .
* Why . . .
* Who is . . .
* What does this section (fill in detail) mean . . .
* Do you think that . . .
* I don't get this part here . . .

Clarify Something

* Oh, I get it . . .
* Now I understand . . .
* This makes sense now . . .
* No, I think it means . . .
* I agree with you. This means . . .
* At first I thought (fill in detail), but now I think . . .
* This part is really saying . . .

Make a Comment

* This is good because . . .
* This is hard because . . .
* This is confusing because . . .
* I like the part where . . .
* I don't like this part because . . .
* My favorite part so far is . . .
* I think that . . .

Make a Connection

* This reminds me of . . .
* This part is like . . .
* This character (fill in name) is like (fill in name) because . . .
* This is similar to . . .
* The differences are . . .
* I also (name something in the text that has also happened to you) . . .
* I never (name something in the text that has never happened to you) . . .
* This character makes me think of . . .
* This setting reminds me of . . .

FIGURE 7.2 *Stem starters for Say Something comments*

3. *The partner's job is to offer a response to what was said.* In particular, the partner should try to answer questions. Any questions that can't be answered should be noted on paper so they can be brought to the entire class.

4. *Dependent readers often need help in making their Say Something comments.* Unlike skilled readers, they often have nothing to say about what they've read. So don't think that simply because you've told them to "say something," they'll immediately start having insightful conversations about the text. I find that if I provide beginnings of statements, what I call *stem starters*, students are more likely to make a comment. Figure 7.2 offers a list of stem starters for each category.

5. *Students first need to practice using Say Something on very short texts*—just a few paragraphs or short poems. This allows them to become familiar with the strategy before they start using it with assignments.

6. Remember, as with all strategies, you must model often how to do it. Modeling a Say Something one time is not enough.

This strategy is helpful to dependent readers, though it often starts slowly. The following recorded conversation shows you what happened the first time I ever had students try this strategy:

GARY: You first.
LONNIE: Not me. [Long pause.]
GARY: You going to tonight's game?
LONNIE: Yeah. You?
GARY: Yeah. Read?
LONNIE: Yeah.

Questions and Answers

1. *Should students be allowed to choose their Say Something partners?*
Sometimes yes, sometimes no. I make sure that students understand that this is work time, not visit time. If I see students together and know that they are saying something about anything other than the text, then they know they've lost the privilege of working together again for a while. But I try to let friends work together. Secondary students are so connected to their friends that putting them with someone they never hang out with almost assures failure for the strategy.

2. *Should everyone do a Say Something?*
No. This strategy is for students who don't think about the text or what they understand (or don't understand) as they read the text. Independent readers already question the text, predict what will happen next, clarify their understanding, comment to themselves or others, and make connections as they read.

3. *Is the strategy graded?*
You can't get a 100 or an 88 on a Say Something. But sometimes students are more likely to do something if they believe that they are getting graded, so I give participation grades. Plus, I have them reflect on their

own Say Somethings after about every third one by answering these questions:

- a. How has using Say Something changed how you read?
- b. What's something you discovered through Say Something with the story you just finished?
- c. What type of comment do you make the least often? The most often?
- d. What do you want to do to make your Say Something comments more powerful?
- e. What do you need me to do to help you use this strategy more effectively?

4. *Can Say Something be done without a partner?*

It certainly works best with a partner, but it can be done alone. Wallis (1998) calls this type of Say Something a Say Something—Silently and explains that with this variation, students decide where they will stop and then, when reaching that point, write their comment. Then they exchange papers and respond to each other's comments, again in writing. Students can also say something silently by writing notes to themselves. They can later reflect on what they have written.

Rereading

ME: What's wrong, Ben?
BEN: I didn't get the story.
ME: Did you reread the parts you didn't get?
BEN: Why?
ME: To help you understand them.
BEN: Why would reading the same stuff again help me get it?

Just like Ben, many dependent readers don't think "reading the same stuff again" does them any good. That is partly because they operate under the misconception that skilled readers read something once, read it somewhat effortlessly, and "get it" the first time, every time. *Re*reading doesn't look any different from reading, so struggling readers don't see how many times proficient readers pause, loop back a few sentences, reread up to a point, reflect, start over completely, and then perhaps proceed slowly. Moreover, as we discuss texts with students, we rarely bring up the issue of how often we reread, why we reread, how the rereading differs from the reading, or how we know what sections to reread. Therefore, dependent

Take time to reread sections of a novel

readers don't hear teachers or other more skilled readers talk about the sentences, passages, or even chapters that they sometimes reread several times to construct meaning. We need to help these students understand that rereading is something that all good readers do and that it is an important strategy to use when trying to understand a text.

Step Inside a Classroom

MR. BELL: Alright guys, let's look at the beginning of Chapter 5; that's what you're going to read tonight. [The students are reading a novel titled *Stick and Whittle* by Sid White.] Before you get into your literature circles to discuss what you read last night, I want us to talk a moment about something I want you to do tonight as you read this chapter. Okay, this chapter is only eight pages so I want you to read it three times tonight. When you get to the end the first time, I want you to stop and jot down any questions you have, predictions you have, or responses you have. Then read that same chapter. This time, I want you paying specific attention to information about Stick. What do you know about him at the end of that chapter that you didn't know before? Finally, I want you to read the chapter one more time, this time focusing on finding out about Whittle. After each reading, jot down notes about what you learned about those two characters.

S1: Why can't we just do that all the first time, Mr. Bell? This is boring.

Mr. Bell: Sometimes you can. But right now, just for these eight pages, I want you to practice rereading, to see how each time you reread you can pick up new information. It's like this. How many of you can name at least three songs that you love to hear on the radio? [Almost all students nod their heads or raise their hands. Several start talking about those songs.] Good. Now, how many of you know the words to those songs? [Students nod. Some start singing.] Alright guys. Now, how many of you learned all those words the first time you heard it? [Students shake their heads no.] Now, how many of you discovered you could sing the words but still didn't really know what those words were saying?

S2: Oh my gosh. That is so true. There was this one song and I just loved it because of the melody I guess but then I learned all the words, I mean really learned them, you know started thinking about them, and then, like I couldn't believe what they were saying, you know? Then I didn't like it at all.

Mr. Bell: That's right. The more you heard the song, the more you learned about it. The same thing happens with reading, guys. The more you read something, the more you learn about it. And as we read the same thing, we can shift our attention. Like you shifted from just hearing the melody to memorizing the words to really understanding what the words were saying.

S1: So you want us to memorize the chapter?

Mr. Bell: Not hardly. I want you to shift your attention as you read the chapter each time. The first time, read it to get an overall impression, to see if there is something you don't understand. The second time, focus on Stick and the third time, focus on Whittle.

Students then moved into literature circles and began discussing the book up to that point. The next day, students had interesting comments about their rereadings.

Mr. Bell: Alright guys. Who did their rereading? [Most hands go up.] Okay. What happened each time you reread?

S3: The first time I read it, I didn't get any of what was going on on page, page 82. But then, by the third time, I had figured it out. I was impressed.

S4: It was weird, like the first time, I thought I had understood everything and then when I read it again, even though you said to focus on Stick, I was really thinking about Brings the Rain and about that battle at Sand Creek and I hadn't thought about that at all the first time I read it. It was like it was there for the first time.

S5: You know, here, here on page 79 where it says, "Whittle stepped forward, doffing his derby and bowing to the girl," well the first time and maybe even the second time I don't think I even noticed that because, well because I think like doffing, you know what is that, so since I didn't understand it, I just went on over it. But by the third time, well you know you said to focus on Whittle and so I was but also, by then, I understood so much more it was like now I could think about what I didn't understand. Whatever it is, it's probably like being pretty polite because he's bowing and all.

Debriefing the Strategy

The students in this class were learning the value of rereading. Mr. Bell didn't wait until a student said he was confused about a particular part of a text, then offer him the vague advice of "reread it." Instead, he wanted students to discover how rereading allows them to see things in the text they simply can't see on the first read. Mr. Bell did a couple of things to make sure this would succeed. First, he asked them to reread a short chapter. No one wants to reread twenty-five pages; but eight pages is probably manageable. Second, he gave students specific things to do with each rereading.

Putting the Strategy to Work

Rereading is probably the number one strategy independent readers use when something stumps them in a text. It's probably the last strategy dependent readers use. That's because independent readers believe it's their job, as a reader, to figure out the text. If they didn't get it the first time through, then they simply need to try again. Dependent readers neither believe they can figure it out nor that they are expected to figure it out. Rereading can move from a quick suggestion to a powerful way to read strategically with a little instruction from us.

> You try it! Read the poem found in Figure 7.3 three times. After each reading, rate your understanding of the poem on a scale of 1 to 10 with 1 being low and 10 meaning you could write the Cliff Notes for the poem. Don't consult a dictionary, thesaurus, online resource, or even ask a buddy. The point is to show you that even without consulting outside resources, your comprehension will probably improve. After each rating, jot down one or two questions you have. When you've completed this, think about how you altered your reading each time you went through the text.

> *Rereading is probably the number one strategy independent readers use when something stumps them in a text. It's probably the last strategy dependent readers use.*

1. *First, prove to students that rereading is valuable.* Do this by giving students a short text and asking them to reread it three times. Keep it short enough that they can do this in class. Ask them to rate their understanding of this text on a scale of 1–10 after each reading (1 is low and 10 is high). Discuss their rating when they are finished. Most students will see that their scores improved either between the first and second readings or second and third or after each rereading. Discuss

Huswifery
by Edward Taylor

Make me, O Lord, thy Spinning Wheel complete.
　　Thy Holy Word my Distaff make for me.
Make mine Affections thy Swift Flyers neat
　　And make my Soul thy holy Spool to be.
　　My Conversation make to be thy Reel
　　And reel the yarn thereon spun of thy Wheel.

Make me thy Loom then, knit therein this Twine:
　　And make thy Holy Spirit, Lord, wind quills:
Then weave the Web thyself. The Yarn is fine.
　　Thine Ordinances make my Fulling Mills.
　　Then dye the same in Heavenly Colors Choice,
　　All pinked with Varnished Flowers of Paradise.

Then clothe therewith mine Understanding, Will,
　　Affections, Judgment, Conscience, Memory,
My Words, and Actions, that their shine may fill
　　My ways with glory and thee glorify.
　　Then mine apparel shall display before ye
　　That I am Clothed in Holy robes for glory.

Ratings:

1st Reading　　　2nd Reading　　　3rd Reading

FIGURE 7.3 *Rereading for understanding*

I've used the following poems for this: "The Secret" by Denise Levertov; "The Sacred" by Stephen Dunn; "The Journey" by Mary Olive (better for high school); the first few verses of "The Raven" by Edgar Allen Poe; "Daily" by Naomi Shihab Nye; "Legal Alien" by Pat Mora; "Ain't I a Woman?" by Sojourner Truth; as well as political cartoons, comic strips from the newspaper, and ads from magazines.

with students why this happened. Figure 7.4 shows you one sixth-grader's reasons for why his scores went up after rereading.

2. *Next, model your thinking as you reread a text.* Read a short passage aloud and think through what was happening in the text. Then reread it and think through it again. Let students hear how your thinking changes as you reread a text.

3. *Then give students specific tasks as they reread.* Dependent readers aren't aware of the power of rereading, so they don't know what the rereading should accomplish. To help them with that, you might do what Mr. Bell did and have students brainstorm instances when it is helpful to reread. Figure 7.5 shows you one student's list.

4. *Finally, after students have reread, review what happened.* This move from rereading to reviewing highlights the value of rereading.

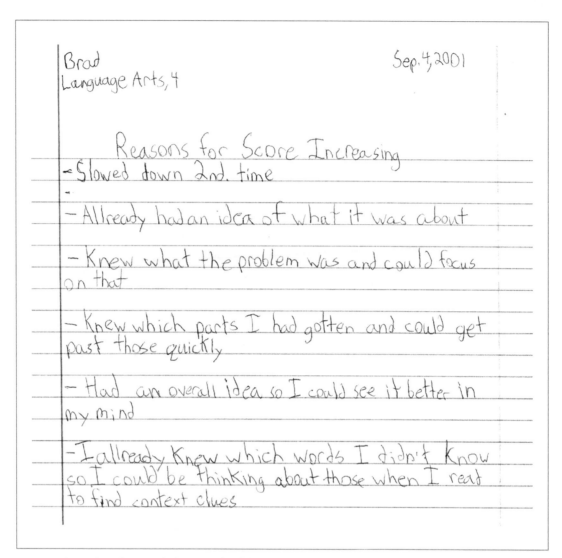

Brad
Language Arts, 4

Sep. 4, 2001

Reasons for Score Increasing
- Slowed down 2nd. time
-
- Allready had an idea of what it was about

- Knew what the problem was and could focus on that

- Knew which parts I had gotten and could get past those quickly

- Had an overall idea so I could see it better in my mind

- I allready knew which words I didn't know so I could be thinking about those when I read to find context clues

FIGURE 7.4 *Brad's explanation for how rereading helps*

Questions and Answers

1. *When you do the part where students rate their understanding three times, do scores ever go down instead of up?*
    Yes. If you are working with students who really don't care about success in school, then that might happen. I've told some students to reread something only to have them just move their eyes over the same text. If students don't put a greater effort into understanding the second time they read, then nothing will happen. Also, if you choose a really difficult text, students might not put forth the effort needed for the

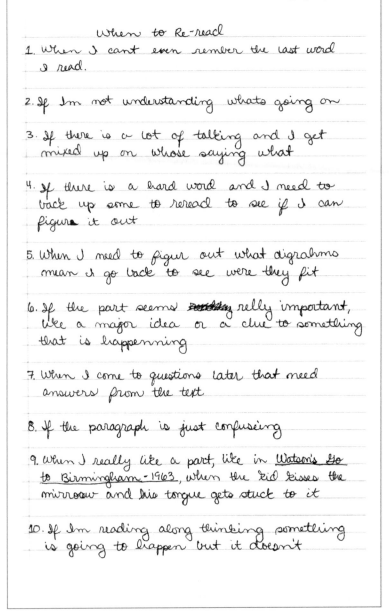

Alexis
L. a. - 3rd
2-7-00

When to Re-read

1. When I can't even rember the last word I read.

2. If I'm not understanding whats going on

3. If there is a lot of talking and I get mixed up on whose saying what

4. If there is a hard word and I need to back up some to reread to see if I can figure it out

5. When I need to figur out what digrahms mean I go back to see were they fit

6. If the part seems ~~sumthy~~ relly important, like a major idea or a clue to something that is happenning

7. When I come to questions later that need answers from the text

8. If the paragraph is just confuseing

9. When I really like a part, like in <u>Watson's Go to Birmingham - 1963</u>, when the kid kisses the mirroaw and his tongue gets stuck to it

10. If I'm reading along thinking something is going to happen but it doesn't

FIGURE 7.5 *Alexis' notes for when to reread*

rereading to be helpful. As mentioned earlier, the text should be one that you know they will understand better with repeated rereading. Also, very good readers sometimes notice something they missed the first time (or second time) that then confuses them and so they rate their understanding with a lower score. In fact, they know more because now they know what they don't know!

2. *How important is it to make the list of reasons to reread?*
   I think this list is critical. It's not just the list of *when* to reread, but what to do *while* rereading. For instance, if students discover they weren't paying attention through an entire section, then they probably need to reread very carefully. However, if they need to reread to find one fact, then they probably can skim many parts of the text.

A last comment about rereading. When my daughter, Meredith, was in eighth grade, her English teachers assigned her class to read *To Kill a Mockingbird*. Meredith read it and when she finished, she told me how much she enjoyed it. "It's a really, really good book, Mom." When Meredith went to high school the next year, her ninth-grade English teacher assigned the same book. Meredith, who enjoys reading, reread the entire book. This time, when she finished, she told me once again how much she liked the book. Then, between Meredith's ninth- and tenth-grade years, we moved, and she changed high schools. And that year, in tenth grade, her English teacher required that they all read *To Kill a Mockingbird*. When Meredith finished the book for the third time, she sat beside me in my study, crying. "Mom, this is the most important book I've ever read," she said and then went on to describe what made this book so powerful to her. Finally, done talking about the book, she wiped tears off her face and then said, "But you know, Mom, I like this version of this book so much better than the one I read in eighth grade." I had to work hard not to laugh. She had decided that in eighth grade she must have read an abridged version; I wanted to hug her and tell her that when she was in eighth grade, she was abridged, just not quite all here yet. And suddenly I thought of all her buddies from eighth grade who had not followed her on to the same two high schools and, having only read *To Kill A Mockingbird* one time, still see it as "a really good book."

I wonder how often we, as English teachers—the people who should most see the value in rereading important texts—convince students that there is *no* value in rereading novels. We say things like, "No, you can't use a book you've already read for your book report," instead of, "If you reread it, you can use it." We argue with one another in the teachers' workroom, telling each other, "No you can't teach that book in eighth grade because we read it in seventh grade." Yet we intuitively understand the incredible value of rereading because we know that every time we reread *Romeo and Juliet* or *The Giver* or *Holes* or *Esperanza Rising* or *Tears of a Tiger* or *Local News,* we understand more about the text. Yet we become frustrated when students don't see the same things in a text that we do when they read it the first time through. I have to ask what would be the harm in revisiting some texts over all three years in middle school or four years in high school? More important, what would be the advantages? I think the advantages far outweigh any disadvantages.

I'm not suggesting that all students should do is reread; however, why not spend that first three weeks of school, when we should be getting to know our students as readers and writers, rereading a novel they read the previous year? Or why not, during December, give students the opportunity to look back through their literature textbooks and find a short story or poem they want to reread? "But they already know how it ends," you think. Please remember, these are the same kids who went to see the movie *Harry Potter and the Sorcerer's Stone* five times—in a row. These are the kids who rented *Jaws* to watch it repeatedly one weekend. Knowing the ending isn't the issue for them. The primary reason kids don't want to reread is because they sometimes don't want to be forced to do the same activities they had to do the first time around. They don't want more vocabulary lists, more lists of questions to answer, more tests to take, more dioramas to make. The second reason students don't want to reread a text is because they didn't enjoy it the first time. That's particularly true when we're forcing students to read classics that were not written for thirteen- or fourteen-year-old students to begin with. If students balk at everything you have them read, then it's probably time that you review what you are requiring them to read. Students prefer rereading—just watch a four-year-old choose bedtime stories. And they understand more of the text each time they reread.

I'm going to propose that each time a reader rereads, she revises her understanding of the text. The first read of a story, a chapter, a poem, a novel, a web page, a letter—any sort of text—yields the first draft of understanding. Readers revise that draft through every rereading. That process of read, revise, read, revise lets me suggest that the reading process is actually more like the writing process than the *writing* process. We've all seen student writing enough to know that at some point the revision of the writing begins to have a reverse effect; the revision, instead of making the writing better, makes it worse. "Stop!" we cry out. "Use the previous revision." But with reading, every revision results in some additional layer or dimension of understanding,

The first read of any sort of text yields the first draft of understanding. Readers revise that draft through every rereading.

whether that is an additional question or new connection or sudden clarification or thought on how to fix up what is still confusing. Viewing reading as revision is a powerful way to understand reading—but one that requires that we encourage rereading of texts rather than discourage it.

Think-Aloud

It happens all the time. You ask students to tell you something about what they've read, and they meet your request with blank stares. They seem to know nothing about the text, but they maintain they've read it. Many of these students have done what they consider reading: their eyes have traveled over the words from left to right and from top to bottom; they've even turned pages at the appropriate time. What they haven't done is pay any attention to what those words mean; they haven't been thinking about what they are reading, noting what they don't understand, deciding what they should do to make the text make sense. That's when a strategy called Think-Aloud can help.

The Think-Aloud strategy (Davey, 1983; Olshavsky, 1976–77) helps readers think about how they make meaning. As students read, they pause occasionally to think aloud about connections they are making, images they are creating, problems with understanding that they are encountering, and ways they see of fixing those problems. This oral thinking not only helps the teacher understand why or how a student is having difficulty with a text but also allows the student to analyze how he is thinking about his reading. This type of metacognitive practice builds independence in reading.

Step Inside a Classroom

I sat in the middle school reading lab with DeDe for about fifteen minutes, listening to her read aloud *Belle Prater's Boy,* a novel by Ruth White (1997, New York: Yearling). DeDe's teacher had asked me to work with her because it appeared to the teacher that DeDe could answer literal-level questions about a text but not much more. DeDe was a fluent reader who had few, if any, problems with word recognition. That fluency, however, had not translated into better comprehension.

I asked her to read aloud a portion of *Belle Prater's Boy* (which she did well) and then tell me what that section was about. She offered a quick retelling that indicated she wasn't sure about the sequence of events, about what was motivating the characters, or about what the effect of some actions would be. It appeared that DeDe's teacher was correct: this student needed help with comprehension, not word recognition. The next day, I met her in the lab again and told her that today I'd be reading a part of the novel aloud and that I had two goals while reading it: First, I told her I wanted to share this excellent story with her and begin discussing who this story was really about—Belle Prater's boy (Woodrow), his cousin (Gypsy), or Belle Prater (Woodrow's mother, who suddenly vanishes). This first goal was intended to pose a question that the teacher had said she wanted the students to explore while reading this book. Second, I explained that I wanted DeDe to learn a strategy that would help her understand a text better as she read. I told her that her job, when I finished reading, would be to tell me what I did while I was reading to help this text make sense. She nodded warily and I began.

First, I spent time commenting on the cover: "Well, as I look at the title and the illustration, I get a little confused. The title says 'Belle Prater's Boy' but there's a boy and a girl on the cover, so he's probably the boy, but is she Belle Prater? I really don't think so because she looks about his age, or at least not old enough to be his mother. It sort of looks like there are mountains in the background, but they are all covered with lush green trees. That doesn't remind me of the Rocky Mountains, but is more like the Smokey Mountains or the Appalachian Mountains. And there's a house down here in the corner, so the story must have something to do with home—leaving home or going home or maybe running away from home or maybe something good or bad happens in the home."

Here I'm using features about the cover to note what is confusing me.

Here I make a connection.

At this point, I make a prediction.

Here, I'm using facts from the text to make a prediction about some things that might happen in the story.

Now I'm using some information from the text to clarify a confusion I had about the cover art.

Using what I know about pronouns, I clarify my confusion by predicting that the word *her* is connected to Belle.

I continued my think-aloud by starting on page 1 of Chapter 1. When I paused to think aloud, I laid the book down on the table; when I read, I held it up. I was trying to give some sort of visual cue that I was thinking about the text, not reading it. After reading the first sentence, I paused:

"Oh, here, with the first sentence, I see that it's 1953. That's almost fifty years ago. That tells me right away that I bet some of the things that happen in this story are going to seem very old-fashioned and out of date. And look, it says, 'my Aunt Belle,' so maybe the girl on the front is Aunt Belle's niece, and that would make the boy and the girl cousins." I read the second sentence, then paused again to make another statement:

"Well, this was confusing, right here, where it says, 'her husband, my Uncle Everett, told the sheriff.' The first sentence sounded like the girl was talking, but now her husband is talking. And who is 'her'? 'Her' must be Aunt Belle. So, Aunt Belle and Uncle Everett go together. Does that mean Everett is the dad of the boy who is on the front cover? And look at what the sentence said about going outside to the toilet. I don't think that most people had outside toilets even in 1953 unless they lived way out in the country. Maybe that's right, though, because look at how Uncle Everett said 'figgered' instead of 'figured.' The author must have done that to give us a hint about either how educated he is or where he lives."

I point out that the author is using an event (going outside to the toilet) and a particular word (*figgered*) to give me a hint about the setting and a character.

I read the first three pages, stopping quite often to think aloud, or to do what Wilhelm (2001) calls "reporting out." As I reported out, I consciously tried to predict what might happen next, clarify what was going on, note what parts of the text were confusing me, visualize the scene, or connect what I was reading to what I know. If I needed to reread something, I said, "I better reread this part," or if I thought that the best way to figure something out was to read further, I said, "Maybe when I read on, this part will make more sense." Figure 7.6 shows you a bit more of this think-aloud.

Text	Comments
"Uncle Everett, a coal miner, and Aunt Belle, along with their boy, Woodrow, lived way far in the head of a long isolated holler called Crooked Ridge, near the town of Coal Station, Virginia, where the Appalachians are steep and rugged."	So, I guess Woodrow is the boy on the front? Maybe. There is so much information just on this first page. I'm not sure what a holler is. I think about holler meaning shout, but that's not it. It's someplace to live because it says Woodrow lived at the head of it. I guess that means the beginning of it. And there's the Appalachians. I thought those mountains on the front looked like the mountains you'd see there.
"According to Uncle Everett, Aunt Belle was barefooted and wearing only a thin nightgown. Her two pairs of shoes and all her clothes were still in their rightful places. There was no evidence of foul play and no indication that she went traipsing off to somewheres else."	Boy, this is sounding like a great mystery. Maybe even a murder mystery. I predict that the story is about figuring out what happened to Belle. The author is giving a lot of hints about how these people live and how much money they have. She only has two pairs of shoes. That's not very many. *Traipsing* is a word you don't hear very often. Sort of like *figgered*. I bet the author used it to show me that these are real country people. I wonder where she went and if Uncle Everett had anything to do with it. Or maybe, you hear about kids who are committing terrible crimes, maybe her son, Woodrow, did something to her.
"Mama reminded me how privileged I was, how fortunate, and I didn't doubt her word one bit, except when a certain nightmare came to haunt me . . . It had something to do with a dead animal, and I would wake up sobbing or screaming."	I wonder if Gypsy is dreaming about what happened to her Aunt Belle? Is she connected to her aunt's disappearance in some way? I'll have to wait to see if that's right, but whatever it turns out to be, I predict that this dream is important in some way. The author has mentioned it too early in the story for it not to be important.

FIGURE 7.6 *Think-aloud for* Belle Prater's Boy

When I paused at one point, DeDe interrupted me and asked, "Why are you doing all that?"

"I'm just saying aloud all what my mind is thinking while I read this."

"You're kidding, right? You're thinking all that while you're reading?"

"Sure. That's what good readers do. They have like a conversation in their mind while reading—asking questions, answering those questions, making predictions, making connections, visualizing the scene."

"Not me. I just read it. You know?"

"Well, why don't you try it, just once, with this next part. Just read it aloud and why don't you stop after this sentence and then either ask a question about something you don't understand or comment on something that now makes sense." She nodded slowly and then began.

Dede stops to question something she doesn't understand.

"*Woodrow had lived way up in the head of that holler with his mother and father without any plumbing or even a refrigerator, and he and I had always gone to different schools.*" There's that holler again. You know, you noticed when you were reading. Here it is again. I'm still not sure what it is. Like a hole maybe? But why would you live at the beginning of a hole? I don't know. And there's more of those hints, you know, like you were saying, like hints from the author about them being poor because it says they didn't have any plumbing or a refrigerator. That's really poor.

Notice how quickly she picks up the term *predict*.

"*I couldn't wait to visit Woodrow that spring night when he moved in next door. I wanted to know if he had any secret knowledge or theories about what had happened to his mother.*" So Gypsy thinks it's a mystery, too. Um, I predict that he, um Woodrow, that he knows where his mother is.

She paused for a moment and said to me, "This is hard work. You know, this is like you really have to think about every word."

"Yeah," I said. "But what do you notice as you are doing all that thinking?"

"Well, it's really different, like, you know, like it's like the story has all this stuff in it, that if you really pay attention it's all there or at least there are hints there. But this is really hard work. You do this all the time?"

Debriefing the Strategy

Good readers have a constant dialogue with the text as they read, although they usually do it silently. Think-alouds provide struggling readers with a structure on which to build this dialogue; they learn to think about their reading and to monitor what they do and do not understand.

As students use this strategy, they

- predict ("I bet that . . . " or "I wonder if . . . " or "I think that . . . ")
- picture the text ("From this part here, I can see . . . " or "I imagine that . . . ")
- make comparisons ("This reminds me of . . . " or "This part is like . . . " or "This is similar to . . . ")
- monitor their comprehension ("I don't get this . . . " or "This confuses me because . . . " or "This is a difficult part because . . . ")
- decide how to fix up (repair) comprehension problems ("Maybe I better reread . . . " or "Maybe I need to keep on reading to see if . . . " or "I better look this word up because . . . " or "Maybe I better consider that . . . ")
- comment on what they've read ("I like this because . . . " or "This part is sad because . . . " or "If you think about it . . . ")
- connect what they've read to what they already know ("This reminds me of . . . " or "I know that this part in the text is right [or wrong] because . . . ")
- question what is happening in the text ("I wonder why the author . . . " or "What's happening here . . . " or "Is the character going to . . . ")

Any of these comments indicates that the student is actively engaged with the reading. That's the goal. As students use this strategy more and more, that internal dialogue with the text becomes more natural, proving to students the connection between reading and thinking. As DeDe later explained, "All this thinking is really the whole point of reading. I mean if you aren't thinking it, you aren't reading it."

Putting the Strategy to Work

1. *First, model thinking aloud.* This is truly a strategy that isn't just taught but is shown—again and again. In fact, I've found that every time we switch genre or form, I've got to model a think-aloud. In other words, I can't presume that just because I've modeled how I think through a poem, students know how to think through a persuasive essay. And after I've modeled how to think through a persuasive essay, that doesn't mean they understand how to think through an argumentative essay or the section of their history book that compares the Civil War to the Revolutionary War.

2. *Before you begin to think aloud, tell students that as you read a passage aloud, you will be stopping to think through what you are reading.* Tell them

to listen for when you predict, visualize (or use the word *picture*), question, clarify, connect, comment, monitor your understanding, or identify ways to fix up your misunderstandings. Remind them that skilled readers constantly have this sort of dialogue with the text as they read.

3. *As you read the text, stop frequently to talk about how you are analyzing what happened in the text.* Some people advocate doing a "cold reading" for your think-aloud, one where you've never seen the text before so that students observe as real a think-aloud as possible. This is good to do occasionally; however, I find it more important to have studied the text I'm going to use for the think-aloud so I can plan where I will stop and what I will say.

4. *As you stop to report out, give students a verbal or visual cue that you're switching from reading the text to thinking aloud.* I like to shift how I'm holding the book. Other teachers say they like to turn their bodies a slightly different direction. Others say they start each think-aloud comment with, "Thinking now," or "My turn." Do whatever works well for you.

5. *Sometimes, as you report out, jot your comments down on a transparency as you make them.* Then when you've finished your think-aloud, let students go back and decide if you were predicting, commenting, noting your confusions, deciding how to fix up what confused you, questioning, clarifying, or visualizing as you read. This level of metacognitive analysis helps students understand what you, the more skilled reader, are doing and why you are doing it.

6. *After you've modeled thinking aloud a few times, have students try it on a portion of text with a partner.* Give students a short amount of text to think aloud. As they read to one another, circulate through the room to see how they are doing. Expect to hear some of them say, "I don't know what to say." That's better than nothing. They'll get better. If students have a very difficult time, you can scaffold this practice for them by cueing exactly where in the text you want them to stop and exactly what word, phrase, or sentence you want them to report out on. You can even tell them that after they read that particular section, they are to describe the scene they see (visualizing) or discuss how this relates to something they know (connecting) or what the text tells them about the character or setting (clarifying). Your job at this point is to support them. Be ready to step in with prompts if they need them. The partners will learn how to be effective from your examples. They can also

capture comments that the readers make on sticky notes. Then, both the reader and partner can study the notes to see what types of comments the reader made.

7. *Provide ample opportunities for students to practice thinking aloud.* This is a strategy that requires constant practice—after all, it's what proficient readers do constantly.

8. *Give students a chance to reflect on how the think-aloud has changed their reading habits.* Figure 7.7 shows you a think-aloud assessment I use with dependent readers.

Questions and Answers

1. *What do I do if students make comments for every sentence?*
   Sometimes that's necessary. But if you think students are stopping too often, then check your modeling to make sure you are showing students how to chunk their reading; it's important for them to see how to stop after every few sentences or even a paragraph to make comments.

2. *Is it helpful to tell students what kind of comments to make?*
   Generally, the answer is no. However, dependent readers sometimes need that extra scaffold of knowing exactly where in the text to stop, exactly which part of the text to respond to, and exactly what type of comment they are to make. This type of cued think-aloud focuses students' thinking. Your job is to monitor their ability to work with cues so you know when to remove them.

3. *What if students' comments are questions they have about the text? Should I answer their questions?*
   Not as the think-aloud is in progress. Often, confusion about what is going on in the text—whether that means wondering what a specific word means, which character is speaking, or what is happening next—is cleared up as the student continues reading. That's when you'll hear comments like, "Oh, I get it," or "I bet that part meant . . . ," or "It must have been this character who said. . . ." Remind partners to keep track of questions and to see if the reader can clarify his own questions as he moves through the text.

4. *Isn't think-aloud similar to the Say Something strategy?*
   It's the role of the partner that is the biggest difference between these two strategies. In the Say Something strategy, two or three readers work

Name _____ Date _____

Think-Aloud Self-Assessment

PART I. Read each statement below. Put a 1 by the items you do often, a 2 by the items you do sometimes, and a 3 by the ones you do rarely.

When I pause to think aloud . . .

_____ I make my mind try to visualize the scene. (visualizing)

_____ I try to figure out which parts have confused me. (monitoring comprehension)

_____ I compare what has happened now with what happened previously. (comparing)

_____ I ask questions about what's going on in the text. (questioning)

_____ I make myself connect what I know to what's happening in the story. (connecting)

_____ I make comments about what I like or don't like. (commenting)

_____ I anticipate what a character might do next. (predicting)

_____ I make comments about what the author is doing to give me hints about the characters or plot or setting. (commenting)

_____ I wonder what the author wants me to figure out at this point. (questioning)

_____ I try to figure out if I need to reread a section. (identify fix-up solutions)

_____ I predict what will happen next. (predicting)

_____ I try to imagine what is happening in the text. (visualizing)

_____ I think about characters or events to see how they are alike or different. (comparing)

_____ I ask myself how this is like something else I've read or maybe a song I've heard. (connecting)

_____ I try to figure out if I should read on. (identify fix-up solutions)

_____ I stop and ask myself if I understand what I've read so far. (monitoring comprehension)

PART II. Look at the numbers you put in the blanks in Part I and then answer the questions in Part II.

1. What do you do most often when you think aloud?

2. Why do you think you do that the most?

3. What do you do the least?

PART III. Complete the following statements to help you plan what you'll do in your next think-aloud.

1. Think-alouds help me because . . .

2. I need to keep practicing (predicting, connecting, comparing, visualizing, monitoring comprehension, identifying fix-up solutions, commenting, questioning) because . . .

3. In my next group of think-alouds I'll . . .

FIGURE 7.7 *Think-aloud checklist for dependent readers*

together, with one saying something one at one point in the text and the others responding. When they reach the next stopping point in the text, they switch roles. In the think-aloud strategy, one person is doing the reading and the thinking aloud. The partner's role is to capture the statements on paper or sticky notes and, when the think-aloud is complete, discuss with the reader what he or she did during the process.

5. *Do students always have to do a think-aloud orally?*
   Not at all. You can have students think through a text by responding to it on sticky notes. I've watched Robert Probst do this with teachers during staff development workshops. He gives teachers a poem on a large sheet of paper and has them read it, encouraging them to make notes all over the paper about their understanding of the poem. I've been so impressed with this that I recently taught my graduate students this same process. Figure 7.8 shows you one of the think-silently posters that one of my graduate student's eleventh-grade class made after reading a poem by e. e. cummings.

Strategy Snapshots

Say Something, Rereading, and Think-Aloud were described in detail to provide you with rich descriptions of how the strategies look in the classroom. In the next section, you'll find eight additional strategies that, though described in less detail, are no less important in helping dependent readers understand how to construct meaning during reading.

Double-Entry Journals

Many of us have had students respond to what they've read in some form of a journal; others of us have had students take notes while they read a text. Double-entry journals combine both techniques, giving students a powerful way to take notes and respond at the same time. Have students fold notebook paper in half lengthwise. They label the top of the left-hand column "Notes from the Text" or "What's in the Book" and the top of the right-hand column "Notes from My Mind." or "My Response." As students read the text, they record on the left-hand side a passage or a word from the text with the page number. On the right-hand side, they make their comment about that passage. This might be a question or a connection or a visual symbol to help them remember something. Figure 7.9 is a portion of DeDe's double-entry journal that she kept while reading *Belle Prater's Boy.*

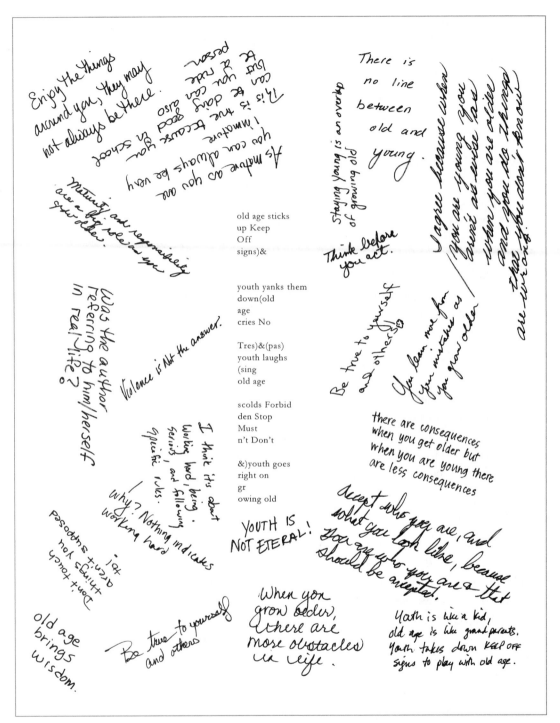

Enjoy the things around you, they may not always be there.

As mature as you are you can always be very immature.

This is true because I am doing good in school but you can also be a rude person.

Maturity and responsibility are a big role as you grow older.

Was the author referring to him/herself in real life?

Violence is Not the answer.

old age sticks
up Keep
Off
signs)&

youth yanks them
down(old
age
cries No

Tres)&(pas)
youth laughs
(sing
old age

scolds Forbid
den Stop
Must
n't Don't

&)youth goes
right on
gr
owing old

I think it's about working hard, being serious, and following specific rules.

Why? Nothing indicates working hard

Don't touch that stuff don't touch that stuff

old age brings wisdom.

Be true to yourself and others

There is no line between old and young.

Staying young is an overlap of growing old

Think before you act.

Be true to yourself and others

You learn more from your mistakes as you grow older

I agree because when you are young you aren't as wise but when you are older and you do things that are wrong you don't know

there are consequences when you get older but when you are young there are less consequences

Accept who you are, and what you look like, because you are who you are & that should be accepted.

YOUTH IS NOT ETERAL!

When you grow older, there are more obstacles in life.

Youth is like a kid, old age is like grandparents. Youth takes down KEEP OFF signs to play with old age.

FIGURE 7.8 *Class example of a think-silently*

DeDe

Book	Response
(31)	
"When it came to washing my hair, I'd rather clean than vomit" (31)	Oh my gosh, she is like so much a tomboy
"Y'all didn't have a piano in that li'l ol' shack, didja?" (33)	She can be pretty rude, calling his house a shack
"Is that a bottle of your homemade blackberry wine I see there on the sideboard? (34)	What's a sideboard? And is this wine like real wine they made out of blackberries?
Everything on p. 36	This was weird. Did this really happen or was he just making it up? I'm confused

FIGURE 7.9 *DeDe's double-entry journal*

Logographic Cues

A logograph is a visual symbol. Many traffic and pedestrian signs are logographs. When drivers see the yellow triangle that has a squiggly line going down the center, they know to slow down because the road ahead has curves. When pedestrians see a sign that has a circle with a diagonal drawn through it, they know to not walk in that direction. Logographic cues are designed to offer readers a high-utility message in a minimum amount of space. Readers can design their own logographs to insert into texts as they read to become "signposts" that show them the direction the text is taking. They can draw these logographs on sticky notes and adhere the notes to the

FIGURE 7.10 *Mary Helen's logographic cues*

texts or they can make a double-entry journal and instead of writing in the response column, they can draw their logographs. Students should design their own logographs so that the picture has meaning for them. You might start, however, by brainstorming some symbols that could be used to show characters, conflict, or setting as well as symbols to show questions, clarifications, or inferences. Figure 7.10 shows you Mary Helen's logographic cues she developed while reading *Mr. Tucket* by Gary Paulsen.

Bookmarks

Everyone knows what a bookmark is—even dependent readers. Playing on the word *mark* in *bookmark,* teachers at Lanier Middle School and I created different types of bookmarks for students to use while reading. Some teachers ran these bookmarks off on bright card stock; others copied them

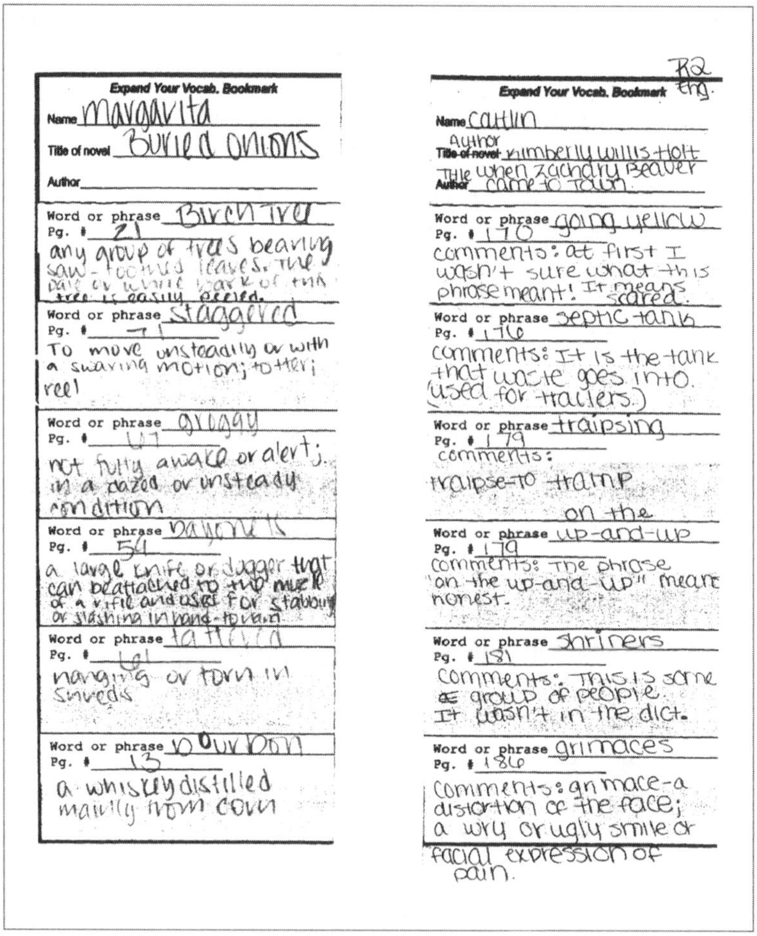

FIGURE 7.11 *Completed bookmarks*

on regular white paper; still others distributed index cards or newsprint, showed students a template, and said, "Make your own." Though the bookmarks looked different from class to class, the result was the same—students were marking things of interest as they read texts. Here's a list of the bookmarks students used and Figure 7.11 shows you some completed ones. You can find templates for each of these in Appendix C.

◆ *Mark My Words:* A bookmark for recording interesting or unusual words you encounter while reading. Every five or ten days, spend ten minutes of class time reviewing what words students recorded. Put the words on chart paper you've put up somewhere in the room. Discuss what the words mean as you write them. As a class, choose two or three that everyone

wants to try using for the next week. Give bonus points every time someone uses one of the words correctly.

♦ *Marking Time:* Use these bookmarks to mark how the setting changes as
the book or short story progresses. Excellent for a history class where
students might need to track the movement of an army during a
particular war.

♦ *Question Mark:* These bookmarks are for students to record their questions as they read. Make sure they put the page number by the question
so they can revisit that part of the text to see what caused the question.

♦ *Mark Who?:* Students can record information about characters on these
bookmarks.

♦ *Mark the Bold:* These are excellent bookmarks for students to use while
they read their content area textbooks—or any book that has a lot of
boldfaced terms. As students come across a boldfaced word, they record
that word on the front of the bookmark. Then they turn it over to the
back (which is titled "Talk the Bold") and write what that term means
in their own words. Once a week or so, have students review the terms
they've collected on their bookmarks and then "talk the bold" by reviewing with one another what they said the words meant. (One student
labeled this activity "a very bold move.")

ABCs of Comparing and Contrasting

Janet Allen reminded teachers how to use ABC boxes to help students
organize information during vocabulary study. While I had never
thought to use these boxes for vocabulary study, I have encouraged
students to use this simple graphic organizer to record information about
characters as they read a text. For instance, as Anne read the short story
"The Most Dangerous Game," she wrote the two main characters'
names, Rainsford and Zaroff, at the top of the worksheet. Then as she
read the selection, she recorded adjectives that described Rainsford in the
correct ABC boxes in pencil. She jotted information about Zaroff in pen.
When she finished the story, she discovered that her page was filled with
words that gave her good information about both characters and she
could easily see how they were alike and different. She was ready to write
an essay on these two characters. Figure 7.12 shows you her ABCs of
comparing and contrasting.

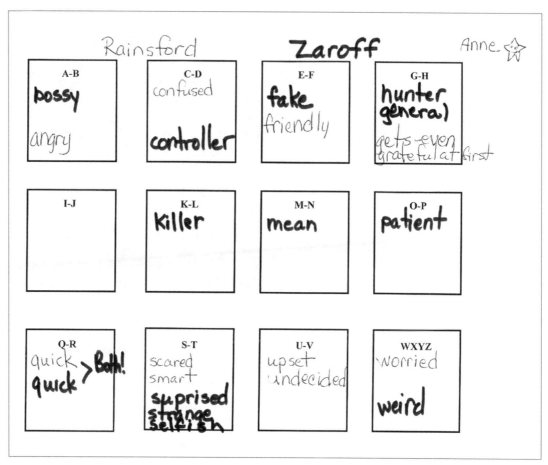

FIGURE 7.12 *Anne's compare/contrast chart*

Post-it Notes

The principal asked me what he could buy his teachers to really help them help their students this year. For a moment I entertained all sorts of responses, but then settled on the practical: "Buy boxes and boxes of Post-it Notes. Get the little ones that come in bright colors and look like flags. Get the standard size we all see. Get some of the index-card-sized ones that have lines on them. And, don't forget some of the huge ones—the ones teachers can hang on walls." He did it and soon students were "writing" in their textbooks. Students used them to flag what they didn't understand or particularly liked. They used them to jot down notes about characters or in history class about events or in science class about experiments. As students finished chapters or stories, they took the sticky notes off the pages of their text and put them onto notebook paper that they then kept in their notebooks. Teachers used Post-it Notes as

Students can use Post-it Notes to mark specific passages in a novel

they moved from group to group listening in on discussions. They could write anecdotal notes on the pads, and then at the end of the day, put them into individual student folders. This was a fast way of creating a running record on many students. So, students use these notes as they construct meaning during reading and teachers use them to help them preserve their own thoughts about students' progress during discussions.

Character Bulletin Boards

I'll never forget the student who said, "When I read, I don't see it and I don't hear it." I cannot imagine at all what it means to not hear a text as you read silently. Add to that the inability to visualize the text, and suddenly we understand why kids would say that reading is boring! Illustrations, especially character illustrations, are very helpful as these reluctant readers try to form a picture in their minds of the people in the book. When books don't provide illustrations, I think it's important that we spend some time discussing what these characters might look like, dress like, walk like, and even talk like. Making character bulletin boards gives students quick references to characters as they read a novel. Students can draw pictures of the characters for these bulletin boards. They can add descriptions such as "funny guy" or "always sad" or "seems to get in trouble easily" by writing comments onto index cards and adding cards to the bulletin board. Students' comprehension is improved while they read if they have texts or classroom materials that help them visualize the plots and characters.

Syntax Surgery

Sometimes hearing us think through a text isn't enough for students, especially for our dependent readers. They need to see our thinking, see how we made connections in the text. That's when something called Syntax Surgery can be helpful. To do this, copy a paragraph from a text onto an overhead transparency. Then, as you do your think-aloud with this passage, connect the words that are related with circles and lines. Especially show how pronouns are related to nouns or other pronouns. Figure 7.13 is an example of a Syntax Surgery that I did while working with middle schoolers. The

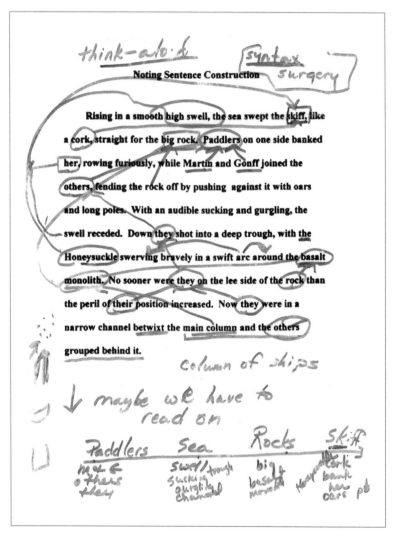

FIGURE 7.13 *Syntax Surgery on a passage from* Redwall *by Brian Jacques*

paragraph is from *Redwall* by Brian Jacques. Note at the bottom of the transparency, we then put words into groups—words about paddlers, the sea, rocks, and the skiff.

Signal Words

Signal words (or phrases) are words that signal what is about to happen next. Some signal words tell readers about the sequence (*later, next, before, first*); others tell them about a similarity (*likewise, in addition to, in the same way*); and some indicate a contrast (*however, on the other hand, although*). Dependent readers often overlook these clues. We must help them see how often they occur in a text and help them understand what information they provide about the text. Figure 7.14 offers a list of signal words to share with your students. You can put these up on chart paper in your classroom. As you think aloud a text, be sure you show students how you use those words to help figure out what is happening in the text.

Sequence Words	Restatement or Synonym Signal Words	Contrast or Antonym Signal Words
after	also	alternatively
afterward	as well as	although
ahead of	by the same token	apart from
all through	correspondingly	but
as	equally	by contrast
before	equally so	contrary to that
beforehand	especially	conversely
during	for example	despite
earlier than	in that	even though
first, second, third . . .	in the same way	however
finally	just as	in contrast
following	likewise	in spite of this
later	similarly	nevertheless
now	such as	nonetheless
prior to	these	notwithstanding
sooner than	too	on the other hand
subsequently		regardless
then		some . . . , but others
throughout		still
while		then again
		yet

FIGURE 7.14 *Signal words*

Reflections

DeDe had it right: "All this thinking is really the whole point of reading. I mean, if you aren't thinking it, you aren't reading it." Students often don't know how to do all this thinking. For too long we've told them to "think carefully" about what they've read without showing them how to do that thinking. And showing means bringing conversation—sometimes noisy conversation—into the classroom. It means demanding that students talk about the text before they complete it. Ben said, "I never used to worry about comprehending until I finished the story and came to that page of questions titled 'Comprehension Check.' I thought that's when I was supposed to think about it. Now I know that you have to think as you read it. If you wait until you're done, you've waited too late."

Jane agreed with him and then added, "You know, when you understand about things like predicting and connecting and figuring out fix-up solutions, then you know what the good readers have been doing all this time. Man, I thought they were just reading. No way. They were doing a ton of stuff. Now I can do it, too."

* * *

Dear George,

As your class finished reading The Pigman, *I asked if John and Lorraine were responsible for Mr. Pignatti's death. Two students immediately started talking, each offering an opinion. I watched you stare at them. After class, you slowly gathered your books, appearing to want to ask me a question. "What's up, George?" I asked. "How'd they know all that? I mean, this book didn't say whether or not they did it. How'd they know all that stuff to say?" You looked so bewildered. "Well, George, they read it," I answered. "Did you read it?" I watched you frown, resigned. "Yeah, but I must've read wrong. I never get the same stuff they get." I wish I had known what I know now, George. You could have answered that question, that one and many more.*

* * *

8

Extending Meaning
After-Reading Strategies

◆ ◆ ◆

Dear George,

The year I was in eighth grade, we read A Tale of Two Cities. *I'll never forget that book, not because it was a great story, which I didn't discover until years later, but because we had to draw a portrait of each character and answer twenty-five questions for each chapter. Each chapter. By Chapter 15, I hated that book. Then years later, I found myself teaching you, and one day realized that I, too, had told you all to draw portraits of the main characters from the book we just finished. ("They love to draw, so they will have fun," I rationalized to myself.) Then I had you answer questions—not twenty-five, but probably too many. ("This will show me what they understand," I convinced myself.) You turned in your folder with all your work for this novel. No portraits. No answered questions. Just an empty folder. "Where's your work, George?" I asked. You shrugged. "Did you do any of it?" I asked. You shrugged again. "Come on, George. Why didn't you do any of it?" "It was stupid," you said.*

Later, I told Anne what happened. "So, was it stupid?" she asked. I shook my head no. "Why not?" she asked.

"Because his answers would have shown me what he understood about the story," I said.

"Really?" she responded, then asked, "Instead of asking George what he did understand, shouldn't you be helping him figure out how to understand?"

"We had already finished the story, Anne," I said. "I needed him to show me what he understood."

"Just because the book is done, doesn't mean the thinking is done," she replied. I borrowed your gesture and just shrugged.

◆ ◆ ◆

Once the Text Is Read

Anne was right: just closing a book doesn't close off the thinking that shapes our understanding of a text. After-reading activities typically measure how much a student has comprehended a text. In that context, comprehension is a product. I'm going to suggest that if we instead view comprehension as a process, then meaning making extends to activities that occur once the book is read.

This chapter examines after-reading activities that help students focus on constructing meaning. These strategies encourage students to

- question what they don't understand or what is confusing in the text
- monitor their understanding of the text
- identify ways to fix up what has confused them in the text
- clarify what has confused them
- comment on the text or their understanding of the text
- connect what they are reading to other texts or personal experiences
- visualize the text
- compare or contrast one part of a text to another
- summarize what they have read
- identify main characters, major events, and details
- identify conflicts or main problems in texts
- see causal connections in a text
- make inferences and draw conclusions
- distinguish between fact and opinion

Scales

There are fish scales, piano scales, the famous scales of justice, and the dreaded bathroom scales. None of those will help kids understand what they are reading. The scales that help students make better sense of the texts they read are scales that help students make comparisons, recognize contrasts, draw conclusions, and distinguish between facts and opinions. They are particularly beneficial for students who need assistance organizing their thoughts or who benefit from seeing information arranged in graphic form. Scales are primarily a post-reading tool; however, they could be used before reading as part of an Anticipation Guide (see page 74 for a discussion of Anticipation Guides) or during reading to help students see changes as the plot and characters develop.

Likert Scales

Likert scales require students to read a statement, decide how much they agree or disagree with it, and then mark or circle the term that indicates that level of agreement. Likert scales often focus on generalizations about characters, themes, conflicts, or symbolism. The best items don't have clear-cut answers found in the book. For instance, if you've read *The Watsons Go to Birmingham—1963* by Christopher Paul Curtis, then you know that one topic in the book is the racial discrimination African Americans faced in this country during the 1960s. A Likert scale item that says, "Racial discrimination

1. Kenny and his family should not have gone to Birmingham, Alabama, when they did.

   _____

   strongly disagree   disagree   agree   strongly agree

2. You can do some bad things and still be a good person. Consider Byron as you answer this.

   _____

   strongly disagree   disagree   agree   strongly agree

3. Throughout the book, Kenny calls his family The Weird Watsons. This was an accurate description of his family.

   _____

   strongly disagree   disagree   agree   strongly agree

4. After the bomb goes off at the church and kills two little girls, Byron tells Kenny, "How's it fair that even though the cops down there might know who did it nothing will probably ever happen to those men? It ain't. But you just gotta understand that that's the way it is and keep on steppin'." Byron's advice to Kenny to accept what happens and just get on with life is good advice.

   _____

   strongly disagree   disagree   agree   strongly agree

5. Not everyone can be a hero; only people with very special talents can be heroes.

   _____

   strongly disagree   disagree   agree   strongly agree

FIGURE 8.1 *Likert scale for* Watsons Go to Birmingham—1963

in the 1960s was a problem in this country," probably wouldn't result in a lively discussion. However, a statement that says, "Kenny's father made a mistake in taking his family to Alabama during this time of unrest," would encourage conversation. Figure 8.1 shows one part of a Likert scale for *The Watsons Go to Birmingham—1963.*

Semantic Differential Scales

Semantic differential scales place opposite character traits (strong/weak, optimistic/pessimistic) at opposite ends of a scale, then ask students to decide how much of the trait a character possesses. These scales focus on character development and can be used to track character changes through a story. Figure 8.2 shows a semantic differential scale for the two characters in Langston Hughes' short story "Thank You Ma'am." The issue, as with the Likert scale, isn't whether students mark the correct term, but why they make their choices. Students can use the scale to track character development by rating a character both at the beginning and at the end of the story.

Step Inside a Classroom

"What'd you put?" the tall, fourteen-year-old boy asked the girl sitting beside him.

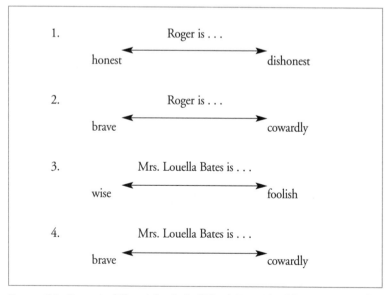

FIGURE 8.2 *Semantic differential scale for "Thank You Ma'am" by Langston Hughes*

"I put *strongly agree*. What'd you say?" the girl said, leaning closer to him to see his paper.

"Strongly agree? How'd you get that?" he said. "I put *disagree*."

"Disagree? How could you disagree? Of course he disturbed the universe; that's what he did the whole book," she said, tapping the item on the Likert scale that said, "In spite of the book's ending, Jerry did disturb the universe."

"Aw, come on. He's bleeding his guts out on the football field at the end and telling his so-called friend to never disturb the universe and saying that they won. They've probably killed him. And nothing's changed at the school. The teachers still don't care what Archie and his gang do and Brother Leon is still as mean as ever. What got disturbed?"

"He made a statement. He stuck by his principles. He never gave in," she responded.

"Sure, he gave in, here at the end," he countered, opening his book to the last page. "Plus, you can't disturb the universe if nothing changes. Think of it this way: if you do something to somebody and that person doesn't notice it, then you didn't disturb them. Only when they notice it did you disturb them," he said, sitting back in his seat, stretching his long legs, and smiling.

"No, not really," said another girl sitting across from them. "Lots of times people disturb me, and I just don't want to let on that they are bothering me, so I just sit still and hope they will stop."

"Yeah, but then they really didn't disturb you enough to change anything," he countered.

No one said anything for a minute, then the boy asked, "Okay, what'd you put for the next one?" and the conversation continued.

After hearing these students discuss the Likert scale they had completed for Robert Cormier's *Chocolate War*, I talked with their teacher about her students' experiences using scales. What pleased her most about the conversation was that two months earlier, the boy leading the discussion didn't participate in discussion groups.

"What changed?" I asked, after hearing about this young man's previous behavior.

"I was using a lot of novel guides that had questions for each chapter, and most of the time he wouldn't do those. When I asked him why, he said, 'What's the use? I'd just get all the answers wrong anyway.' After I started using Likert scales, he told me that they seemed more opinion-based, so how could he get them wrong? Now kids talk more about why they've marked what they did, and with more talk going on, the kids are learning more about the book."

"So are you saying that such scales made him a better reader?" I asked.

"He still has reading problems, but he is talking more about what he has read, so he's just more interested. The Likert scales have made him think more about what he's reading, and that's what is helping him understand better—not that he's filling in some bubbles. Using the scales has given him a way to join our classroom conversation."

Debriefing the Strategy

When this teacher started using scales as a way to help students shape their thoughts, the students started talking more about what they had read. When I asked students in the class what they thought about using Likert scales, one said, "They are easier than real questions because you don't have to look through the story for just one right word for an answer, but you get to use your mind."

Another said, "They are okay. Some are pretty hard because you don't know what the right answer should be and you can't find it in the book." These kids are right—responding to items on a scale is both easier and harder than responding to typical questions because the answer must come from their own minds.

Scales encourage students not only to think about but also to engage in discussions on what they've read. In addition, as students discuss the reasons for their choices, they draw conclusions, make inferences, use the text as support, and make connections to their own lives.

Putting the Strategy to Work

I teach scales by modeling one for students. After we've read something together (anything from a selection in their anthology to a picture book), I complete a scale, making sure to explain how I arrived at my opinions based on evidence from the text. What's important to remember with scales is that not only must students respond by marking to what extent they agree or disagree, they must also explain their choice by citing evidence from the text, from personal experience, or from outside knowledge.

Questions and Answers

1. *How do I know what kind of scale to use?*
    Think about your objective. If you want students to analyze a character, use a semantic differential scale. If you want students to decide how

There are several word pairs that work well in semantic differential scales:

strong/weak
kind/cruel
brave/cowardly
honest/dishonest
bold/shy
wise/foolish
selfish/unselfish
happy/sad
mature/immature
sharing/stingy
forgiving/vindictive

much they agree or disagree with statements that are generalizations about a story's themes, symbolism, or conflicts, use a Likert scale. More important than the type of scale you use, though, are the statements or pairs of words that you use. Choose word pairings or statements that require reflection and that have no obvious choice.

2. *How many items should I include for each scale?*
I've found that ten items—a favorite number for many teachers—can be too many for struggling readers. Remember, the point is to defend the answer. Ten defenses are about five or six too many. I'd work toward scales that have four to six items.

3. *What should students do after completing the scales?*
In the previous classroom example, students discussed and defended their responses in small groups. They could also write about or create visual images of their responses, stage debates with others who had different opinions, interview each other about their responses, or write editorials about the characters. These are only a few ideas, however; there are many other follow-up activities that students could do.

4. *How do I assess students' responses to the scales?*
You are evaluating their reasons for their markings. I assess on a three-point scale:

> 1 = Your explanation didn't even begin to convince me.
> 2 = I'm somewhat convinced, but still a little hesitant.
> 3 = I buy into everything you've said!

Whichever type of scale you decide to use, remember that as students make their choices, they will be analyzing, synthesizing, and evaluating information. They will be making inferences, making comparisons, and drawing conclusions. And they will be using their knowledge from the text to explain their decisions.

Somebody Wanted But So

"Okay, group. Let's get started," Ms. Stemmons said to her class as she moved to the front of the room, ready to begin her lesson on "The Necklace" by Guy De Maupassant. "Let's look at what you read last night." Moans emerged from the back right corner of the room, but everyone else began digging through backpacks, pulling out their literature anthologies. "Who remembers the title?"

"Something about a necklace," one person said.

"Yeah. 'The Necklace,'" another said.

"Okay. Who can give a quick summary?" she asked.

Twenty-three heads looked down. Several students began thumbing through the pages. A few looked into their backpacks. Most just sat very still.

Summarizing a short story or a novel appears to be too overwhelming for many students, who either offer nothing or restate everything in the story. SWBS, or Somebody Wanted But So (MacOn, Bewell, and Vogt, 1991), offers students a framework as they create their summaries. Students read a story and then decide who the *somebody* is, what that somebody *wanted*, *but* what happened to keep something from happening, and *so*, finally, how everything works out.

SWBS also moves students beyond summary writing. As students choose names for the *Somebody* column, they are really looking at characters and trying to decide which are the main characters. In the *Wanted* column, they look at events of the plot and immediately talk about main ideas and details. With the *But* column, they are examining conflict. With the *So* column, they are looking at resolutions.

Students can help one another create class-generated SWBS statements

Step Inside a Classroom

"Anyone?" Ms. Stemmons said. She waited a few more seconds and then wrote four words on the chalkboard like this:

Somebody   Wanted   But   So

Then she said, "Okay, name a somebody from this story."

"The lady, uh, Loisel," a girl said.

"Right," Ms. Stemmons said, writing that name on the board under the word *Somebody*. "Mrs. Loisel. Who was somebody else?"

"Her husband," another girl said. "Mr. Loisel."

"Good," the teacher said and wrote, "Mr. Loisel," under "Mrs. Loisel." "Now, who can tell me what Mrs. Loisel wanted?"

"She wanted to be rich," a boy said.

"And she wanted to go to that dance," another student said.

"Yeah, but she didn't have the right clothes . . . ," a girl began saying.

"Wait a second," Ms. Stemmons said, interrupting her. "Don't get ahead of me," she said as she wrote, "wanted to be rich," and "wanted to go to the dance," under the *Wanted* column. "Okay, now, Shelly, what did you say?"

"But she didn't have the right clothes and jewelry and stuff."

Ms. Stemmons wrote, "but she didn't have the right clothes and jewelry."

"I get it," a boy on the front row said. "Put 'so she bought a dress and borrowed a necklace' under that last column, that *So* column." Ms. Stemmons did that.

Now the board looked like this:

Somebody	Wanted	But	So
Mrs. Loisel	wanted to be rich and wanted to go to the dance,	but she didn't have the right clothes and jewelry,	so she bought a dress and borrowed a necklace.

"So, is that the whole story?" the teacher asked.

"Wait, don't you think that just saying that she bought the dress isn't enough?" a girl in the middle of the room asked.

"Well, that's what she did," another responded.

"Not really," the girl said. "She made her husband feel guilty so he gave up his money for her."

"Yeah," several agreed.

One spoke louder than the others and said to Ms. Stemmons, "Under the *So* column, can you change that to 'so she shamed her husband into giving her money to buy a dress'?"

"Okay," Ms. Stemmons said and made the change. "Is that the end of the story?" she then asked.

"No. She lost the necklace and had to work really hard to pay it back," a student said.

"Yeah, but then she found out that it was like cubic zirconia or something. You know, fake," another said.

"Can you make that fit into the chart?" Ms. Stemmons asked as she added the word *THEN* to the board.

"Okay," one of the boys from the back right corner said. "Mrs. Loisel, or however you say her name, wanted to give back the necklace after she wore it but she had lost it, so her and her husband had to find a new one and then borrow money to buy it so she could return the replacement to her friend." Ms. Stemmons took down what he said, so now the chart looked like this:

Somebody	Wanted	But	So
Mrs. Loisel	wanted to be rich and wanted to go to the dance,	but she didn't have the right clothes and jewelry,	so she shamed her husband into buying her the dress and she borrowed a necklace.
		THEN	
Mrs. Loisel	wanted to give back the necklace after she wore it,	but she had lost it,	so she and her husband had to find a new one and then borrow money to buy it so she could return the replacement to her friend.

"And then what happened?" Ms. Stemmons asked after she had read everything on the chart.

"Put down they had to take on extra jobs to pay back the borrowed money, and one day ten years later, she saw her friend and wanted her friend to know the truth, but her friend told her it was a fake, so she and her husband had done all that work for nothing."

After Ms. Stemmons finished writing that statement, everyone looked at the chart for a moment.

"That's pretty cool," one student said.

"Does it work every time?" another asked.

"What about Mr. Loisel? If you started with him, would everything change?" another one asked.

"Could you get it down to one statement, you know with no *thens*?" another wondered.

Ms. Stemmons waited until the comments stopped, then she divided the class into groups of three or four students. She told two of the groups to figure out what the SWBS statement would be for Mr. Loisel. She told two more groups to choose some other stories they had read that year and see if SWBS would work for them. She told the final two groups to see if they could get the SWBS statements that were on the overhead projector down to just one SWBS statement. Students immediately went to work. Here's what three students said while writing an SWBS statement in which Mr. Loisel was the "somebody."

ERIN: Okay, so we got that Mr. Loisel wanted to make his wife happy, but she constantly wanted what he couldn't afford, so both of them ended up miserable.

CATHERINE: This one was like more general than what we did for Mrs. Loisel.

MARGARET: Yeah, this is more of a general summary than a real plot summary like the one on the board. Should we do it like that one?

ERIN: No, I like this one better. This is a better summary of the meaning of the story.

MARGARET: So what would that be for Mrs. Loisel?

CATHERINE: Um, Mrs. Loisel wanted people to think she was rich, so she borrowed what she thought was an expensive necklace, but she lost it and had to spend the rest of her life earning money to repay it, so she ended up poorer than when she began.

ERIN: That one still has a lot of the detail. I guess maybe it has to since it is the one that focuses on the main character who was doing everything. Maybe?

CATHERINE: Yeah, but Mr. Loisel was important, too. He was important because he was so opposite of her. He wanted to do things to make his wife happy, but she wasn't too worried about making him happy. He must have really loved his wife a lot to put up with how she acted.

MARGARET: He should have told her to repay it herself or to be honest with her friend.

CATHERINE: I think he should have told her to grow up. I mean, he gave up that gun he wanted to buy, and he even got her the invitation to begin with. She was just so stingy that she always wanted more.

Debriefing the Strategy

Ms. Stemmons' class has given you a glimpse of what a powerful strategy Somebody Wanted But So is. Her students, a mixed group of proficient and struggling readers, all enjoyed the strategy and participated in the discussion that ensued after their group work. None of these students wanted to offer a summary of "The Necklace." However, once the framework SWBS was offered, students were not only willing to summarize but also were interested in the summaries they were creating.

As the girls in the preceding dialogue created the SWBS statement for Mr. Loisel, they noticed how some summaries are detailed and others are general. Plus, through SWBS, they began a discussion on character differences and character motivations. This single strategy not only provides a scaffold for writing summaries, it also helps students to identify main ideas and details, recognize cause and effect relationships, make generalizations, identify character differences, and understand how shifting the point of view emphasizes different aspects of the story.

Putting the Strategy to Work

I either introduce the strategy with a short story, like Ms. Stemmons did, or with a picture book. Generally, students of all levels learn this strategy quickly and are able to use it on their own within a short period of time. SWBS can be used both to practice writing and evaluating summaries and to talk about literary elements.

1. *Teach students how to use this scaffold by modeling how you create a Somebody Wanted But So statement.* I often choose a narrative poem like "Sarah Cynthia Sylvia Stout Would Not Take the Garbage Out" or "I Cannot Go to School Today" (both by Shel Silverstein) or "Grandmother Grace" (Ronald Wallace) to teach this. Read the poem aloud and then discuss with students which somebody to consider, what that somebody wanted, what occurred that caused a problem, and so what eventually happened. Make sure students understand that when they are finished, they should have written one sentence that offers a summary of the text. Figure 8.3 shows Lauren's and Eleanore's SWBS chart for *Freak the Mighty* by Rodman Philbrick.

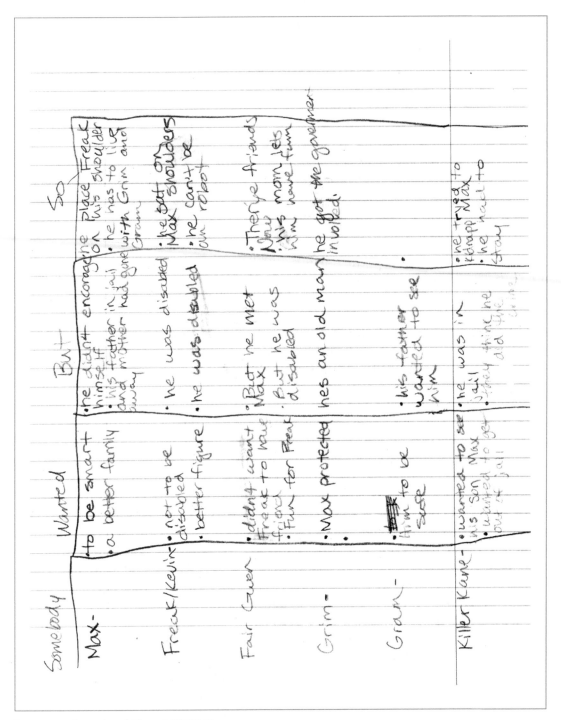

FIGURE 8.3 *Lauren's and Eleanor's SWBS Chart*

2. *Next, if the text is long, remind students they may need to break it into chunks,* connecting the statements with words like *then, later, and,* or *but.*

3. *Remember, you can use this to teach students about point of view as they change the character in the* Somebody *column.*

Questions and Answers

1. *SWBS does look simple, but don't kids come up with different statements for the same story?*

   Yes, they certainly do, but I don't see that as a problem. You look at the statements and figure out which students are still at the and-then-this-happened stage (recognizable by many SWBS statements strung together by the word *and*) and which are able to generalize; you quickly see which students do not recognize cause and effect relationships; you see which students understand main ideas and which don't; you see which ones can distinguish main ideas from details. You use students' statements to evaluate their progress and to help you decide what you need to teach next.

2. *Can't this strategy be used for more than teaching how to summarize?*

   Absolutely. As students complete an SWBS chart, they are looking at characters, events, conflicts, and resolutions. They write summaries from different points of view, they evaluate which summaries are the best, and they note how changing the *Somebody* column changes everything else. They have to identify main events, recognize cause and effect relationships, and decide which characters are worth discussing. I've even seen teachers use it to encourage students to predict what will happen next. To use SWBS for prediction, simply say to students, "Well, if this is what has happened so far, what do you think so-and-so will want to do next?" or "What will be the next conflict, or what will get resolved next?" As students create those statements, they are using prior information from the story to make an educated guess about what will happen next.

3. *Does SWBS work with nonfiction?*

   SWBS is a scaffold for a narrative text structure. You can experiment with different headings for expository text. For instance, if students are reading a science text that focuses on causal relationships, you might use these words as labels: Something Happened . . . Then This Occurred.

   Somebody Wanted But So might well be one of the most powerful summarizing tools you teach your students. Struggling readers have limited experience with narrative text structures, so they haven't seen how all stories contain a discussion of a character who does something, encounters a conflict, and then reaches a resolution. However, when they use it often enough, dependent readers can eventually drop this scaffold when they realize that, as one seventh grader said to me, "It is so cool how all stories are just a bunch of Somebody Wanted But So statements strung together." Cool indeed!

Retellings

"So tell me what happened in the story," I asked Easton.

"Well, uh, well, it was like this man or, um, this guy, and, and they, the guy and his, uh brother, goes to, to uh, well they like leave and then some stuff happens."

Stuff happens. That about summed up the story as far as Easton was concerned. While I'll admit that the general notion that "stuff happens" in a story is accurate, the phrase seems to lack the specificity most of us want in a discussion of a piece of literature. But this level of summary is what many students offer us on a consistent basis. To move students past the "stuff happens" response, consider using a strategy called retelling (Tierney, Readence, and Dishner, 1995). A retelling is an oral summary of a text based on a set of story elements, such as setting, main characters, and conflicts. Students use retellings to help them be more specific in their summarizing, get more organized, discover main ideas and supporting details, and become aware of their audience, use of language, and personal responses to the readings.

Step Inside a Classroom

It was late September, fifth period. Some of the twenty-eight sixth-grade students were reading silently, others were writing in response journals, and two students, in opposite corners of the classroom, were speaking into tape recorders. They were giving retellings of books they had recently finished reading. One of the students, Amelia, was a struggling reader. Her Iowa Test of Basic Skills reading scores placed her at about the twenty-eighth percentile in reading comprehension. While Amelia was a fluent reader, she had a lot of difficulty keeping the text organized in her mind, keeping events in the story in sequence, and recognizing what events were most important. In late September, Amelia gave the following retelling after reading Lois Lowry's *Number the Stars*:

Okay, there are soldiers and the family, it escapes, but the soldiers are going to catch . . . Well, they hide stuff in a casket and the dogs, first she is supposed to take this basket to the boat, and then, like, uh, the dogs and soldiers stop her and the basket, it like has hidden stuff—okay—but the cocaine kept the dogs from sniffing it and then her friend gave her the necklace and she kept it.

This retelling lacks organization, details, and continuity. It reveals that Amelia has trouble sequencing events as well as organizing her thoughts to present important facts: characters, setting, main ideas, conflicts, and supporting details. Her teacher, therefore, began modeling retellings, gave Amelia a rubric (outline) to follow when she gave retellings, and provided lots of opportunities to practice retelling. More than four months later, Amelia gave the following retelling of Katherine Paterson's *Bridge to Terabithia*. The italicized elements are aspects of retelling that Amelia had worked on specifically.

It was these two kids and they wanted, you know, to race. Okay. Wait. *This is a retelling for* Bridge to Terabithia, *which is about a boy and a girl and, uh, they are friends and, uh, one dies. And it was at the beginning of the school year.* Okay. One of the kids, a boy, and his name was Jess and he wanted to win the race so he was like running every day and then at school he met this girl and she was new and they are in the country. *In the country, that is the setting.* And the girl's name is Leslie. *So Jess and Leslie are the main characters and the setting is the country.* And there are some other characters. Like Marybelle and Jess' parents and his other sisters and Leslie's parents. And so then they become friends and when they go into the forest over to a little island she says to imagine that he is the king and she is the queen and they name the land Terabithia and they like go there to play. He likes it but doesn't tell anyone that they go there. And they are not boyfriend and girlfriend but just friends. And that is like cool. And his dad is mean to him. *That is one of the problems of the story, that his dad doesn't like that he does art but Jess likes to do art.* And his dad treats his sisters like really nice and Jess is like, you know, jealous about his dad. So then one day Jess goes with his teacher to look at some art pictures and Leslie goes to play without him and she is killed because the bridge to their island is just a tree that has fallen over this creek. Okay. It is really raining and she drowns. And so then Jess has to

Amelia stops herself to provide an introduction for the listener.

Now she remembers to give us the setting.

Amelia thinks to provide the characters' names purposefully instead of in a haphazard approach.

She inserts a comment about the conflict at this point.

find out and he is really sad and then he is worried it is his fault and stuff and his dad was almost kind of nice to him, well just a little. *Okay that's another problem that Leslie has died. This is like the main problem.* And then Jess takes his little sister there to play but he makes the bridge safe and he tells her about Terabithia. And so that is the end. *And the main problem was that Leslie died and the other problem, but not the main problem, is that Jess' dad doesn't want him to do art.* And there was a bully but that was earlier and that was not a main problem.

Amelia continues to identify problems that occur in the story and labels this one the main problem.

Amelia attempts to provide a closing statement.

That's a big difference between September and February. The first retelling has no structure, unity, main ideas, or supporting details. The second one, while certainly not without its problems, is much better.

Debriefing the Strategy

Like many struggling readers, Amelia had difficulty recalling what she had read and retelling that information in a logical, coherent manner. However, by comparing Amelia's first retelling in September with the one in February, we see that giving Amelia a structure to follow does allow her to share information in a logical way. Now her teacher knows that Amelia can absorb information; she just has trouble processing that information in a way that lets her share it meaningfully with others. The retelling strategy provides a scaffold that allows students like Amelia to understand the components of a good retelling, to use a rubric or guide to create their retellings, and to see improvement over time.

Putting the Strategy to Work

Using retellings effectively means modeling them frequently, incorporating a rubric students can use to plan their own retellings, assessing students' retellings over time so they can see both growth and areas that need work, and finally, using students' retellings as a way to inform instructional practices.

1. *Begin by modeling a retelling.* Modeling is integral to this strategy's success. Read a short story or a picture book to students; then retell it. You'll need to have looked over the rubric you want to use (we'll discuss rubrics in a moment) and to have practiced this retelling. Then, put a copy of the rubric on the overhead projector and discuss your retelling as a class. Model a retelling every day for several days, letting students score it. Occasionally, give a poor retelling, making sure you

discuss with students what made it poor. Even after students begin to give their own retellings, continue modeling them from time to time, especially when you change genres.

2. *Use a rubric to plan and evaluate retellings.* Think of a retelling rubric as an outline for what you want to hear in the retelling. Figure 8.4 is an example of one retelling rubric, but you can also write your own. The main thing is that students see the rubric before they give their retellings. They shouldn't have to guess what's important. I've even seen some teachers let students use the rubric as they give the retelling.

3. *Chart students' progress over time.* There's nothing students like better than to see their own progress. For a progress chart to be meaningful, you need to be the one who assesses the retelling, using the same rubric each time. Figure 8.5 shows you one student's progress. Notice that between Ian's first and ninth retellings, he had a steady increase in scores, except for January. That makes sense; a lot of time had elapsed between the December and January retellings. But look how quickly his score began climbing again. By February, he was making progress. His last two retellings, both in early May, had scores of 23 and 25. Ian made a lot of progress during the year, and he loved plotting the progress on his chart.

4. *Use retellings to plan instruction.* Ian's teacher used these rubrics to help him see what he needed to work on in his next retelling. Evaluating students' rubrics also helped her decide what she needed to mention to the entire class. For instance, when she noticed that several students were still not starting the retelling with a good introduction or they weren't making connections to something in their own lives or to other texts, she knew she needed to model how to do that.

Questions and Answers

1. *Why is a good introduction for the retelling important?*
Most of the time, when students start telling us about a text they've read, they presume we know everything that's already in their heads. It's part of their egocentric nature—if they know it, then of course we should know it. So they just begin—anywhere. They might forget to mention the title or the author; they might not think to give a brief overview— even something as simple as "I'm going to give a retelling about the story 'Cinderella.'" The fact is, if students are having difficulty providing all the information the listener needs to really understand what's going on

Retellings Rubric

Name _____   Date _____

Text _____   Selected by _____

Directions: Use the following checklist to rate the retelling. For each item below, circle a number from 0-3 in the appropriate column. On this scale, 0 means the retelling didn't include the item at all, and 3 means the retelling completely and successfully included the item.

Does this retelling

1. have an introduction that includes the story's title and setting?	0	1	2	3
2. give the characters' names and explain how the characters are related to one another?	0	1	2	3
3. identify the antagonists and protagonists?	0	1	2	3
4. include the main events?	0	1	2	3
5. keep the main events in the correct sequence?	0	1	2	3
6. provide supporting details?	0	1	2	3
7. make sense?	0	1	2	3
8. sound organized?	0	1	2	3
9. discuss the main conflict/ problem in the story?	0	1	2	3
10. explain how the main conflict/ problem was resolved?	0	1	2	3
11. connect the story to another story or to the reader's life?	0	1	2	3
12. include the reader's personal response to the story?	0	1	2	3

Total Score _____

Comments from listener about the retelling:

Suggestions for the next retelling:

FIGURE 8.4 *Retelling rubric*

Name _Ian_____ Class _____

Retellings Progress Chart

	Sept.	Oct.	Nov.	Dec.	Jan.	Feb.	Mar.	Apr.	May
R13									25
R12									23
R11								20	
R10							18		
R9						17			
R8					13				
R7				16					
R6			14						
R5			12						
R4		9							
R3		8							
R2	7								
R1	6								

FIGURE 8.5 *Progress chart*

in the retelling, chances are you are seeing the same problem in their writing. Once they begin to include an introduction, you know that they are aware of an audience that isn't familiar with the story.

2. *So does that mean that retellings will help students in their writing?*
   I've certainly found that they do. But that's only when teachers have used them often in the manner described earlier. If you really want to focus on students' writing, you might want to look at Hazel Brown and Brian Cambourne's book *Read and Retell* (1990). With their approach, retellings are always written, and the focus of the retelling is on the author's craft, whether that is character development or use of setting. I don't suggest using this approach with struggling readers until they

understand the art of retelling; for someone who is already struggling, having to write the retelling greatly reduces its fluency and elaboration.

3. *So, then, how do you listen to all of the retellings?*

    You need to reduce the number of retellings you listen to. First, think about who needs to be doing retellings. Do you already have students who can find the main idea and supporting details, organize their thoughts about a text, and relate events in the correct sequence? If so, those students don't need this strategy. They've already internalized what to do. Second, when you start a new strategy, start small. Choose five or six students from one class. You don't have to sit and listen to them as they give their retellings; you can have students record the retellings on a cassette tape and listen to them later.

4. *Should I listen to all the retellings any one student does?*

    I don't think that's necessary. Listen to one or two a month. Otherwise, let students score themselves from recordings they make, or let students score each other's retellings.

5. *How many retellings should students be doing?*

    How often students do retellings is up to you. One teacher arranged her class time so that when her ninth-grade students came into the classroom on Mondays, Tuesdays, and Wednesdays, the first thing they did was to read silently for ten minutes. On Thursdays and Fridays, they got with a partner and used the time to do a retelling. The more often students have a chance to practice the strategy, the better the results.

6. *As students keep practicing, should I keep modeling?*

    As students learn the strategy, you will need to model less often. I'd suggest, though, that you model retellings as students encounter new types of text structures. For instance, if students will be reading a selection that has a flashback, those who don't understand how to sequence will not know how to retell the selection without seeing it modeled.

7. *And one more time, just what are the benefits?*

    By learning how to give a good retelling, students figure out how to sequence, discuss connections, organize their thoughts, and identify main ideas, supporting details, characters, and setting. The retelling is simply the vehicle that allows those things to occur.

Ian and his classmates had a successful year with retellings because his teacher modeled them often, made sure students understood all the components of the rubric, charted their scores over time, and used their performance on retellings to plan instruction for individuals and the entire class. Ultimately, these dependent readers began to use retelling as a way to identify what they didn't understand in the text.

Text Reformulation

One night when my daughter was twelve, she handed me her history book, pointed to a particular passage, and said, "I don't get it."

"Don't get what?" I asked.

"What it's trying to say," she replied, thumping the opened page of her book.

I took the book, read the passage, and then put the expository passage into the framework of a narrative example. "Well, Meredith, it's like this. Pretend that . . . ," I began.

Ten minutes later she replied, "That is so cool. Why didn't the book just say it that way?"

"What way?" I asked.

"Like that. Like a story. Now it makes sense."

I thought about that exchange for a long time. "What had really happened?" I asked myself. Eventually, I realized that all that had happened was that I had taken a piece of text and transformed it into another type of text.

Students work in small groups as they reformulate a text

I reformulated the expository text structure to fit the narrative one she was more familiar with.

Text reformulation, or Story Recycling (Feathers, 1993), is a strategy in which students transform a text into another type of text. Whether students turn expository text into narratives, poems into newspaper articles, or short stories into patterned stories such as ABC books, reformulating texts encourages students to talk about the original texts. In addition, reformulations encourage students to identify main ideas, cause and effect relationships, themes, and main characters while sequencing, generalizing, and making inferences.

Step Inside a Classroom

Seventh period. Late April. The ninth graders were all reading Richard Connell's "The Most Dangerous Game." Some were reading in the Reading Café, a corner of the room with a rocking chair, two beanbag chairs, a small round table covered in a blue tablecloth, and two wicker chairs with cushions. Some were at the writing station—a table with three word processors, a printer, several thesauruses, and a handbook on usage. Several other students were talking with the teacher. A few were at listening stations, wearing headsets and reading along with the cassette tape of "The Most Dangerous Game." The rest were in small groups working on their text reformulations. In one of these groups, we see Catherine (a fairly proficient reader), Matt (a weak reader), and John (an excellent reader) working together to reformulate this story into an ABC alphabet book.

CATHERINE: Okay, read what we've got.

MATT: Okay. A is for Africa and Amazon where General Zaroff once killed animals. B is for . . .

JOHN: Wait a sec. I don't think we should say he killed them. He hunted them.

CATHERINE: Well, what's the difference? If you hunt them, then you kill them.

JOHN: No. That's the point. Look here at this part where he says, "I am speaking of hunting." And then Rainsford says, "What you speak of is murder." See, that's the point—that one sees going after men like hunting, and the other like murdering or killing. But both would see hunting animals as okay, so you don't call it killing, you call it hunting. See?

MATT: Okay. So hunted. Now, B is for boredom that Zaroff begins to feel. C is for—well, we don't have a good C yet. D is for Death Swamp where Rainsford almost dies. E is for the escape that Rainsford must do. F is . . .

JOHN: Wait—I was just thinking for S . . .

Here John makes a clarification.

She doesn't understand John's comment and questions him.

John works to explain the conclusion he's drawn about the difference between hunting and killing.

Matt, not as high-level a thinker as John, is more secure working through this in a sequence.

CATHERINE: S? We aren't up to S.

JOHN: I know, but when Matt said about how Rainsford was trying to escape, I was thinking about how he was in the room at the end and like how he started to fight and then he won and did he really escape?

John questions the text and begins to draw another conclusion about what it means to escape.

MATT: You mean did he get off the island and then come back?

JOHN: No, like did he, did he really . . . I mean. Well, S should be for switch because what I'm wondering is, did he become Zaroff and is he going to just start killing people? So, did he escape from Zaroff, or did Zaroff's ways like, you know, turn Rainsford into Zaroff?

CATHERINE: Oh, I get it. If Rainsford had gotten off the island, then why did he come back?

MATT: Well, he had to come back because he couldn't just keep swimming, but when he came back he had won, and maybe he didn't have to fight with Zaroff. So, yeah, did they switch?

Matt talks through John's idea until he, too, sees the implications of what happened to Rainsford.

JOHN: Yeah. And so then maybe C could be for confusion?

CATHERINE: Maybe, but I don't know.

MATT: Well anyway, that's good for S. Now, F is for fear because Rainsford, he felt a fear he had never felt before.

Another group was still trying to decide how to reformulate the text. As you try to picture this group, think terminally cute: perfect ponytails, perfect makeup, perfect nail polish. And very surface readers. They can answer literal-level questions, but when they need to infer or generalize, they begin to have trouble.

CINDY: I think we ought to do the Brown Bear pattern. You know, like "Rainsford, Rainsford, what do you see? I see Zaroff looking at me. Zaroff, Zaroff what do you see? I see Rainsford running from me."

Cindy begins to evaluate how to reformulate this text.

MEGAN: I don't know. That seems really hard to get everything in. Like the first thing that happened wasn't Rainsford looking at Zaroff.

Megan focuses on sequencing.

CINDY: Okay, so we'd just have to start earlier, like "Rainsford, Rainsford, what do you see? I see a black night looking at me."

MEGAN: Yeah, but then how does the black night see something?

We see Cindy accepts the suggestion and shows that she can reorder her thinking. Her statements also show that she can see cause and effect relationships.

JENNIFER: Well, what about "This is the island that Zaroff built. This is the game that Zaroff plays on the island that he built." [Pause.]

MEGAN: Okay, like "This is Rainsford, the man that Zaroff hunted that is part of the game that Zaroff plays on the island that he built."

What type of thinking does Megan's comment show us?

CINDY: Yeah. But you don't say how Rainsford got there.

MEGAN: You could say, "This is the way that Rainsford fell off the ship in the middle of the night and the game that he plays on his island that he built."

CINDY: [Pause.] This is going to get really long.

What type of thinking is Cindy making visible at this point?

Text Reformulation   161

MEGAN: Well, not if we pick like the really important parts.

JENNIFER: Okay, that's what we need to do. So what is like important?

CINDY: Like falling off the ship . . .

What does this comment show us?

Debriefing the Strategy

As the students worked through their reformulations, they returned to the text, reread portions, argued over meanings, questioned whether something was important or not, and listened to each other's interpretations. Text reformulation encourages dependent readers to think critically about the text without overwhelming them. The teacher never has to tell students to "find the main idea" or "make an inference"; students simply do these things while working on their reformulations. As students begin the process of reformulating, they must analyze and evaluate not only the text but also the writing they are creating about the text.

Eventually, students begin to see how form influences the message. One student said, after doing several reformulations, "This story had to be done like an ABC book because it was true, and that's what ABC books are—just telling you something, like A is for apple. And because everything happened in this story bam, bam, bam—just one thing after another. That's what happens when you read an ABC book; you just turn those pages one right after another."

Putting the Strategy to Work

1. *First, introduce students to the types of texts they can use as patterns when they reformulate a text.*

   1. Fortunately-Unfortunately Stories: "Fortunately I set my alarm clock last night. Unfortunately I forgot to turn it on. Fortunately my little brother woke me. Unfortunately he used his new water pistol. . . ." These linked texts help students with cause and effect and with sequencing.
   2. If-Then Stories: "If the dog chases the cat, the cat will run up a tree. If the cat gets stuck in the tree, you'll have to get her down. . . ." You might bring in *If You Give a Mouse a Cookie* or *If You Give a Moose a Muffin,* both by Laura Joeffe Numeroff, to read as examples of If-Then stories. Again, use this pattern when students have trouble keeping events in the correct sequence or misidentify cause and effect relationships.

3. ABC Book Structure: "A is for _____ because _____.
B is for _____ because _____."
This structure works when students encounter a text with a lot of terms or when they need to pull out facts to remember.

4. Cumulative Tale Structure: Give students an idea of this structure where a new sentence is added to previous sentences all the way through the text by sharing picture books like *The Napping House* by Audry Woods, *The Twelve Days of Christmas* illustrated by Jan Brett, or the folktales *The House That Jack Built* or *I Know an Old Lady Who Swallowed a Fly*. This structure certainly helps students with prediction (they must know what will happen next to plan their next statement) and with sequencing.

5. Repetitive Book Structure: In this structure, the reader sees a text structure that repeats throughout the book, as in Bill Martin Jr.'s popular *Brown Bear, Brown Bear, What Do You See?* or *Polar Bear, Polar Bear, What Do You Hear?* This structure helps students see cause and effect connections.

2. *Model several types of reformulations.* Some students always choose to do patterned text reformulations; other students, though, begin to explore various types of reformulations. Students might try the following reformulations:

- all kinds of texts into patterned texts, comic books, letters, or interviews
- poems into stories or letters
- stories into plays, radio announcements, newspaper ads, or television commercials
- plays into poems or newspaper stories
- expository into narrative
- diaries or memoirs into plays, newspaper articles, or television newsmagazine scripts

3. *Decide whether you or the students will choose the type of reformulation.* I wouldn't suggest dictating that yourself all the time; part of the power of the strategy comes from deciding exactly what type of reformulation works best. Sometimes, though, you might want students to work on cause and effect relationships; in that case, ask them to reformulate using the Fortunately-Unfortunately or If-Then pattern. Other times, you might want them to look at characterization; in that case, I'd suggest using an interview reformulation.

If you want students to practice main idea and details, have them recycle the story into the ABC pattern.

4. *Provide opportunities for practice and evaluation.* Text reformulation must be used repeatedly for students to realize its full benefits. These reformulations can be used to evaluate students' progress, but make sure you don't penalize students for something they've omitted in their reformulation if you didn't tell them to include it. If you want to see whether they are identifying cause and effect relationships, remind them to include that in what they write.

Questions and Answers

1. *How often should students reformulate a text?*

   I can think of nothing worse than knowing that every time I read something, I am going to have to rewrite it into some other form. So, every time is too often. Close to every time is also too often. On the other hand, twice during the school year is too seldom. I suggest that you don't think in terms of a number, but instead, introduce the strategy, model it several times using several different types of reformulations, and then make it one way for students to demonstrate that they can identify main ideas, sequence events, generalize, infer, analyze, and synthesize.

2. *So just by reading their reformulation, can I tell if they've used those skills?*

   Probably. If the reformulation puts events in the selection out of sequence, then you'll know that sequencing didn't occur. However, sometimes the reformulation will not include an example of a particular skill, such as making an inference. Does that mean the students can't infer? No; all that means is that the reformulation doesn't show you that skill.

3. *What about students who hate to write? Won't they hate this strategy?*

   That's a great question because struggling readers often don't like to write. There are several things to consider when you tell these students to do something that requires writing. First, when students say they don't like to write, often they mean exactly that—they don't like to put pen to paper. It rarely means that they don't like to make up stories. So, give them alternatives to *writing down* the story. For instance, perhaps students could record their text reformulation rather than write it. If students are working in groups, the student who doesn't mind writing could be the scribe, or students could take turns writing. Second,

> Abraham Lincoln, Abraham Lincoln, what do you see?
> I see unhappy slaves looking at me.
>
> Unhappy slaves, unhappy slaves, what do you see?
> I see Northern soldiers fighting to rescue me.
>
> Northern soldiers, Northern soldiers, what do you see?
> I see my Southern brother shooting at me.

FIGURE 8.6 *Text reformulation for information from eighth-grade Civil War unit*

sometimes students who don't like to write have trouble deciding how to say what they want to say. The patterned texts offer these students a scaffold, relieving them of worries about form. Third, keep text reformulations an option: optional activities are generally received more favorably than required activities.

4. *Can this strategy be used with expository text?*

Reformulating expository text to narrative text is the best way to use this strategy. Be sure to share this one with the social studies and science teachers. Figure 8.6 shows you how two students from a resource class used text reformulation to write about what they learned from a unit on the Civil War.

It Says—I Say

Dependent readers often have difficulties making inferences. (To read much more about how to help students make inferences, look at Chapter 5.) This strategy, called It Says—I Say, is simply a visual scaffold that helps students organize their thoughts as they move from considering what's in the text to connecting that to their prior knowledge.

Step Inside a Classroom

"When you finish reading," Mr. Arlin said, "answer the questions at the end of the story. If you need to, use the It Says—I Say chart."

"Tell me again when we need to use it," the girl in the third seat of the fourth row said.

It Says—I Say—And So

Question	It Says	I Say	And So
1. Read the question.	2. Find information from the text that will help you answer the question.	3. Think about what you know about that information.	4. Combine what the text says with what you know to come up with the answer.

FIGURE 8.7 *It Says—I Say chart*

"Okay, everybody, look this way," Mr. Arlin said, walking to the large chart that hung on the wall (see Figure 8.7). "Remember, people, we've been using this chart to help us answer certain questions. Anybody remember what kind of questions?" Mr. Arlin asked.

Silence. This was a class of sixteen students, all fourteen or fifteen years old, all of whom read at about a fourth-grade level. All were in the class because they had repeatedly failed the reading portion of the achievement test. Many had repeated a grade. Mr. Arlin worked well with these kids and often got responses from them when other teachers got nothing.

"Winner leaves class two minutes early. So, I'll ask again, what kind of questions . . . " He had not even finished the question when a boy in the first row answered him.

"Uh, you know, those inferred questions."

"Good job, Isaac. Get your Get-Out-of-Class-Early pass off my desk," Mr. Arlin said. "Now, who can tell us what inferential questions are?"

A tall young man said, "Questions where we have to use the chart." Everyone laughed, including Mr. Arlin.

"Sorry, Benjamin. You'll have to do better than that," Mr. Arlin responded.

"Oh, you know, like those kinds of questions where the answer isn't there in the book, so you gotta think about it, and you gotta already know somethin' about it," Benjamin said.

"That's it," Mr. Arlin said. "Now, some of the questions at the end of this story aren't answered directly in the story. That doesn't mean that the story is dumb, that the questions can't be answered, or that you are stupid; it means you've got to think about the question differently. You must take what's in the story, combine that with what you know, and then come up with your answer."

"Mr. Arlin, I don't get it," a girl in the second row said.

"She wasn't here when we did it, Mr. Arlin," another girl quickly interjected.

"Okay, who remembers 'Goldilocks'?" he asked.

"I do," another boy said. "Like Goldilocks, she went into the three bears' house and she ate their porridge and sat in their chairs and broke the baby's chair and went to sleep in the baby's bed. So I could ask you, 'Why did she break Baby Bear's chair?'"

"Because it was a baby chair, so it was little and she was big so she was too heavy and it broke," a boy called out.

"Marcus," Mr. Arlin said to the boy who offered that answer, "come up to the board, and using the It Says—I Say chart, show us how you came up with that great answer."

Marcus walked to the board and filled in the chart as shown in Figure 8.8.

"Okay, people," Mr. Arlin said. "Look here, because this is correct. Marcus wrote down the question and the information from the story. But remember, the story doesn't tell you that she is too big for the chair, so Marcus had to think about how kids are bigger than babies, how they weigh more, and how they can break baby furniture because it isn't strong enough to hold heavy people. Then he made his inference and answered the question. Goldilocks breaks the chair because she is too heavy for it."

"Cool," the girl who had been absent replied.

"Okay. Are we ready to read?" No noise. "Finish reading, then answer the questions. Students who use the chart correctly will get a special congratulatory handshake from me."

Laughter and moans erupted as students opened their books and settled down to read.

Question	It Says	I Say	And So
Why did she break Baby Bear's Chair?	Story says she sits down in the baby chair but she's no baby.	Baby chairs aren't very big because they're for babies and she is bigger and so she weighs more.	And so she is too heavy for it and it breaks.

FIGURE 8.8 *Marcus' It Says—I Say chart*

It Says—I Say—And So

Question	It Says	I Say	And So
Was Johnson right to refuse the money?	The story says that he was "sure the money had come to Peterson from bad ways."	I think that bad ways must mean that Peterson got the money illegally and if Johnson took illegal money then he could get in trouble.	And so I think he was right to refuse the money.
	And it says that Johnson "always knew right from wrong and never wanted to be the one doing wrong even though wrong followed him around like a little puppy."	I think that since Johnson doesn't want to do wrong and since he knows this money is wrong then he would feel bad if he took the money.	

FIGURE 8.9 *Karen's It Says—I Say chart*

The next day, students came back to class with most of the questions answered. As they discussed their answers to the questions that required an inference, students shared their charts. Here's how one student modeled her answer for another student:

FAITH: What'd you say?

KAREN: Well, I thought it was hard. But I made my chart like this. [She lays down her paper that has the chart shown in Figure 8.9 on it.]

FAITH: Yeah, I got that about the money coming from bad ways, but I didn't put that part about not wanting to do wrong.

KAREN: Yeah, that just seemed important, or why not take the money even though you know it's stolen?

FAITH: Yeah, that's what helps you know he is not going to take it. Okay, that's why I couldn't see if he should have taken it or not, since they needed the money and all, but you're right about how he never wanted to do wrong. Then you know that he was right. That's good.

After observing students using the It Says—I Say strategy, I asked Mr. Arlin why he had Marcus write his answer on the board using the chart's structure, even though he had given the right answer.

"Marcus is a bright young man. I didn't know if he answered the question about why the chair broke because he remembered that example from a few days ago, because he made the inference on his own, or because he understood how to use It Says—I Say as a way to structure his thinking. What I do know is that I've got students in my class who don't understand how to make inferences. They needed to see how Marcus got to that answer. By having him put the answer on the board, following the chart's structure, those students were able to see how an inference is created."

"So some of your students' answers to inferential questions can be found just in the text?" I asked.

"I'm not really sure," he said. "But I do know that once questions move beyond the literal level, the students flounder. With this strategy, though, they are seeing how to think."

Debriefing the Strategy

Seeing how to think. I liked his phrase, and I believe it is an accurate description of what the It Says—I Say chart does for students. Mr. Arlin's students, like many struggling readers, generally responded to inference questions with comments like, "There's no answer in this story for this question," or "How am I supposed to answer this? The answer isn't here," or "This is a dumb question," or even "I'm too stupid to answer this question." These students spend so much effort just getting through the text, just keeping up with the literal details—characters, events, setting— that making an inference as they read is the last thing that happens, if it happens at all. Therefore, when they encounter a question that requires an inference, they don't know where to begin. They need a scaffold, something that helps them internalize the process of how to infer. The It Says—I Say chart helps students finally see a structure for making an inference.

These students spend so much effort just getting through the text that making an inference as they read is the last thing that happens, if it happens at all.

Putting the Strategy to Work

You won't be surprised when I say that repeated practice is the key to success when using It Says—I Say. In the previous classroom example, Mr. Arlin had to go over the strategy with students again, even though he had obviously talked with them before about how to use it. He also had hung the It Says—I Say chart in the classroom so that students could refer to it.

1. *Introduce the strategy to students using a short, familiar story such as "The Three Bears" or "The Three Little Pigs."* Ask a few literal-level questions, questions that Taffy Raphael calls Right There Questions (Raphael,

1982). Then, ask a question that requires students to make an inference. If a student answers it correctly, great—now ask that student to explain how the inference was created. Pull out the It Says—I Say chart that you'll have already made (that's the chart in Figure 8.7) and ask that student to fit the answer into the chart. Or, if no one can answer the question, you answer it, putting your answer into the chart.

2. *Model the strategy regularly.* As with everything we teach, modeling is the key. Remember that struggling readers often need multiple models over an extended period of time. But you don't always have to be the model. In Mr. Arlin's classroom, Marcus did the modeling. The next day, Karen and Faith shared their answers to inference questions. That sharing became another form of modeling. As Faith saw how Karen worked through the answer, she came to understand not only how Karen reached her conclusion but also why she couldn't "see" the answer.

Struggling readers often say things about not being able to visualize what is happening in the text—and that might include not being able to visualize the connections between what is happening in the text and what is already in their minds. Those connections are what form inferences. The It Says—I Say chart is the visual form of those connections. Eventually, you want students to do that visualizing in their heads; until then, when asked to make inferences, they may need the extra support of this strategy. With it, you'll be able to *see* their thinking, and they'll be able to *see* the connections they need to form.

Questions and Answers

1. *Is it important to quote from the text in the* It Says *part of the chart?*
Yes. Since the *It Says* column refers directly to the text, the more direct quotations students use, the better. In Figure 8.9, Karen wrote a comment in the *I Say* column for each quotation from the text. That's important. Then she reached one conclusion.

2. *Doesn't this chart get lengthy?*
It can. That means you need to look ahead at the questions you want students to answer. If there are six questions and all six require an inference, that's probably too much writing for struggling readers (who are also often struggling writers). If that's the case, consider having students work in pairs or small groups to answer some questions. Also, remember that as soon as you see that students can make inferences and tell

you how they have reached those inferences, they don't need to complete the chart repeatedly. The chart is a scaffold to be used as needed.

3. *How do you make sure students get all the important information on the* It Says *part of the chart before they go on to the rest of the chart?*

The answer has to do with good teaching. Remember, the purpose of the chart is to give students a scaffold or support system as they figure out how to think inferentially about a text. Some students might need an even stronger scaffold than just the chart; they might need to be told how many items to list under the *It Says* column. So, you might need to look ahead at the questions, think about the answers, and tell students that for a certain question, they should find one, two, or three items from the text for their *It Says* column. Eventually, you want them to be able to do that on their own, but in the beginning, you might have to provide that support.

4. *How can I tell whether a student can't make an inference or just got the wrong answer?*

I generally see that students who have trouble making inferences either don't answer questions that require inferences, complain about the question by saying that it has no answer or the answer isn't in the book, or give an answer that is unrelated to the text. Those students need the chart.

5. *What happens when kids use the chart?*

The purpose of the It Says—I Say chart is to help students see the connection between information in the text and information in their heads. Once they can do this, I'd eliminate this scaffold.

Strategy Snapshots

Scales, Retelling, Somebody Wanted But So, Text Reformulation, and It Says—I Say were described in detail to provide you with rich descriptions of after-reading strategies that can extend the meaning-making process. In the next section, you'll find three additional strategies that, though described in less detail, are no less important in helping dependent readers understand how to construct meaning after reading.

Sketch to Stretch

Capitalize on many students' art ability by using this strategy, called Sketch to Stretch (Harste, Short, and Burke, 1988). With this strategy, students work

I put Bo in the nest with the baby mockingbirds because they often felt defenseless like he would feel.

FIGURE 8.10 *Student's sketch to stretch for* To Kill a Mockingbird

independently or with a partner to create symbolic sketches of their interpretations of the text. On the back of the sketch, they write an explanation of their sketch. As students gather in small groups, they share their sketches. Others respond to a sketch before the artist discusses why she drew what she did. Figure 8.10 is one student's Sketch to Stretch for *To Kill a Mockingbird*.

Save the Last Word for Me

Dependent readers are often reluctant to offer their opinions because they anticipate being wrong. Save the Last Word for Me (Short, Harste, and

Burke, 1996) offers even the most reluctant of speakers a forum in which their comments are heard. After reading a text, students choose passages they like and copy each passage on a card. Then, on the reverse side of that card, they write why they liked that passage. Once students have completed this, they get into small groups. One at a time, they read the passages they selected. Other students comment on what they liked or didn't like about each passage. Then, the student who wrote it on his card gets to have the last word as he reads his reason for choosing that passage.

Most Important Word

To encourage what often becomes a lively debate (yes, even with struggling readers!), ask students to choose what they consider to be the most important word from the text they've just read. This strategy, first proposed by David

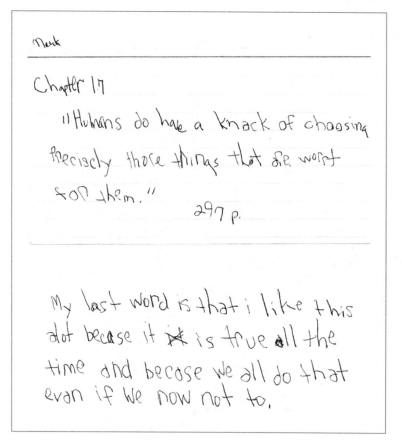

Figure 8.11 *Most Important Word chart*

Bleich (1975), forces students back into the text to consider what was the most important aspect of that text. Be warned, some students might say that the word *of* or *the* is the most important because it occurs the most often. Kids will laugh, but once you've sent that student off to actually *count* how many times those words occur (or something equally boring) while the rest of the class discusses other, more important, choices, that level of response will soon cease. If you want to, tell students they can't choose a character's name or a word that is in the title. When students have made their choices, make sure they can point to places in the text where the word is used and explain why they chose that word as most important. Variations include having students find the most important chapter and most important passage.

While skilled readers will enjoy discussing and debating the most important word, struggling readers often need a more structured approach to deciding on their word choice. Consequently, I give them a Most Important Word form to complete. You can find a template for this form in Appendix F.

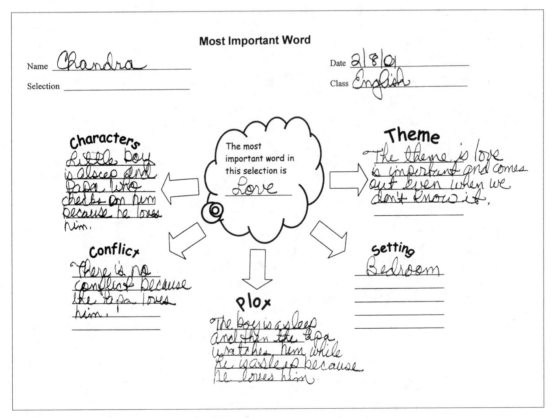

FIGURE 8.12 *Chandra's Most Important Word form*

With this form, students consider how the word affects the characters, conflict, plot, and setting. From that, they use this word to help them formulate a theme statement. Chandra, an eighth grader, used this form after reading a poem titled "The Sacred" by Robert Coffin (see Figure 8.12). She chose love as the most important word and after thinking about how this word affected the characters, the conflict, the plot, and the setting, she concluded that the theme for this poem is, " . . . love is important and comes out even when we don't know it."

Reflections

I'm most frustrated when I visit classrooms in which the teacher obviously still views comprehension as a product and not a process. I know that's what's going on when the after-reading activities are limited to answering the questions at the end of the story or completing the fifty questions that came with the novel's study guide. That limited vision is particularly damaging to dependent readers. These students, more than any others, need activities that bring the invisible process of comprehending to the visible level. The strategies in this chapter extend the meaning-making process to after-reading activities, thus helping dependent readers figure out "how to get it" throughout the entire reading process.

Dear George,

I picked up a note you had been writing during class. It was late spring and you, like all the students, were more interested in counting how many days until school was out than anything I might say. I expected your note would be to a buddy, asking him what he wanted to do that day after school, or maybe even what his summer plans were. Instead, I found a note to your grandmother. In part, it said, "Grandma, I need to know if I can come live with you. Maybe if I was in a diferant school things wuld be diferant. Its just to hard here. If I culd come live with you I culd help you with stuff and I wuld be real good. I think I just need a place to start over."

I thought you'd been thinking about ending the year. Instead, you were looking for a way to begin again. I wonder how many times I misread your thoughts, misunderstood your actions. I wonder how long it took me to understand that endings and beginnings are always connected.

Vocabulary
Figuring Out What Words Mean

* ◆ ◆ *

Dear George,

How many times that year did you say to me, "What's this word mean?" and how often did I respond, "Use the context clues," or "Look it up." I hate to tell you, but that was my stock advice to students for several years, more specifically until my fifth year, when one particularly perceptive young lady asked me, "And just which context clues would those be?" I looked at the sentence; I looked at the surrounding sentences. Finally, I burst out laughing as I admitted, "Well sweetheart, I don't have a clue."

As she and I stood there laughing over that moment, I slowly realized that when it came to vocabulary instruction, I really didn't have a clue.

* ◆ ◆ *

Learning New Words

If you want to see if your students recognize effective versus ineffective vocabulary instruction, ask them to write recipes for terrible vocabulary lessons and recipes for great ones. You'll probably find a wide range of recipes for great vocabulary instruction; you'll most likely discover that their recipes for ineffective instruction all look the same. Turn them loose with recipe cards after you've reminded them about the vocabulary they'd find in recipes. Figure 9.1 shows you the recipes two eighth-grade boys created.

For many of us, vocabulary instruction, like spelling instruction, tends to be one of those things we know we ought to be doing, but generally don't know much about doing; consequently, we fall back on how we were taught vocabulary: On Monday, teacher gives students the vocabulary words; during the week, students memorize definitions of vocabulary words; on Friday, teacher gives test on vocabulary words; on Friday afternoon, students forget definitions of vocabulary words. Some of us get creative and let students choose their own vocabulary words—those words that students were supposed to identify as new to them while reading their literary texts. This was supposed to provide ownership of the words and make vocabulary instruction more meaningful. It only took my struggling readers about one week to figure out that if they were honest and listed all the words they didn't know, they would have very long lists; so instead, they didn't choose any.

Vocabulary Casserole

Ingredients Needed

20 words no one has ever heard before in his life
  1 dictionary with very confusing definitions in it
  1 matching test to be distributed on Friday
  1 teacher who just wants students quiet on Mondays copying words

Mix 20 words onto blackboard. Have students copy each word and then look them up in the dictionary. Make students copy down all the definitions. For a little spice, require that students write words in sentences. Leave alone all week. Top with a boring test on Friday.

Perishable. This casserole will be forgotten by Saturday afternoon.
Serves: No one

Vocabulary Treat

Ingredients Needed

5–10 great words that you really could use
  1 thesaurus
    map colors and chart paper
  1 game like jeopardy or bingo
  1 teacher who thinks learning is supposed to be fun

Mix 5 to 10 words into the classroom. Have students test each word for flavor. Toss with a thesaurus to find other words that mean the same. Write definitions on chart paper and let us draw pictures of words to remind us what they mean. Stir often all week by a teacher who thinks learning is supposed to be fun. Top with a cool game on Fridays like jeopardy or bingo to see who remembers the most.

Serves: Many

FIGURE 9.1 *Recipes for vocabulary instruction*

Others of us decided that vocabulary workbooks were the way to go. Now students didn't even have to copy words off the blackboard; there they were, twenty words, neatly printed in two columns at the top of the left-hand side of the page, with four exercises (A, B, C, and D) on the next three pages. These exercises had students define the preselected words, match to synonyms, match to antonyms, and figure out derivations. If you did one exercise a day, you could still get to the vocabulary test on Friday and be ready to start a new unit on Monday.

One eleventh-grade AP English teacher recently told me that her students actually like the vocabulary study books, do well on the tests, don't forget the words, *and* score very well on the vocabulary portion of the SAT, thank you very much. For a moment (okay, a long moment) I coveted her job. She had *my* job, the job I presumed I'd have when I finished my under-graduate degree. But then I snapped out of it and remembered that I actually like working with dependent readers. So, I asked her how much reading her kids did. She began clicking off the novels—*Turn of the Screw, My Antonia, Wuthering Heights, The Great Gatsby, Death of a Salesman, Oliver Twist,* and the list went on. And that was just the required reading. They read an additional eight novels on their own, a plethora of short stories, and many, many poems. I wondered if the ninth graders I was working with that semester had read eight novels—ever. I asked her if she thought their wide reading had anything to do with their rich vocabulary. She stared at me. I asked her if she had ever tried a year not using the vocabulary workbooks to see if those students scored as high on the SAT as students who had spent a year working through vocabulary workbooks. She walked off.

Then, two weeks later, she found me in the library. "Okay," she said, "I asked my students how much vocabulary they actually learned from the workbooks." She paused. I waited. "We had a really interesting discussion, as most said that they liked doing the workbooks because they required so little thinking. One kid said, 'It's good TV homework.' They said that they didn't really remember the words they learned from there. One said, 'If when you ask how much vocabulary we learn from the books means how much we learn so that we really use it, then I'd have to say, not much. If you mean do we learn it for the tests, then sure, because it's for a grade. But I don't ever really use those words.'"

"Are you surprised?" I asked her.

She waited a minute. "I don't know. At first I thought I was, but then I had to admit that I've always known that these kids are going to do well on their SATs just because of how much reading they do, how many discussions they've had." She stopped, then said, "I guess I never knew what else to do."

Vocabulary Instruction: What Else to Do

I thought for a while that this might be the shortest chapter in this book, perhaps the shortest chapter ever written. I wanted it to say simply, "Vocabulary instruction—see Janet Allen's book *Words, Words, Words* (1999)." While I've decided to expand beyond that comment, I still want to encourage you to read that book. In it, Janet offers many ideas for helping with the vocabulary development of all levels of learners. I only wish she had written this book back in the early 1980s instead of the late 1990s!

What I want to do in this chapter is tighten the focus a bit beyond where Janet goes and talk specifically about vocabulary development for students who are reading far below middle school or high school standards. So, in this chapter, I'll share with you the specific vocabulary instruction that I've found to be effective for dependent readers. *Effective* means that students learn the words, use the words, and remember the words. What follows are eight suggestions that have led to students learning, using, and remembering new words. These suggestions are based, in part, on the research by Adams and Cerqui (1989); Allen (1999); Baker, Simmons, and Kameenui (1995); Baumann and Kameenui (1991); Nagy (1988); and Vacca, Vacca, and Gove (2000).

Suggestion #1: Assign Word Study, *Not Word* Memorization

I was in a middle school specifically to help the language arts teachers with vocabulary instruction. As the principal explained to me, the teachers were spending a lot of time teaching vocabulary, and he was spending a lot of money on vocabulary workbooks, but they just weren't seeing any results. The words weren't showing up in students' writing; students seemed to have forgotten the words as soon as the weekly test was done; and there didn't seem to be much difference on standardized test reading comprehension scores, which he felt ought to be improving if students were indeed learning lots of words. "More important," he said, "our poorest readers, who are getting the strongest dose of vocabulary instruction, are still our poorest readers."

I met with the language arts teachers, twelve of them. As we talked, I discovered that some of the teachers used vocabulary workbooks to supply lists and activities while others pulled vocabulary words from the novels and short stories that their students read. Whichever method, all agreed that students had between fifteen and twenty words to learn each week. Students were expected to learn the words by looking up the definitions in the dictionary and writing them in their vocabulary notebooks or by completing the exercises in the workbook. It all sounded very familiar. We looked at some of the words from a previous week's list that one eighth-grade class had to know. This twenty-word list included words such as *anaphoric, anathema, guileless, taciturn, veracity,* and *verve.*

As we looked at the list, I asked what folks saw as the biggest problem. Several responses were offered:

"These are really tough words."

"There sure are a lot of words."

"Apart from the book [vocabulary book], I'm not sure where the kids would ever see these words again. Maybe that's a problem."

One teacher *disagreed* that this list of twenty words was too many for kids. She explained, "These lists are for our worst readers. The problem for most of them is that they can't understand the stories because they don't know what most of the words mean. If we don't give them a lot of words, they'll never catch up." She was so passionate about wanting these kids to "catch up" that she convinced several other teachers to agree with her. Finally, all twelve agreed that twenty words a week was a reasonable number of new words to learn if these students had any chance of moving forward in their reading comprehension.

After they decided on that number, I asked if they'd be willing to do something as an experiment. They were wary. I asked them if they'd be willing to learn the twenty words two weeks prior to the students' being introduced to the words so that for two whole weeks before the words were formally introduced, they, the teachers, would use the words repeatedly in class. We talked about this for a while. They all agreed that if students heard them use the words, it might make a difference.

One teacher, Jan, explained that once, while she was teaching a class, the district language arts supervisor had come into her classroom and announced, in front of her students, that she needed to rewrite some curriculum material she had submitted so it would conform to a certain format. Later, another teacher came into the class, and while they were talking about what had happened, the visiting teacher said, "She is so persnickety. You just have to do it her way." Jan explained to us that her students must have overheard that comment because the next week, when she was explaining the format for the

While my biggest concern about this list of words was that it was at a frustrational level—meaning the list was much too difficult for the students and therefore truly defeating and overwhelming for them—these teachers focused on other issues. I decided to go with their discussion and see where it would lead.

book report, one student said, "You sure are being persnickety." Many other stories followed as teachers shared how students certainly did mimic the language they heard. (Any of you who are parents know that children certainly *do* use the language they hear—and sometimes at the most inopportune times!) So, they all agreed to give this a try.

I then reminded them that their learning/using/introducing weekly schedule would have to look like this:

	Learning	Using with students	Introducing in a list
Week 1	Learn List 1		
Week 2	Learn List 2	List 1	
Week 3	Learn List 3	List 1 and 2	
Week 4	Learn List 4	List 2 and 3	List 1
Week 5	Learn List 5	List 3 and 4	List 2

Suddenly, they didn't like this quite as much, but they stuck to their decision to give it a try. We agreed to meet in four weeks. By then, they would have learned four lists, would be using words from two lists, and would have introduced formally the words from the first list. I recorded our conversation when we reconvened.

ME: Well, how'd it go?

T1: Fine. It was fine.

T2: Okay.

[Silence.]

ME: Everyone doing okay with keeping up with the words?

T1: Yeah, it's fine.

[Silence.]

ME: Anyone want to add to that?

[Silence.]

T7: Well, I thought this was a little hard.

T6: I am so glad you said that. This is ridiculous. There is no way I can keep up with all these words.

T9: Oh. Good. I thought I was the only one.

T4: And it's not just how many words, it's the words themselves. I mean, do you know how many of these words I just never use? *Fortitude.* I mean, I just don't ever use that.

T8: Oh, did ya'll see that word *jaundiced*? I was trying to figure out how I was going to talk about a baby being jaundiced, and then I looked it up and it said it was cynical. I didn't know that.

These teachers continued their discussion for about twenty minutes, all beginning to share how difficult it was to keep all the words straight, how silly it was to learn some of the words, how many of the words they never used at all, and how completely overwhelmed by the whole experience they were. One teacher summed up everyone's feelings: "When we started this, I thought, 'No big deal. I've got a good vocabulary, so I can do this in a snap.' But by the third week, I was in tears. It's too many words, and it's words I don't use, and all I could think about was how much I dreaded Monday because I knew I'd have to start learning another list of words. And I'm supposed to be the smart one. I can't imagine how the kids in my class must feel!"

Then a critical thing happened. Another teacher responded, "Yeah, but the kids don't feel that bad because they don't ever really have to use the words. . . ." She stopped, her words hanging in the air. No one said anything, but folks nodded in dawning understanding. She continued, "Oh my God, that's it, isn't it? I never really expected that they'd learn them to actually *use* them. It never bothered me that there were so many because I always must have known deep down that they were only learning them for a test. Not to really ever use them."

Her powerful words shook the group, and we were all quiet for a moment. Finally, I asked what they thought they should do. They agreed that they really did want kids to learn words so they could use them and that twenty words were too many: "If it's too many for us, then it's got to be too many for the kids, you know, too many to really learn and use and remember." Over the next few weeks, we experimented to determine what a reasonable number really was. We finally decided that eight words was a reasonable number to learn and use on a regular basis in order to familiarize students with them prior to their introduction in a vocabulary workbook lesson or a reading selection. A few teachers felt like they could manage ten. A few others wanted to stick with five. Some varied between five and eight, depending on the words. Most of the teachers decided not to use the workbooks since students might be confused about why they were only studying some of the words. Those teachers used the workbooks as a resource to create the lists. Other teachers kept using the workbooks and just told kids which words in each list they had to learn that week.

The results: students began using the words long before they were introduced in the workbooks, and when they got to the workbooks, the students made comments like, "Look, we know this word already," or "These lists are getting easier," or "Oh, they think this word is important just like you do." Students remembered the words longer, as borne out by

Effective vocabulary instruction means students use words they learn

unit test scores. Furthermore, students began using the words in both their oral language and their written language.

> LESSON #1: Students learn more words when we focus on
> fewer words and use those words in our own speech.

Suggestion #2: Teach Students How to Use the Context as a Clue

In a very unscientific study (no control variable, no written record, no strict data analysis—just sitting in a restaurant with a lot of English teachers in Detroit during the National Council of Teachers of English Annual Convention), I asked about twenty teachers to ask as many teachers as they could during the next two days the following question: When it comes to vocabulary instruction, what piece of advice do you give to students most often? Two nights later, we met at the same place and shared our results. We had either fifty responses or twenty-five hundred. I lost count. Okay,

Discerning the meaning of unknown words using context clues requires a sophisticated interaction with the text that dependent readers have not yet achieved.

so the methodology lacked rigor. What was interesting to me, though, was the number one response: "I tell kids to use the context clues."

Let's consider the usefulness of this advice. Yes, we tell students to use context clues . . . often. The problem with that is, discerning the meaning of unknown words using context clues requires a sophisticated interaction with the text that dependent readers have not yet achieved. Consider the following sentences:

> The jaundiced voters doubted whether they believed the politician; like so many other politicians, this one offered promises that the voters didn't think he would keep. Their pessimistic attitude frustrated the candidate as he tried to explain that he was sincere in his promises.

If the word we want students to define from the context is *jaundiced*, then what context clue or clues do we expect them to use? The best clue comes in the second sentence, where a synonym for *jaundiced* is offered—*pessimistic*. You probably saw that right away. But you're a reader who makes all sorts of inferences while reading. Look at what skilled readers must do to get to that clue:

- Readers must infer that *their* in sentence 2 refers to *voters* in sentence 1.
- Readers must recognize that *pessimistic* is describing *attitude* in the same way that *jaundiced* was describing *voters*.
- Then, they have to make the inference that there's a semantic connection (not just syntactic) between *jaundiced* and *pessimistic*.
- Next, from that inference, they have to see that *pessimistic* is a synonym for *jaundiced* and from that infer that *jaundiced* means *pessimistic*.
- Finally, if they don't know what *pessimistic* means, they must use all the information in both sentences to infer that voters aren't happy with politicians. That means they must know the words *candidate, frustrated, sincere*, and *politicians*—all difficult words for some dependent readers—and they must infer that the candidate is a politician.

All that must happen even when there is a direct clue (a synonym) to the meaning in the sentence. Here is a passage with less than direct clues. Focus on the word *loquacious*.

> Tara's dad couldn't believe his ears. Finally, he folded his newspaper in half, set it on the coffee table, and got up from his chair to leave the room. As he got to the door, he said, "I never thought that I'd

tell my loquacious daughter that she is DRIVING ME NUTS!" His daughter finally moved the phone from her mouth and said, "You say something, Daddy?" before he walked out, shaking his head.

Here the clues are much more subtle. A very skilled tenth grader (pre-AP English class; assistant editor for the school newspaper; all A honor roll) provided this think-aloud for defining *loquacious* from this sentence:

> Well, I thought I had heard that word before, but thought it was like to do with being loco, you know crazy. But that, I don't know, maybe that's it because it says she is driving me nuts, like crazy. But then I looked back to that first sentence and where it says "couldn't believe his ears" rather than his eyes, then that got me thinking about hearing, you know because it's usually "couldn't believe his eyes." So ears have got to be important or like the author he wouldn't have changed it. And then later it says that when he said you drive me nuts that then the daughter, she like moved the phone from her mouth and that means that she was talking. And like talking and hearing, they have to do with each other. And my sister, oh my gosh, she is always on the phone talking and that can drive you nuts. So, maybe like loquacious, it means like talking, a lot.

I can't begin to count all the inferences that student made to define that word from the context. But what's readily apparent is how active he was in constructing that knowledge. It's that level of activity that is sometimes missing from dependent readers.

By contrast, a ninth-grade struggling reader looked at *loquacious* in the same passage and offered this think-aloud:

> Well, it's something about the girl, the daughter. And see how these words are capital, you're driving me nuts, well that must be important because it's in capitals and it's about the girl, too. So, so, you know if you're like really bothering someone you say you're driving me nuts. So, it means, it is like, what is it when you really bother someone? You're like a pain. Annoying. That's it. Maybe it could mean annoying.

The biggest difference between these two readers is that the first reader was willing to move beyond the single sentence where the word occurred to infer the meaning; in fact, he was willing not only to move beyond but also to look back to preceding sentences. He understood that "context" extends beyond the immediate few words after the word in question. The less-skilled reader, however, viewed context in a limited manner. I suspect that was supported by many worksheet pages in which he practiced using context clues where the clue did occur in the same sentence as the target word. Those contrived practices rarely help prepare students for the types of clues they will encounter in real texts.

Note that both readers were willing to move beyond the passage to try to bring in their own background knowledge. The first reader made a connection to his own sister who talks on the phone a lot; the second reader talked about hearing the phrase "driving me nuts." The difference, again, is that the first reader made a connection beyond the sentence where the target word occurred. The second reader limited his thinking about the word to that single sentence.

So, the first problem we see with context clues is that the clues are subtle and require a lot of inferencing from readers. Second, context clues may give some readers some idea about the word's meaning, but that usually isn't sufficient for inferring specific meanings (Vacca, Vacca, and Gove, 2000; Nagy, 1988; Baumann and Kameenui, 1991). In other words, context clues can sometimes give us the gist of the meaning, enough perhaps to complete that one reading, but not enough to allow students to define a word so that they can use it on their own in other situations.

Does that mean we should abandon teaching context clues? I don't think so. I do think it means we must recognize that using the context as a clue is something that requires lots of practice, something that separates dependent from independent readers, something that is much harder than we may have realized. And actually, I think that we will better understand how difficult this is if we'll stop using the term *context clues* and instead use the phrase I offered in the preceding sentence: "using the context as a clue." That more accurately describes what skilled readers do.

As readers use the context as a clue to figuring out unknown words, they'll see that sometimes authors offer very direct clues. Pointing out these clues can sometimes be helpful:

◆ definition/explanation clues
◆ restatement/synonym clues
◆ contrast/antonym clues
◆ gist clues

Example of a definition clue: *A symbol is something that stands for something else.* Here, the reader learns what the word *symbol* means simply by reading the sentence.

Definition or explanation clues are the most direct clues an author offers readers. With this type of clue, the author actually defines the word for the reader, generally in the same sentence.

Restatement or synonym clues are clues that explain unfamiliar words in the text by restating them in simpler terms or by using synonyms. This type of clue is often used in content area textbooks. Unlike definition clues, restatement clues may or may not appear in the same sentence as the unfamiliar word.

Contrast or antonym clues offer an opposite meaning for a word. These clues often require that students catch and understand the signal word. Like restatement and synonym clues, the contrast or antonym may appear in the same sentence or a subsequent sentence.

Gist clues are the most subtle type of clue an author can offer readers. With these clues, the meaning of a particular word must be inferred from the general context—or the gist—of the passage. Sometimes readers must read an entire passage before they understand the meaning of the word. A good example of gist clues was found in the *loquacious* passage. *Loquacious* was never defined or restated, nor was an antonym offered. Instead, readers must infer the meaning by understanding the gist of the passage. Using gist clues to define unknown words is difficult at best for dependent readers; overwhelming at worst. Be sure to think aloud passages that require readers to discern meanings of unknown words via inferencing. Students must hear how you piece together all the parts of the puzzle to understand how to use these subtle clues to create meaning.

> LESSON #2: Teaching students *how* to use the context as a clue requires that students see relationships among words and can make inferences about the passage.

See Chapter 5 on making inferences for more specific ways to help students infer meaning from contextual clues.

Suggestion #3: Teach Word Parts

Teaching some words directly via word lists and teaching students how to find the meaning of other words indirectly via the context are both

---

Example of a restatement clue where the restatement is in the same sentence: *Cowboys often wore chaps, leather trousers without a seat, over their pants to protect their legs from thorns.* Example of a restatement clue that occurs in another sentence: *The food was bland. In fact, everyone called it tasteless.*

Example of a contrast clue: *Chad is calm and quiet, but his brother is boisterous.*

Here's another example of a passage that requires that readers understand the gist to define the unknown word, *precipice: John burst out of the woods and found himself at the edge of a precipice. Clinging to a boulder, he gazed down dizzily at the blue ribbon of river below.* The word *precipice* isn't defined, restated, or put in contrast with other words. Therefore, readers must figure out what that word means by reading the passage and thinking about the other information in the text. "If he's gazing down, he's up high. And, if the river looks like a blue ribbon, he must be very high. Boulders are very big rocks, usually on mountains. A precipice must be someplace up high, on a mountain, at the edge of something where you can see over to what's below."

important. However, we can't directly teach the meaning of all words, and sometimes the context just leave students clueless; therefore, we also must help dependent readers increase their word knowledge by teaching them how words work. In other words, let's teach them the meanings of prefixes, roots, and suffixes. When students learn those meanings, they can unlock the definitions of many words.

Teaching Latin and Greek roots isn't a new instructional strategy for most of us. What might be new, though, are the following two suggestions.

TEACH SPECIFIC ROOTS AND AFFIXES

My experience with dependent readers suggests that they need to learn a few specific roots, prefixes, and suffixes in a year. Few might mean six or it might mean fifteen, depending on the level of the student. The next year, students review those while learning another group.

The goal, therefore, is that we do some vertical planning in our schools so that in middle school or high school, the language arts teachers from all the grades know which roots and affixes constitute the "master list" for the school and, more specifically, which ones will be introduced at which grade level. No longer should one teacher decide to do a unit on roots and affixes because she likes word study while the next three teachers say they just don't take the time to do that; word study should be something teachers across grades embrace so that students have repeated opportunities for learning and relearning. Start with the most common roots, prefixes, and suffixes listed in Appendix D. Then, for high school or advanced middle school students, introduce the much longer list of roots in Appendix E.

VOCABULARY TREES

The second recommendation has to do with *how* you teach root words. Instead of simply giving students a list of roots with their definitions and examples of words that include those roots, have students build vocabulary trees. (Figure 9.2 shows you what a vocabulary tree looks like.)

To build a vocabulary tree, choose which root word you want students to study and have them write it in the root of the tree. Under the root, students write its definition. In Figure 9.2, for example, the student has written *tract* in the root area of the tree with "to pull, drag" written underneath. In the trunk of the tree, students write a key word that you provide that uses that root. Under the word, students write the definition of the word. Then, in the branches that come off the trunk, students write as many other words as they find that use that root. In this case, the student found *detract, subtract, traction,* and *contract*. Students define the word and copy a sentence

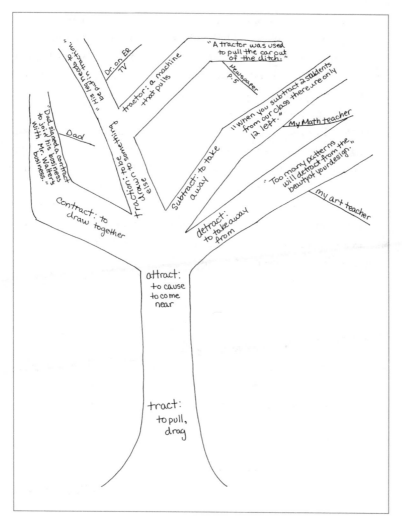

FIGURE 9.2 *Vocabulary tree*

that uses it. This could be a sentence they heard, one they read, or one they said themselves. In the twigs off the branch, they record where they heard or found the sentence.

Students can build these trees on their own in the vocabulary section of their binders. In that case, I check them about every two weeks and give points for added twigs or branches. They turn in vocabulary trees every six weeks (or whatever the grading period is) for a major grade. Grades are based on the number of branches they have. While it's probably not in vogue to mention giving students numerical grades for such a project, my students often won't do anything unless they are sure it counts toward their grade.

Students can also build class trees. In this case, draw a tree (with lots of branches!) on some colored butcher paper from the art department and mount it on a wall where lots of students can add words to the branches and can read what other students have offered. In one school, the vocabulary trees became so popular with two teachers that they moved them into the hall and the students began to compete to see which class could "grow" a bigger tree. To make sure that students aren't just adding words without learning them, you can require that a certain number of the words show up in their writing. Again, the more of these words *you* use, the more of the words the students will begin to use.

Vocabulary trees are great for teaching roots—mostly because you can put the root in the root of the tree and then see how that root can branch out. It's a nice way of making this concept very concrete to students who often need those tangible connections.

> LESSON #3: Do some vertical planning with teachers in your school to determine which roots and affixes will be systematically taught in which grades. Use graphic organizers such as vocabulary trees to help students learn roots.

Suggestion #4: Turn Vocabulary Study into a Word Hunt

When vocabulary study is about testing students on long lists of words they've probably never heard before, then we've most certainly taken the fun, the joy, the delight out of finding new words. Many of us became English teachers because we love words—we love finding new words, saying funny-sounding words (every time I say piccadilly—not often, I admit—I smile), or figuring out unusual words. (When I ran across *durbar,* I decided that since the root *bar* means admission, then this word must have something to do with letting someone in or seeing people. When I looked it up, I found that I was close; it's a formal reception held by an Indian prince.) We enjoy how words sound one against the other; we smile at the images they create and pause at the memories they invoke. We collect words like some collect coins. We are, most certainly, wordsmiths.

Word Collection

To pass that love of words on to others, we must do more than "study vocabulary." We must delight in the vocabulary that authors offer. I do this with dependent readers by giving them opportunities to collect words they like, don't understand, think sound funny, think look funny (*hors d'oeuvre* always shows up there!), or that invoke a particular memory or image. They put these words onto bookmarks that one teacher from Lanier Middle School labeled "Mark My Words" bookmarks. Read more about these bookmarks on page 130 and see Appendix C.

Every seven or ten days, we take about fifteen minutes of class time to share the words we've all collected. As students call out their words, I record them on a big sheet of chart paper, and we talk about them. If we can, we use what we know about root words and affixes to figure out meanings. If we can't, and if I don't know what someone's word means (I had no idea what *isinglass* or *deckle* meant), then somebody becomes our "sleuth" and looks it up for us. Finally, as a class, we choose two or three (and sometimes even four) words that we all want to use for the next few weeks. Such choices have included *cadence, stooge, doublet,* and *essential.* They've sometimes included words that surprised me—words I presumed teens would know: *quicken, surveyed, appetite, preference, monotone,* and *consistent.* Such choices from students remind me that dependent readers are, in fact, dependent on us because they know so few words. This simple activity has helped students become wordsmiths and has helped me remember not to assume anything when working with struggling readers.

> *We enjoy how words sound one against the other . . . we are, most certainly, wordsmiths.*

Words Across Contexts

A second way we play with words is an activity I call *Words Across Contexts.* Students spend time looking for words that have different meanings depending on the context. They create questions that follow this format:

What would the word	a. give one example
[insert word] mean to	b. give second example
	c. give third example (optional)

For example, one student provided the class with these questions:

1. What would the word *jersey*	a. a dairy farmer?
mean to	b. someone from New England?
	c. a football player?
	d. a seamstress?

2. What would the word *driver*
   mean to

   a. Tiger Woods?
   b. a movie star?

3. What would the word *surf*
   mean to

   a. a kid on a beach?
   b. a techie?
   c. someone watching TV?

4. What would the word *volume*
   mean to

   a. a kid with a stereo?
   b. someone who writes
      encyclopedias?

To help students keep up with their words and examples, I give them a template to complete. Once they have found one or two good examples, they put them on a blank transparency and share them from the overhead projector with the entire class. You can find a copy of this template in Appendix F.

> **LESSON #4:** Take advantage of students' sense of discovery and play by making use of word puzzles.

Suggestion #5: Use Graphic Organizers

In one class I visited, students spent about forty minutes of their ninety-minute class looking up words in the dictionary and copying definitions. These fifteen sixth graders had all scored below the twenty-second percentile on the reading portion of the Iowa Test of Basic Skills. None had ever passed the reading portion of the state standards test. I would say that the teacher's instructional strategy for teaching these students this list of words (look them up, copy the definition, use them in a sentence) was less than effective. As an example, for the word *courageous,* almost every student copied this dictionary definition: "having or characterized by courage." Sentences that these students then wrote included:

◆ He was having courageous.
◆ Characterized by courage he was courageous.
◆ He was having a courageous character.
◆ He was full of courageous.

Students complete graphic organizers to help them learn new words

Across the hall, another teacher had a similar group of sixth-grade students. Her students were studying the same list of words. This teacher, however, was using a graphic organizer, one that I had adapted for dependent readers from an organizer Janet Allen presents in *Words Words Words* called Words in Context (1999, p. 140). My adaptation consisted of reducing the number of blocks and ovals students had to complete and providing specific space for students to write the definition and to practice using the word in a sentence. This second teacher had divided her twenty-three students into groups of three and had given each group two words and two blank transparencies of the graphic organizer (see Figure 9.3). Students completed the graphic organizer for each word and then presented their word to the class on the overhead projector. At that time, the entire class completed graphic organizers for each of the words presented. That night, for homework, students completed the practice section for each word. The next day, we saw a range of sentences from them for the word *courageous*:

◆ The fire men who went into the World trade bilding were courageous.
◆ My brother shows couregousness when he plays football.

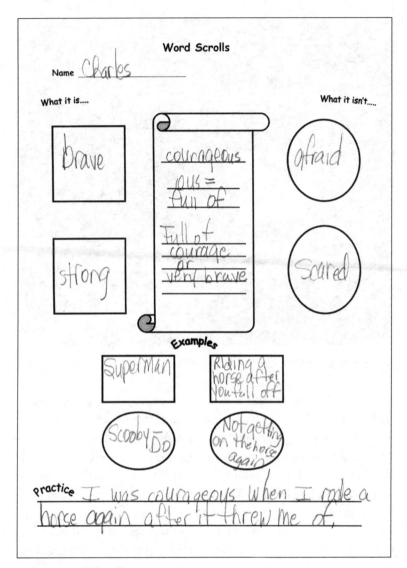

Word Scrolls

Name Charles

What it is.....

What it isn't.....

brave

strong

courageous
ous =
full of

Full of
courage
or
very brave

afraid

scared

Examples

Superman

Riding a
horse after
you fall off

Scooby-Doo

Not getting
on the horse
again

Practice I was courageous when I rode a
horse again after it threw me of.

FIGURE 9.3 *Word scrolls*

♦ When it was a storm and my parents were gone, I was courageous and stayed home by myself.
♦ The courageous girl went into the hanted house.

Later, when students were tested on the words, we saw that students who had simply copied definitions remembered far fewer words than students who had completed the graphic organizers. Graphic organizers help dependent readers organize information and see relationships that they otherwise might not see. There's a copy of this graphic organizer in Appendix F.

Suggestion #6: Use Logographic Cues

Creating logograph cards can help students learn vocabulary words. On one side of the card, students write the vocabulary word; on the other side, they write the definition and draw a logograph that suggests the meaning of the word. For instance, a student might draw someone falling off a cliff for the word *precarious* or a ghost for the word *apparition*. A vocabulary logograph can be anything that helps a student remember the meaning of a word, and since this will vary from students to student, it's important that students always create their own logographs for vocabulary. For additional ways to use logographs, see page 129.

Some students also create logographs to help them remember where they originally saw the word. For instance, Sarah, a skilled reader, drew a heart next to vocabulary words from *Romeo and Juliet*, a single red mark next to words from "The Scarlet Ibis," Braille dots next to words from *The Miracle Worker*, and a simple birdcage next to a selection from *I Know Why the Caged Bird Sings*. Figure 9.4 shows you Sarah's logographic card for the word *precarious*, which she found while reading "The Scarlet Ibis."

Sarah explained why she likes to use vocabulary logographs:

> We get all these words from stories and we have to learn them. The lists get really long and it all starts to run together. With these pictures, I just look at that one picture and I can remember the word much better . . . It's faster and helps me see it better in my mind.

Logographs act as a powerful scaffold to comprehension for some students. As students decide what symbol would best represent an idea in the text, they are encouraged to think critically about what they are reading.

LESSON #6: Let students create logographs as a tool for
remembering words.

FIGURE 9.4 *Sarah's logographic cue card*

Suggestion #7: Read Aloud and Use SSR

Jim Trelease quotes a line from the Albany (New York) Area Reading Council's brochure: "All babies are born equal. Not one can speak, count, read, or write at birth, but by the time they go to kindergarten they are not equal!" (*The Read-Aloud Handbook*, 2001, p. 36).

That difference in speaking, counting, reading, and writing ability when children enter kindergarten hinges on the amount and type of interaction the parent or primary caregiver has had with the child. Children from homes rich in conversation have heard more than 45 million words by the time they are four. Children from homes that lack these rich conversations have heard as few as 13 million words (Hart and Risley, 1996). This is not to suggest that the former have heard 45 million different words; in fact, they've probably heard the same 10,000 to 20,000 words repeatedly. (For example, think of how many times you said the word *up* or *more* or *go* or *no* to a toddler.) In fact, in conversation, adults tend to use a basic vocabulary of about 5,000 words, with another 5,000 used less often (Trelease, 2001). "Beyond that ten thousand mark are the rare words, and these play a critical role in reading. The eventual strength of our vocabulary is determined not by the common ten thousand words but by how many *rare words* we understand" (p. 17).

Hayes and Athens (1988) explain that we encounter more of these rare words in printed text than we do in oral speech. In fact, adults, when talking to other adults, will use about 17 rare words for every 1,000 words. Adults, when talking to a ten-year-old child, will use only about 11 rare words for every 1,000 words. Television shows offer about 22 rare words per every 1,000. However, a children's book uses 30 rare words for every 1,000; an adult book uses 52 for every 1,000; a comic book (Yes! Archie lives!) uses about 53 rare words for every 1,000; and a scientific paper uses as many as 128 rare words per every 1,000.

We quickly see that talking with children, though critical, isn't enough. Watching television certainly doesn't expose children to enough rare words either. Children need to be exposed to written text over long periods of time. In other words, we've got to read aloud to children long before they enter school and continue that practice long after first and second grade.

The landmark study, *Becoming a Nation of Readers* (Anderson et al. 1985) called reading aloud "the single most important activity for building the knowledge required for eventual success in reading" (p. 23). Studies by Livaudais (1985), Beers (1990), Martinez and Roser (1985), and Anders and Levine (1990) show that reading aloud

- builds background knowledge—an essential ingredient for comprehension
- improves listening comprehension—a precursor to reading comprehension
- improves listening vocabulary—this store of words informs your speaking vocabulary and reading vocabulary
- builds vocabulary—of both common and rare words
- creates interest in reading

- improves students' understanding of sentence structure and usage
- improves students' ability to visualize the text

As middle and secondary teachers, we often forget the power of reading aloud to students, relegating this powerful instructional strategy to a special treat on rainy days or something we see as the responsibility of elementary school teachers. We also worry that if we read aloud to students, we are keeping them dependent, not fostering their own reading abilities.

I'd agree with that to a point. If we never give students a chance to read on their own, then, yes, their silent reading will never improve. On the other hand, if we combine silent reading with reading to them to accelerate achievement in all the areas in the previous list, then we've built a program that moves students toward reading success. Plus, if students need to read a text that is far above their instructional level, hearing the story aloud, either from the teacher or on tape, will provide a way to improve reading skills and give them access to content.

Reading aloud can take many forms. You can read aloud an entire text by reading a portion of it each day. You can read and tease, reading students a small portion of a text to lure them into reading the rest on their own. Teri Lesesne (1998, p. 252) offers these guidelines for reading aloud:

- Let students respond to the reading every day but do not turn this session into a skill lesson.
- Establish a regular schedule for reading aloud. Reading aloud to students is most effective when it is done on a regular basis.
- Reading daily for ten minutes or every other day for fifteen minutes is optimal. Initially, you may have to begin with a shorter period of reading aloud and work up to the full ten to fifteen minutes as students become accustomed to the routine.
- Preview all material to be read aloud. Not only will this make the presentation more effective, it will avert any uncomfortable situations that might occur because of language or events not appropriate for your students.
- Vary the material to be read. Read nonfiction as well as fiction. Be sensitive to the diverse needs of your students. Sometimes choose books that have males as main characters and other times choose those with females. Include books that show students characters of various ethnic backgrounds.

You should also remember that *you* don't have to do all of the oral reading in the classroom. Let students do paired reading. Here, two students sit and read the text together. They can decide how to divide the reading, taking turns as they choose. You can let students pick a partner or you can purposefully pair a stronger reader with a weaker one. You can also do paired reading with the entire class. This variation means you'd read a part of the text aloud and the class would respond in unison on the next portion. What you're trying to avoid is the round-robin reading that many of us remember from our own elementary school days. You know the one—taking turns up and down the rows with each student reading one paragraph aloud; the problem is, students count ahead to their one paragraph, rehearse it so they'll get it right, and then tune out.

You might also decide to use readers theater. Readers theater allows a small group of students to perform a text. The students sit at the front of the room and read the script. No actions, props, or memorizing is required. You can find many prepared scripts in a book by Latrobe and Laughlin titled *Readers Theater for Young Adults: Scripts and Script Development*. I've also found several by going to <*www.google.com*> and entering the term "readers theater."

Finally, the flip side of reading aloud is silent reading. Giving students time for daily, uninterrupted, sustained silent reading is critical. Studies show that giving students as little as fifteen minutes a day for SSR (sustained silent reading) can impact attitudes, vocabulary, fluency, and comprehension. Yet, few middle and secondary teachers give students time to read in class. "We've got other stuff to cover" is the common response. The Commission on Reading, the group that prepared the report *Becoming a Nation of Readers*, found that teachers could pick up approximately two hours per week of time for students to read by spending less time on worksheets and workbooks. No one would ever expect the school football team to get better without actually playing football or the band to improve without actually playing instruments. But for some reason, many of us do expect students to become better readers without actually having time to read. The logic fails and, eventually, so do students.

This next comment might trigger some debate. The literature I've read on sustained silent reading and the people I've heard speak about this all suggest that the teacher must be reading silently with the students. I disagree. While I do find it beneficial to let kids see you reading along with them (that's that all-important modeling), when you first start the program,

I also think those same fifteen to twenty minutes represent valuable time in which you could

◆ conference with a student about a paper
◆ hold a guided reading group to work on a specific comprehension strategy
◆ interview a new student about reading interests
◆ talk with a student about his or her reading progress
◆ meet with a small group of students to work on phonics or spelling
◆ meet with one or two students who have been absent

What the time shouldn't be used for is grading papers, cleaning out the file cabinet, running off a test, catching up on lesson planning, or visiting with a teacher. That only sends the message that sustained silent reading time is a time for them to be busy so you can do other things. Just remember, it's your call. If one day, you are eager to get back to that book you've been reading, then by all means, join them. If, however, you have students who would benefit from an individual conference with you, do that. It's been my experience that students who see that you are serious about reading and about helping them become better readers are perfectly happy to accept both alternatives.

Reading aloud and SSR programs take time, but that time yields great rewards. Chapter 14 offers resources for keeping up with new titles, and Appendix M offers many titles your students might enjoy.

> LESSON #7: Incorporate reading aloud and sustained silent reading into your instructional program.

Suggestion #8: Ask the Right Question

For years I taught vocabulary either as a reaction (A student would tell me "I don't know this word," and so I would tell him) or in isolation (I gave out lists of words that had little to do with what we were reading and had students look them up and define them). Now, as I work to weave vocabulary study into the fabric of what we are studying, I've discovered that I need to figure out what the student doesn't know about a word before I can begin to teach him what he does need to know. Certain questions we might ask students about words yield different answers. As you read the following chart, you'll see that the left-hand side gives you a list of teaching objectives while the right-hand side offers questions you can ask to assess specific word knowledge.

Information you are looking for	Question to ask
To discover if the student has heard the word or has used the word	Read the word to the student and then ask "Have you ever heard this word?" "Do you have any ideas about what it means?"
To discover if the student knows how to use the word	"Can you use the word in a sentence?"
To discover if the student knows what words he doesn't understand while reading	"What words caused you problems while you were reading this section?"
To discover what students know about prefixes, suffixes, or roots	"Can you figure out what this word might mean by looking at this part?"
To discover if connecting the word to a larger context helps the student with the word's meaning	"Can you figure out what the word might mean if I tell you it is related to _____?"
To discover if the student can use the context as a clue to figure out the meaning	"Can you reread that section and from the other sentences figure out what the word might mean?"

As students answer those specific questions, we know how instruction should proceed. For instance, Ricardo, a ninth grader, read fluently, but often didn't understand what he was reading. As an English Language Learner, I suspected his problem in comprehension came from a limited English vocabulary. One day, as he read his literature book, I stopped him often to point to some words and ask the questions in the above list. For instance, as he read *reinvent*, I asked, "Can you figure out what *reinvent* means by looking at this part?" and I pointed to the prefix *re*. He shook his head no. I followed up with "Do you know what the word *invent* means?" He thought for a moment and said, "Like to discover something?" We continued talking about the word *invent* and then as I told him what *reinvent* meant I asked him if he understood what the prefix *re* often did to a word's meaning. He said, "I thought it was just another word, you know, another word to learn." Obviously, I needed to spend time helping Ricardo with the role and meaning of affixes.

At another point, after he finished a lengthy paragraph, I asked him, "Were there any words you didn't understand?" He looked back through the paragraph and pointed out four or five words. His ability to point out what he didn't know put him ahead of many of my other students.

Finally, after he read a paragraph with the word *civilian*, he stopped and said, "Here's another one I don't know." I asked him if he could read the paragraph again to get an idea as the context provided a strong clue. He read it again, slowly, and said, "Here, at this next sentence, it says about the people so maybe it is something of people?"

From asking specific questions, I learned a lot about how Ricardo processed information about words and, therefore, what to teach him next. Ricardo could identify what he didn't know, when prompted would return to the context to figure out the meaning, and needed some information on affixes (or at least the prefix *re*!). Asking the right question at the right time often gives us just the right information to keep a student's learning moving in a meaningful direction.

> LESSON #8: Ask students specific questions about their word knowledge and use their answers to help inform your instruction.

◆ ◆ ◆

Dear George,

No one ever wants to relive that seventh-grade year. It's so tough in so many ways. But how I wish you and I could step back in time and do that one again. We could have done so much with vocabulary; instead, I pushed you through the red level of that workbook we used. Toward the end of school, as we finished the last unit, you asked if we were done with that vocabulary book. As I stood in the doorway talking with an eighth-grade language arts teacher, I nodded my head yes. You walked to the garbage can and threw it away and muttered something that I'm quite sure wasn't a prayer. The other teacher told you that you couldn't get rid of it that easily. You asked her what she meant. She explained that in eighth grade you'd have the yellow-level book. "Same stuff?" your small voice asked. "Yep," her throaty voice replied. Your eyes welled with tears that you quickly wiped away. "I give up," you whispered and sat down, head on folded arms. "It'll be okay," I said, kneeling beside you. "Really?" you asked. "Which part will be okay? Not knowing how to do these stupid books or not knowing how to read or not knowing any of the answers that any teacher ever asks? Just which part do you think will be okay?"

Your words caught me by surprise. And then I knew that all year long, my words had left you needing so much more. Words matter, but how teachers help students learn words and learn about words matters more.

◆ ◆ ◆

10

Fluency and Automaticity

❖ ❖ ❖

Dear George,

You sat beside my desk one day after school struggling through a short story. I read a few sentences; you read a few sentences. Your finger pointed to each word as you said it, slowly, one . . . word . . . at . . . a . . . time. For you, reading was a slow and laborious process. Many times, I found myself simply telling you the word just so you'd finish. Once, as we sat together in our classroom during lunch, eating sandwiches and reading a portion of a short story aloud that I knew you'd never get through on your own, I said, "I think it would make more sense to you if you'd just read it a bit faster."

"Now why didn't I think of that," you replied with a slow grin and then continued your word-at-a-time approach. I heard echoes of that conversation recently when I listened to a beginning teacher suggest to a tenth grader that he seemed to be reading very slowly. "No duh," he said. "Miss," he continued, "I'd love to read faster, but this is as fast as the reading brain works."

Slowly, like your reading, I came to understand the role of fluency in becoming an independent reader.

❖ ❖ ❖

The Rhythm of Reading

Automaticity is that ability to do something quickly without a lot of conscious thought about the task. For instance, as I type these words, I don't consciously think about where each key is located on the keyboard; in fact, when I try to recall the location of individual keys, I begin making errors. Also, I think of my daughter as she learned to drive. Coordinating looking in the rearview mirror, putting the car into reverse, pressing the accelerator slowly, and keeping the steering wheel lined up in the direction she actually wanted to go while moving backward required all of Meredith's attention—along with a lot of prompting from her dad (her mother was too afraid to be in the car). There was very little that was automatic as she was learning to drive in reverse (actually, there wasn't that much as she drove going forward either!). Now she's done this so many times that she's beginning to develop some automaticity.

Reading automaticity refers to a reader's ability to recognize words without conscious decoding. It means readers recognize words as whole units, and they recognize the words quickly and accurately. The word *window* is seen as a unit—window, not /w-i-n-d-o-w/ or even /win-dow/. Sounding out words a letter at a time or syllable-by-syllable slows a reader, disrupts fluency, and that interrupts meaning. It's important to remember that students don't develop automaticity via decoding but rather through repeated exposure to a word they can decode. Said another way, just because students can sound out a word doesn't mean they automatically recognize it. For students who are quickly becoming independent readers, they may need to see the word about ten times before it moves into their bank of easily recognized words. However, our dependent readers who are struggling with word recognition may need to see this word as many as forty times. That's four times as many exposures as our fluent readers need. Consequently, these students, more than any others, must have repeated and regular opportunities to read stories at their independent reading level (Samuels, Shermer, and Reinking, 1992).

Automaticity—rapid and accurate word recognition—leads to fluency. Fluency—the ability to read smoothly and easily at a good pace with good phrasing and expression—develops over time as students' word recognition skills improve. Students lacking fluency read slowly, a word at a time, often pausing between words or phrases; they make frequent mistakes, ignore punctuation marks, and read in a monotone. Fluent readers know the words automatically, and therefore move easily from word to word, spending their cognitive energy on constructing meaning.

As you read the following two transcripts, ask yourself which student has good word recognition skills but lacks automaticity and fluency and which one lacks automaticity and fluency because word recognition skills are still developing.

Independent level of reading: Students can recognize 95 percent of the words in the text and comprehend 90 percent or more without any assistance from the teacher. **Instructional level of reading:** Students can recognize 90 to 94 percent of the words and comprehend 75 percent or more of the text without assistance from the teacher. This level, as the name implies, is the level of text we should use to instruct students in either word identification procedures, vocabulary, or comprehension strategies. **Frustrational level of reading:** Students recognize fewer than 90 percent of the words and comprehend less than 50 percent of the text. At this level, students are too frustrated by the text to learn from the text.

Fluent readers know the words automatically, spending their cognitive energy on constructing meaning.

Step Inside a Classroom

ANTWAN

I listened intently as Antwan, a first grader, read the sentences aloud that I jotted down on a dry erase board. If you'll read aloud these same sentences, pausing every time you see a diagonal mark, you too can hear how Antwan's reading sounded.

> I/ saw/ my/ friend/ at/ the/ park./ He/ said,/ "Do/ you/ want/ to/ play/ with/ me?"/ I/ said,/ "Yes!"/ We/ went/ down/ the/ slide,/ and/ then/ we/ played/ chase./ We/ had/ a/ great/ time.

As Antwan read, his finger pointed to each word and his head nodded at each word. He paused between words and completely ignored the pausing or intonation that the question mark, period, exclamation point, and comma would suggest. Using a monotone, he lacked any expression in his reading. When he finished reading, he said, grinning, "I did real good, didn't I?"

ME: You certainly knew all the words.

ANTWAN: Yep, I'm a good reader.

ME: Can you tell me what this was about?

ANTWAN: Well, it wasn't a very good story, now was it? There are these two boys and they are at the park and one says play with me and the other says okay and so they go on the slide and then play chase at the end. [Pause.] I wonder why they didn't go on the swings? Swings are my favorite thing to do at the park. We have a park that's close to my house, and when we go there, I always get on the swings. I can go real high and then jump out of the swing.

ME: Sounds like you really like to swing. [He nods.] How did you decide that this was about two boys at the park?

ANTWAN: Huh?

ME: You said it was about two boys who were at the park. But in the story, I don't see where it says boys. [Antwan studies the passage.]

ANTWAN: Yeah, here. It says, "I."

ME: So if I read it and say, "I," then is it about girls?

ANTWAN: [Slowly shaking his head.] No. It's about two boys. Because here [points to the word *he*] it says *he* and why would he want to play with a girl? No. It's two boys.

ME: I don't know about that. I'm thinking it could be about a girl who plays with her friend who is a boy.

ANTWAN: Well, that's just because you're a girl.

ME: Oh. Okay. I think it's my turn to read this aloud, now. Okay? [He nods.] I want you to listen to how I read it.

ANTWAN: Good. You go now.

ME: I saw my friend at the park./ He said, "Do you want to play with me?"/ I said, "Yes!"/ We went down the slide, and then we played chase./ We had a great time./

ANTWAN: You're a good reader, too.

ME: Why do you think that?

ANTWAN: Because you got all the words right. Like me.

ME: Did you think my reading sounded any different from your reading?

ANTWAN: Nope. You got all the words just right.

ME: I think I heard a few more pauses between your words than I had between my words. What do you think?

ANTWAN: [Paused for a moment.] I think you're a lot older and can do some reading stuff that I can't do. When I'm old, I can do that stuff, too.

I actually think Antwan won't have to wait until he's my age (which until my conversation with him I had not really considered to be "old"!) to do some of the "reading stuff" I can do. Antwan is a beginning reader who, though he has good word recognition skills, lacks automaticity and fluency. He certainly understands what he has read and is even willing to offer his opinion on the value of the text ("Well, it wasn't a very good story, now was it?"). With repeated practice, his automaticity will continue to improve, leading to better fluency.

Why share this first grader's transcript in a book for middle and secondary teachers? First, I share it because I love his retelling. He's quite sure the two characters must be boys. That egocentric interpretation of the text will give way to more objective reading as he develops as a reader. Also, I share his transcript because Antwan reads like many of the dependent readers we teach every day. The same is true for the next student, also a first grader. The difference is both students read at a very appropriate level for first graders. We delight in their attempts and their successes when they are six years old. But when they are sixteen and read this way, we understand how defeated they must feel and wonder what we must do to accelerate their achievement.

SOPHIE

I/ s-s-aw/ my/ fr-ien-d/ at/ the/ p-ark/ he/ s-says/ do/ [Appeals by saying, "What's this word?" I ask, "Have you ever seen it before?" She responds, "I don't think so." I tell her the word.] you/

w-w-will/ to/ p-pl-ay/ wi-th/ me/ I/ s-says/ yes/ we/ ww-ent/ d-d-did/ the/ s-sl-ide/ and/ th-en/ we/ play-ed/ c-ch-ase/ we/ had/ a/ gr-greet/ time.

Sophie, like Antwan, pointed to each word with her finger. Unlike Antwan, she often segmented the words, pulling individual sounds apart from the remainder of the word. She rarely, after segmenting the sounds, blended them to create a meaningful unit. For instance, look at the second word in the passage—*saw*. She said /s/-/s/-/aw/ and then never put those sounds together to say /saw/. You see the same with *friend*. She said /fr/-/in/-/d/ but never blended those segmented sounds to get /friend/. She also paused between words, read with no expression, and avoided all punctuation signals. When I asked her to tell me what it was about, her retelling lacked detail:

SOPHIE: At the park, when they go to the park, at the park they are on the slide.
ME: Who's at the park?
SOPHIE: The children.
ME: Do you remember how many children?
SOPHIE: [Pause.] No. A lot. They are all at the park.
ME: What did they do after they went on the slide?
SOPHIE: [Pause.] They played. [Pause.] Like maybe they just played.

We can easily see the difference between Antwan's and Sophie's reading. Antwan has good word recognition skills. Sophie has developing decoding skills and is still relying on segmenting sounds to decode words. Her attention to segmenting sounds is distracting her from reading for meaning. To improve Sophie's word recognition and comprehension, she needs an easier text because this text is a frustrational-level text for her. This one is too difficult for her to practice fluency and build automaticity so that we can focus on comprehension issues.

Measuring Fluency

Typically, when looking at beginning readers, researchers have measured fluency by oral reading rates (Allington, 2001). Reading rates usually increase faster during the elementary school years than during the middle and high school years. Furthermore, the more a reader reads, the more her reading rate will improve. So, students in classrooms that provide big blocks of time for sustained silent reading, as well as students from home environments that encourage home reading, show more gains in reading rate than students who do little reading at school or home. We should also expect that reading rates vary as the content changes (magazines might be read faster than physics books), as motivation and interest change, and as background knowledge changes. In fact, the ability to vary that rate is a sign of a proficient reader and exemplifies what fluency is really all about—accurate, smooth, expressive reading that allows for comprehension of the text. So, while gaining speed in reading rate is important, speed alone does not equal fluency. Fluency is also determined by accuracy, phrasing, and intonation (Clay and Imlach, 1971).

A look at various tables of reading rates will show different rates for the same grade levels (Harris and Sipay, 1990). Most often, these differences occur because of the difficulty or ease of passages students were asked to read. A look at some of the reading rates as reported by Barr et al. (2001) offers you a good range of rates showing how much they can vary. When middle schoolers or high school students fall below these minimum average oral or silent reading rates, then I've got to look carefully at their fluency and automaticity and work at improving their reading rate.

Why is it important to improve a student's reading rate? Well, let's do a little math to see how a slow reading rate affects middle and high school students. First, notice on Figure 10.1 that the typical silent reading rate for a sixth grader is 160–190 words per minute.

Here's the problem: You read at a rate of 60 words per minute. You have 10 pages of homework to read. Each page of homework has 500 words (social studies textbook, science textbook, literature book). How long will it take you to complete your homework? Got it? You'll spend 83 minutes, or

Grade	Oral	Silent
3	70–120	90–120
4	90–140	110–140
5	100–150	140–170
6	110–150	160–190

FIGURE 10.1 *Reading rates*

Source: Derived from information in Barr, R. et al (2001). *Reading Diagnosis for Teachers: An Instructional Approach.* Boston: Allyn and Bacon.

1 hour and 23 minutes just reading 10 pages. And that's presuming that it's 10 pages that are at your independent level. Now, let's say you have 20 pages to read—a typical amount for many high school students. Reading time is now at 158 minutes, or 2 hours and 38 minutes. That's more than 2½ hours just to read your homework—not complete the assignment, mind you, just to read the pages. Compare that with the student who reads about 275 words per minute (the average WPM rate for skilled readers in grades 9–12). That student will spend 18 minutes reading 10 pages or about 36 minutes reading 20 pages. With little effort, you can understand how a slow reading rate affects a student's attitude toward reading.

Improving a student's reading rate doesn't automatically mean a student's attitude toward reading improves or that comprehension improves. However, I've found that when I can help a student become a faster, more fluent reader, then attitude and comprehension often show progress.

To determine a student's reading rate, keep in mind that you are measuring both accuracy and speed. To determine a silent reading rate, follow the following steps:

1. Choose a book at the student's independent reading level.
2. Give the student some background knowledge on the book by providing a very brief summary.
3. Have the student begin reading the book silently.
4. Time the student for one minute. At the end of the minute, have the student stop reading and count the number of words that were read in that one minute.
5. Repeat this two more times.
6. Add the three numbers and divide by three. That gives you an average silent reading rate.
7. Make sure you follow up with some general questions about what was read. If the student can't answer your questions that you believe he should be able to answer after reading the passages only one time, then the rate tells you little.

I like to determine a silent reading rate and an oral reading rate. Oral rates are generally slower (we simply can't read aloud as fast as we read silently), but offer a better understanding of the phrasing, expressing, and intonation that a student is using while reading. To determine a student's oral reading rate, follow these steps:

1. Choose a passage with at least 200 words. Give the student an overview of the passage.

2. Tell the student to begin reading at a rate that's comfortable for her.

3. Tell her if she makes a mistake, she should certainly go back and correct it. Tell her that if she comes to a word she does not know at all, she should try to figure it out on her own. If she can't, you should wait about three seconds and then either tell the student to skip it or tell the student the word.

4. As the student reads, you need to follow along on your own copy and take note of all errors (technically referred to as miscues). Any miscue that is corrected should be noted as such. If the student inserts words that aren't there (text says "drove fast" and student says "drove very fast"), that's a miscue. If the student omits words (text says "drove very fast" and student says "drove fast"), that too is a miscue. If the student skips a word because she doesn't know it, or if you have to supply the word, that's a miscue. If the student simply repeats words, do not count repetitions as miscues.

5. Decide how many minutes you want the student to read (one to five minutes) and then when finished, divide the number of words read by the number of minutes.

6. Next, tally the uncorrected miscues. Divide that number by the total number of words read. So, if the student made 9 miscues on the 150 words she read, the proportion of miscues is 6 percent. Now, subtract that 6 from 100 (100 being perfect accuracy) to get an accuracy rate of 94. Remember, the instructional reading level is an accuracy rate of 90 percent to 94 percent.

7. Rate the student's fluency. I rate students on a scale of 1–3. Level 1 indicates that the student reads a word at a time, pauses often, still sounds out many words, uses a monotone, ignores punctuation, and lacks any sort of meaningful phrasing. Level 2 shows that the student manages some fluency in some phrases, still pauses occasionally to repeat words or sound out words, responds to some punctuation, and uses some expression. Level 3 shows good phrasing, nice expression, some repetitions but those are to correct miscues, smooth (not choppy) reading, and intonation that indicates an understanding of what is being read.

8. Check the student's comprehension by asking questions and asking the student to retell the passage. Remember, good accuracy with low comprehension means that the passage is too difficult for instructional purposes.

Miscue analysis research reveals that unskilled readers, when compared to skilled readers, make fewer attempts to self-correct errors, overrely on graphophonemic cues, substitute words they know for words they don't know even when that word doesn't make sense, and try to correct all errors—even substitutions or omissions that did not change the meaning. This last tendency suggests an overreliance on graphophonemic cues (i.e., word-by-word sounding out) and less concern over semantics (i.e., meaning).

Improving Fluency

If I see that a student is scoring far below the average reading rates, then I know I must help the student with fluency. Sometimes fluency problems are not a result of poor word recognition or a lack of automaticity. Sometimes children have tracking problems with their eyes. If students constantly lose their place while reading, tracking might be a problem. If you suspect this, make sure you let parents know immediately so they can get their child to the ophthalmologist. Other times, students are simply easily distracted. They aren't paying attention to what they are reading—whether silently or orally—and so they lose focus. If you hear a lot of "ums" in-between words while students are reading aloud, that may be the problem. Other times, students slow down as they read an unfamiliar text. If that's the case, consider doing more pre-reading activities to help students prior to reading the activity. When the issue is, however, that students simply have not developed the fluency they need, try the following techniques.

Suggestion #1: Improve Students' Knowledge of High-Frequency Words and Sight Words

Sight words are generally considered to be those words that students need to learn by sight because they don't follow regular decoding rules (i.e., *have, does, give, been*). *High-frequency words* are those words that students need to know by sight because they appear so often in texts that automatic recognition is helpful. Both sight words and high-frequency words need to be words that students recognize instantly. Blevins (2001), building on the work by Johns (1980), Fry, Kress, and Fountoukidis (1993), Adams (1990), and Carroll, Davies, and Richman (1971), offers these numbers:

> Of the approximately 600,000-plus words in English, a relatively small number appear frequently in print. Only 13 words (a, and, for, he, is, in, it, of, that, the, to, was, you) account for over 25% of the words in print and 100 words account for approximately 50%. . . . The Dolch Basic Sight Vocabulary contains 220 words (no nouns). Although this list was generated over 40 years ago, these words account for over 50% of the words found in textbooks today. (pp. 49–50)

There are many lists of both sight words and high-frequency words. The Dolch Basic Sight Vocabulary and Fry's Instant Word List are two of the more common lists. Both lists are included in Appendix G. You can find many additional word lists by going online to *<www.google.com>* and entering "high-frequency words" in the search line.

Spend some time making sure your nonfluent readers know these words. It takes very little time to call a student to a conferencing area of the room and simply run through the words. If this looks like out-of-context reading, that's because it most certainly is. I want to see how quickly students can recognize the most frequently seen words in the least contextual environment. I've found that if a student can quickly recognize *because* written alone on an index card, then he generally can recognize it in a sentence. If a student can't recognize the word in isolation, then he may or may not be able to recognize it in context. I want students to definitely be able to recognize it in context—not sometimes, not when the contextual clue is obvious enough, but all the time.

As I'm working with individual students, we don't try to read all the words in one day. Instead, I select ten words that I want to see if the student knows. As I find words the student can't quickly recognize, I have the student write those on his own index cards. Students keep their index cards in a pencil pouch at the front of their notebooks. These index cards serve as a student's personal word bank. I've tried organizing those cards in small file boxes, but found stacking the boxes in the classroom took too much space and students were reluctant to carry them between their lockers and the classroom. Pencil pouches work fine. Now when I send home the yearly supply list at the beginning of the year, I require two pencil pouches—one to actually hold pens, pencils, erasers, markers, Post-it Notes, and scissors; the other to hold their word banks.

As students progress in word knowledge, these word banks can hold index cards that have vocabulary words. We review those cards daily until they can say the words quickly. Some will correctly point out that students have simply memorized a pattern of letters. Sure. I know that. That's why as students review their words *out* of context, they are also reading lots of texts and finding those words *in* context. The index card drill is just to remind both the student and me of particular words that he needs to learn to recognize automatically.

High-frequency words can be reinforced with word walls. Word walls are a powerful way to get words in front of students for constant reinforcement. Find a space on your wall where you can put up words, arranged alphabetically. The words need to be written large enough that students can see them easily from a distance. Also, don't build a word wall prior to the first day of class so that it is on the wall when students arrive. That word wall would belong to you. Instead, have the portion of the wall you'll be using marked and divided into a grid labeled with letters of the alphabet so that students know where to put specific words, and then build the word wall with the students. Now it's theirs. For a high-frequency word wall, I often ask students to look at a few pages of text and find some words that appear over and over. They find words like *of, a, the, at, that, but, have, very, would, about, had,* and *if* with little trouble. I (or a student) write one word on a card (again, use big print and a marker), and then we put the word under the correct letter.

Ask students to find high-frequency words in books they read and books you read to them.

If this sounds much too easy for your students, then don't do it! This is for that group of students who don't recognize the word *you* when they see it or for the kids who stare at the word *were*, wondering what it is. This is not something every student needs.

Finally, help students learn high-frequency words through lots of reading. This is difficult because students who need help reading high-frequency words are our slowest readers, so giving them time to read means giving them *lots* of time to read. Often, we worry that we should be doing so many other things besides just watching kids read. The truth is, though, if we don't give these slowest readers time to read, they will never become better readers. Again, this practice must be at their independent reading level.

Suggestion #2: Give Students Varied Opportunities for Hearing Texts

Students need to hear fluent reading in order to become fluent readers. Make sure as you are reading aloud to students, you are modeling good expression, good phrasing, and good pacing. Keep in mind that you can model fluent reading by reading aloud just a few pages from the chapter students are reading or the short story they are about to read. Smith (1979) reminds us that when students listen to a teacher read aloud a few pages of a text they are about to read on their own, and follow along as the teacher reads, these students then complete the story with better fluency and accuracy.

Echo reading in small or large groups improves fluency. In echo reading, the teacher reads aloud a short passage, modeling strong phrasing, and then students repeat the same passage, mimicking his reading. As with comprehension instruction, begin an echo reading lesson with specific information: "As I read the following passage, note how I raise my voice at the end of sentences that are questions." Again, if you think your students don't need this level of practice, then move to other strategies.

Choral reading is similar to echo reading except the teacher isn't reading the passage first with students echoing afterward. Choose a few lines that offer a specific reason to be read aloud. Perhaps there's a section of dialogue between two characters, one who is whispering while the other is shouting. One part of the class can read the shouting character's words while the other responds with the whispered text. The point of choral reading is to work on a specific aspect of fluent reading.

After any type of oral reading—whether it be a read-aloud from you, echo reading, or choral reading—ask students what they noticed about how the dialogue was read, how statements and questions were read differently, how excitement was added, how a character's emotions were captured through stress and intonation. Ask what they noticed about the phrasing and the pacing. Remember, in the beginning, their answers might vary between the ever-ready "I don't know" to the frustrating shoulder shrug. Then, you have to model answers. It also might mean you aren't exaggerating the reading enough. Students must "hear" the features you want them to understand.

Suggestion #3: Teach Phrasing and Intonation Directly

It's one thing to model fluent reading and another to directly teach students how to use correct phrasing and intonation. You can do it by putting a series of sentences on the overhead projector and having students read them (choral reading, echo reading, or from individual volunteers) following the directions you give. The goal is to show students that how you read a text can make a difference in what you understand about the text. Don't assume that nonfluent readers naturally understand this. The reality is, they probably don't give phrasing and intonation much thought. You've got to show them directly how stress on certain words can make a difference in meaning. Try it with this example:

1. Read the following sentences aloud. In each sentence, stress the word that is underlined:

    <u>You</u> read the book.
    You <u>read</u> the book.
    You read <u>the</u> book.
    You read the <u>book.</u>

2. Now, in the margin, note how the change in stress changed the meaning of the sentence.
3. Read the sentences aloud again. This time, pay special attention to the end punctuation.

    You read the book!
    You read the book?
    You read the book.

What's the difference between the first and second sentences? How did your voice change as you read each sentence?

Suggestion #4: Have Students Reread Selected Texts

One of the best ways to improve fluency is through the repeated rereading of texts (Samuels, 1979). Let the student read an instructional-level text aloud. You time him for a prearranged number of minutes (one to five is fine). Afterward, discuss any miscues the student made and count the number of words per minute the student read accurately. Record this on a chart. Then let the student reread this passage two more times. As students reread, they are focusing on correcting the miscues they made previously and improving their phrasing and rate. Recording the data gives students a record of their reading rate improvement over time.

Suggestion #5: Prompt, Don't Correct

Often when nonfluent readers read aloud, their reading is interrupted not only by their own pauses but by other students (or teachers) who tell them the word that is causing the pause. Whether done out of kindness, offered out of frustration, or offered because we don't know other strategies, telling the dependent reader the word encourages more dependence. On the other hand, letting the student stare at the word indefinitely doesn't help either. The alternative to correction is prompting.

Prompting means giving the student the prompt he needs to decode the word successfully on his own. The simplest prompt is "Read that again." Sometimes starting the phrase or sentence over again gives the student an opportunity to either get the word or correct a decoding. Other times, the prompt needs to be more explicit:

- Can you divide the word into syllables and sound it out that way?
- Do you see a part of the word you recognize?
- Can you get your mouth ready to say the first few letters?
- What word would make sense at this point?
- Can you try sounding it out slowly to see if that helps?

If none of those prompts help, then you need to tell the student the word and have the student start that sentence again, reading the word without your prompt. Providing the word and then letting the student read on doesn't benefit the student.

The goal with prompting is to move away from correcting. I've seen students read aloud, pausing between words to wait for the teacher's nod of

When I don't know what a word is I can . . .

- look for little words that are in it that I do know
- look to see if there are parts of the word I do know like -tion or pre- or -ing
- go back and reread the sentence and think about what word would fit
- get my mouth reading to say the first few sounds
- try to sound it out
- try to divide it into syllables and then try to pronounce the syllables
- ask the teacher to help me with the word

FIGURE 10.2 *An eighth-grader's ways for figuring out words*

approval. I've watched other students read until they come to a word they don't know, pause, wait for the teacher to insert the correct word, and then read on, never saying the word that gave them trouble aloud. Correcting rarely fosters independence. Prompting so that the student is in control of figuring out the word contributes to independence. You can strengthen the power of prompting by asking students, when they've finished reading, to identify what they did when they came to a word they didn't know. Let them keep a list of strategies they use. Figure 10.2 shows you one eighth grader's list of strategies for tackling words she doesn't know.

Final Points About Fluency

Nonfluent readers are most often nonfluent because of a lack of practice with reading. We cannot confuse teaching about reading with the act of reading. Flash card drills, placing words on word walls, listening to a teacher read aloud, following along in a text while listening to an audiotape of the same text—these teaching strategies are not reading. Struggling readers must have a lot of time to read at their instructional or independent level. Furthermore, we must examine our own instructional practices with these students. Ask yourself the following questions:

We cannot confuse teaching about reading with the act of reading.

- ◆ How often do I give students instructional or independent-level texts to read?
- ◆ How much time in my class do I give students to read?
- ◆ How often do I read aloud to students?

- When struggling readers read aloud, do I correct their mistakes or prompt them to correct their own mistakes?
- What prompts do I offer students beyond "sound it out"?
- How often do I use echo reading or choral reading?
- How often do I discuss with students why I read a certain passage a certain way?
- Do I remind students to transfer what they've been doing with oral reading to their silent reading?
- Do I ask students to pause while they are reading silently to reflect on how the reading sounds in their mind?
- Do I give students specific instructions before they begin to read silently about how the reading should sound in their mind?

As you reflect on those questions, you'll probably find ways to improve some of your instructional practices. What's rewarding about reading instruction is that as we become better teachers of reading, students become better readers.

Dear George,

I was listening to my son, Baker, read aloud a part of The Golden Compass *the other night. "Slow down, Baker," I said. "You're going so fast, I can't understand all the words." "But Mom," he replied, "I'm hurrying to get to the good part. Just listen faster."*

Just listen faster. I had to laugh. I thought for a moment about talking to him about phrasing and expression, but then, luckily, that moment passed. Instead, I realized he was urging me to keep up with him, go at his pace because he had someplace important to go and he wanted me to get there with him. Just eleven years old, he sometimes reminds me of you in that wonderful innocence that marks this thing called childhood. Like you, he needs me to listen to his words, follow his direction, and let him set the pace. As a teacher, that's tough when thirty of you sit in a classroom, all needing one teacher to listen faster, listen better. That's the part of teaching that's an art. You can't learn it in a methods class, test it in a midterm exam, or evaluate it during a principal's quick walk through the classroom. But you can see it in the students' eyes; kids know when you're one who listens.

CHAPTER ELEVEN

Word Recognition
What's After "Sound It Out"?

◆ ◆ ◆

Dear George,

I wonder how many times I told you, "Just sound out the word." "Just sound out what?" you responded one day in frustration. "The word, George, sound out the word," I replied, equally annoyed. You stared at it and finally said, "I don't hear any sounds. I don't know what you're talking about."

◆ ◆ ◆

When Kids Can't Read the Words

I hesitate before writing this chapter.

In the previous decade, educators, researchers, and policy makers studied the reading development of young children with an intensity never before experienced in this country. That attention has, depending on who is talking at that moment, either brought us greater clarity in how young children become skilled, fluent, and proficient readers or offered a smokescreen to obscure best practices. Much of this conversation has centered on the role of explicit phonics instruction, moving the great debate in phonics from journal pages to politicians' podiums. It was hard to find a candidate in the most recent national political races who did not address taxes (they all promised to lower them), hate crimes (they were all against them), and phonics (they were all for it).

At the dawning of the new millennium, that discussion intensified. In December 2000, the *Report of the National Reading Panel: Teaching Children to Read* was published (Langenberg et al., 2000). This report was intended to provide clarity to our understanding about the most effective reading instruction in early grades, specifically examining phonemic awareness, phonics, fluency, and comprehension. After determining a strict definition of what type of studies would be reviewed, a subgroup of the National Reading Panel focused on thirty-eight phonics studies that used either an experimental or a quasi-experimental design in an attempt to discover to what degree a causal relationship exists between phonics instruction and reading achievement.

Subgroups of the National Reading Panel were formed to study phonemic awareness, phonics, fluency, and comprehension.

The hundreds of pages of the *Report of the Subgroups* and the less detailed *Executive Summary* led to a flurry of articles and listserv debates as proponents of explicit, systematic phonics instruction lauded the panel's findings and opponents criticized its focus on experimental and quasi-experimental research, the validity and generalizability of its conclusions, and the differences between the findings in the *Report of the Subgroups* and the *Executive Summary* (Garan, 2001a, 2001b, 2001c; Ehri and Stahn, 2001; Shanahan, 2001). Tension mounted and phrases like "the war on reading" sometimes felt like an attack on individuals rather than strikes against illiteracy and aliteracy. Consequently, to talk about word recognition now, in the year 2002, means entering into a national debate that on the best of days opens oneself to national criticism and on the worst of days stands you in the line of not-so-friendly fire.

So, as my teenage daughter would say, "Why go there?" I look at other well-respected and highly informative professional texts written to help teachers who work with struggling readers and notice that this chapter is missing (Allen, 2000; Wilhelm, 2001; Schoenbach et al., 1999; Tovani, 2000). The reason is readily apparent—each of those was written to address comprehension. I, too, thought of doing the same, but I kept remembering George. There were words he just couldn't read. Simple words: *were, because, there, special*. Harder words: *independence, advocate, unbelievable*. I had one strategy to offer him: "Sound it out, George." I had one way of explaining that strategy: I sounded out words for him. And I had, though I didn't know it then, little chance of helping him if that was the depth of my instructional acumen.

Though the majority of middle school and high school struggling readers do not struggle because they lack word recognition skills, there are students for whom this is the problem. For these students, though they might also need help with comprehension strategies, fluency, and vocabulary development, unless we are also willing to address their word recognition deficits, we are not providing them all the instructional support they need. Thus, though I hesitate at writing this chapter, I remain committed to including it in this book. Indeed, when kids can't read, we sometimes must help them figure out the words.

Does that mean that these middle and high school struggling readers need the same explicit phonics instruction that some advocate for beginning readers? The National Reading Panel's report offers no guidance in this area, as it selected studies that focused on students in grades K–6. The National Reading Panel (NRP) found, that phonics instruction for older readers (older meaning up to grade 6) who are developing normally was less effective than phonics instruction in earlier grades, but how does that extrapolate to what phonics instruction (type and degree) should be offered in middle and high school for low-achieving students? Members of the NRP have been quite clear that the *Report of the Subgroups* did not find that older struggling readers would benefit from explicit phonics instruction (Shanahan, 2001). While some schools would provide anecdotal evidence that suggests placing struggling readers into explicit phonics programs is beneficial (and longitudinal data will tell us the long-term gains of such moves), most of us would agree that the phonics instruction we might offer middle and high school students should not mirror the instruction they received in elementary school. In fact, we know that students who struggle with word recognition do not become fluent and proficient readers just because we give them additional phonics instruction (Stahl, 1997). Chall and Popp (1996) explain, "There is also considerable evidence that reading development depends on wide reading of connected text, the development of fluency, and the growth of vocabulary, knowledge, and reasoning." Indeed, as we address the needs of older struggling readers, we must look beyond phonics instruction to the larger category of word recognition and then place such instruction within the context of a classroom environment that encourages—even requires—the following:

"There is also considerable evidence that reading development depends on wide reading of connected text, the development of fluency, and the growth of vocabulary, knowledge, and reasoning" (Chall and Popp, 1996).

- extensive reading at students' instructional and independent reading levels
- many opportunities for discussions about the readings
- ongoing opportunities for writing
- a strong read-aloud program
- direct strategy instruction in comprehension
- meaningful vocabulary development

This chapter offers an explanation of the word recognition activities I have used (or taught teachers to use) with middle or high school students to help them become fluent readers. Anecdotal evidence and test scores (both from teacher-made tests and state-mandated tests) indicate that these strategies, used in conjunction with fluency strategies, vocabulary instruction, and comprehension instruction, help students with word recognition.

To better understand some of the word recognition strategies, we need a common vocabulary. These terms, defined in the following list, are not presented here so that you might spend valuable instructional time determining if students know what a diphthong, digraph, or phoneme is. Instead, this definition of terms is offered to provide clarity to activities described later in this chapter.

Building a Common Vocabulary

1. WORD RECOGNITION: *Word recognition* is a broad term that encompasses the many ways students can access print: decoding or sounding out, recognizing prefixes, suffixes, and root words; looking for small words inside big words; knowing words by sight; using the context to figure out meaning that leads to word recognition.

2. HIGH-FREQUENCY WORDS: High-frequency words are words that occur often in our written language. Students need to be able to recognize these words quickly. Appendix G offers a list of high-frequency words. You can find similar lists by going to <*www.google.com*> and entering "high-frequency words" in the search line.

3. SIGHT WORDS: Some use the terms *sight words* and *high-frequency words* interchangeably, meaning *sight words* are words that readers should know by sight, without sounding them out. Others use *sight word* to mean a high-frequency word that lacks a predictable grapheme-phoneme (letter-sound) correspondence so the word cannot be decoded following anticipated rules. For instance, *have* is often considered a sight word because the letter *a* makes its short sound instead of the long sound a reader might anticipate by looking at the silent *e*.

4. DECODING: This term is often used interchangeably with *word recognition*, but I suggest that's an overgeneralization of this word. Decoding refers to understanding the letter-sound code. A synonym for this word could be *sounding out*. When teachers say a student can't decode, that means the student can't recognize words via sounding out.

5. PHONICS: The term *phonics* refers to the rules or, more accurately, the *generalizations* that help readers understand under what conditions certain letters or letter combinations will make certain sounds. Appendix H offers a list of the most common phonics generalizations. The purpose

of providing this list isn't so you can require struggling readers to memorize these generalizations; instead, the list is for your own knowledge.

6. GRAPHEMES: Graphemes are the letters of our alphabet. We have twenty-six graphemes in our written alphabet.

7. PHONEMES: Phonemes are the smallest unit of sound. The word *cat* has three graphemes (*c, a,* and *t*) and three phonemes (/c/, /a/, and /t/). Remember, when a letter is placed between diagonal marks, say the sound of the letter, not the name of the letter. The word *little* has six graphemes (*l, i, t, t, l,* and *e*) and four phonemes (/l/, /i/, /t/, /l/). The word *shoe* has four graphemes *(s, h, o,* and *e)* and two phonemes (/sh/ /ü/). This lack of one-to-one correspondence between graphemes and phonemes makes our language a difficult one to decode. Figure 11.1 provides a list of the various phonemes in our language and the graphemes that represent those sounds.

8. VOWELS: The graphemes *a, e, i, o,* and *u* are vowels. Vowels can make long sounds (*a*pe, *ea*t, b*i*ke, h*o*pe, t*u*ne), short sounds (*a*t, b*e*d, *i*t, h*o*p,

---

Consonant Sounds

1. /b/ (bib)	10. /n/ (nest)	19. /sh/ (ship)
2. /d/ (dot)	11. /p/ (pat)	20. /th/ (this)
3. /f/ (fun)	12. /r/ (ran)	21. /th/ (thin)
4. /g/ (go)	13. /s/ (sun)	22. /hw/ (where)
5. /h/ (hot)	14. /t/ (take)	23. /zh/ (measure)
6. /j/ (jelly)	15. /v/ (vase)	24. /ng/ (sing)
7. /k/ (kite)	16. /w/ (wish)	
8. /l/ (let)	17. /z/ (zebra)	
9. /m/ (mat)	18. /ch/ (child)	

Vowel Sounds

25. /ă/ (bat)	32. /ī/ (bike)	39. /ou/ (mouse)
26. /ĕ/ (bed)	33. /ō/ (hope)	40. /oi/ (boy or soil)
27. /ĭ/ (pit)	34. /yū/ (tube)	41. /ô/ (ball)
28. /ŏ/ (hot)	35. /ä/ (father)	42. /û/ (bird)
29. /ŭ/ (fun)	36. /ə/ (ago)	43. /â/ (fair)
30. /ā/ (make)	37. /o͞o/ (moon)	44. /ä/ (car)
31. /ē/ (meet)	38. /o͝o/ (book)	

FIGURE 11.1 *Phonemes in our language*

r*u*n), a sound called schwa (in *a*larm, the first *a* makes the schwa sound), an /r/ sound when the grapheme *r* follows the vowel (ca*r*, te*r*m, bi*r*d, ho*r*n, bu*r*n), and other sounds when combined with other vowels (so*i*l).

9. *y* AND *w*: The letters *y* and *w* sometimes act as vowels. *Y* functions as a vowel either on its own (b*y*, friendl*y*) or by teaming with another vowel (sa*y*). *W* functions as a vowel by teaming with another vowel (co*w*, pa*w*, o*w*n).

10. VOWEL TEAMS: A vowel team is a combination of vowels (two or sometimes three), or a combination of a vowel and one or more consonants, that makes one single sound. For example, *ou* makes the sounds you hear in *sound, should, you,* and *though; ea* makes the sounds you hear in *team, head,* and *steak; igh* makes the sound heard in *high* and *night.* The terms *digraph* and *diphthong* are often used instead of the term *vowel team.* A vowel digraph is two vowels (and occasionally three) that create a single sound (*ee* in *sweet* or *ew* in *pew*), while a *diphthong* is two vowels that produce two sounds that glide into one another. The *oy* in *boy* or the *ou* in *out* represent diphthongs. The *ea* in *create* is not an example of a diphthong. Figure 11.2 offers examples of vowel sounds.

11. CONSONANTS: The remaining graphemes are called consonants. Your students might be interested to know that all vowels can function in a word as a consonant. For instance, in the word *azalea*, the *e* takes on the /y/ sound. Can you figure out other examples? Crossword puzzle fans certainly know the answers!

12. CONSONANT TEAMS: When two or three consonants appear together and create a single sound, they are a consonant team. These consonant teams are often called *consonant digraphs.* Some consonant digraphs create a new sound, one not otherwise represented by a single grapheme. For instance, the digraph *sh* makes the sound heard at the beginning of *ship.* Other digraphs create a sound that can be represented by a single grapheme. For example, the digraph *ph* makes the /f/ sound. Still others are combinations in which one of the letters is silent: *kn-, gn-, pn-, wr-, gh-* (at the beginning of a word), or *-mb.* Figure 11.3 lists the most common consonant digraphs. (Vowel digraphs are listed in Figure 11.2.)

13. CONSONANT BLENDS: Some consonants can be combined (clustered) to create sounds that blend together. Unlike digraphs, which cannot be sounded out separately, blends can be segmented. So, you could not

Letter	Short Sound	Long Sound	R-Controlled	L-Controlled	Latin A
a	mat	make	car	all (only affects a)	father
e	fed	feet	term		
i	it	bite	fir		
o	on	boat	horn		
u	us	use	turn		

Vowel Diphthongs

Spelling	Example
ou	house
oy	boy
oi	soil
ow	cow

Vowel Digraphs

Spelling	Example	Spelling	Example
ai	pain; air	ou	trouble; house
ay	day	au	author
ea	meat; head	aw	paw
ee	sweet; steer	oo	mood; book
ey	key; convey; geyser	ei	weigh; receive; foreign; seismic
oa	float	ie	relief; lie; patient
ow	grow; plow	ew	grew; sew
oi	boil	ui	fruit; guild

FIGURE 11.2 *Vowel sounds*

sound out *child* by saying /c/ /h/ /i/ /l/ /d/, but instead, must keep the *ch* together to get the /ch/ sound. However, you can segment the cluster *tr* in *trip* to get /t/ /r/ /i/ /p/. Blends are consonant clusters (generally two, but occasionally three) that can be segmented, one from the other. Figure 11.4 lists the consonant blends.

14. **RIMES:** A rime is a vowel and any consonants that follow it in a syllable. In the word *cat*, *-at* is the rime. In *sight*, *-ight* is the rime.

Sound	Spelling	Examples
/ch/	ch	child
	ch	beach
	ch	catch
/k/	ch	choir, chemistry
/sh/	ch	Chicago, chef
/sh/	sh	ship
	sh	fish
/th/	th	thank, thin, three
	th	this, then
/hw/	wh	when, why, where
/ng/	ng	sing, bank
/f/	gh	laugh
	ph	phone
/n/	kn	knight
	gn	gnat
/g/	gh	ghost
/m/	mb	lamb

Because there are always exceptions to rules, some single consonants and consonant-vowel combinations make a sound more normally made by a consonant team. These exceptions include the following:

/zh/	s	vision
	s	measure
	g	garage
	z	azure
	ti	equation
	x	luxurious
/sh/	s	sure, sugar
/sh/	ti	nation
/sh/	ci	facial

FIGURE 11.3 *Consonant digraphs*

15. **ONSETS**: The consonant prior to the vowel. In the word *that, th-* is the onset and *-at* the rime; in *school, sch-* is the onset and *-ool* is the rime.

Knowing terms such as these is important, not so much because we want to teach them to children but because they give us a common vocabulary and allow us to understand questions that parents, principals, and policy makers ask about phonics. For instance, parents ask if we're going to "teach phonics." I'm not convinced that the majority of these parents are asking if we're going to teach the phonics generalizations; sometimes I'm not

Beginning Blends

R-Blends

br	break
cr	crash
dr	drip
fr	free
gr	grow
pr	print
tr	truck

L-Blends

bl	black
cl	click
fl	flag
gl	glass
pl	place
sl	slip

S-Blends

sc	scout
sk	skate
sm	small
sn	snake
sp	space
st	stop
sw	sweep
tw	twin
qu	quick

Ending Blends

-ct	act
-ft	gift
-ld	old
-lp	help
-lt	colt
-mp	lamp
-nd	hand
-nk	bank

FIGURE 11.4 *Consonant blends*

-nt	ant
-pt	slept
-sk	mask
-sp	clasp
-st	test

Three-Letter Consonant Clusters

sch	school
scr	scream
spl	splash
spr	spring
squ	squeak
str	stream
thr	thread

FIGURE 11.4 *continued*

For much more detailed information on phonics, I recommend the following three books: *The Sounds and Spelling Patterns of English: Phonics for Teachers and Parents* by Phyllis E. Fischer (1993); *The Violent E and Other Tricky Sounds* by Margaret Hughes and Dennis Searle (1997); and *Teaching Phonics and Word Study in the Intermediate Grades* by Wiley Blevins (2001).

sure that they know what they are asking. They are simply frustrated at their children's problems with reading and *phonics* is a word they've heard. We can't answer their questions with any degree of confidence if we don't know what the words mean. A look at the following incident illustrates this point.

Step Inside a Classroom

I was the speaker at a PTO meeting in a middle school several years ago. About hundred parents and teachers came for my talk. The topic was "Helping Your Middle Schooler with Reading." At one point, a mom raised her hand and asked, "Don't you think schools ought to be teaching more phonics?" I asked her to tell me specifically what she meant. "Well, don't you think all these problems that some kids are having with reading in middle school are because they didn't learn enough phonics in elementary school?" Some parents nodded their heads in agreement.

Still wanting her to be more specific, I asked, "Which reading problems are you referencing?"

She responded, "You know. Kids just can't understand what they read."

This mom meant well. And although I don't know this for a fact, I'll bet her child was having some sort of reading comprehension problem and she was looking for a reason. Phonics—either too much of it or not enough—often gets to carry the blame for all reading woes. As I looked around the room, I saw the principal of the elementary school that fed into this middle school and the language arts supervisor for the district. I saw middle school language arts teachers, and I saw a lot of parents waiting for my answer. I said, "Actually, if the issue is that students are having trouble *understanding* what they are reading, then I'm not too sure if teaching students that 'when two vowels go a'walkin', the first one does the talkin' helps that child understand how to make an inference or summarize what she's read or predict what might happen next in the text. So, if you're asking me if teaching more phonics will help students comprehend better, I have to say, I think the answer is no. Does that mean I think students don't need to understand the sounds letters make? Not at all. I think that's an important part of the reading process. It just isn't the entire process, and it doesn't mean students can automatically understand what they've decoded." All were quiet, so I continued:

"Phonics—understanding what sounds a letter can make under certain conditions—is a part of what students need to know to be able to read. It's one of the cues, or clues, they use to figure out the words. They also use the context—the other words—to help figure out a word. Look at this." On the overhead projector, I wrote this sentence: *She got in her _____ and drove to town.* "What goes in the blank?" I asked.

Almost everyone responded, "Car."

"That's right, and you were able to figure that out not because of your knowledge of phonics, but because of the context. The word *drove* suggests one type of vehicle. The word *in* is also important. What goes in this blank?" This time I wrote, *She got on her _____ and rode to town.* "Is it still car?"

People shook their heads no. Some called out the word "bicycle"; others said "scooter."

"Now, we don't know for sure unless we cross-check by sounding out at least a portion of the word." I put the letter *h* at the beginning of the blank. "Now, will *bicycle* work? Will *scooter*?"

People shook their heads no. One dad called out, "It's horse."

"*Horse* might work, I say, because horse starts with /h/ and the letter *h* makes the /h/ sound."

Another parent asked, "So, you're saying that context is as important as phonics?"

I responded, "I'm saying that if we don't use them together, we can make mistakes that keep us from understanding what we read. Here's an example." On the overhead, I put the following sentence: *The boy saw a cardinal.* "I watched two first graders read a very simple book that had one sentence per page with a picture that was directly related to the sentence. So, on the page that said, 'The boy saw a puppy,' there was a puppy. When the first reader came to this page, he said, 'The boy saw a/ saw a/.' His finger paused under the word *cardinal.* He looked at the picture and saw a beautiful red bird; then he looked back at the word and read, 'The boy saw a red bird.' I asked him what word on the page said *red*. He said, 'Well, actually, *red* isn't on the page, but this word [pointing to cardinal], I don't know this word, but it means *red bird*. What's that bird called?' I told him the word, and we looked at how the word I said matched the print on the page. When he reread the book and came to that page, he read, 'The boy saw a/ a/ a car-car-di-cardinal.' Then he said, 'Yep, that's a red bird all right.' When the second boy came to that same page, he read, 'The boy/ saw/ a c-c-ar-d/ [pause] card,' and then he continued to the next page. I stopped him and asked him to read it again. He did, and again, he identified the word as 'card.' 'Look at the page and tell me if that makes sense,' I said. He looked at the picture of the red bird. 'I don't know,' he said. That student was so overrelying on sounding out that he was forgetting to cross-check his result with meaning. Unless we break him of that habit now, he's going to have problems all through school—one of those kids who decodes words but doesn't know how to make sense of the text."

The parents all nodded. I concluded, "We can't say any one cueing system, like phonics, is more important than another, like semantics. We have to show students how they work together. That means we need to be teaching them together. Yes, students need to know how to sound out words, but at the same time, they've got to know how to use the context and their own background knowledge to predict or confirm that decoding."

The meeting concluded and as I walked to my car, one middle school teacher stopped me and thanked me for the answer. "My degree is in English," she said. "I've never taken a beginning reading class, so I don't know this stuff about phonics. I wouldn't have known how to answer her question." We talked about how phonics is often offered as the panacea for all reading problems, and then she said, "Yeah, but some middle schoolers really do need help figuring out words. What are we supposed to do with them?" The suggestions in this next section offer some direction for tackling that question.

Suggestions for Students Who Lack Word Recognition Skills

When I'm working with middle school and high school students who have trouble with word recognition, I look for four things:

◆ I want to see how many high-frequency and sight words they can quickly identify.
◆ I want to see if they can read single-syllable words but not multisyllabic words.

- I want to see if, when they are reading multisyllabic words, they are guessing at the word based on the first few letters or if they are reading through the entire word, just very slowly.
- I want to see what they know about letters and sounds.

Once I know the answers to these basic questions, I have some idea of where to start. Wherever I start, though, I must work within the regular classroom setting—28 to 35 students; a class that lasts 45 minutes, 55 minutes, or 90 minutes, depending on the school district; and a core curriculum that must be covered. In some places, students reading far below grade level may be in a special intervention program in addition to the regular English/language arts class. That can be an ideal situation. But in many places, there are not the additional funds to purchase materials or hire teachers for such classes. Consequently, it's the language arts teacher who must accelerate the student's reading achievement (while covering the required curriculum, of course). What follows, therefore, are not the same suggestions I might offer for teachers working with students in an intensive reading program; instead, these are suggestions that any English/language arts teacher can implement.

Suggestion #1: Teach High-Frequency Words

This topic was discussed in Chapter 10. Automatic recognition of high-frequency words is critical for fluent reading. These words are often difficult for beginning readers or older struggling readers to decode because many do not follow the regular sound-letter relationships. For instance, consider *of, have, done, said, do, been*—all words that stray from expected letter-sound correspondences. High-frequency words are the words readers often confuse: *were/where; was/saw; from/for; for/of; what/that; with/them; on/no.* Chapter 10 offers more discussion on high-frequency words and how to teach them to students.

Suggestion #2: Teach Common Syllables

Much like teaching high-frequency words, teaching common syllables is important because these syllables occur so frequently that students need to be able to recognize them automatically. You can find a list of the most common syllables in Appendix I. Sharing this list at one time is overwhelming. Choose five or ten syllables and, like with high-frequency words, have students read them to you. When they can't identify a syllable, have students add that syllable to their personal study list. Make sure students spend time looking through texts to find those syllables in words. Transferring the ability to recognize the syllable on a flash card to a syllable in a word is critical.

Suggestion #3: Assess What Your Students Know About Sounds and Letters

When it's apparent that students' reading problems aren't vocabulary, comprehension, or fluency issues, but instead word recognition, spend some time with those students asking them to name the letters (graphemes) in specific words. Ask them to identify what sounds those letters make. You're listening to hear what letter-sound correspondence knowledge each student has. I've met some students, especially second language learners, who don't recognize all the letters and certainly don't know all the sounds those letters can make.

You don't need a special assessment form to do this, nor do you need a lot of time. Just point to some words and ask students to tell you what letters are in the word and what sounds those letters make. You can also show them consonant diagraphs such as *sh, ph,* or *th* and blends such as *tr, st,* or *bl* and ask students to tell you what sounds those pairs of letters make. You can show them vowel teams such as *ai* or *ee* and ask them what sound the vowels would make. Put these letter combinations into the context of a word. The small number of students who can't recognize letters and lack even a basic knowledge of the sounds those letters make probably need specialized help.

Suggestion #4: Teach Rime Patterns

Once called "word families," rime patterns help readers identify chunks of words quickly. Instead of decoding phoneme by phoneme, readers decode by onset and rime. In the word *hop, h* is called the onset and *-op* is the rime. Students don't decode *hop* as /h/ /o/ /p/ (which is often difficult to blend) but instead decode it as /h/ /op/. Using rime patterns to help children learn to decode by analogy (if the letters *a* and *t* sound like /at/ in *cat* then they probably sound that way in *bat, sat, that,* and *flat*) has received considerable attention (Gaskins and Elliot, 1991; Cunningham, 1995; Wylie and Durrell, 1970; Fox, 1996). Rime analysis is a helpful way for beginning and older struggling readers to build word identification and automaticity.

It certainly helped Cody, a sixth grader who knew very few words automatically and labored through decoding each word phoneme by phoneme. His teacher began teaching him rime patterns. Cody practiced identifying these rimes in words over and over again for the first six weeks of school. He repeatedly read *The Cat in the Hat*. Finally, he announced, "Now I understand

These thirty-seven rimes make five hundred words (Wylie and Durrell, 1970)

A		E		I		O		U	
-ack	back	-eat	seat	-ice	nice	-ock	sock	-uck	duck
-ail	pail	-ell	bell	-ick	sick	-oke	smoke	-ug	rug
-ain	rain	-est	west	-ide	hide	-op	drop	-ump	jump
-ake	take			-ight	might	-or	for	-unk	skunk
-ale	male			-ill	will	-ore	core		
-ame	name			-in	win				
-an	can			-ine	fine				
-ank	tank			-ing	sing				
-ap	nap			-ink	drink				
-ash	rash			-ip	dip				
-at	sat								
-ate	late								
-aw	saw								
-ay	day								

FIGURE 11.5 *Most commonly used rimes*

how words work." Figure 11.5 offers the list of thirty-seven rimes from which students can form more than five hundred words (Wylie and Durrell, 1970). Remember, the goal is to teach students to transfer that rime pattern to other words. You can't presume that because you show them *-at* in *cat* they'll see it in p*at*tern or c*at*erpillar or even b*at*. Therefore, plan some time to work with an individual or small group a few times per week for ten minutes or so to practice transferring the rime pattern to other words.

The easiest way to work with these patterns is to show students a list of words that have the same rime (*blush, brush, crush, flush, rush, hush*) and ask them what's the same in each word. Once they identify the letters *u, s,* and *h,* ask what sound that letter group makes. Say each word for them, or with them, as needed. Ask them what part of each word had to change to make the new word. They'll probably say something like "the beginning changed and the end stayed the same." I usually tell them that the beginning part is called the *onset* and the ending part is called the *rime*—just so we have a common vocabulary. Then, have students brainstorm other words that have the same rime. Sometimes they give us words that rhyme but don't share a rime. For instance, if the rime is *-ed*, then students might think of the word *said.* Simply explain that a rime allows a word to rhyme. Sometimes words rhyme because the rime is the same (*top* and *stop*) but other times the rime is different (*rain* and *vein*). Spend time searching a text for other words that contain the rime you are studying. Have students discuss how spotting the rime helps them read the word. Finally, you can make rime walls. Rime walls get words on the wall so they are visible to students. To create a rime wall, put one rime on each of several (three or four) index cards and mount them on the wall. Under each rime, list the words that can be made from those rimes. Add additional rimes to your rime wall as students easily recognize the ones you've already introduced. Here's how one student used rimes:

CINDY: [Looking at the word *grandfather.*] Um, well, like, okay there's *and* so, *and.* Okay, /gr/-/and/. Grand. And, and, okay there's *at,* oh and there's the word *her,* I know that word. *Her.* So, *fat. Her.* Grandfat-her? [She paused and looked at me.]

ME: Have you ever heard a word like "grandfat-her"?

CINDY: [Shaking her head no.] I don't think so.

ME: I wonder which part doesn't sound right.

CINDY: The second part. *Fat-her.* [Pauses.] Oh. Look. It's the *th,* see like on our chart, *th* says /th/ [makes the sound heard at the beginning of the word *there*]. So, it's not *fat,* it's /th/-/er/. Oh, *father.* Grandfather.

ME: Grandfather.

CINDY: Yeah. Now that makes sense.

Suggestion #5: Teach Chunking

Chunking a word means dividing long words into more manageable chunks, though some students will confuse the word with *chucking* and think you're suggesting they toss it away! Sometimes those chunks are syllables; often they are smaller words or prefixes and suffixes that we hope students recognize. This seemingly easy suggestion helps many readers work through long words. A look at two transcripts reveals the power of this suggestion.

Step Inside a Classroom

SEAN

When Sean, a sixth grader, saw the word *effectiveness,* he said, "Well, there's n-e-s-s and that says /nes/, and there's t-i-v-e and that says /tiv/, so /tivnes/. So . . . okay, it's just this little part here [pointing to *effect*] that . . . hmm. What do I do now?" He looked at me.

Just when you think all is going well . . .

JEFF: [Looking at the word *manipulate*]. You want to know what rhymes with this word?

ME: No, I want you to think about the rimes we've been talking about [pointing to the rime wall] and see if any of those patterns can help you figure out this word.

JEFF: I don't see this word on the wall.

ME: No, but look at the end of the word. Do you see that -ate pattern up there?

JEFF: Yeah.

ME: So, what's the word?

JEFF: Up there on the wall?

ME: Yes.

JEFF: Ate.

ME: So, can that help you with how this word [pointing to manipulate] sounds at the end?

JEFF: No.

ME: Well, what about this part of the word [pointing to *an* in manipulate]?

JEFF: Yeah. An.

ME: Right. So, how can you use that to help you say this part of the word [pointing to *man* of manipulate]?

JEFF: Can't. Different word.

ME: Can you get your mouth ready for those first couple of sounds?

SEAN: Oh, yeah. [Moves his mouth back and forth as he mouths first /e/ then /f/. Grins.] Oh, /e-fec-tivness/.

Notice from Sean's think-aloud that he looked for what he knew and then moved to the rest of the word. Later, when I asked him how his reading was changing, he said, "Used to, when I came to big words, you know, long words, then I just stared at them. They were so long. I'd just try to start at the first letter and sound them out, but then the sounds wouldn't make any sense because the words, there were so many letters. But now, I look at long words, and I tell myself to just chunk it—look for the parts I already know."

JASMINE

Jasmine, an eighth grader, offered this think-aloud as she struggled through a word:

JASMINE: [Looking at *meaningful*.] Boy, this one is long. Um. /m/. No wait, there's -f-u-l and that says /ful/. Right. And, there's -i-n-g and that's, you know, /ing/. So this part here [puts her index fingers around the letters *ingful*] says /ingful/. So that just leaves this [moves index fingers to border *mean*]. Well, e-a-n, that's like in *bean*—see right up there on the wall [points to rime wall that has words arranged by onset–rime]. So, /m-ean/. Oh, *mean*. /Mean-ing-ful/. Meaningful.

ME: That's good, Jasmine. Meaningful. How'd you figure that word out?

JASMINE: Well, at first I was getting lost. It's so long. But then I saw some parts I already knew, and then I looked at this part here and recognized it. So I was, I guess, you know what we called chunking. Yeah, I was like chunking it.

ME: What would you have done last year, before you had learned about chunking?

JASMINE: You know, other teachers, you know my reading, it's not too good, because all the words, you know, they are like so long. And other teachers they are always like going "sound it out" and so you just try to go through all the letters, but sometimes then the word, it isn't like making any sense. So, mostly, I was just stopping. Just stop. If you stop, somebody will tell you the words.

ME: What about this year?

JASMINE: Well, now, you know, now it's like I've got some other ways, you know, like I can chunk or find parts that I know. Now it's like big words are really just a lot of like small parts put together.

Note, if Sean didn't already have the word *effectiveness* in his listening vocabulary, then he wouldn't have connected /e-fec-tivnes/ to the target word. This underscores the importance of reading aloud to students to build the background knowledge and vocabulary knowledge they need to help with word recognition.

Not all students explain themselves as well as Jasmine or remember what we've discussed as well as Jasmine. Mike, a ninth grader, proved that as he looked at the word *certainly*. "/K/-/k/-/ke/. I don't know," he said.

"Do you see any parts of the word that you already know?" I asked, hoping he'd remember -*ly*, since we had just finished discussing it yesterday for about the millionth time.

"Nope," he said.

"Look carefully," I encouraged. "Do you see any parts you could chunk?"

"I'd like to chunk the whole thing," he replied confusing *chunking* with *chucking*.

Suggestion #6: Teach Rules About Syllables

When students can sound out single-syllable words, but stumble through multisyllabic words, then I find that teaching them how to divide a word into syllables can be helpful. It can also be confusing. To understand where to make syllable breaks, students need to recognize some basic patterns. Help students see those patterns by showing them how to transform any word into a spelling pattern, or code, that uses three letters—C, V, and *e*. C stands for any letter that's a consonant; V stands for vowels; and, *e* stands for the silent *e* at the end of some words (*make, life*). So, the spelling pattern CVVC might stand for *boat* or *meal*. CVC could stand for *cat* or *hop*. CCVCe is the pattern for *close*, while CVCC is the pattern for *fish*. Once students can see how C, V, and *e* can represent spelling patterns, we discuss how a word divides into syllables between those Cs and Vs (see Figure 11.6).

The only reason I'd ever work with students on dividing a word into syllables is to help them figure out the vowel sounds. Vowel sounds are generally

---

1. Every syllable must have a vowel sound (not just one vowel, but a vowel *sound*).

2. Vowel teams should not be separated into different syllables: ai, ay, ea, ee, oa, ow, oo, oi, oy, ou, ie, ei.

3. Consonant teams should not be separated into different syllables: ch, ck, ph, sh, th, wh, tch.

4. If a word has two consonants between two vowels, divide between the two consonants. So, VCCV divides as VC CV as in *al-bum* or *rab-bit* or *con-tain*.

5. If a word has one consonant between two vowels, divide between the first vowel and consonant. So, VCV divides as V CV as in *pi-lot* or *o-val* or *a-loud*.

6. If the word has one consonant between two vowels and that consonant is an X, divide after the X. So, VXV divides as VX V as in *Tex-as* or *ex-it* or *ex-act*.

7. If the word ends in Cle (as in possible), the Cle form the last syllable. So, *bu-gle*, or *ta-ble*, or *lit-tle*, or *syl-la-ble*.

FIGURE 11.6 *Generalizations for dividing words into syllables*

what cause the problem for readers, not consonants (though the letter *c* certainly represents enough sounds to give some novice readers fits). Once students can see the pattern, they can sometimes identify the sound the vowel should make in that pattern. For instance, the spelling pattern CV means that the vowel will makes its long sound (*no, go, by, he*) while the CVC pattern results in a short vowel sound (*tap, red, sit, top, run*). Figure 11.7 offers a list of spelling patterns and the typical vowel sounds found in those patterns.

Long Vowel Sounds

Pattern	Example
CV	my
CVV	see
CCV	she
CCVV	flee
CVVC	rain
CVCV	baby
CVCe	take
CVVCe	leave
CCVCe	these
VCe	ate

Short Vowel Sounds

VC	at
VCC	end
CVC	run
CVCC	past
CCVCC	think
CCVC	stop

*Note: there are, of course, exceptions to these patterns. For instance:

- CVVC is also the pattern for *head, said,* and *been*—all words with a short vowel sound.
- CVCe is also the pattern for *give, love,* and *have*—all words with a short vowel sound.
- CVCC is also the pattern for *told, bold,* and *sold*—words with a long vowel sound.

FIGURE 11.7 *Spelling patterns and resulting vowel sounds*

This is difficult and tedious, and I recommend it only when you've found time to work consistently with an individual or small group of students over a long period of time. You must explicitly teach them the rules for putting words into syllables and the patterns for long and short vowel sounds, and recognize there will always be exceptions.

Suggestion # 7: Teach Students to Use the Schwa Sound

The schwa sound is the vowel sound that is unstressed in a multisyllabic word. You've seen it identified in dictionaries as the upside down and backward *e* /ə/. For example, in the word *civil,* the second *i* makes the schwa sound (/uh/).

Many students become frustrated with decoding multisyllabic words because what they understood about how vowels work in single-syllable words often isn't true in multisyllabic words. In those longer words, the vowel sounds often take on this schwa sound. Consequently, if students can get through the first syllable (usually the stressed syllable) and can figure out the consonants and then just say /ə/ for the remaining vowels, they usually come close to the correct pronunciation of the word. Give students these guidelines:

1. Get your mouth ready for the first few letters.
2. Look for prefixes, suffixes, and consonant blends and digraphs that you already know how to say.
3. Look for rimes, vowel teams, or vowel diphthongs you recognize.
4. See if you can read the word now. Ask yourself if you've heard that word before and if it makes sense with what you're trying to read. If not, then try the next step.
5. Read through to the first consonant after the first vowel, and then read on through to the end, pronouncing the consonants and using the /ə/ sound for the remaining vowels. Ask yourself if you recognize the word now and see if that word makes sense with what you are reading.

Suggestion #8: Teach Students to Get Their Mouths Ready

First-grade teachers involved with an intervention program called Reading Recovery know this suggestion well. It requires that you remind the student to get his mouth ready to read a word that is causing him to pause. I started using this suggestion with middle and high school students several years ago after using it successfully with first graders, though I wasn't sure what the results would be. I was pleased at what I found. First, reminding students to "get your mouth ready" forces students who normally sit and stare at an unknown word to actually do something. Telling them to get their mouths ready for the first couple of sounds helps them remember that *they* are in charge of figuring out the word—they are active agents, not passive recipients. Second, this suggestion helps students get a running start into the word. Often students can recognize the first syllable of a word. As they read the sentence up to the word that is unknown and then read the first few letters of that word, often they then can predict what the entire word should be as they combine semantics (what the sentence is about) with graphophonics (letter-sound relationships). They can then confirm that prediction by seeing if the letters in the remainder of the word fit with the word they have in mind and completing the sentence to see if that word fits the context.

So, when students say, "I don't know this word," I say, "Show me how you can get your mouth ready." To see how effective this can be, read this sentence again, getting your mouth ready for each word, as if you were going to read each word aloud. You'll quickly see that your mouth changes position, and by putting your mouth into the correct position, you begin to focus on the sounds that are in that word. As one student explained, "Used to I just stare at the word, I guess like hoping that poof! I'd just figure it out. But now, I tell myself 'get your mouth ready.' I don't know, remembering to get my mouth ready helps me hear the sounds in the word."

Students practice a variety of word recognition strategies as they read on their own

But remember: don't confuse word recognition with word knowledge. You'll see what I mean as you try this hint with the following word: *cor-plucantly.* Though you might have been able to get your mouth ready for the first few sounds—perhaps even all the sounds—it probably didn't help you know what the word means. This is a hint to encourage active participation in word recognition, that's all.

Step Inside a Classroom

CONNER

As Conner read the sentences, "He was huddled into a corner. He was too afraid to move," he paused at *huddled.* He just stared at it and then looked at me. Prior experience told him that if he waited long enough, the teacher would tell him the word.

Instead, I said, "Get your mouth ready to say those first few letters."

He looked back at the page. He whisper read /hud/ and then he started reading again: "He was hu . . . ." He stopped and looked at me. I asked him to cover up the *hud* part of the word and to get his mouth ready to say the rest of it. He looked at it and said "dl." I asked him what the end sound would be and to move his mouth to that sound. He made the /d/ sound and then said, "dled." I told him to read the sentence again, trying the entire word. He read, "He was hud-dled," and then said, "Oh *huddled*, he was huddled." He finished the selection, and then I asked him to reflect on how he figured out the word. "Well, you know, I kept trying to make my mouth like say the sounds. Usually, I just look at the word, but looking doesn't really help you hear the sounds."

Lest you think all students appreciate this advice, read what Ruth, a junior in high school, said after I reminded her to get her mouth ready: "Oh, do I need more lipstick?"

Benjamin, another junior, replied, "My mouth is always ready!"

Robert, a seventh grader, answered, "Ready for what?"

Suggestion #9: Teach Prefixes, Suffixes, and Root Words

When helping disabled readers with word recognition, remember that studying prefixes, suffixes, and root words not only helps with vocabulary but helps them move through big words quickly. Turn to page 187 for information on teaching these word parts and see Appendixes D and E for lists of prefixes, suffixes, and roots.

Suggestion #10: Use Instructional-Level Texts

Students need practice on word recognition with texts that are at their independent and instructional levels. When students must read certain texts that you know will cause word recognition problems, then I suggest you accept that you won't be improving word recognition with that text. Focus on what you *can* do with that text. I had to teach *The Tell-Tale Heart* to two eighth graders who simply could not get through the words in that text. So, I recorded the story for them, gave them headsets, and had them do a read-along—follow along in the text as I read it to them. Occasionally, on the tape, they heard me say, "Stop and discuss what's happened so far." Together, they talked about characters and events. Because I took away the burden of word recognition, they were able to concentrate on meaning.

Reading aloud to students or letting them listen to the text on audiotape is not offered as a replacement for word recognition. Nor should it replace all of the reading students should do. However, when the text is too tough for some students, then tell yourself that with that text you won't focus on word recognition. Instead, instruction for students will focus on literary elements, comprehension, or vocabulary. Then, make sure you create some time for students to practice word recognition and fluency with texts that are at their independent and instructional reading levels. (These terms are defined on page 205). See Chapter 14 for information on how to find books for students who struggle with word recognition.

Keeping It in Context

Working with adolescents who have difficulty with word recognition is difficult on good days, beyond frustrating on bad days. And that's for us—the folks who already can read. I sometimes try to imagine what it would be like to be thirteen, fourteen, fifteen, or sixteen years old and not know how letters and sounds work. When I think that way, I understand negative attitudes, flip remarks, books left in lockers, bored expressions that announce, "This is dumb."

For some, the reaction is to put these students into intensive, scripted phonics programs. The reality is, however, phonics programs for middle and high school students rarely achieve the results we want; research shows that explicit phonics instruction much beyond first grade does not create fluent readers (Ehri et al., 2001). Word recognition is critical, but students can learn to recognize many words by learning about prefixes, suffixes, and rimes. They can learn some basic vowel rules (r-controlled, vowel teams, diphthongs) and about consonant blends and consonant digraphs without moving into scripted intervention programs. But none of that will matter if we fail to give them plenty of opportunity to read at their instructional and independent levels, give them repeated chances to hear us read aloud while they follow along, and teach them how to cross-check cueing systems so that as they sound out words (phonics), they are asking themselves, "Does this make sense?" (semantics). They need to be in classes that encourage lots of writing, lots of reading, lots of talking about their reading and writing. And they need to know that we have confidence that they can become better readers. They don't have confidence, I promise you that; we've got to have enough for us (to sustain us each day) *and* them (to encourage them each day). I don't think I realized how important this was until one teacher told me how she really had not expected her eighth graders could get better at word recognition:

> I left your workshop yesterday a little angry at you. When you said we had to believe that kids really could get better at word recognition, I thought, "Well, just what does she think I've believed all this time?" Last night, though, I really thought about what you said and thought about some of my students and asked myself if I really and truly, really *really* believed I could help those students become better readers. Suddenly, I realized I didn't. I didn't have enough confidence in what I might be able to do to really convince these kids they could be better readers. We were going through some motions—mostly looking at comprehension things to help them on the TAAS. That was all. Why wasn't I doing more? I asked myself. In part because I didn't know what else to do and in part because I didn't think whatever I did would make a difference.

What you do with word recognition can make a difference. But before you can ever convince your struggling readers of that, you've got to believe it first.

◆ ◆ ◆

Dear George,

"Stay after school," I said to you. "I'll help you with this chapter." So, that day in February, we sat side by side at a conference table at the back of the room. I listened to you struggle through words. Finally, you said, "This book is too hard. The words are too long. It's just too hard." Then you pushed the book and your notebook off the tabletop. "I just don't care," you said, not worrying that someone might hear you, for the school day had ended a good hour earlier. "I just don't care, anymore," you said again,

beginning to cry, hating yourself for crying, hating me more for seeing you cry. You stood up, then sat back down, completely defeated. I sat still, not sure what to do. "George, I'll help you. You can do this," I said. You looked up. "No. The book is too fucking hard," you said. I'd never heard that word from a kid before, never considered I'd hear it at school. I jumped up, sure I was supposed to do something, but before I could say anything, you looked at me and said, "It doesn't matter what you do to me or what you say to me. Don't you get it? It's not the fucking book. It's me. I'm just too dumb."

When kids can't read, I've finally learned, they take the failure personally. Though they might say a book is boring or a teacher is bad, those are just the words they dare to say. What they rarely share is what you finally blurted out that cold winter day: "It's me. I'm just too dumb." George, you showed me that day that becoming a reader shapes who we are, how we see the world, and how we see ourselves in this world. Tragically, failure to become a reader shapes our perceptions as well.

◆ ◆ ◆

12

Spelling
From Word Lists to How Words Work

Dear George,

On the first day of class, you completed an interest inventory I had distributed. On it, you wrote, "I relly like to swim. I like to play basket ball. I am hopeing to go to basket ball camp this sumer. Theirs not much more to say." I couldn't believe the spelling mistakes. At first, I thought you were simply in a hurry. Later, I decided your spelling mistakes weren't about inattention but were instead about inability. Struggling reader. Struggling speller. I saw both weaknesses, yet never took the time to think about how one influenced the other.

Why Discuss Spelling in a Reading Book?

Many us of remember spelling instruction from elementary days that looked something like this: Get the list of words on Monday. During the week, alphabetize the words and write them three to five times. Write them in sentences. Then, take the spelling test on Friday. At the same time, many of us might remember reading instruction that had us separated into groups (red birds, blue birds, and swallows). We might remember round-robin reading, worksheets, SRA kits, and controlled readers. What most of us probably won't remember, though, is any sort of connection between spelling instruction and reading instruction. Reading was reading and spelling was spelling and that was that.

That division continues today even though we know that as spelling knowledge improves, word recognition improves (Adams, 1990; Ehri,

1980, 1997; Invernizzi, 1992; Bear, Invernizzi, and Templeton, 2000; Ganske, 2000). Logically, we should be able to see the connection: as children read, they connect sounds to letters; as they write, they connect letters to sounds. Understanding this relationship means that now, as we teach students how to spell, we recognize that we are helping them with the decoding process; in turn, as we help them with the decoding process, they are learning more about spelling. As you observe your students carefully, you'll probably see that students who struggle with word recognition struggle with spelling.

Stages of Spelling Development

For a much more detailed explanation of spelling stages and for information on how to assess your students' spelling ability, I suggest three sources: the March 2002 issue of the NCTE journal *Voices from the Middle*; *Words Their Way* by Bear, Invernizzi, Johnston, and Templeton (2000); and *Word Journeys* by Ganske (2000).

Research shows us that spelling is a developmental process (Reed, 1971; Beers, 1980; Beers and Henderson, 1977; Schlagal, 1989; Templeton, 1983, 2002). Children advance through stages as their understanding of letter-sound relationships broadens. At the earliest stage, children lack any awareness of letter-sound relationships; at the most advanced stage, children manipulate Latin and Greek prefixes, suffixes, and roots to spell words correctly. As we understand the features of each stage, we understand what types of instruction we should offer (Templeton, 2002). Figure 12.1 offers a basic overview of the five stages.

Understanding these stages offers us guidance for helping students. For instance, consider how three students, all in sixth grade, spelled the word *striped*. John spells the word *strip*, failing to use any vowel markers to indicate that the *i* is making its long sound. He's still spelling at the letter-name stage. Millie's spelling, *striep*, indicates that she has moved into the within-word stage; she knows that she needs two vowels in this word to indicate that *i* will make its long sound. Will appears to have progressed even further in this stage, as he has spelled the word correctly. Without more words, we don't know if Will has advanced to the next stage or not.

In Figure 12.2, we see how three students spelled twelve words. As you study this list, first you see that the target words move from single-syllable, short vowel sound words to two-syllable words with unusual vowel sounds. As you look at Reed's spelling, you see that he is still misspelling short vowel sounds, isn't sure how to spell digraphs or blends, and is spelling long vowel sounds simply with their letter names (*fram* for *frame*, for example). As the words become more complex (*nation* and *squirrel*), his spelling deteriorates so that he begins to omit vowels, relying only on consonants, as an emergent-level speller would. At what stage would you place Reed?

1. **Emergent:** This stage marks children's first attempts at writing. These children are in preschool, kindergarten, and perhaps first grade. It is marked by a range of behaviors from scribbles to pretend writing (marks that look like letters but aren't) to random letters. Children at this stage put letters on a page without any attention to the letter-sound relationship. As they progress through this stage, they begin to pay attention to the sounds that particular letters make. By the end of this stage, children may write a word using its initial and final consonants.

2. **Letter Name:** Students at this stage spell using the names of letters to spell words. These students are generally in grades 1 to 2. So, they spell *make* as *mak*. The word *drive* might be written as *jriv* since the /dr/ sound puts your mouth in a similar position as it is in when you say the letter *j*. The word *bed* might be spelled *bad*; again, the student is searching for the name of the letter that most matches the /ē/ sound. If you say the /ĕ/ sound (as in bed) then say the letter *e*, you'll see that there is very little relationship (from your mouth's point of view) between the /ĕ/ sound and the /ē/ sound. Students spell long vowel sound patterns with the name of the letter and don't worry about any sort of vowel marker that would indicate that the vowel is saying its long sound. Short vowel sounds are generally spelled incorrectly following this pattern: short *e* changes to *a*; short *i* changes to *e*; short *o* changes to *i*; and short *u* changes to *o*. Short *a* is usually spelled correctly. Digraphs and blends are often incomplete at this stage, so, *that* is spelled *tat* or *hand* is spelled *had*.

3. **Within-Word Pattern:** At this stage, students spell short vowel sounds correctly and are trying to spell long vowel patterns correctly. Students are generally at this stage between grades 2 and 4. At the letter-name stage, the word *team* might be spelled *tem*; however, you know a student has moved into the within-word stage when you see the child trying to use a vowel marker. At this stage, *team* might be spelled *teme* or *teem* and then eventually *team*. Students also begin to experiment with how to spell r-controlled

FIGURE 12.1 *Overview of spelling stages*

vowels. Often, they reverse the vowel and the *r* so the word might be spelled *brid* instead of *bird*. As students move through this stage they also secure how to spell some of the more complex digraphs and blends such as *str* or *scr*. Toward the end of the stage, they turn their attention to unusual vowel teams such as *ou* or *aw* or *oi*.

4. **Syllable Juncture:** Students reach this stage between grades 3 and 8. By this point, students are spelling most vowel patterns for single-syllable words correctly. The issue at this stage is how to spell multisyllabic words. In this stage, their attention is focused on how to add suffixes correctly, in particular when to double the final consonant before adding *-ed* or *-ing*. Students at this stage might spell *hoping* as *hopeing* and *hopping* as *hoping*. These students are also figuring out how to spell the vowels in the unstressed syllables of a word. So, they might spell *sample* as *sampul* or even *sampal*. As they progress through this stage, they move to the correct spelling. This stage marks a good time to focus on prefixes and suffixes so that students can understand why *really* is spelled with two *l*s or *misspelled* is spelled with two *s*s.

5. **Derivational Constancy:** This stage might begin as early as grade 5 for some or not until grade 8 for others. For most, it extends through adulthood. Words studied at this stage are words that are derived from the same root. For instance, when students see the constant relationship between *compose* and *composition*, they are more likely to spell *composition* correctly. Other relationships include *haste* and *hasten*; *express* and *expression*; *design* and *designation*; *consume* and *consumption*. Students at this stage also learn about assimilated prefixes (also called absorbed prefixes). Assimilated prefixes are prefixes where the consonant has changed to match the first letter of the root to make the word easier to say. So, instead of in+literate for *inliterate*, the letter *n* assimilates to the *l* and the prefix changes to *il*; therefore, the word is *illiterate*. Or, the prefix *sub* changes to *sup* so the word is *suppress* instead of *subpress*.

FIGURE 12.1 *continued*

Correct Word	Reed	Rosa	Jimmy
bed	bad	bed	bed
cap	kap	cap	cap
with	wet	with	with
sheep	sep	shepe	sheep
train	jran	trane	train
frame	fram	frame	frame
couch	koth	coch	couch
hurt	hrt	hert	hurt
making	makng	makeing	making
hoping	hopng	hopeing	hoping
nation	nasn	nasheon	nashun
squirrel	skrl	skwerl	squirle

FIGURE 12.2 *Comparison of three spellers across twelve words*

Rosa, unlike Reed, is spelling short vowel sounds correctly. Additionally, she can spell the digraphs /th/ (*with*) and /sh/ (*sheep*) and /ch/ (*couch*) correctly. She also has spelled the blend /tr/ correctly (*train*). When you look at her attempts to spell words with long vowel sounds (*sheep, train,* and *frame*), you see that she is not spelling those long sounds with only their letter names (*shep, tran, fram*), but instead is trying to mark those long vowel sounds with a second vowel. She understands something must happen but isn't quite sure what it is. She appears to have one pattern—add silent *e*. Therefore, she has spelled *frame* correctly; however, that might be lucky rather than deliberate. When we look at how she is trying to spell more complex vowel sounds (*couch* and *hurt*), we see that she still has trouble. As you continue to look through her test, you see that she continues with the pattern of adding silent *e* to words (*makeing, hopeing*) and becomes very confused by the time she reaches *nation* and *squirrel*. At what stage would you place Rosa?

Jimmy is further along in spelling development than either Rosa or Reed. We see that he doesn't have trouble until he reaches the last two words. At what stage would you place Jimmy?

Now, here's the most important question: How fair would it be for these three students to share the same spelling list? Reed needs to continue working on short vowel sounds, digraphs, and blends, while Jimmy is ready to consider how to spell suffixes and vowels in unstressed syllables of multisyllabic words. Rosa needs to learn how to spell long vowel sounds and unusual vowel sounds in single-syllable words. Giving them all the same list means

Reed is still at the letter-name stage. Rosa is at the within-word stage. Jimmy is at the syllable-juncture stage.

somebody will be too challenged and someone else won't be challenged enough. It's this one-list-fits-all mentality that results in memorizing words

The problem isn't with the spelling list; the problem is in presuming that all students should have the same list.

rather than understanding how words work. When students simply memorize for the test on Friday, that knowledge is generally gone by Monday. Sometimes we've been frustrated with spelling lists because it appears that giving students lists of words hasn't improved their spelling ability. The problem, however, isn't with the spelling list; the problem is in presuming that all students should have the same list.

Does that mean that if you have twenty-five students, you must create twenty-five spelling lists? No! There are only five stages of spelling. And though each stage breaks into early, middle, and late, the reality is that by middle and high school, most students fall into either the within-word or syllable-juncture level. (A few might be at the letter-name stage or the derivational-constancy stage.) In that case, you may need only two or three lists.

Does that mean kids will compare lists and wonder why some students have some words and others have other words? Probably. It's our job to remind kids that everyone progresses at different rates. Listen carefully for put-downs ("You've got baby words" or "Oh my gosh. You're still spelling those little words.") and stop those quickly. With middle schoolers (usually much worse at put-downs than high school students), I often ask everyone to take off one shoe. We line the shoes up across the front of the room and

Students work collaboratively on a spelling sort

compare all the sizes. The differences are vast. That doesn't mean some are "bad" sizes. It just means some folks have grown faster than others. I then ask students how comfortable they would be if they had to wear a shoe that was obviously the wrong size. I remind them that learning is supposed to fit their needs like shoes fit their feet.

As you plan your time for the week, set aside twenty- to twenty-five-minute blocks of time at least twice a week for students to work on spelling via word sorts. I find that a word sort is an effective activity for helping students discover a particular spelling pattern. You can find one example of a word sort on page 19 of this book. There, Haley is sorting words to discover when to double the final consonant before adding *-ing*. You now understand that Haley's work is indicative of the syllable-juncture level. As you read the next transcript from a seventh-grade classroom, look at the words the students are sorting and decide the level of each group. In this example, students are numbered within groups labeled A, B, C, D, and E, so A1 would mean the first student in group A, while B3 would mean the third student in group B.

Step Inside a Classroom

ME: Okay folks. A and B groups, you'll be reading silently for the next twenty minutes. C group, you'll be working with me. D and E groups, you'll be working on word sorts. Check the board up here if you can't remember which group you're in today. [Students look to the blackboard at the front of the room where I've written four, five, or six names under each group label. Groups A and B each have six students.]

A3: Can we sit on the floor?

ME: You know where silent readers can sit.

C2: Do we need our books?

ME: Yep, bring your books and move on back to our big table. [Four students move to the back of the room where we have one conference table. They sit there and open the novel they are all reading, *The Giver* by Lois Lowry.]

D1: Can we work with the people in E group?

E2: No way. We're doing a different sort. Yours is like way too hard.

D1: Can we?

ME: Nope. You know that. Get your words and see how far you can get on your sorts.

Groups A and B took a minute to settle down and begin reading. Group C turned to a chapter I asked them to find, and they spent a few minutes skimming that chapter. I walked over to the floor where groups D

	Group 1	Group 2	Group 3
	terrible	believable	returnable
	horrible	achievable	breakable
	edible	excitable	remarkable
	visible	debatable	comfortable
	legible	notable	transportable
	possible	observable	avoidable

FIGURE 12.3 *Word sort for group D*

and E had spread out index cards, one word on each. I made sure a tape recorder was running near each group. I returned to group C, where we spent the next fifteen minutes or so talking about inferences that they made while reading that chapter.

Students in group D are trying to figure out when to use the suffix -ible and when to use -able. They are learning to generate a rule rather than memorize words.

D2: Where'd we get on Tuesday?

D3: Here. I got it. They were like this. [See Figure 12.3 for this group's words and how they arranged them.]

D1: Yeah. That's right.

D2: I don't get it. Why aren't all the *-able* words together? Put them like this.

D3: No. Don't mess them up. Put them back. See they've got to be in different groups because all these, they all end in *e*.

D2: End in *e*?

D1: Yeah. Take off the *-able* and see you'd have to put on an *e*.

D2: Oh yeah. Okay. So are we done?

D3: No. We have to get the rule for when you have, when you know it's *-ible* and when it's *-able*.

[Pause.]

D1: So like if you have to take off an *e*, it's like *-able*.

D3: Yeah, but then what, why is it, then on this group why is it *-able* because they don't end in *e*?

D2: But look, look at these words. Okay. See, like here if you take it off, it is a word, even without an *e*. See, *remarkable*. You can take off the *-able* and you have *remark*.

D1: Yeah, yeah, yeah, that's it. See here. Okay. All of them like here are just words. So add *-able*.

D2: Okay, so if it's a word or a word if you put back on the *e*, then you add -*able*.

D3: So on these, why is it -*ible*?

[Pause.]

D2: Is it because these are more unusual words? You know, like *edible*.

D1: But *terrible* and *horrible*. That's not unusual.

D2: Yeah.

[Pause.]

D3: Maybe it's because they don't end with *e*, you know, if you take off the -*ible*.

D2: But some of the -*able* words don't end with *e*.

D1: Yeah, but if you take off the -*ible*, then, oh, look, that's, look, they aren't words, they don't make any sense.

D2: So, what does that mean?

D3: Does it mean if the word isn't really a word, then add -ible?

As the D group worked on their sort, the E group worked on theirs.

E1: Here's how we had the words. [This student spreads their words into three groups on the floor. See Figure 12.4 to see how these students sorted their words.]

E4: I don't get it. What are we supposed to do?

E2: Look, see all these? They end with -*tch* and all these, these all end with just -*ch*. And so, and so we have to figure out why.

E3: They just do. You know. Like they just do.

E1: I don't think these go here. I mean they end in -*ch*, but listen, listen if you say them, then okay, listen *each, beach, search,* and then *punch, inch,* and *bunch.* They don't sound the same. Like you know *b-unch.* The vowel, it's different.

Students in this group are trying to understand how to know if a word ends in the /ch/ sound and whether to use *ch* or *tch*. Again, the point is to see how words work, not to memorize a spelling list.

each	crunch	match
coach	lunch	notch
beach	inch	hutch
peach	wrench	stretch
teach	punch	sketch
	pinch	watch
	perch	catch
	search	fetch
		ditch

FIGURE 12.4 *Word sort for group E*

E2: Yeah, they are like these. See how all these have a short vowel sound? But oh, here it is. These end with *-nch* and these with *-tch*.

E4: So some of them end with just *-ch* and some with *-tch* and some with *-nch*. Okay. Is that it?

E1: No. Listen. See you can look and see that's how they end. But why is that?

E4: Oh.
   [Pause.]

E4: Is it like if it's long, you know, the vowel, then it's *-ch*?

E1: Yeah. That's good. And if it's short, then it's *-tch*.

E2: What about *bench* and *inch* and *punch*?

E1: Maybe if it's *-nch,* it's short. Or, I guess, if it's short, then it's *-nch*.

Understanding Sorting

Both groups were working on a sort that was matched to their spelling developmental level. Students in group D finally generalized the rule that if the root can stand alone, add *-able*. Sometimes, they noted, the final *e* must be dropped before adding that suffix. If the root can't stand alone, add *-ible*. This was an appropriate word sort for this group because everyone in this group could spell all the short and long vowel patterns in single-syllable words, could spell unstressed vowels in multisyllabic words, could spell digraphs and blends, and could understand which letters to drop and which letters to retain when adding a suffix. They needed to focus on figuring out how to tell the difference between the *-able* and *-ible* suffixes. By contrast, the students in group E were not ready for this sort. They were still confusing *-tch* with *-ch* at the end of some single-syllable words.

It's hard to have students practice word sorts if you aren't sure what patterns go with which stage of spelling development. You'll find some ideas for word sorts in Appendix J.

Both *Words Their Way* (Bear, Invernizzi, Johnston, and Templeton) and *Word Journeys* (Ganske) offer spelling diagnostic tests to help you understand students' spelling levels.

Suggestions for Improving Spelling

Although determining students' stage of spelling development and then designing activities that move them from one stage to the next, such as word sorts, are the most beneficial steps to take, they aren't your only choice for improving students' spelling. The following strategies can help students focus on words—but only if you are consistent in your requirements.

ache	any	break	can't
again	been	built	choose
always	beginning	business	color
among	believe	busy	coming
answer	blue	buy	cough
could	here	read	too
country	hoarse	ready	trouble
dear	hour	said	truly
doctor	instead	says	Tuesday
does	just	seems	two
done	knew	separate	used
don't	know	shoes	very
early	laid	since	wear
easy	loose	some	Wednesday
enough	lose	straight	week
every	making	sugar	where
February	many	sure	whether
forty	meant	tear	which
friend	minute	their	whole
grammar	much	there	women
guess	none	they	won't
half	often	though	would
having	once	through	write
hear	piece	tired	writing
heard	rays	tonight	wrote

FIGURE 12.5 *Spelling demons*

1. Spelling Word Walls: Post a list of spelling demons that all students are required to spell correctly at all times. You can find lots of spelling demon lists by going online to <*www.google.com*> and entering "spelling demons" into the search line. Figure 12.5 offers one list of spelling demons that I particularly like, mostly because this list was first published in 1917 in the Merrill Speller, Book 1. It seems some words will always cause problems!

2. Homonym Lists: Some students continually confuse words like *principal* and *principle* or *to, two,* and *too.* I find that students get more confused rather than less confused if we distribute lists of homonyms and require them to take tests on them. Instead, when you notice a problem, correct it. If a student writes *rights* rather than *writes,* check to see if it was simple confusion or if the student really doesn't know the

difference. When they don't know the difference, you might have to look for helpful mnemonics.

For instance, many a student has remembered to spell the head of a school as *principal* because the last three letters spell *pal*. Some remember to how to spell *too* correctly when they think that if you eat too much dessert, your derriere might look like the two *o*s. Others remember that *where* is the correct spelling when they mean the location (see the word *here* inside it?). *Wear* is connected to what goes on your body—including your *ear*! *Their* is easy to remember as the word that shows possession if you can see the word *heir* in it. *There*, the word that focuses on location, has the word *here* in it. As students latch on to hints that help them remember spellings, post them on chart paper so the class can review them from time to time. To find extensive lists of homophones (words that sound the same but have different spellings and meanings such as *their* and *there*) and homographs (words that are spelled the same but have different meanings such as *bear*—an animal—and *bear*—to support) go to <*www.google.com*> and enter either of those words in the search box. The best way to teach homophones and homographs is to study the words in context. Learning long lists of pairs of these words is more confusing than helpful. Consequently, look for when students are using the wrong word and use that as the moment to teach the correct word in that context. Finally, remember that it's not only homophones and homographs that students confuse. Some words are very close in spelling or sound and students confuse them as well—words like *affect* and *effect* and *adapt* and *adopt*. See Appendix K for a list of commonly confused words.

3. Thematic Spelling: As you study a theme, a genre, or a topic, make sure you create a word wall that shows those words. In one ninth-grade class, students were studying character development. The teacher built a word wall that used adjectives to describe characters. In an eighth-grade language arts class, students were reading *The Diary of Anne Frank* and studying the Holocaust. They built two word walls: one displayed words they learned about WWII, Hitler, and concentration camps; the other displayed words that were connected to prejudice.

4. School Words: School words are the words students should spell correctly to function well at school: teachers' names; courses; school district name; school name; months of the year; days of the week; numerals; function words like *assignment, homework, exam, complete, essay,* and *composition.* Do something with these words early in the year—from a Friday spelling bee to spelling baseball (as you pitch out the

word, students who spell it correctly move from first to second to third to home base to score points for their team) to a bulletin board.

5. Spelling Rules: Make sure you know the most common spelling rules. It's hard to help students with the rules if we don't know the rules. Appendix L offers a list of the most common spelling rules.

6. Spelling Patterns: Look for patterns of spelling mistakes that students make. When you can identify the pattern, then you'll know better what to teach.

• • •

Dear George,

Years after I taught you, an eighth grader named William slipped me a note. It said, "I had this techer in fith grade and she said we wouldnt do spelling any more that year becase spelling isnt important becase any one can spell. That made me feel real bad becase my spelling, it isnt so good. I think that may be spelling isnt importunt to pepole who can spell good. But if you cant spell good, spelling is real umportunt." A few weeks later, he wrote a final note to me: "You say to techers dose spelling count and thay say that spelling allways counts and thay take of if you spell it wrong but then they dont tech you to spell it right escept to make you take more tests. If spelling does count so much then why dont thay tech you to do it an not just keep telling you to do it. Teching and telling are not the same thing." William is right: when you can't spell, spelling is really important. As long as our spelling instruction is about giving a list on Monday and a test on Friday, we'll continue to see students like you and William—disabled spellers.

• • •

Creating the Confidence to Respond

◆ ◆ ◆

Dear George,

"Why won't you ever participate?" I asked you quietly as I stood at your desk. You said nothing. "I can't help you if you won't at least try," I said. You picked up your pencil and started drawing on the margin of your paper. "I know you've got things to say about some of the stuff we read," I said. You finally looked up at me. "You think I'm going to say something so you can tell me it's wrong or the know-it-alls can laugh at what I say? No way." "George, has anyone in here ever made fun of anything you've said?" I asked. "No—because I never say anything," you replied. I smiled at your logic. "George, who's ever laughed at something you said?" You looked at me with dismay, suddenly far wiser about what happens in schools than I, a first-year teacher. "You don't know nothin' if you think kids don't make fun of you when you're dumb." I knelt beside your desk. "George, you're not dumb." You interrupted me. "Yeah? What do you call it when you can't do the work everyone else can? I call it dumb." "You've got to try, George. Just try," I whispered. You never even looked up. You just shook your head and whispered back, "No. No I don't."

◆ ◆ ◆

The Power of Confidence

I love to visit first-grade classrooms. The energy there is contagious. In first grade, students don't raise their hands to answer questions; instead, they shoot their hands into the air, wave them wildly back and forth, stand on one leg as they lean their bodies across their desks, and snap their fingers while blurting out either, "Miss! Miss! Miss!" or "I know! I know! I know!" You finally choose one to call on ("Okay, Julie, what's the answer?") and watch as all students turn to face her to see if she'll get it right or leave something unsaid for someone else to supply. No student is surprised when her answer is, "Um, um, well, I don't remember." No one laughs; everyone understands. The goal is to be called on—answering the question correctly (or at all) is the bonus. "Yes!" first graders shout as they throw their hands back into the air and begin shouting, "I remember, Miss, I remember!"

I'd give a lot to see that level of energy in middle schools and high schools. Generally what I find in these schools is that a very few students offer to participate while most sit slumped in their seats, eyes vacant, staring at someplace I don't see. Their expressions rarely change and then only to move from boredom to condescension. Where does that first-grade energy go? Where does that willingness to be a part of the conversation, actually to dominate the conversation, go? When does that spark in their eyes—that demand that you listen to them—disappear? When does apathy replace activity and a reluctance to learn replace an insistence for always knowing more?

When does apathy replace activity and a reluctance to learn replace an insistence for always knowing more?

These difficult questions are more easily answered when we remember that as students move through the grades, they come to value their peers more and more. Fitting in, finding a group, and forming relationships with peers become more valuable than stickers on homework papers or nods of approval from the teacher. If that need for peer approval begins to escalate (as early as third grade for some students) at the same time that reading problems become more evident, then students find themselves more and more reluctant to take risks in reading in front of their peers. At the very moment we need them telling us, "I got lost at this part," or asking, "How do you say this word?" or demanding, "How do you know that's what the character looks like?" they begin to retreat behind a wall of silence, stares, and sullen behavior. "They won't try," we say. Instead, we fail to see that they are trying—they are just trying at what matters the most: keeping some form of respect with their peers.

When Students Lack Confidence

If reading problems continue to grow throughout the elementary school years, students reach a point where the effort they must exert to find even minimal success with reading is not worth the embarrassment they face in

Helping students develop social and emotional confidence requires patience on our part.

the process. For some of these dependent readers, it becomes easier to make fun of those who like to read, to treat reading with disdain, and to convince others, as well as themselves, that reading "don't do nothin' for nobody." These students arrive in middle school and later in high school disengaged— from reading, specifically, but often from learning in general.

We can help these students become more skilled readers; we can help them find books they can read and will enjoy reading. But unless we help them rebuild that confidence that's been missing for many of them since second or third grade, then we've addressed only part of their reading struggles.

Though we can say (and should say), "You can do it!" on a daily basis, the reality is that unless students believe us, they won't do it, won't even attempt to do it. And students won't believe us unless we create opportunities for success. The suggestions outlined in this book thus far address students' cognitive confidence. As discussed previously in Chapter 2, social and emotional confidence almost always improves as cognitive confidence improves. So, the foundation for success is improving their comprehension, vocabulary, and/or word recognition skills. What follows are additional suggestions that help students develop social and emotional confidence as readers.

Keep Your Expectations High

Ask your students who struggle, really struggle, with reading what they think the problem is. Some will quickly dismiss the question, but others might say, "The books are too hard"; others will respond, "I'm too dumb"; a rare few will explain, "I just need to try harder." Guess which ones will be easiest to reconnect to reading? That's right, the ones who think that this problem can be overcome if they just try harder. That's an incredible attitude for an adolescent to have, and when we discover a student with this "I can do it" attitude, we treasure it.

Watch students when you return a test. If the grade is low, some cram the paper in their notebook or backpack while muttering, "This was dumb," or harsher comments like "Bitch," or "This sucks." Others get quiet or work to hold back tears, frustrated once again at failure. And then that rare few stare directly at the items they missed and remark, "If I had only studied that part, I'd have gotten it." These kids believe in themselves. These tenacious kids expect that eventually they'll overcome any struggle—and they generally do.

However, these children are few and far between. As we watch other students struggle with reading (specifically) and learning (in general), our first reaction is often that we need to make the curriculum easier. If kids can't read *Moby Dick,* we reason, then let's either rewrite it so that it's easy enough, give them a summary to read, or, perhaps, just give them an easier book altogether and never read that classic at all. You're fooling yourself if you think middle school and high school students don't know when we've dumbed down the curriculum. They say things like, "Yeah, the kids in Mrs. So and So's class, they read the important stuff. We just read baby stuff in here," or "Our class doesn't read hard stuff. The teacher thinks we can't do it." They say these things because they hear us say (often with the best of intentions), "This story is really hard, so we're going to skip it," or "Instead of reading all of this play, we're only going to read certain parts. I'll just tell you about these other parts because they are really confusing." They see on our blackboards that one class must write an "essay" about what they've just read, but in their class, they will only write a "paragraph." They ask why and we say, "We haven't gotten to essays yet in this class. You just concentrate on seeing if you can write a paragraph." They see that students in first period must read five books outside the class during the quarter. They aren't expected to read any.

"Why don't we ever have homework in here?" an eighth grader asked his teacher.

"I'm just excited if I can get you guys to do class work," the teacher explained.

"I can do homework," the student replied.

The teacher said, "You know what, let's just see if you can get some of it right with me here to help you."

The teacher meant well, but as the student told me later, "What she was really saying was that the kids in this class are too dumb to do it at home."

Step Inside a Classroom

Having high expectations doesn't mean tossing students work they absolutely can't accomplish. It means helping them achieve *their* highest levels. It means not backing away from some tasks just because you recognize you'll have to provide a lot of scaffolds on which to build their success. It means believing that if you provide the right support, they really can be successful. The twenty students in one eighth-grade classroom asked why they couldn't read *Huckleberry Finn* like the students in the advanced language arts class. These students were in this particular language arts class because their reading scores on the Iowa Test of Basic Skills were in the fiftieth percentile or lower. The teacher told them the novel was very difficult. "So, do you think we're too dumb to do hard stuff?" one girl asked.

"Okay," the teacher said, "we'll read it, but I expect you to work hard."

And they did read it. The teacher did an incredible job of frontloading information students needed to be successful. Students read some sections aloud in paired reading; the teacher read aloud other chapters. Some students with word recognition problems listened to parts of it on tape. Students read independently and stopped often to think aloud their confusions, predictions, or clarifications with peers or the teacher. They kept double-entry journals and used bookmarks and sticky notes to keep up with questions, unusual vocabulary, and comments they wanted to make. They used logographic cues and the ABC chart to keep up with how the characters were changing. At the end of each chapter, they wrote Somebody Wanted But So statements for several characters. They met daily for about ten minutes in small groups to discuss what they understood, what they didn't understand, and what they were going to do to figure out what they didn't understand (a nice adaptation of the K-W-L chart). They completed It Says—I Say charts to help make inferences. (See Chapters 6, 7, and 8 for explanations for all those strategies.) And they finally finished the book. At that point, they said they wanted to take the same test that the kids in the advanced class took. They did and all scored between 80 percent and 94 percent on the test. As students looked at their tests with incredible pride, one said, "I guess now we're just as smart at those other kids."

Another said, "Yeah, maybe we're even smarter."

A third remarked, "Being smart is hard work, but it sure feels good once you've done it."

After a moment of silence, another said, "I guess now we've got to keep it up. What's the next book they're going to read?"

By the end of the year, these students had read all the same texts as the students in the advanced language arts class had read. At that point, one asked, "So, should our report card say Adv LA (advanced language arts) instead of just language arts?" The teacher agreed and talked with the principal. He agreed and these students suddenly found themselves in an advanced language arts class.

What's important to remember is that the success these students had with these texts was tied to the work the teacher was willing to do in providing the necessary scaffolds. For those who needed it, she continued to teach word recognition strategies with material at their instructional level. She didn't expect word recognition, automaticity, and fluency to improve with a reading of *Huckleberry Finn*. She helped these students gain access to this text by taking away the word recognition constraints and then didn't back away from the time she needed to help them with decoding. Then for all students, she provided a lot of support in comprehension. When they finished the novel, she wrote:

> I don't think I've ever worked this hard. I've always just given the students in this class easier books to read. But this was incredible. In spite of working harder than I've ever worked, I feel more excited to go into this class than ever before. These kids can do this work. I think I've never expected that they could really do hard work, so I never pushed. But it's really not just pushing. It's about using all those strategies we've been talking about. It's that self-fulfilling prophecy: Kids will do what we tell them they can—or cannot—do. Our next stop: *Romeo and Juliet*!

Create a Classroom That Encourages Risk

I'm often asked to give speeches. I say yes, but invariably, that speech becomes a workshop. During a workshop, I'll explain something, participants will try it, and then we'll discuss what happened. It's during the "participants try it" phase that I ask teachers to share what they've written or share their thoughts about what they've just read. Almost always, when I ask the who-will-share question, there is a moment of silence. Teachers look down, suddenly very interested in the papers in front of them. Some will even decide this is the perfect time to take a break. Finally, a brave soul will say, "Well, I'll share."

At some point in the workshop, we reflect on that moment, that first time I ask teachers to share. "I sense some hesitancy," I recently said to a group of teachers in Florida. Silence. "I wonder why that is?" I asked.

One teacher answered, "It's hard to speak up. I worry 'What if I'm wrong?' I don't want to be embarrassed." Many others nodded their heads in agreement and suddenly the room was abuzz with talk—talk about how hard it is to provide answers when you are so worried about being right or, more important, wrong.

One teacher finally spoke out over all the others: "We just don't know each other real well, aren't sure what you want us to say, and certainly don't want to appear dumb in front of you or anyone else in here."

"So, how are those feelings different from the feelings your students have in your classroom?" I asked. Silence, again. I continued. "I know it's hard to speak out. But you have college degrees. You are the skilled readers and writers. You stand in front of others every day and explain critical concepts. Yet you are hesitant to read a paragraph you've written aloud. Is it unreasonable to expect that the twelve-year-olds or fifteen-year-olds would feel more confident about participating than you do?" I went on to explain, as I do to all groups, that my point is simple: We often become frustrated when students won't join in discussions, speak up to answer questions, take part in debates, or volunteer to read what they've written. Yet, we understand why we—the most skilled in the classroom—are reluctant to do the same things when put in the same situation. I want us to hold on to that feeling of "What if I get it wrong?" and use that to help us understand why students sometimes are reluctant to participate.

I use the same structure in workshops that I do in classrooms. I give participants/students three opportunities for participation:

◆ They have the opportunity for personal reflection that they can choose to share with no one or perhaps only with me.
◆ They have the opportunity for small-group discussion with others whom they choose.
◆ They have the opportunity to speak up in the large-group setting.

Often, at the beginning of a workshop, teachers choose the first option. By the end of the workshop, all teachers are doing the second option and many have moved to wanting to talk in the large-group discussions. We've built a community over the three hours or three days or whatever and begun to trust one another. With that trust comes a willingness to take risks. And with risk taking comes a powerful vehicle for testing new ideas, trying out what you understand and don't understand, and a willingness to say, "Let me try." You can encourage this community and risk taking in your classroom by doing the following.

Make Sure Students Know One Another's Names

First-grade teachers win the prize on this one. Students enter their classroom on the first day of first grade to find their names everywhere: taped onto desks and chairs, on lost-teeth charts, on birthday bulletin boards, on welcome trees hanging from the classroom door, on beginning-of-year word walls, on rulers, pencil boxes, and welcome notes from the teacher. The student is made to feel as if he or she certainly belongs in that room, as does everyone else. By the end of the day, they know every classmate's name. By contrast, I see middle school and high school teachers who never even learn their students' names, much less worry if students learn each other's names. It's certainly harder to do this when you have 150 or more students instead of 22. However, the effort we put into learning their names and making sure they learn each other's names is critical. It's easy for students to argue, disagree with, or make fun of "that kid on the third row," but a little harder to be rude to Jeff or Tonya or Mac.

Celebrate the Diversity in Your Class

It's hard for adolescents to embrace differences. Teenagers want to be treated as individuals at the same time that they want to look like, dress like, sound like, and act like those in their crowd. It's an interesting dichotomy that adults can't understand, and I'm sure, at times, is just as confusing to teens. So, when you look across your classroom and see the various ethnic groups, hear the many languages, recognize the various economic groups sitting in your room, and see that you've got "techies," "jocks," "preppies," "goat ropers," "science geeks," and "rappers" all in one room, you might need to spend some time making sure students value their differences. Sometimes simply asking, "What would high school be like if everyone were a sports star?" gets a conversation going. One football player began with the opinion, "It'd be great," but then later said, "Well, maybe not. If we were all good at football, I might not get to play and who would watch?"

"What's the advantage of having multiple languages in a school?" one teacher asked her class, whose twenty-eight students represented eleven languages.

One young woman responded, "If we all spoke the same language everywhere, then, for sure communication would be easier, but life would be duller." In short, look for the diversity that sits in your classroom and help students see it and celebrate it.

Do Not Tolerate Put-Downs

Adolescents are great at one-liners that can reduce another student to tears or humiliation and, at times, intense feelings of alienation.

"I've got an idea," one student says.

Another responds, "So?" or "You? An idea? I don't think so." Sometimes students zing each other without words. Smirks, rolled eyes, hushed laughing do as much damage as words do. Other times, students commit their put-downs to print with slam books, passed notes, or emails that outline who not to invite to parties, to sleepovers, or to study sessions. Girls are particularly notorious for this type of hurtful behavior.

Eliminating negative comments is difficult and sometimes takes more energy than we may want to invest. One teacher told me, "I know they are mean to each other. They are just going to have to work it out. The world is filled with mean people and you've got to learn to ignore it." Another said, "If I spent time fixing how kids treat one another, I'd never get anything done. Nothing." Still a third explained, "I think it's just a natural part of growing up. The best thing we can do as teachers is ignore it."

I have to disagree. The best thing we can do is stop it. When children are belittled by their peers, something happens that is hurtful almost beyond repair. When it happens in front of an adult, an adult who is supposed to care, and the adult does nothing, then the damage is even greater. Let students know that in your classroom, belittling remarks—through written language, oral language, or body language—will not be tolerated.

To understand more about why girls behave the way they do, read an excellent book titled *Odd Girl Out: The Hidden Culture of Aggression in Girls* by Rachel Simmons (2002). Through interviews with thousands of adolescent girls in America, this book provides insight into the spiteful behavior of some girls, the alienation that behavior causes others to feel, and suggestions parents and teachers can use to help girls act with more respect toward one another.

Step Inside a Classroom

One teacher bought a bell—the type on hotel registration counters. She placed it on her desk and said, "Every time one of you says something mean, you're acting like a real ding-a-ling. You do it so much and so often, you don't even hear it. In this class, we will treat each other with respect. Every time you make a statement or do something that makes you sound like a ding-a-ling, I'm going to ring this bell. The first day you go all class period with no ding-a-lings, you get to go to lunch five minutes early. The first time you go all week with no ding-a-lings, you all earn a hundred for a major test grade. When we've gone a month with no ding-a-lings, we'll have a pizza party with a movie." These eleventh graders just moaned.

That day, she must have rung the bell more than fifty times. Kids were testing her—hard. She didn't flinch but just kept ringing the bell. By the end of the week, the bell was beginning to get annoying. Students were beginning to tell each other, "Oh man, don't say that; she's gonna ring that bell." And she would. During the third week, when the class went a whole period with no ding-a-lings, the entire class burst into applause. But succeeding that one day didn't mean they had it made. Every time, every single time, there was the hint of ding-a-ling behavior, she rang the bell. Over time, the negative behavior slowly went away. One day, after about four days in a row of no bell ringing, the class talked about what was happening. One student remarked, "Ding-a-lings [now the class term for negative comments or gestures] become so common that you don't even hear them. Now, I hear them so much in my other classes that I'm amazed how awful they really are."

Another said, "It's like this class is now safer. You know that people are going to respect your ideas. They may not agree with them, but they are going to let you know that in a better way."

A final student said, "When folks are dissin' you, you can't be focusing on anything but how they are acting. And you got to act a certain way back, you know, to let them know that you won't take no disrespect. Now, now with that gone, you are focusing on what they are really saying."

You can make class rules, set class guidelines, and certainly model respectful behavior. But the most important thing you can do is to be vigilant. Walk the halls and eat in the cafeteria. We gave up a lot when we gave up lunch duty. If you want to know how some students are treated, go back to the cafeteria. Who never has anyone to sit with? Who is pushed—literally—out of a seat so a "good" kid can sit there? Who stands alone at the end of the cafeteria line wanting anyone to say, "Hey, sit here with me"? Who takes a book to the lunchroom so he'll look busy and not alone? Who watches the clock to see when this torturous time will end? When we retreat to the teachers lounge or stay in our classrooms during lunch, we most certainly are giving ourselves a needed break, but we're missing the dynamics that control how some children feel all day.

Your zero tolerance of disrespectful comments and behavior is critical if students are going to be willing to join the conversation in the classroom. As we encourage students to speak out, remember that our own words must convey that same respect. Comments like, "Oh, I see you've finally decided to try your hand at some homework," can sound funny, but actually point out what a student hasn't been doing and *may* be viewed as a negative remark. Some teachers use sarcasm quite well as a way to interact with students. If that's your style, just always be on the lookout for when sarcastic remarks become hurtful ones.

Provide Various Ways for Engagement

Moffet (1968) tells us that as we are developing as writers, first we write for ourselves, then for a known audience, and then for an unknown audience. I believe students benefit when we provide the same layered approach to classroom participation. First, we need to give students the opportunity to form their thoughts, mull them over, and decide what they want to say or ask about what they've read. Second, opportunities to share in small groups—groups that, preferably, the students choose—give students chances to try out ideas in intimate settings. Finally, taking part in the classroom discussion—or now, the online discussion—allows students to test their thoughts against the backdrop of a larger community.

Examine your methods for interaction and make sure they include opportunities to

- keep a personal response log
- write response notes to a trusted friend
- join in very small groups (two or three people) to discuss very specific questions
- take part in larger literature circles
- join classroom discussions
- try online discussions
- listen to discussions in other classes

Encourage an Aesthetic Response

Students can't fully enter what Smith calls the "literacy club" (Smith, 1988) when they won't enter the conversations of that club. When they won't talk about texts or their responses to texts, when they won't take risks by asking questions or expand their own boundaries by entertaining ideas that differ from their own, then they stay on the fringes of the club. And as we all know, when you aren't an active member of a club, eventually membership in the club isn't valued at all.

While entrée to the literacy club comes from learning how letters and sounds work, active and continued membership is a result of meaningful interactions with texts, and those meaningful interactions most often occur when we read aesthetically.

Aesthetic and Efferent Stances Toward Reading

Rosenblatt (1938/1983) explains the difference between an aesthetic stance toward reading and an efferent stance. She tells us that readers might take an efferent stance toward reading when their goal is to carry information *from* the text. They assume a more aesthetic stance when the goal is to live *through* the text. Rather than thinking of these stances as an either/or situation, think of them as two points on a single continuum. Sometimes we read with a stance more toward the efferent; other times we lean toward the aesthetic.

Avid readers show an ability to move easily along this continuum, something I've identified as stance versatility (Beers, 1990). This stance versatility allows readers to begin reading their history assignment with an efferent purpose (to be able to answer the questions on the review sheet), but then, getting caught up in the battle being described, to shift to a more aesthetic stance (living through the danger, the hunger, the fear, the cold), only to finish and, as they answer questions, reread the text with an efferent stance (Where exactly did the battle take place?). Likewise, they begin the short story or novel in their literature class with an aesthetic stance and then, when needed for assignments, shift to an efferent stance. Even if certain avid readers can't stand reading about battles and read the entire chapter in their history book with an efferent stance, they recognize their distance from the text as distaste for history, not a dislike of reading. Then, when they pick up a text they *do* like—whether that is the science book or a poem by Nikki Giovanni—they switch easily to that aesthetic stance.

By contrast, struggling readers, as well as reluctant readers, often lack this stance versatility. They read everything with one dominant stance, an efferent stance. This belief that the purpose of all reading—whether a great work of literature or a recipe in a cookbook—is simply to gather information causes an attitude that distances the reader from the text. This is particularly a problem when students are reading fiction and literary nonfiction in their language arts classes. As they finish reading Chris Lynch's *Slot Machine* or Avi's *The True Confessions of Charlotte Doyle* or Gary Paulsen's *Nightjohn* or Patricia McKissack's *Black Hands, White Sails*, we ask them, "Did you like it?" and they stare at us and reply, "Do we need to write our answer in a complete sentence?" We cry as we read aloud Karen Hesse's *Out of the Dust* or Yukio Tsuchiya's *Faithful Elephants,* and they file their nails

Kylene talks to students about aesthetic response

and want to know, "Do we have to know this for the test?" We read with them *At Her Majesty's Request* by Walter Dean Myers and ask, "Can you believe this child's life?" and they ask if that's a true or false question. We are living through the moment of the text, feeling the excitement, the pain, the fear, the joy of the characters, and they are living for the bell to ring. There is, to borrow a line from Cool-Hand Luke, a failure to communicate.

What we must do with those students is help them read a text with an aesthetic stance. For these kids, reading is about letting their eyes skim over the words on the page. Until they are willing to bring the text closer, let the ideas and issues, conflicts and contests, triumphs and tragedies of the text become a part of who they are, they'll never discover what that text means to them.

That's hard to do, however, if we continually give them tests or lists of questions that focus not on their thoughts about the text, but instead on what we perceive their interpretation of the text to be. But if our goal is to create lifelong readers, not just school-time readers, then reading must be about something more than answering questions at the end of the chapter or book. We must support and nurture an aesthetic stance to reading as much as an efferent stance. In part, we do that by the types of questions that we ask. Figure 13.1 offers a list of questions that allow students to respond to a text by examining what the text meant to them.

An excellent article that discusses a response-based view of teaching literature is "A Response-Based View of Literature in the Classroom" by Lee Galda (*The New Advocate*, 1(2), 1988, pp. 92–102). Three outstanding texts are *Response and Analysis: Teaching Literature in Junior and Senior High School* by Robert Probst (1988); *The Reader, the Text, the Poem: The Transactional Theory of the Literary Work* by Louise Rosenblatt (1978); and *How Porcupines Make Love II: Teaching a Response-Centered Literature Curriculum* by Purves, Rogers, and Soter (1990).

Questions to Encourage a Personal Response to the Text

1. What are your first thoughts about this text? What in the text caused those thoughts?
2. What emotions or feelings did you have while reading the text? Identify the parts that caused those feelings.
3. Did anything in this text remind you of anything in your own life?
4. Did this text remind you of any other texts? Movies? Plays? Why?
5. If you could talk to the author of this text, what would you ask about or comment on?
6. If you were going to recommend this text to someone, who would it be? What in the text would that person like?
7. What confused you or surprised you in this text?
8. As you read this text, describe how you felt. For example, were you bored, caught up, thinking about characters, thinking about how you might react if in the same situation, enjoying the author's writing style, or enjoying the humor or suspense?
9. Did you like the cover of the book? Why or why not? If not, how would you change it?
10. Did you like the title of the book? Why or why not? If not, how would you change it?

Questions to Encourage Reflection About the Plot

1. What went on in this story?
2. What parts of the plot did you find to be the most significant? Why?
3. What were the turning points in this plot for you? Why?
4. What was the most important word in this text? Why?
5. What idea or image or situation meant the most to you as you read this text? Why?
6. What did the author of this text do that helped you enjoy the story? That made you not enjoy the story?
7. If this story were to continue, what do you think would happen next? Why?
8. If you could change the ending, would you? How would you change it?
9. If you were to draw a picture that represented what you found to be important in this text, what would you draw? Why?
10. Evaluate this plot on a scale of 1 to 4 with 1 being "Not worth recommending" and 4 being "Everyone should read this" and tell why you gave it the rating you did.

FIGURE 13.1 *Questions to ask students*

Questions to Encourage Reflection on the Characters

1. Which character or characters did you most enjoy? Why?
2. Which character or characters did you least enjoy? Why?
3. Do any of the characters remind you of yourself? Which ones? Why?
4. Did you think the characters were believable? Why or why not?
5. Which character or characters did you think learned the hardest or most important lessons in this text? Why did you choose that character?
6. What surprised you most about any of the characters?
7. If you could take on the qualities of any of the characters in this text, what qualities would those be?
8. Which character changed the most in this text? How did that character change? What did you learn about that character in watching that change? What did you learn about yourself?
9. If this text were to be made into a movie, which movie stars would you cast in which roles? Why?
10. If you were to eliminate a character from this text, which character would you choose? Why? How would eliminating that character change the text?

Questions to Encourage Reflection About the Setting

1. What was the setting of this text?
2. Was the setting important to the text? Why or why not?
3. How could you change the setting without changing the outcome?
4. How could you change the setting so that it would affect the outcome?
5. Does this setting remind you of a place you know?
6. Which events in the text are most connected to the setting?
7. How did the author let you know what the setting was?
8. Did the setting affect what the characters did or didn't do?
9. If you could talk to the author about the setting of this book, what would you ask?
10. If you were to write a story, would you choose the setting first or think about characters and the conflicts they would face and let that dictate the choice of setting?

FIGURE 13.1 *continued*

Questions to Encourage Reflection About the Theme

1. What message did you take away from reading this text? Why?
2. Which passage in the text would you consider most significant or most important? Why? Did that passage help shape what you considered to be the message of this text?
3. If you were talking with the author, can you speculate what the author might say the theme is? What is in the text that gives hints to that?
4. How do the title, chapter titles, and/or cover illustration help you determine a theme for the text?
5. How do the changes the main character undergoes help you make a decision about the message of this text?
6. Talk with someone else who has read the same text. What does that person see as the message? If you see different messages, discuss what caused those differences.
7. The plot (the series of events in the text) and the theme (the lesson or message you take away from text) are not the same. Think of the text you just read. What is the plot? What is the theme? How does the plot relate to or affect the theme?
8. What affected your interpretation of the theme the most: the plot, the characters, or the setting?
9. If you were to draw the theme symbolically, what would you draw?
10. Think about several texts you've enjoyed. Do they share similar themes? Different themes? If they share similar themes, what does that tell you about what you are looking for in a book or story?

Questions to Encourage Reflection on the Point of View, Author's Style, and Author

1. Who told the story in the text you just read? Was the narrator a character in the story or an omniscent narrator? How did the narrator affect your reading of this story?
2. How would the text have changed if a different character had told the story?
3. Can you speculate on why the author chose the narrator he or she did to tell this story?
4. How did the author make the story come alive in your mind? What specific words or phrases did the author use to help you see events, characters, and the setting vividly?
5. Find a section of the text that you particularly liked. What did the author do to help you like that section?
6. Look at the beginnings of chapters. What did the author do there to make you want to read the rest of the chapter? Also look at the endings. Did the author do something special to make you want to read on to the next chapter?
7. Is there a particular phrase or sentence in the text that you thought was particularly well said? What is there about that passage that makes it stand out in your mind?
8. Did you like how this author wrote this text? What did you like or not like? Consider things like setting description, use of dialogue, characterization, explanation of conflict, foreshadowing, symbolism, as well as length of chapters, length of sentences, choice of chapter titles, and use of illustrations.
9. Would you want to read another book by this author? Why or why not?
10. What other writer or writers does this author remind you of? Why?

Figure 13.1 *continued*

Recognize the Stages of Literary Appreciation

Margaret Early (1960) and Robert Carlsen (1954) helped us understand how students move from an unsophisticated appreciation of literature ("It was a really good book") to a sophisticated appreciation ("The language created images that made the book come alive"). When we understand these stages and recognize, therefore, that students at different stages enjoy reading for different reasons, then we can allow students to respond to literature in a way that most honors the stage they are in and nudges them gently to the next stage.

Carlsen outlined five stages of literary appreciation. In the first stage (about grades 3–7), students read at what Carlsen calls the "unconscious delight" stage. In other words, they are absorbed in the plot, and when we ask why they liked it, they respond (at best), "Well, first this happened and then this happened and then this happened." We quickly see that their attachment to the text and to the enjoyment of reading is at the subconscious level.

In the second stage (about grades 7–9), students who have been given the opportunity to read widely for pure enjoyment begin to read with a different goal. Now they want to experience the plot or conflict or setting vicariously. They live through the characters' lives, experiencing each character's triumphs or tragedies. A lot of our girls who are reading Lurlene McDaniel books are right at this stage.

At about ninth grade, we see a shift as readers begin reading books with characters that mirror or reflect their own concerns. This stage makes sense when you think of fourteen- and fifteen-year-olds and their intense preoccupation with themselves. We suddenly also understand why young adult literature, with characters like the readers, will appeal more readily to students than adult classics.

The fourth stage of literary appreciation emerges (for students who have continued to have wide reading experiences) about the junior year in high school. At this time, readers again shift their major purpose for reading. Now they hunt for books that allow them to ponder life's bigger issues. At this stage in their lives, they are willing to discuss issues such as right and wrong, retribution, forgiveness, love, hate, envy, selflessness. Now, they'll read *To Kill a Mockingbird* not just for the plot and characters but also to discuss man's inhumanity toward man, what it means to be our brother's keeper, or if we are indeed all created equal.

Finally, at the fifth stage, often not ever seen, but usually not seen before college years, students read to enjoy the expression of the words. At

Students in this first stage enjoy series books. While parents and teachers sometimes discourage avid reading of series books like The Babysitters Club, Encyclopedia Brown, or The Hardy Boys, we should remember that almost all lifetime readers can recall reading series books about this point in their lives. These books seem to provide a critical link to becoming a lifetime reader.

this most mature level of literary appreciation, the focus is not on the character or plot or even theme but on the author's choice and arrangement of words. We all experience this from time to time as we read certain texts and mark a passage, saying, "I love the way she wrote that."

Implications of These Stages

These stages matter a lot when we realize two things:

1. We can't force students from stage to stage. They will only proceed from one stage to the next if they have lots of opportunities to read. With those opportunities, their focus or purpose naturally shifts.

2. At different stages, students value different things. At the first stage, students most value the plot. At the second and third stages, students value characters and (third stage) conflict. At the fourth stage, their interest shifts to theme. At the final stage, their enjoyment comes from literary devices. When we see that, we see that our questions about what they read ought to respect their purpose for reading. That's not to say you can't ever ask a sixth grader something about the character or conflict. But it is to say, you ought to start by asking them to tell you what they liked best about this book, what part of the plot they enjoyed the most. Likewise, you certainly can ask seventh or ninth graders about theme, but just realize that's not their main focus. Let them talk about characters and conflicts and then use that discussion to lead to a discussion of theme.

Use Appropriate Literature

Appropriate literature means two things. It means you need to have access to some very easy texts for some of your students who have word recognition problems. These students must have an opportunity to practice word recognition, automaticity, and fluency with texts at their instructional level. Plus they need a chance to read on their own with independent-level texts.

Appropriate also means sometimes choosing young adult literature over classics. Young adult literature offers students the chance to read about characters, conflicts, and situations they relate to more quickly. When we want students, especially our reluctant readers, to read, we need to give them the literature that most appeals to them. Again, look at Appendix M for many suggestions of books.

The following are some articles that you might find interesting if you want to learn more about young adult literature.

"Adolescent Literature and the English Curriculum" by Robert Probst. *English Journal*, 3, pp. 26–30. 1987.

"Deep Down Beneath, Where I Live" by G. Robert Carlsen. *English Journal*, 43(5), pp. 235–239. 1954.

"Classroom Talk About Literature: The Social Dimensions of a Solitary Act" by Kylene Beers and Robert Probst. *Voices from the Middle* 5(2), pp. 16–20. 1998.

Give Students the Smart Words

Recognize that many times reluctant readers are reluctant to speak up because they don't know what to say. Those of us who love to read are never at a loss for what we want to say about a book. More than that, we've participated in enough conversations about books that we've learned to phrase our remarks so that we sound intelligent. Dependent readers and reluctant readers, on the other hand, have little experience joining the talk. Therefore, they sometimes need help in framing their comments. Harvey Daniels' excellent book *Literature Circles: Voice and Choice in Book Clubs and Reading Groups* (2002) helps us give students entrée to that literary discussion. I jump-start that discussion by helping students make a list of phrases they can use to help describe literary elements like characters, plot, and theme. See Figure 13.2 for a list you might use.

We make charts that we keep on the wall for several months with these descriptors and others. The purpose of such comments is simply to give students a way to describe what they are thinking about the words. I began using this chart after one student told me, "I just don't know the same smart words as other people."

The next day, when he came in, I handed him the chart you see in Figure 13.2, just written by hand on a sheet of paper. "See if this helps," I said.

The next day, he tentatively raised his hand while the class was discussing the novel they were reading and said, "I thought the ideas in the plot were well developed. That's because I really understood why she was afraid to have this stranger living at her house, but still wanted him there."

Three students replied, "Yeah, I agree." This eighth grader just grinned.

Provide Time for Sustained Silent Reading

As students move through school years, their resistance to reading grows. For some, that's not because they've decided they don't like reading; rather, they've just found other things that interest them more for the moment. But for many others, the demands and expectations we place on reading far exceed their abilities. It's no wonder they choose not to read. But it is our obligation to keep them connected to reading. One powerful way to do that is to provide time in class to read. This sustained silent reading time offers students a chance to read what they want to read. This type of free-reading approach creates students who are more likely to read outside the school

When students lack words for talking about selections they've read, it's hard for them to enter into literary conversations. Let them use this chart to help them find the words they need to move them past the "It was boring" or "I really liked it" stage of conversation.

Words to Describe the Plot

POSITIVE	NEGATIVE
realistic	unrealistic
good pace from scene to scene	plodding
suspenseful	predictable
satisfying ending	frustrating ending
subplots tied together well	confusing subplots
well-developed ideas	sketchy ideas

Words to Describe Characters

POSITIVE	NEGATIVE
Original	Stereotyped
Believable	Unbelievable
Well-rounded	Flat
Multidimensional—change and grow	Static—remain the same
Well-developed	Flawed

Words to Describe the Theme

POSITIVE	NEGATIVE
Important message	Unimportant message
Subtle	Overbearing
Unique	Overworked
Powerful	Ineffective
Memorable	Forgettable

Words to Describe the Author's Writing Style

POSITIVE	NEGATIVE
Descriptive, filled with metaphors	Boring, no imagery
Original	Filled with cliches
Lively, full of action	Slow-moving
Poetic or lyrical	Clodding, jumpy

FIGURE 13.2 *Building social confidence*

setting (Pilgreen and Krashen, 1993). Read more about the value of SSR in Chapter 9, p. 196.

Getting kids who love to read to embrace sustained silent reading time is easy; making sure struggling and/or reluctant readers are reading is more difficult. Chapter 14 offers specific information on how to help those students find the right book.

Confidence and Aliteracy

Just as we sometimes incorrectly presume that all students who struggle with reading struggle for the same reason, we also sometimes incorrectly decide that all readers who are reluctant to read are reluctant for the same reason. These students who can read but choose not to read—aliterates—make up a growing number of the population. The tremendous concern with aliterate behavior is twofold. First, as these students use their reading skills less and less, their skills become diminished (Beers, 1990, 1996a, 1996b; Decker, 1985; Mikulecky, 1978; Wilson, 1981). Second, as some choose not to read, our nation faces a division between "the knowledgeable elite and the masses":

> Aliteracy reflects a change in cultural values and a loss of skills, both of which threaten the processes of a free and democratic society. Literacy . . . knits people together, giving them a common culture . . . and provides people with the intellectual tools used to question, challenge, understand, disagree, and arrive at consensus. In short, it allows people to participate in an exchange of ideas. A democratic nation is weakened when fewer and fewer citizens can participate in such an exchange. Aliteracy leads inexorably to a two-tiered society: the knowledgeable elite and the masses. It makes a common culture illusory or impossible; it erodes the basis for effective decision making and participation in the democratic process. (Baroody, 1984, p. ix)

Seen in this light, aliteracy is not only an academic problem but also a societal concern. Frank Smith (1988) suggests, "One of the great tragedies of contemporary education is not so much that many students leave school unable to read and write, but that others graduate with an antipathy to reading . . . despite the abilities they might have" (p. 177).

Types of Aliterates

In studying why some students would choose not to read (Beers, 1990), I found that there is no single type of aliterate student. Instead, we see a range of aliteracy:

1. *Dormant Readers:* These students like to read and call themselves readers; however, because of schedules and conflicting interests, they simply don't make the time to read (just like many teachers who find that between September and May there is little time for recreational reading). While dormant readers look like reluctant readers in school (these kids often will choose visiting with friends or doing homework over reading), they indeed do like to read. These students in particular benefit from time to read in class.

2. *Uncommitted Readers:* These students are what I often call "a book-at-a-time" readers. In other words, if we hand them the right book, they'll read it—and probably enjoy it. They won't, however, search for books on their own. They have positive attitudes toward reading, just don't see it as something that really interests them. As we work with these students, we must stress the enjoyment of reading.

3. *Unmotivated Readers:* These students have a very negative attitude toward reading as well as a negative attitude toward students who like to read. They are our most difficult to reconnect to reading because they don't value the act or the people who enjoy reading. To begin to help these aliterate students, we must work from their interests.

4. *Unskilled Readers:* Dependent readers often have a negative attitude toward reading simply because it is so difficult for them. As we help them become better readers, if all we do is focus on skills, they will most likely keep their negative attitudes. If students do not recognize the emotional benefits of reading, they likely will never become lifetime readers.

All types of aliterate students benefit from a curriculum that encourages an aesthetic stance toward reading, provides time for sustained silent reading, and allows for various levels of engagement. It takes some special effort to connect unmotivated readers to books. In the next chapter we'll look at specific text features that appeal to these students as well as specific motivational strategies you might try with them.

Reflections

As we connect reluctant readers to texts, we are helping them build the confidence they need to fully enter into the community of readers. This level of connection requires patience and tenacity on our part. Our dependent readers don't believe they can succeed and they don't believe they have anything to offer. You must believe for them.

◆ ◆ ◆

Dear George,

You brought me a present one day, a well-worn copy of The Little Engine That Could. *After class, you stood at my desk and said that you knew how much I liked books, and you had been at a garage sale with your mother where you saw this book for a dime. You thought I might like it. You handed it to me and said, "And besides, it's about always trying." You grinned. "And you know how you are with trying." I smiled. "And anyway, I thought you might like it."*

Nope. I loved it.

◆ ◆ ◆

CHAPTER FOURTEEN

Finding the Right Book

Dear George,

You told me on more than one occasion how much you disliked reading: "It's boring and I hate it," you'd say. "Oh come on, George. You don't really hate it," I'd say. "No? I'd rather clean bathtubs than read a book," you explained. I looked at you, stunned. "Okay, so you hate it," I agreed. "But you shouldn't. What don't you like about it?" I asked. "It's boring. Nothing happens," you replied. "That just means you haven't found the right book," I countered. "I just read the ones you teachers hand me," you said. You started to walk away, then turned and said, "So do you really think if I had the right book, I'd like to read?" Then you grinned, flashing your new braces, and finished your question: "Or at least like it better than cleaning bathtubs?"

Book by Book

In her book *Bird by Bird*, author Anne Lamott explains the title of that book. It seems that once, when they were both children, her brother put off writing a report on birds until the night before it was due. That night, overwhelmed with all he had to do, he asked his dad how he was ever supposed to finish. His father replied that he should do it bird by bird. I thought that was the perfect response, and I've used it with my own son. ("But, Mom, how will I ever get all this picked up?" Baker whines, looking across the wasteland formerly known as his bedroom floor. "Lego by Lego," I respond.) Thinking back, I realize that that was how I tried to connect students to reading: book by book. We'd try one, and if that didn't work, we'd try another. "You'll love this," I'd say as a student would warily eye the book in my hands. "It's such a great book," I'd encourage, pushing the book toward the student.

"Why?" the student would challenge, retreating gradually until he was trapped: me on one side, an entire shelf of Joan Lowery Nixon books on the other; the student had no choice but to take the book and run.

And book by book, I'd sometimes make a match that would result in a slight shrug and a mumbled, "It was okay," but rarely (ever?) that "*Wow! Now I love to read!*" response that I kept anticipating. The problem was, as I finally discovered while taking a graduate class taught by Dr. Richard Abrahamson, that I was handing students books that *I* loved instead of focusing on what the students might enjoy.

Part of the problem was that as an avid reader, I didn't think like a *non-reader*. I thought like a female who loves thick, complicated, intricately detailed, complex relationship stories. As a teen, that meant romances and mysteries; as an adult that means, well, romances and mysteries. Somewhere along the way, science fiction became a favorite, and somehow or another, poetry joined my must-read list as well. I find myself as eager to read a new novel by Lori Aurelia Williams or Pamela Muñez Ryan as I do one by Joyce Carol Oats, Wally Lamb, or Barbara Kinsolver. I revisit young adult classics such as Robert Cormier's *Chocolate War*, Sue Ellen Bridgers' *All Together Now*, Walter Dean Myers' *Fallen Angels*, or Robert Lypsite's *One Fat Summer* with the same excitement as rereading *Return of the Native*, *To Kill a Mockingbird*, or *Anna Karenina*. I eagerly await Orson Scott Card's next book and would stand in line for any amount of time to hear Maya Angelou read anything. Anything. And for years, I thought if I loved it, my students would, too.

Wrong.

Though my students might appreciate the fact that there are certain books that mean a lot to me, this, I finally discovered, in no way meant those books would mean anything to them—especially to my nonreaders. I had to realize that my first requirement for a book—something really, really long so I could be lost for days, perhaps weeks, between the covers— was their first criteria for *not* reading a book. I had to learn to think short. Think short. Think short.

I also had to learn that while I wanted lots of characters, nonreaders often wanted few. I wanted a complicated plot; they wanted straight-forward. I wanted to grapple with the biggest human issues set upon the individual human heart and consciousness while they wanted *Captain*

Summertime Reading

Summer offers us some precious moments for reflection. Share some of those times with these titles you might have missed or simply want to revisit. Because of the publication dates, this list (most of it young adult literature) might be found more easily in libraries than in bookstores. Still, if you don't know young adult literature, start with these titles— you'll soon realize you've been missing some excellent reading.

Homeless Bird by Gloria Whelan

One Bird by Kyoko Mori

Othello by Julius Lester

Out of the Dust by Karen Hesse

Parrot in the Oven by Victor Martinez

Rain Catchers by Jean Thesman

Send Me Down a Miracle by Han Nolan

Shabanu: Daughter of the Wind by Suzanne Fisher Staples

The Starlite Drive-In by Marjorie Reynolds

Words by Heart by Ouida Sebestyn

Underpants. I wanted them to love what I loved. They simply wanted a book that was better than cleaning bathtubs.

And yet, that wasn't quite true.

Derrick explained, "I don't like to read because it's slow and there's just other stuff to do, so if I'm going to read something, I need it to be something that's like important to me, something that really matters, you know, can really change your life."

Carter said, "When I read, it's like it's a waste of time, you know, a do-nothing. So, if I'm going to read, it like better be for a good reason, you know? Like to really teach you something. Not like a history book or anything. Who cares what's in there? I mean how can that help you with anything? All that stuff is like two thousands years old. I mean it's gotta be like now, you know, to help you like right now."

David reported, "Reading sucks. You just sit. You turn the pages. You answer these questions. You take a test. You start over. But if I could find a book that explains just why it's fair that white folks get all the advantages while everybody else has to work for minimum wage, then that would be a good book. But white folks probably control who all does the publishing so they wouldn't let a book like that get out. But I'd read that book. I sure would."

Text Features

If we can't use ourselves as guides for what makes a good book, then we're left with using what students tell us. If we listen, we'll hear very specific criteria for what makes a book appealing to a reluctant reader. Start with the comments from Derrick, Carter, and David. These boys have let us know they want books that give them information that fits into their world. They want it to help them with the issues they face right now. Look at what several students say about books they'd want to read:

> "I've never really liked to read very much, you know. It's like, well, it's just boring. But if I had to like really read a book, you know like really had to read one, then I'd want one that is funny and not too long. I can't stand long books. They just go on forever. But I don't mean like a joke book. I mean like, well do you watch *Friends* on TV? That's like so funny. That's the kind of funny I mean." (Mandy, tenth grade)
>
> "I guess if I had to pick a kind of book to read, it would be one where it was either a mystery or maybe like a funny story.

Mysteries can be pretty good. But they can't be long and they can't be so hard that you can't ever figure them out." (Traci, ninth grade)

"If I had to read a book, I'd want a real-life book, you know something about something that really happened, and I'd want it to have real photographs to, you know, show you like what was going on. That would be good." (John, tenth grade)

"I don't really like to read, but I do like those books where you can sort of read starting at any point, like those Guinness books; those are good because you can skip around." (Rich, seventh grade)

"I'm probably not going to read it, you know, whatever it is, but if I was going to, then I like books where you feel like you are the character. You know, you are right there. And with a lot of excitement. It can't be boring. Stuff has to be happening. Like

Students like to read when we let them read what they like

right away. I really don't want to have to read pages and pages and pages before anything even happens. I mean that is so do-nothing." (Erin, eighth grade)

"Well, it ought to be good, I mean really good, and short. And I need to be able to understand it, so like no really hard words. That's when it gets the most boring, when you don't understand it. So it needs to have a lot of understandability in it." (Byrd, sixth grade)

I encourage you to ask your reluctant readers the same question I had asked each of those students: If you absolutely had to read a book, what would it need to be like for you to enjoy it? Be ready for a lot of "I dunnos," and realize that's probably an honest answer. Many of these students have never read enough to know all they could expect to find in a book. So, you might want to make a list with them of things they would like in a book.

The comments from these students as well as hundreds of others have helped me understand what reluctant readers are looking for in a book. The next section outlines important text features for reluctant readers.

Fiction

THIN BOOKS AND SHORT CHAPTERS
Reluctant readers don't only want thin books, they want the chapters in those thin books to be short. Thin books suggest students don't have to invest a huge amount of time to finish them. Short chapters mean students don't have to spend much time at any one sitting. Of course, the Harry Potter books are the obvious exception to this. Interestingly, though, it's been the younger reluctant readers who have been most willing to forge through the hundreds of pages of those books; our older reluctant readers said they'd "just see the movie."

WHITE SPACE
Reluctant readers are easily overwhelmed with a text. Too many pages or too many words on a page encourage reluctant readers to read that book reluctantly. Wide margins and an open font tell a reluctant reader that he can move through this book quickly.

SOME ILLUSTRATIONS, ESPECIALLY OF CHARACTERS
Reluctant and struggling readers often complain that they can't see or visualize the text. Consequently, when we can provide books that offer illustrations—even small ones at the beginnings of chapters—we help these readers connect with meaning.

Your list of text features might include the following:

- humor
- mystery
- faraway settings
- few characters
- lots of characters
- short chapters
- long chapters
- illustrations and photographs
- a book about made-up events and made-up people
- a book about real-life events or real people
- boys as the main characters
- girls as the main characters
- books about things that happen now
- books about things that have happened in the past
- books about things that might happen in the future

Well-Defined Characters

Reluctant readers don't want to have to guess who is the narrator or who is doing what. For instance, many avid readers love Avi's *Wolf Rider* or Louis Sachar's *Holes*. Furthermore, if we read those two aloud, many reluctant readers enjoy them as well. But the beginning of *Wolf Rider* is a bit confusing for students who are easily frustrated with a text; likewise, *Holes* requires that readers be willing to fill in the holes as they read—something reluctant readers are reluctant to do.

Plots with a Lot of Action That Begins Right Away

"I can't stand pages where nothing happens," an eighth grader told me. "I want Lights! Camera! Action! from the first page!" This fellow isn't unlike many aliterate students. If they have to work through pages of character description or setting description before they find any action, then they probably will put the book away. This is why many, many reluctant readers start off loving Gary Paulsen's *Hatchet*. In the first twenty or so pages, Brian leaves home, watches the pilot on his small plane have a heart attack and die, lives through a plane crash, and finds himself alone in the Canadian wilderness. That's a lot of action in a very few pages! However, many reluctant readers find themselves skipping later parts of the *Hatchet* because "it just doesn't have enough doing stuff in it" as one fifth grader reported. Most avid readers would disagree with that—but then we've got to remember that what avid readers want and what reluctant readers want don't always match.

Mysteries

Most students enjoy a great whodunnit mystery. This is even true for our most reluctant of readers. The critical issue is in the level of complexity. Avid readers often prefer mysteries that offer minute detail. Reluctant readers want more obvious clues. This is because reluctant readers read with less engagement than skilled readers.

Funny Books

We should all write notes to Dav Pilkney, Gordon Korman, Paula Danziger, Jon Sciezska, Jack Gantos, Ellen Conford, and Chris Lynch for providing readers with characters, situations, and settings that keep us all laughing. As we remember that humor always plays off some level of inference, we should be delighted when we see readers chuckle over something funny. Reading is often a tedious event for reluctant readers; reading something funny lightens the moment and, as one student explained, "makes me forget I'm even reading."

CHARACTERS THEIR AGE OR ONLY SLIGHTLY OLDER

While there are certainly exceptions to this (think about Jonas in *The Giver* or Harry in any of the Harry Potter books), most readers are looking for characters who are their age or up to two years older. Many times, when struggling readers complain that we've given them "baby books" to read, they aren't complaining about the length (they like short, remember?) or the white space on the page or the use of illustrations. Their concern is the age of the character. Fourteen-year-olds just don't want to read about eight-year-olds.

CHARACTERS WHO FACE TOUGH CHOICES

"If I'm going to spend time reading, I want to see something really important happen," one student explained. Sometimes adults shy away from books in which characters face tough situations, but students don't. As one young man told me once about tough books, "I want to meet these characters on the pages of a book before I have to meet them in real life. In a book, if it gets too intense, I can just walk away; in real life, I probably won't have that option."

REALISTIC LANGUAGE

Fragments, run-ons, short sentences, and slang all help create what readers call "real talk" or "slang lang" in a book. Reluctant readers aren't looking for literary language; they are looking for language that speaks to them. They want characters to talk the way the situation demands. They want short sentences that keep the action moving. They want dialogue that isn't stilted. Interestingly, run-ons bother them when not a part of a character's speech. Fragments don't.

A word about profanity: sometimes realistic language means characters utter words we'd prefer not to hear or read. This is particularly true in some young adult literature for older teens. Likewise, some classics deal with issues—adultery in *The Scarlet Letter*, for instance, or abuse in *I Know Why the Caged Bird Sings*—that some readers will find uncomfortable. Our job is to evaluate the novel, be it an adult classic or young adult newcomer, to see if the situation or the language is gratuitous. When that's the case, you might want to think twice about recommending the book. And always remember that the books you require for all students to read must pass a far different standard than books you might have available in your classroom library, which might be different from those that are in the school library, which are certainly different than those in a public library. The issue isn't censorship, but appropriateness. Interestingly, students report that the language in books isn't what encourages them or discourages from using or not using profanity. That comes from the language they hear from their parents and their peers.

AN EASILY DEFINED CONFLICT

This is not the same as a superficial conflict. Reluctant readers prefer books in which characters face tough choices and therefore face tough conflicts. They simply want that conflict to be obvious.

Nonfiction

VISUAL FEATURES

Reluctant readers enjoy informational books with a large number of photographs, illustrations, drawings, charts, and diagrams. When reluctant readers read informational books, they use the visual aspects of the book not only to help them create meaning but to help them visualize the text, thus sustaining an active level of engagement with the text. Our concern that they are just looking at the pictures is probably an oversimplification of what they are really doing: using all the text features they can to help this text be more meaningful to them.

TWO-PAGE SPREADS

Reluctant readers enjoy informational texts that give them a lot of information in a confined amount of space. The Dorling Kindersley books such as the Eyewitness Books offer a format that often appeals to reluctant readers. Readers open the book to any page and on the left-hand side, at the top of the page, they find basic information on the topic. On the rest of that page and the facing page, they find other information linked to brightly colored charts, diagrams, drawings, illustrations, and photographs. When readers turn the page, they discover another topic. This format appeals to a reluctant reader's desire to get a lot of information quickly.

BEYOND THE BOOK FORMATS

Many times when reluctant readers tell us they don't want to read, they mean they don't want to read the 150-page problem novel we've chosen for them. However, when we expand our notion of what makes an acceptable text to include magazines, computer guides, Nintendo and Game Boy guides, web sites, newspapers, instruction manuals (that would be instructions for completing a Lego kit or fixing the motorcycle, not for finishing

When reluctant readers tell us they don't want to read, they mean they don't want to read the novel we've chosen for them.

the science fair project), driver's education material (which I'm always very pleased to see kids reading!), comic books, graphic novels (those novels told in comic book form), *TV Guide,* puzzle magazines, and newspaper comic strips, then we see that many of our nonreaders are indeed readers.

INDEX, TABLE OF CONTENTS, HEADINGS, AND BOLDFACED TERMS

While reluctant and struggling readers never seem to notice these features in their social studies or science textbook, they adore them in informational texts. Students who choose informational texts do so because they want information—sometimes very specific information. They like being able to read the book "out of order," moving to sections that are important to them. They like being able to turn to an index to find the single page they need.

THIN BOOK

While finding a thin book is less critical with an informational book than with fiction, it does make a difference for some readers. Other readers recognize that a book like *The Top Ten of Everything* is only long if they want to read all of it.

HIGH-INTEREST TOPICS

While you can probably find a thin book with a great index, wonderful boldfaced headings, and superb photos, if the topic is cell division and no one has asked for that title, you'll have a hard time convincing reluctant readers it's worth their time. Students who want to read informational books are looking for specific information—information that interests them. It's critical that you help students learn how to navigate a library so they can find that section of books that they want to read.

VOCABULARY DEFINED AT POINT OF USE

By their very nature, informational books often contain specialized vocabulary. Students prefer books that define unusual terms at the point of use rather than in the back in a glossary.

WANDER-AROUND BOOKS

This unusual term came from an eleventh-grade boy who explained, "I really don't like to read unless it's a book I can just wander around in, you know, one of those where you can start reading it anywhere and stop anywhere." At the time, he was reading David MacCauley's *The Way Things Work,* a perfect example of a wander-around book.

BIOGRAPHIES

In addition to informational texts, many reluctant readers are interested in true-life stories of current sport figures, celebrities, musicians, and politicians. Some are interested in historical figures as well. Like with other nonfiction, these biographies need to err on the side of short, be filled with photographs, provide a way to find specific information about the person quickly, and use a vocabulary that keeps the text accessible.

Selling the Book to Students

It would be great if bringing in the right book at the right time were enough to connect kids to reading. The reality is, that's not enough. Instead, we've got to sell the book. For many of us, a leisurely stroll through our favorite bookstore with a cup of Starbucks coffee in one hand is enough to connect us with any book. For others of us, a quick, "Oh you'll love it," from a trusted friend sends us reaching for that book. The rest of us like to read reviews to sell us on a book. Now with our reluctant readers . . . well, the sell job is a bit harder. What follows are some suggestions that often encourage even our most reluctant readers to give a book a try.

Suggestion #1: Read Aloud

Chapter 9 describes the cognitive benefits of reading aloud; here we'll focus on the motivational benefits. While many students will tell us they don't like to read, few will tell us they don't like to hear a good story. We need to hold on to that difference and remember the power of reading aloud to our students. Many times the story we begin reading aloud to students will be the one they want to read at home or want to read on their own once we've finished reading it in class. Just remember, when students tell us they like us to read aloud, what they really mean is they want us to act aloud. You can't sit on a stool at the front of your room or hidden behind your desk reading in a rushed voice that reveals little interest in the book. You've got to read aloud with expression, with excitement, with assurance. You need to have read ahead the portion you'll be reading aloud to decide at what points you should whisper or show fear. You can't stumble or words will get lost in complex syntax. Students know when you've prepared, and that level of preparation lets them know just how valuable you think the story really is.

One other point: While first- and second-grade teachers know the value of reading aloud to children, secondary teachers may have forgotten, for it's rarely done on a regular basis in the upper grades. And when teachers do this only occasionally, the value is reduced to one of entertainment. However, if you read aloud on a consistent basis, ask students to summarize what was read the day before, stop occasionally to discuss the action or unusual words or a confusing part, and then, at the end, have students predict what will happen next, you'll have tied this activity to comprehension and vocabulary development. Use this strategy consistently, and you'll see that you've not only connected students to valuable texts, you've also helped them with critical reading skills.

Suggestion #2: Read and Tease

Reluctant readers are less reluctant to read a book if you've read the first chapter—or two—aloud to them. In doing so, you've helped them hear the text. Stop your reading aloud at a particularly compelling point so they'll want to read on to find out what happens. Or lure them in with booktalks. Spend about ten minutes every other week booktalking new books that you suspect your students will enjoy. Booktalks aren't a summary, but rather an advertisement. For instance, for Louis Sachar's award-winning *Holes,* you might say: "What do you do when you find yourself in a juvenile detention facility—in other words, kids jail—with a warden who sends you out into the desert heat every day to dig holes in the ground? What happens when you finally figure out just why he has you doing that? How do you get away when there's no place to get away to? This book tells the story of a teenage boy who faces just that situation. If you like mystery, humor, and survival, you'll definitely like this book."

Go to <*www.google.com*> and enter "booktalks" in the search window. You'll find plenty of sources that provide ready-made booktalks. I'm a fan of Nancy Keane's booktalks, and as of this writing, you can get to her booktalk site either through google (by entering "booktalks") or at <*www.nancykeane.com*>. She has a great book filled with booktalks titled *Books and Beyond* that's available through Amazon.

Suggestion #3: Create Book Jacket Bulletin Boards

Well, we might tell students not to judge a book by the cover, but that's exactly what most of us do. So, make a bulletin board filled with book jackets. Borrow some book jackets from your school librarian or make some color copies of your students' favorite paperbacks. Near the jackets, put sticky notes so students can predict what they think the book will be about. Then, at some point, read the predictions, take the cover off the bulletin board and put it back on the book, offer a quick booktalk, and give it to the student who most wants to read it.

Suggestion #4: Take Students to Your School Library

Two years ago, I surveyed sixty-four high school English teachers and asked them how many took their students to the school library on a regular basis to check out books. The answer: none. "Why not?" I asked.

"No time," they replied.

"Why not?" I asked again.

"I'm too busy teaching students how to read to waste precious time watching them wander aimlessly in a library," one responded. I was dismayed at the response, so I'll repeat what I've already said in this book: The single best way to improve reading interest and reading ability is to read. The best way is not to *learn about* reading, but to actually *do it*. If we don't take all students, but particularly reluctant and struggling readers, to the library on a regular basis, then chances are that when they leave school, being a regular library patron will not be a part of their routine. Public libraries are a major equalizing factor in this nation, so how can we afford *not* to take students to the library?

In my third year of teaching, I spent spring break chaperoning a group of seventh graders on a weeklong field trip to Washington, D.C. This trip was one of those where for every fifteen or twenty students who pay to go, a teacher can go for free. All year long as I talked about this trip with my students, one young boy named Gary talked a lot about going. On the last day to pay for the trip, he came in early and told me he wouldn't be going because his family didn't have the money. As I sat there trying to figure out how to pay for this one child without suddenly finding myself needing to pay for all of them, Gary said, "But it's okay, Mrs. Beers. Mom says that if you'll give us a copy of the itinerary, she'll take me to the library. We'll check out books of the places you'll be seeing. Mom says that on the day you're at the Smithsonian, we'll read about it and on the day you're at the Lincoln Memorial, we'll read about that. Then, mom says, when you get back, you can come over for dinner and you can show us your pictures and I can show you my books because mom says the only difference is you'll take a trip on a plane and I'll take a trip in my mind. So, can I have a copy of the itinerary?" At that point, I'd have given that child anything.

Eventually spring break arrived, and I headed to Washington with sixty seventh graders while Gary headed to the library. When I returned, his mom invited me over for dinner. I went, carrying my photographs. After dinner, we sat in his living room and shared our trips. (I think Gary had a better trip than I did.) As I stood at the door to leave that night, I told his mom that she was indeed the smartest woman I had ever met. She turned to a small table by that front door, picked up her purse, rummaged through it, and removed a small, blue, well-worn library card. She held it up for me to see and said, "There are many things in this life I'll never be able to buy my children, but there is nothing they will ever lack because I have a library card."

I left there wanting the world to be filled with people like Gary's mom. I thought about how this woman didn't just tell her son, "You know we can't afford such a trip," and then dismiss his plea to go. Instead, she gave him an option that showed him a world he would have otherwise missed. Too many of our students don't go home to parents like Gary's mom. But they come to school to people like you, teachers who know the value of reading, who understand that reading opens doors that otherwise might forever remain locked. You are, for so many children, their only chance at ever experiencing a person like Gary's mom. Like her, find the time to take your students to the library. The doors you open to reading will be worth the time you lose in class.

Suggestion #5: Create a Good Books Box

Years ago, while in a library with seventh graders, I noticed that some students always went right to the shelves to select books they wanted to read. Other students headed straight to the couches to just sit. A third group of students wandered aimlessly through the library, thumbing through the card catalogue (these days, that would be scrolling through titles on a computer disk) or walking through the stacks, looking at covers, sometimes selecting a book, most often not. As this particular class lined up to head back to class, I asked one student from that group of wanderers why she hadn't checked out a book.

"Are you going to tell me what all the other teachers say?" she asked.

"I don't know. What do other teachers say?" I replied.

"They all say the library is filled with good books."

"Well, what's wrong with that?" I asked.

"Where are they?" she said.

"Where are what?" I said.

"The good books. I sure don't see them. Just where are they?"

"Tell me what you mean," I said.

"It's like shopping. You go to Foleys [a very large department store] and you can shop all day and never find anything. It's why I shop at The Limited now," she said.

I wasn't quite following her line of thinking. "I don't get it; why do you shop at The Limited?"

"Because it's *limited*. There's not as much to choose from. You can actually find things."

"And tell me just how this connects to finding a good book in the library," I said.

She was clearly frustrated at my inability to follow her reasoning. "The library is like Foleys. You can't find anything," she said and then hurriedly left to catch up with her classmates.

She left me standing there looking around at this middle school library. Suddenly I thought of my grocery store. For some unknown-to-me reason, the store had recently been remodeled. I hated shopping there for a while because I couldn't find the peanut butter or Parmesan cheese or boxes of Equal. And when I couldn't navigate it well, it became a frustrating place. This student was telling me she didn't know the library, didn't know authors, didn't know genres, and therefore, like shopping in a department store that was too large or a grocery store with a new layout, she couldn't find what she wanted.

I asked the librarian to help me with an experiment. I asked her to take a small box—the type that reams of paper come in—and write "Good Books" on the side, and then fill it with eight or ten great books. I wanted her to put the box on a table the next time this class visited the library. She did just that. Two weeks later, this same class arrived in the library. Some kids went directly to the shelves and chose the books they wanted. Others found their spot on the couch. The wanderers kept on wandering. Finally, a boy spotted the Good Books box. He stood staring at it, not touching any books inside. After a while, he asked the librarian what those books were. "Good books," she replied.

"You're kidding," he said, as if he had looked for them for years and suddenly there they were, in a box. Another kid walked by and asked him what he was looking at. "Good books," he answered.

"Really?" the second kid said.

They both stood there. Finally one asked, "So can you like check them out?" The librarian nodded. Eventually, about five students checked out a book from the Good Books box.

On their next visit, the librarian and I waited to see what would happen. As students turned in their books, she asked, "Did you read the book?" Each student nodded. "What'd you think?" she asked.

"It was a good book," each student answered, somewhat amazed. They all stood there, saying nothing. The librarian and I stood there, waiting.

Finally, one student asked, "We were wondering, do you have any more good books?"

And then, this dear, amazing librarian surprised us all when she pointed to another box on a different table and said, "Sure do." We all turned to look at this second box, labeled "More Good Books."

"Cool," one kid said as they moved to look through that box.

I've told the Good Books box story for many years in many places because the lesson is powerful. Until you are comfortable with authors, genres, and interests, it's hard to find a good book. We need to narrow that choice for students. Lining books up along the chalk holder is a great idea; standing some up on a desk works well. Or just tossing them in a box and labeling it "Good Books" works, too. Remember, your goal is to move the students from the box to the stacks, so study what types of books your students choose. I watched this librarian point out to one student who was reading from the Good Books box that she always chose mysteries. Then the librarian pointed out that there was an entire section in the library devoted to mysteries. "Where?" the girl asked.

"Under that huge five-foot sign that says 'Mysteries' hanging from the ceiling over there," the librarian explained.

"That is so awesome," the child answered as she finally saw meaning in that sign for the very first time.

> If you're looking for some great books to put into your Good Books box, talk with your school librarian, or ask students what books they love, or go online to the American Library Association web site at <*www.ala.org*>. On that homepage, click on "ALA Divisions, Units, Governance." From that link, click on "ALA Divisions." From there, click on "YALSA." That takes you to the ALA directory on young adult literature. You'll find wonderful booklists.

Suggestion #6: Know Your Students' Interests

I gave up using long reading-interest inventories many years ago for one simple reason—I wasn't reading them. If you've figured out how to find the time to read them and make sense of them, then by all means keep doing so. Instead, I discovered what works best for me is quick-talks with students. I try to meet with students—especially those who are struggling or reluctant readers—for a few minutes at the beginning of the school year to simply ask them what types of things they like to do and what kinds of books might interest them. I'm looking for enough information that I can steer them in the right direction in the library or choose the right range of books for book-talks. I jot down their answers on a four-by-six-inch index card and then align them in rows on one side of a bulletin board (because if I put them in any sort of box, I'm less likely to read them again). Then I take Polaroid photos of students and mount them on the other side of the bulletin board. The kids and I work on connecting the picture to the corresponding interest card. I'm always surprised at how this is a favorite activity in high school, especially upper grades. As one senior told me, "I haven't thought a teacher cared who I was since second grade. You know, when you're little, they make a big deal out of learning your name and what you like, but in high school, teachers just don't seem to care." I suddenly realized that this young man, in a class with 32 other students, didn't see that the teacher had 5 other classes with just as many students. He didn't know how hard it is for teachers to learn 150+ names, likes, dislikes, strengths, and weaknesses. He saw a classroom of 32 students and expected the same depth of attention and familiarity that he had experienced from his elementary school teachers.

Suggestion #7: Talk About the Authors

Students like the inside story, just like we all do. Read up on young adult authors and share interesting facts with students. A great online source for information on authors is *<www.authors4teens.com>*. Be sure to check out the link to Teri's Corner. A great print resource is *Writers for Young Adults*, edited by Ted Hipple, and *Nonfiction for Young Adults: From Delight to Wisdom* by Betty Carter and Richard Abrahamson.

Finding Books

You can know your students, know what students like in a book, know how to connect kids to books, but if you don't actually know the books, then you've still got a problem. We live in a time when every year there seems to

Students love to hear about authors. Here's a photo of Christopher Paul Curtis at my house for a party. We've convinced him to spend some time autographing books.

be more quality young adult literature published for students, and there certainly is a huge amount of popular adult literature that students want to read. So how do you know what's out there and how do you know what's good? Keeping up is hard to do; the following lists might help.

Turn to Appendix M for several booklists. Use the following sources to update this list.

Review Journals

1. *Booklist.* This journal, published by the American Library Association, is published twenty-two times per year. Though expensive ($79.95 for a year or $145.00 for two years), it's worth every cent. You'll find reviews for adult, young adult, and children's books. Special features such as boxed reviews, author interviews, grade-level suggestions, and starred ratings make this source very valuable. You can subscribe by sending a check to *Booklist*, P.O. Box 607, Mt. Morris, IL 61054–7564 or by going online to <*www.ala.org/booklist/*>.

2. *School Library Journal.* This journal, primarily read by school librarians, not only includes wonderful reviews but has information about how librarians can help connect students to reading. Many of those ideas are very appropriate for classroom teachers. It's also expensive at $109.00 per year for twelve issues. You can subscribe by writing to SLJ, P.O. Box 16178, North Hollywood, CA 91615–6178 or look at the online journal at <*www.slj.com*>.

3. NCTE journals. The National Council of Teachers of English offers three outstanding journals that always provide information and reviews on new books as well as articles to help you with ongoing professional development. You can find information on online copies as well as print copies for *Language Arts, Voices from the Middle,* and *English Journal* at <*www.ncte.org*>. At the top of that homepage, you'll see tabs that say "Elementary," "Middle," and "Secondary." Click the one that fits your needs and then follow the links to the journal for that section. You can also follow the link on the sidebar to "Assemblies" to find information about *The ALAN Review*, a journal devoted to young adult literature.

4. IRA journals. The International Reading Association publishes *The Reading Teacher* and *The Journal of Adolescent and Adult Literacy*. Both of these journals offer some reviews of children's (*The Reading Teacher*) and young adult (*JAAL*) literature. Find out about ordering these journals at <*www.IRA.org*>. From that homepage, on the left sidebar, click on "Publications." Follow the links from there to the desired journal.

Online Booklists

1. The American Library Association web site, <*www.ala.org*>, provides a wealth of information, especially if you are looking for booklists. While some of the lists are restricted to members, you can find out information on the following awards or lists:

   a. Newbery Award: For literary excellence in children's literature.
   b. Caldecott Award: For artistic excellence in children's literature.
   c. Coretta Scott King Award: Award presented to authors and illustrators of African descent whose distinguished books promote an understanding and appreciation of The American Dream.
   d. Pura Belpre Award: Presented to a Latino/Latina writer and illustrator whose work best portrays, affirms, and celebrates the Latino cultural experience in an outstanding work of literature for children and youth.
   e. Printz Award: For literary excellence in young adult literature.
   f. Sibert Award: Presented to the author of the most distinguished informational book for children.
   g. Best Books for Young Adults (BBYA) list: Chosen annually, this provides a list of fiction and nonfiction titles deemed "Best Books."
   h. Outstanding Books for College Bound: This list offers direction for our most skilled readers.
   i. Quick Picks for Reluctant Young Adult Readers: This list, as its title suggests, offers suggestions for students who are reluctant readers, but not necessarily struggling readers.
   j. Notable Children's Books: This list is a companion list to the BBYA list focusing on outstanding books for children.

2. Mystery Writers Organization

   a. Edgar Allen Poe Award: Presented annually in many categories, both adult and young adult, to the outstanding mysteries for the preceding year. Find this valuable list at <*www.mysterywriters.org /awards.html*>. Scroll down the page to find the section on young adult books.

3. Additional Lists

   a. Booklists for Young Adults on the Web: This site, found at <*www.seemore.mi.org/booklists/*>, is especially helpful. It pulls many of the ALA and other booklists to this one site.

b. The Carnegie Library of Pittsburgh's Young Adult Booklist: This site, like the previous one, offers direct links to other sites as well as reviews of favorite books as selected by teens. Visit this site at *<http://alphaclp.clpgh.org/ein/ya/yalists.html>*.

c. Various Lists: I'm hesitant to list more online booklist sites because we all know how quickly web addresses change. So, do what I do and go to your favorite search engine (mine is obviously *<www.google.com>*) and enter "booklists." You'll find current sites that way. Bookmark your favorite and check it often.

◆ ◆ ◆

Dear George,

Sometimes you frustrated me; often you worried me. But many times you entertained me with your honesty, your wit, and your willingness to make fun of yourself. After telling me you'd be happy with a book that was more interesting than cleaning the bathtub, that became our measure of success. I'd give you a book; you'd read through and return it. I'd ask, "So, did it beat bathtub cleaning?" You'd grin and shake your head no. But one day, as our class walked back from the library, you walked alongside of me and said, "You know, that book, that one I just turned in, it was definitely better than cleaning the bathtub."

"You're kidding?" I said, wanting to run back to the library, claim it, and never lose it. "What was it?"

You shrugged. "I don't know. But it was really pretty good." You grinned, walked off, turned around, and said, "I think it was called How to Clean Your Bathtub in Ten Easy Steps."

◆ ◆ ◆

CHAPTER FIFTEEN

A Final Letter to George

* * *

Dear George,

In so many ways, this book is for you.

I know of no one who doesn't occasionally ask of his or her life's course: Why? Why did this happen? Why didn't that happen? Is this the right path for me to follow? I expect that you have, like me, asked those questions. I've often wondered what my life as a teacher would have been like had I not taught you that first year, not met your parents—wonderful people unwilling to ignore their son's difficulties—not seen your struggles and defeats and cautious optimism from your occasional successes. When I identify defining moments in my life, you, dear child, most certainly are one.

I still see you as that child you were in seventh grade. Short, freckled, braces, an amazing smile that was shared generously with friends, hesitantly with me. I know that year you questioned why you struggled so with reading. The question you never voiced, though, was why no one seemed able to help you. But I heard that unasked question, George, and other teachers throughout this nation teaching other students just like you heard it as well. Now, more than ever before, teachers ask—demand—to know what to do when kids can't read. The roll call of those who have added significantly to our understanding of how to help dependent readers is impressive: Cynthia Block, Michael Pressley, Richard Allington, Jeff Wilhelm, Janet Allen, Jo Worthy, Karen Broaddus, Gay Ivey, Stephanie Harvey, Ruth Schoenbach, Cynthia Greenleaf, Christine Cziko, Lori Hurwitz, Ann Goudvis, Rebecca Barr, Camille Blachowicz, Claudia Katz, Barbara Kaufman, Ellin Keene, Susan Zimmerman. The list goes on. I look at the books these people have published, think back to the workshops they have offered, and wonder what I could add to this body of knowledge.

I can add you.

You are the critical element, George. We must, at all times, remember that we don't teach a subject, we don't teach to a test, we teach you—specific children with specific needs. And there's not a teacher out there who doesn't know you. You come from all nations, from all ethnic groups, as a boy or a girl. You are from rich families and poor families. You've seen parents divorce, siblings leave home, and grandparents die. You

> *We must, at all times, remember that we don't teach a subject, we teach you—specific children with specific needs.*

speak many languages. You go to school in small towns and large cities. You steal our hearts, make us cry, help us laugh, and keep us up late at night wondering how we can help.

And we do wonder that, George, that and so much more. We wonder how we can convince you that a single state-mandated test is important when you've arrived at school fearful of failure or hungry or saddened by another night of loneliness. We question how to attend to individual needs when each year classes are more crowded. We ask how to grow as professionals when districts continually restrict the number of days we can attend local, state, and national conferences.

We know we can be a demanding bunch, but we believe our desires are reasonable. We want a school where children are safe, are fed, and for a few hours are free of the fear they sometimes face at home. We want a desk for every child, the right instructional material for every learner. We'd like a classroom where at least once a week, there are no interruptions from the PA system, no one leaves for basketball pictures, debate tournaments, play rehearsals, or visits to the orthodontist. We'd like a school where drive-by shootings, gangs, and drugs are not a part of our students' lives, where our greatest worry is remembering to put out the attendance slip, and where meeting with colleagues to discuss issues and practices is the rule rather than the exception. We want a classroom where getting to the computer lab doesn't mean a five-minute walk via an uncovered walkway, where bathrooms are close and clean, where the lunch period lasts more than twenty-eight minutes, where a forum for students' voices replaces the need for student graffiti. We dream of a school where the principal is more than an administrator, but is truly a principal teacher, where the public trusts us to know more about education than politicians, where parents are interested in their children's activities, where students like you have a chance at success.

Do you have children now, George? If so, then know that we want your children to pass whatever district or state requirements they have before them. We want that for all children—but we want so much more. It's when we want more that teaching becomes hard. Teaching to a single test requires little effort on our part, but such teaching gives students a diminished educational experience. Instead, we want to create lifelong learners who embrace curiosity, who enjoy analyzing ambiguity, and who view education as a journey that isn't about offering the single correct answer but instead is about asking the thoughtful question. We want students who are willing to try one more day because the effort they gave yesterday was valuable to them. And, always, we want to know what to do when kids can't read.

Never doubt that teachers constantly look to research, to practice, to experience to know how best to help students who struggle. Never doubt that we hear your cry. And never doubt that you aren't alone. Twenty years after I taught you, an eighth grader named Derek gave me this note:

> I read *Basher Five-Two*. It was a good book. It was about how this fighter pilot got shot down behind enamy lines and had to survieve by useing survieval skills like eating bugs and diging a hole he could stay in at night and he has ants all over him but could'nt move or make any noises because the enamy soltiers where evarywere. He had to have faith that his troop would come back in to get him and save him. I would like to have the same fathe that he has got because I am down behind enemy lines to. I got things that make me want to cry but if I cry I get puntched and told I'm a crybaby sissy. He has alot of curage because in the tuf times he kept on going. I keep on going alot of times to. But how long would his curage have lasted if noone had come to get him? That's what I want to no. How long does you're curage last when the troops don't come?

Because of you, George, and the journey you started me on, I was ready to help Derek. Teachers across this nation have learned from students like you so they can help others, like Derek. We must know that for so many of the Dereks of this nation, we are the troops. These children sit in our classrooms behind the enemy lines of poverty, hunger, pain, loneliness, and illiteracy. That they dress and come to school at all is a testament to their courage and belief that this day might indeed be a better day. That they look to us for guidance and perhaps survival is a tribute to each teacher of this nation.

George, I must tell you that though I am amazed at the strength and resilience of students, I am continually stunned at the professionalism, dedication, and ability of this nation's teachers. Teachers everywhere should know that as a teacher, I can stand beside them in all that they do; but as a parent, I stand in awe of all that they do. Teachers are, for so many children, Gary's mom, George's hope, and Derek's rescue. To be called "Teacher" might indeed be one of the greatest compliments one could ever receive.

To be called "Teacher" might indeed be one of the greatest compliments one could ever receive.

Dear George, as you and your classmates rushed out of class that last day of school, I stood there, telling you each to have a great summer. I didn't understand how many of you would linger in my heart for so long after you were gone. I didn't know what a privilege it was to have been a part of your childhood for those brief months. And that's what it was, George, a privilege.

Sometimes when I remember you, I am saddened at all we did not accomplish; other times, I am inspired by your courage. But much of the time, I am heartened as I remember that slow nod of your head as that shy grin would emerge. Most days, I am quite sure you found your way in this world, guided by parents who adored you, by friends who admired you, and by teachers who encouraged you. I hold fast to that note you wrote your grandmother, remembering the lesson it taught: endings are indeed beginnings.

❖ ❖ ❖

Coding of Kate's First Time Teaching "Eleven"

Kate coded the discussion she had with students by looking for initiating comments she made (questions), responses students offered, and evaluations she offered of their comments. This IRE procedure for classroom discussions is discussed at length by Cazden (1986).

Kate: Okay. That was a good story. How many of you liked the story? — *Initiating question*

[more than half the students raise their hands] — *Response*

Kate: *Evaluation* Good. Okay. Let's answer some questions over the story. Why didn't the girl want the sweater to be on her desk? Amanda? *Initiating question*

Amanda: It smelled and had germs. — *Response*

Kate: Good. Ben? *Evaluation*

Ben: It embarrassed the girl, you know, having people thinking it was hers. — *Response*

Kate: That's right. Hallie? *Evaluation*

Hallie: It wasn't hers. — *Response*

Kate: That's right; it was smelly and that embarrassed her and she didn't want anyone to think it was hers. Good. *Evaluation*

Kate: So, what did getting the sweater have to do with turning eleven? [no response] ! *Initiating question*

Kate: Um, turning eleven must be important because it's the title. So why is it important that on the day she turns eleven she has this encounter with having to put on the sweater? [pause] Laura? *Initiating question*

Laura: It was like, it was her birthday. — *Response*

Kate:	Good. It was happening on the day it was her birthday. Good. [pause]	— *Evaluating*
Kate:	So what did the author say about turning eleven on that day? William?	*Initiating*
William:	It was . . . it didn't matter.	— *Response*
Kate:	What do you mean it didn't matter?	— *Follow-up*
William:	It's because she was also all those other ages. Ten and nine and eight and so on.	*/Response*
Kate:	Okay. Very good. Do you all agree that it didn't matter that it was her birthday?	— *Evaluating* *Initiating*
	[several students nod; more do nothing]	— *Response*
Kate:	Did it make it worse that this was her birthday?	— *Same initiating question*
	[students look down at their text]	— *Response*
Kate:	Amanda, what do you think?	
Amanda:	I guess it was worse.	— *Response*
Kate:	That's right. Good. Why was it worse? Amanda?	*Evaluating* *Initiating*
Amanda:	I guess because like on your birthday, you know, it's like your birthday and nothing bad was supposed to happen.	*/Response*
Kate:	(Okay.) Also since it's her birthday, she's supposed to be more mature, but see what she's really saying is that she can't just be more mature because she's all those ages, those other ages, and those other ages sometimes come out---that's why she started crying. Okay? See, she's showing that you stay all those other ages even when you turn another year older. Okay?	*Evaluation*
Students:	[most nod]	— *Response*

Comments: Not much discussion. Just me asking questions and some kids answering.

Transcript of Kate's Think-Aloud for "Eleven"

Kate's comments to class prior to reading aloud this story:

Today I'm going to read this story aloud to you and as I do, I'm going to stop some and think aloud what I'm wondering about as I read the story. In particular, I'm going to try to visualize, you know, see what's happening in my mind. And I'm going to try to clarify any part that's confusing. And I'm going to try to predict what might happen next. Okay. Follow along.

Text	Think-Aloud
What they don't understand . . .	Well, here, right at the first sentence, I have to wonder who "they" is. This just seems to start right in. I'm not sure who the "you" or "they" is, but, since it's the first sentence, I can't have missed anything, so I'm going to presume that as I keep on reading, I'll figure this out.
And you are . . .	OK, I think I can clarify what was confusing me. The "you" is anybody, and the "they" is grown-ups. I figured that out because it says "when you wake up on your eleventh birthday," so I know the author is talking about when anybody turned eleven. The "they" therefore would be grown-ups who had forgotten what it would be like to turn eleven. I figured this out by reading on.
. . . like my little wooden dolls . . .	When I read this I can picture or visualize exactly what the author is talking about. I've got a set of Santas that fit, one inside the other. Now that I can visualize that, I can see how you could compare that to growing older, where the younger age still exists inside the older age.
. . . like pennies in a tin Band-Aid box.	This slowed me down for a minute because I've certainly seen Band-Aid boxes, but they aren't tin. This makes me wonder if maybe this is the way they used to come? Maybe this story was written a while ago.

Text	Think-Aloud
I think it belongs to Rachel . . . Mrs. Price takes the sweater and puts it right on my desk . . .	I'm going to stop here and reread that sentence. I'm rereading it because it's the first time I've seen the name Rachel and I'm a bit confused as to who Rachel is. But when I see the part that says "puts it right on my desk," then I have to connect "my" to Rachel and I see now that the narrator's name is Rachel. And Sylvia tells the teacher that the ratty sweater belongs to Rachel. Sylvia must not like Rachel.
"Of course it's yours," Mrs. Price says . . .	I need to pause here. This teacher, Mrs. Price, doesn't want to believe Rachel and that's awful. That reminds me of a time I was in a class at the university and I told the professor that I had forgotten to bring in my assignment and he didn't believe me at all. He thought I just hadn't done it and was looking for an excuse. I was both angry and embarrassed. I really understand exactly how Rachel feels.
I move the red sweater to the corner of my desk with my ruler.	Wow. When I read this part, I have to stop and ask why the moving it with a ruler. But then I get it. She hates it so much that she can't stand to even touch it. That inference is important to make. She's so upset that she doesn't want to even touch it. I bet that the teacher is going to get even angrier at her for not touching it.
. . . put that sweater on right now . . .	OK. I'm going to stop here because I had predicted this would happen. Not only does the teacher get angrier, but now she wants Rachel to put the sweater on. This part is really sad. I can just feel how awful Rachel must feel.
. . . only Mrs. Price pretends like everything's okay.	I really hate this teacher. She's so mean. She should apologize to Rachel. But she's not going to. She's just going to act like it's all okay. I wonder if Rachel's going to tell her parents and her mom call the teacher. Probably not.
. . . so tiny-tiny you have to close your eyes to see it . . .	Now that I'm finished, I want to reread that last paragraph again. I got a bit confused when it said "I wish I was one hundred and two" because the whole thing had been about being younger and now she wants to be older. [Kate rereads this final paragraph.] OK. Now I get it. She's so sad at everything that happened, that she wishes the day was gone far, far away. She wishes that she was like a helium balloon that just disappears in the sky. So, even though things sort of worked out, she's still very sad. I can understand that.

C

Bookmark Templates

Question Mark bookmarks give students a space to write questions as they read the text. As students discuss questions they have captured on their bookmarks, they can write answers on the back of the marks.

? Mark	? Mark	? Mark	? Mark
Name_____ Book_____	Name_____ Book_____	Name_____ Book_____	Name_____ Book_____
Page___	Page___	Page___	Page___
Page___	Page___	Page___	Page___
Page___	Page___	Page___	Page___
Page___	Page___	Page___	Page___
Page___	Page___	Page___	Page___
Page___	Page___	Page___	Page___

Bookmark Templates

Mark My Words bookmarks give students a space to record interesting or unusual words they encounter while reading.

Mark My Words	Mark My Words	Mark My Words	Mark My Words
Name_____ Book_____	Name_____ Book_____	Name_____ Book_____	Name_____ Book_____
Page____ Word	Page____ Word	Page____ Word	Page____ Word
Page____ Word	Page____ Word	Page____ Word	Page____ Word
Page____ Word	Page____ Word	Page____ Word	Page____ Word
Page____ Word	Page____ Word	Page____ Word	Page____ Word
Page____ Word	Page____ Word	Page____ Word	Page____ Word
Page____ Word	Page____ Word	Page____ Word	Page____ Word

Bookmark Templates

Marking Time bookmarks give students a space to record how the setting (both time and place) changes as the story progresses. This is an excellent bookmark for history texts or historical fiction.

Marking Time	Marking Time	Marking Time	Marking Time
Name_____ Book_____	Name_____ Book_____	Name_____ Book_____	Name_____ Book_____
Page ___	Page ___	Page ___	Page ___
Page ___	Page ___	Page ___	Page ___
Page ___	Page ___	Page ___	Page ___
Page ___	Page ___	Page ___	Page ___
Page ___	Page ___	Page ___	Page ___
Page ___	Page ___	Page ___	Page ___

Bookmark Templates

Mark Who? bookmarks give students a space to record information about characters.

Mark Who?	Mark Who?	Mark Who?	Mark Who?
Name_____ Book_____	Name_____ Book_____	Name_____ Book_____	Name_____ Book_____
Page___	Page___	Page___	Page___
Page___	Page___	Page___	Page___
Page___	Page___	Page___	Page___
Page___	Page___	Page___	Page___
Page___	Page___	Page___	Page___
Page___	Page___	Page___	Page___

Bookmark Templates

Mark the Bold bookmarks give students a place to mark the boldfaced terms that appear in their textbooks. They record the boldfaced term on the front of the card and then the reverse side of the card, labeled "Talk the Bold" (see p. 314) they record what they want to say about the term.

Mark the Bold	Mark the Bold	Mark the Bold	Mark the Bold
Name_____ Chapter_____	Name_____ Chapter_____	Name_____ Chapter_____	Name_____ Chapter_____
Page ___	Page ___	Page ___	Page ___
Page ___	Page ___	Page ___	Page ___
Page ___	Page ___	Page ___	Page ___
Page ___	Page ___	Page ___	Page ___
Page ___	Page ___	Page ___	Page ___
Page ___	Page ___	Page ___	Page ___

Bookmark Templates

Talk the Bold	Talk the Bold	Talk the Bold	Talk the Bold
Comments:	Comments:	Comments:	Comments:
Comments:	Comments:	Comments:	Comments:
Comments:	Comments:	Comments:	Comments:
Comments:	Comments:	Comments:	Comments:
Comments:	Comments:	Comments:	Comments:
Comments:	Comments:	Comments:	Comments:

D

Common Roots, Prefixes, and Suffixes

Root	Meaning	Examples
act	do	action, actor, react, transact, enact
aud	hear	audience, auditorium, audible, audition
cred	believe	credit, discredit, incredible, credulous
dic	speak	dictate, predict, contradict, verdict, diction
graph	write	autograph, paragraph, phonograph, photograph, telegraph
loc	place	allocate, dislocate, locate, location
man	hand	manual, manufacture, manuscript, manipulate
mot	move	demote, motion, motor, promote
ped	foot	pedal, pedestrian, pedestal
pop	people	population, popular, populace
port	carry	import, export, portable, porter, transport
sign	mark	insignia, signal, significant, signature
spec	see	inspect, respect, spectacle, spectator, suspect
tract	pull, drag	attract, detract, contract, subtract, traction, tractor
vid	see	evidence, video, provide, providence
volve	roll	evolve, involve, revolve, revolver, revolution

Prefix	Meaning	Examples
ad-	to	adapt, addict, adhere, admit
amphi-	both, around	amphibian, amphitheater
an-	not	anarchy, anesthesia, anorexia, anonymous
auto-	self	automobile, automatic, autograph, autobiography
co-	together	coauthor, cognate, coincide, cooperate, coordinate
de-	opposite	deactivate, deform, degrade, deplete, descend
dis-	opposite	disagree, disarm, discontinue, disgust, dishonest
for-	not	forbid, forget, forego
il-	not	illegal, illegible, illegitimate, illiterate, illogical
im-	into	immediate, immerse, immigrate, implant, import
im-	not	imbalance, immaculate, immature, immobilize, impossible
in-	not	inaccurate, inactive, inadvertent, incognito, indecisive
ir-	not	irregular, irreconcilable, irredeemable, irresponsible
mal-	bad	maladjusted, malaise, malevolent, malfunction, malice
pro-	before	prognosis, progeny, program, prologue, prophet
pro-	forward	proceed, produce, proficient, progress, project
re-	again	redo, rewrite, reappear, repaint, relive
re-	back	recall, recede, reflect, repay, retract
sub-	under	subcontract, subject, submarine, submerge, subordinate, subterranean
trans-	across	transatlantic, transcend, transcribe, transfer, translate
un-	not	unable, uncomfortable, uncertain, unhappy

Suffix	Meaning	Examples
-ade	action or process	blockade, escapade, parade
-age	action or process	marriage, pilgrimage, voyage
-ant	one who	assistant, immigrant, merchant, servant
-cle	small	corpuscle, cubicle, particle
-dom	state or quality of	boredom, freedom, martyrdom, wisdom
-ent	one who	resident, regent, superintendent
-ful	full of	careful, fearful, joyful, thoughtful
-ic	relating to	comic, historic, poetic, public
-less	without	ageless, careless, thoughtless, tireless
-let	small	islet, leaflet, owlet, rivulet, starlet
-ly	resembling	fatherly, motherly, scholarly
-ly	every	daily, weekly, monthly, yearly
-ment	action or process	development, embezzlement, government
-ment	action or quality of	amusement, amazement, predicament
-ment	product or thing	fragment, instrument, ornament
-or	one who	actor, auditor, doctor, donor

More Roots

Root	Meaning	Examples
aero	air	aerobics, aerodynamics, aeronautics, aerate
agr	field	agriculture, agrarian, agronomy
alt	high	altitude, altimeter, alto
alter	other	alternate, alternative, altercation
ambul	walk, go	ambulance, amble, ambulatory, preamble
amo, ami	love	amiable, amorous, amity
ang	bend	angle, angular, rectangle, triangle
anim	life, spirit	animate, animosity, animal
ann, enn	year	annual, anniversary, annuity, biennial
anthro	man	anthropology, anthropoid, misanthrope, philanthropist
apt, ept	suitable	adept, apt, aptitude, inept
ast	star	astronaut, astronomy, disaster, asterisk
belli	war	bellicose, belligerent, rebellion
biblio	book	Bible, bibliography, bibliophile
bio	life	biology, biography, biopsy
brev	shorten	abbreviate, abbreviation, brevity
cad, cas	fall	cadaver, cadence, cascade, decadence
cam	field	camp, campus, campaign, encamp
cap	head	cap, captain, capital, decapitate
cardi	heart	cardiac, cardiology
cede, ceed	go, yield	concede, exceed, proceed, succeed
ceive, cept	take, receive	accept, conception, exception, receive, reception
centr	center	central, eccentric, egocentric
cert	sure	ascertain, certain, certify, certificate
chron	time	chronic, chronicle, chronological, synchronize

Root	Meaning	Examples
cip	take, receive	incipient, participate, recipe, recipient
claim, clam	shout	acclaim, clamor, exclaim, proclaim
clar	clear	clarify, clarity, declaration, declare
cline	lean	decline, inclination, incline, recline
clud	shut	conclude, exclude, include, preclude, seclude
cogn	know	cognate, cognition, incognito, recognize
cord	heart	accord, concord, cordial, discord
cosm	universe	cosmonaut, cosmos, cosmopolitan, microcosm
crat	rule	aristocrat, autocratic, bureaucracy, democrat
cred	believe	credit, credulous, discredit, incredible
cur	care	curable, cure, manicure, pedicure
cur	run	concur, current, excursion, occur, recur
cycle	circle	cycle, cyclone, bicycle, recycle
dem	people	democrat, demagogy, epidemic
div	divide, part	divide, dividend, division, divorce
doc	teach	docile, doctor, doctrine, document
don	give	donate, donation, donor, predominate
duc	lead, carry	aquaduct, conduct, deduct, duct, educate, induct
fac	do, make	benefactor, factory, facsimile, manufacture
fer	bear, carry	conifer, ferry, infer, refer, transfer
fic	make	efficient, proficient, sufficient
fig	form	configuration, disfigure, effigy, figment, figure
firm	tightly fixed	affirm, confirm, firmly, firmament, reaffirm
flect	bend	deflect, inflection, reflection
form	shape	deform, form, reform, transformation, uniformity
fug	flee	centrifuge, fugitive, refuge, refugee
gen	birth	generate, generation, geneology
grad	step	grade, gradual, graduation
gram	letter	diagram, epigram, grammar, monogram
grat	pleasing	congratulations, grateful, gratitude, ungrateful
greg	gather	aggregate, congregation, gregarious, segregation

Root	Meaning	Examples
hab, hib	hold	exhibit, habit, habitat, habitual, prohibit
hosp, host	host	hospice, hospital, hospitality, hostess, host
hydr	water	dehydrate, hydrant, hydrogen
imag	like, likeness	image, imagine, imaginary, imagery, imagination
init	beginning	initial, initiate, initiative
junct	join	adjunct, conjunction, injunction, juncture
jud, jur, jus	law	judge, jury, justice
lab	work	collaborate, elaborate, labor, laboratory
lat	carry	collate, relate, translate
log	word	apology, dialogue, eulogy, monologue, prologue
luc, lum	light	elucidate, lucid, translucent, illuminate, luminescent
lust	shine	illustrate, illustrious, luster
mar	sea	marine, maritime, mariner, submarine
mem	mindful of	commemorate, memory, memorial, remember
merge, mers	dip	emerge, merge, merger, submerge, immerse
meter	measure	barometer, centimeter, diameter, thermometer
migr	move	emigrate, immigrate, immigrant, migrate
mim	same	mime, mimic, mimeograph, pantomime
min	small	mini, minimize, minor, minute
miss, mit	send	dismiss, missile, mission, remit, submit
mob	move	automobile, mobile, mobilize, mobility
mort	death	immortal, mortal, mortician
mut	change	commute, immutable, mutual, mutuation
narr	tell	narrate, narrative, narrator
neo	new	neonatal, neophyte, neoclassic
not	mark	denote, notable, notation, notice
noun, nun	declare, state	announce, denounce, enunciate, pronounce
nov	new	innovate, nova, novel, novelty, novice
onym	name	antonym, homonym, pseudonym, synonymn
opt	eye	optic, optician, optical, optometrist
opt	best	optimal, optimist, optimize, optimum

Root	Meaning	Examples
ord	row, lined up	extraordinary, order, ordinary, ordinal, ordinance
path	feeling	antipathy, empathy, pathology, sympathy
pel	drive	compel, expel, propel, repel
pend	hang	append, appendix, pendulum, suspend
phon	sound	microphone, phonics, phonograph, symphony
phys	nature	physical, physician, physique
plex, plic	fold	complex, duplex, perplex, complicate, duplicate, implicate
plur	more	plural, pluralism, plurality, pluralistic
pod	foot	podiatrist, podium, tripod
poli	city	cosmopolitan, metropolis, police, political
pon, pos	place	exponent, opponent, postpone, proponent, compose, depose, deposit, position
pug	fight	impugn, pugnacious, pugilist, repugnant
pul	urge	compulsion, compulsory, expulsion, repulse
quer, ques, quir	ask	query, inquiry, inquest, quest, question, request
ras	scrape	abrasive, erase, rasp, razor
rect	straight	correct, direct, direction, director, erect, rectify
reg	guide	regal, regent, regulate, regulatory
rid	laugh	deride, derisive, ridicule, ridiculous
rupt	break	abrupt, bankrupt, erupt, interrupt, rupture
san	health	insane, insanity, sane, sanitary, sanitarium
scend	climb	ascend, descend, descendent, transcend
sci	know	conscience, conscious, omniscient, science
scop	see	microscope, periscope, scope, stethoscope, telescope
scribe, script	write	describe, inscribe, prescribe, scribe, descript, script, transcript
sect	cut	dissect, intersect, sect, section
sed	settle	sedate, sedative, sedentary, sediment
sens, sent	feel	sensation, sense, sensitive, sensible, sensory, assent, consent, dissent, sentimental
serv	save	conserve, preserve, reserve, reservoir

Root	Meaning	Examples
sim	like	similar, simile, simulate, simultaneous
sist	stand	assist, consist, resist, subsist
sol	alone	desolate, solitary, soliloquy, solo
solve	loosen	absolve, dissolve, resolve, solve, solvent
soph	wise	philosopher, sophisticated, sophomore
spir	breathe	conspire, conspirator, inspire, perspire, respiration
sta	stand	stagnate, station, stationary, statue, status
strict	make tight	constrict, restrict, strict
struct	build	construct, destruct, destruction, instruct, instruction, structure
sum	highest	sum, summary, summit, summons
surg, surr	rise	insurgent, resurgent, surge, insurrection, resurrect
tact	touch	contact, intact, tact, tactile
tain	hold	attain, contain, detain, retain
ten	stretch	tendency, tense, tension, tent
term	end	determine, exterminate, term, terminal, terminate
tex	weave	context, text, textile, texture
the	god	atheism, monotheism, polytheism, theology
therm	heat	thermal, thermometer, thermos
tort	twist	contort, retort, tort, torture
trib	give	attribute, contribute, tribute
trud, trus	push	intrude, intruder, protrude, abstruse, intrusive
turb	confusion	disturb, perturb, turbulent
urb	city	urban, suburb, suburban
vac	empty	evacuate, vacate, vacant, vacation, vacuum
var	different	invariable, variant, variety, vary
ven	come	advent, convent, convene, convention, invent, venue
ver	truth	aver, veracity, verdict, verify
voc	voice	advocate, convocation, evocation, vocal
vol	will	benevolent, malevolent, volition, voluntary, volunteer
vor	eat	carnivorous, herbivore, omnivore, voracious

Templates

Probable Passage

Title of Selection _____

Characters	Setting	Problem

Gist Statement...

_____

_____

_____

_____

Outcomes	Unknown Words	To discover...
		1. 2. 3.

Name _____ Date _____

Words Across Contexts

1. What would the word _____ mean to

    a.

    b.

    c.

2. What would the word _____ mean to

    a.

    b.

    c.

3. What would the word _____ mean to

    a.

    b.

    c.

4. What would the word _____ mean to

    a.

    b.

    c.

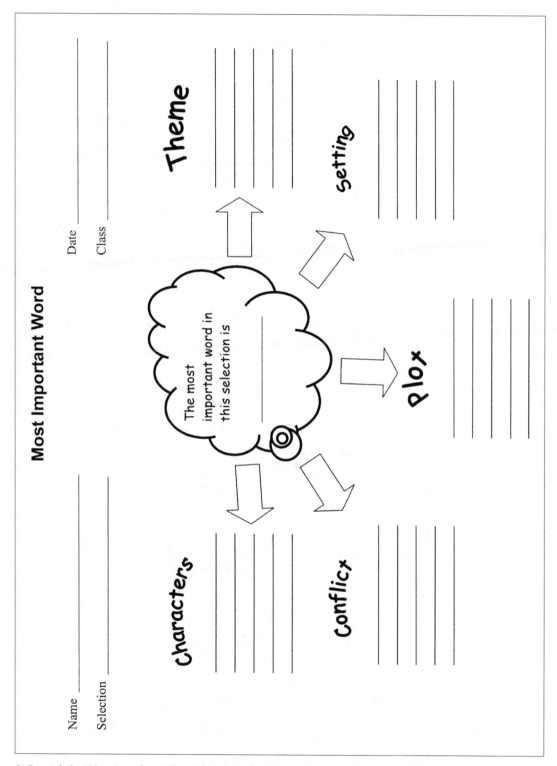

Most Important Word

Name _____

Selection _____

Date _____

Class _____

Theme

setting

Plot

Conflict

characters

The most important word in this selection is _____

Word Scrolls

Name _____

What it is.....

What it isn't.....

Examples

Practice _____

_____

G

Fry and Dolch Word Lists

Fry's Instant Words

The following words are the most common words in the English language (Fry, Kress, and Fountoukidis, 1993). Fry reminds us that "the first twenty-five words make up about a third of all printed material," while the first hundred "make up about half of all written material" and the first three hundred "make up about 65 percent of all written material" (p. 23).

FIRST HUNDRED

the	at	there	some	my
of	be	use	her	than
and	this	an	would	first
a	have	each	make	water
to	from	which	like	been
in	or	she	him	call
is	one	do	into	who
you	had	how	time	oil
that	by	their	has	its
it	word	if	look	now
he	but	will	two	find
was	not	up	more	long
for	what	other	write	down
on	all	about	go	day
are	were	out	see	did
as	we	many	number	get
with	when	then	no	come
his	your	them	way	made
they	can	these	could	may
I	said	so	people	part

SECOND HUNDRED

over	name	boy	such	change
new	good	follow	because	off
sound	sentence	came	turn	play
take	man	went	here	spell
only	think	show	why	air
little	say	also	ask	away
work	great	around	went	animal
know	where	form	men	house
place	help	three	read	point
year	through	small	need	page
live	much	set	land	letter
me	before	put	different	mother
back	line	end	home	answer
give	right	does	us	found
most	too	another	move	study
very	mean	well	try	still
after	old	large	kind	learn
thing	any	must	hand	should
our	same	big	picture	America
just	tell	even	again	world

THIRD HUNDRED

high	never	along	together	sea
every	start	might	got	began
near	city	close	group	grow
add	earth	something	often	took
food	eye	seem	run	river
between	light	next	important	four
own	thought	hard	until	carry
below	head	open	children	state
country	under	example	side	once
plant	story	begin	feet	book
last	saw	life	car	hear
school	left	always	mile	stop
father	don't	those	night	without
keep	few	both	walk	second
tree	while	paper	white	later

THIRD HUNDRED *continued*

miss	watch	let	cut	song
idea	far	above	young	being
enough	Indian	girl	talk	leave
eat	really	sometimes	soon	family
face	almost	mountain	list	it's

FOURTH HUNDRED

body	usually	hours	five	cold
music	didn't	black	step	cried
color	friends	products	morning	plan
stand	easy	happened	passed	notice
sun	heard	whole	vowel	south
questions	order	measure	true	sing
fish	red	remember	hundred	war
area	door	early	against	ground
mark	sure	waves	pattern	fall
dog	become	reached	numeral	king
horse	top	listen	table	town
birds	ship	wind	north	I'll
problem	across	rock	slowly	unit
complete	today	space	money	figure
room	during	covered	map	certain
knew	short	fast	farm	field
since	better	several	pulled	travel
ever	best	hold	draw	wood
piece	however	himself	voice	fire
told	low	toward	seen	upon

FIFTH HUNDRED

done	fly	correct	minutes	machine
English	gave	oh	strong	fact
road	box	quickly	verb	base
halt	class	person	stars	inches
surface	finally	became	front	street
ten	wait	shown	feel	decided

contain	stay	round	deep	noun
course	green	boat	thousands	power
ran	known	game	yes	cannot
produce	island	rule	pair	able
building	week	brought	circle	six
ocean	less	understand	yet	size
force	clear	warm	government	dark
note	equation	common	filled	ball
nothing	ago	bring	heat	material
rest	stood	explain	full	special
carefully	plane	dry	check	heavy
scientists	system	though	object	fine
inside	behind	language	am	include
wheels	hot	shape	among	built

SIXTH HUNDRED

can't	region	window	arms	west
matter	return	difference	brother	lay
square	believe	distance	race	weather
syllables	dance	heart	present	root
perhaps	members	sit	beautiful	instruments
bill	picked	sum	store	meet
felt	simple	summer	job	third
suddenly	cells	wall	edge	months
test	paint	forest	past	paragraph
direction	mind	probably	sign	raised
center	love	legs	record	represent
farmers	cause	sat	finished	soft
ready	rain	main	discovered	whether
anything	exercise	winter	wild	clothes
divided	eggs	wide	happy	flowers
general	train	written	beside	shall
energy	blue	length	gone	teacher
subject	wish	reason	sky	held
Europe	drop	kept	glass	describe
moon	developed	interest	million	drive

SEVENTH HUNDRED

cross	buy	temperature	possible	fraction
speak	century	bright	gold	Africa
solve	outside	lead	milk	killed
appear	everything	everyone	quiet	melody
metal	tall	method	natural	bottom
son	already	section	lot	trip
either	instead	lake	stone	hole
ice	phrase	consonant	act	poor
sleep	soil	within	build	let's
village	bed	dictionary	middle	fight
factors	copy	hair	speed	surprise
result	free	age	count	French
jumped	hope	amount	cat	died
snow	spring	scale	someone	beat
ride	case	pounds	sail	exactly
care	laughed	although	rolled	remain
floor	nation	per	bear	dress
hill	quite	broken	wonder	iron
pushed	type	moment	smiled	couldn't
baby	themselves	tiny	angle	fingers

EIGHTH HUNDRED

row	joined	cool	single	statement
least	foot	cloud	touch	stick
catch	law	lost	information	party
climbed	ears	sent	express	seeds
wrote	grass	symbols	mouth	suppose
shouted	you're	wear	yard	woman
continued	grew	bad	equal	coast
itself	skin	save	decimal	bank
else	valley	experiment	yourself	period
plains	cents	engine	control	wire
gas	key	alone	practice	choose
England	president	drawing	report	clean
burning	brown	east	straight	visit
design	trouble	pay	rise	bit

EIGHTH HUNDRED *continued*

whose	fell	serve	maybe	flow
received	team	child	business	lady
garden	God	desert	separate	students
please	captain	increase	break	human
strange	direct	history	uncle	art
caught	ring	cost	hunting	feelings

NINTH HUNDRED

supply	fit	sense	position	meat
corner	addition	string	entered	lifted
electric	belong	blow	fruit	process
insects	safe	famous	tied	army
crops	soldiers	value	rich	hat
tone	guess	wing	dollars	property
hit	silent	movement	send	particular
sand	trade	pole	sight	swim
doctor	rather	exciting	chief	terms
provide	compare	branches	Japanese	current
thus	crowd	thick	stream	park
won't	poem	blood	plants	sell
cook	enjoy	lie	rhythm	shoulder
bones	elements	spot	eight	industry
tail	indicate	bell	science	wash
board	except	fun	major	block
modern	expect	loud	observe	spread
compound	flat	consider	tube	cattle
mine	seven	suggested	necessary	wife
wasn't	interesting	thin	weight	sharp

TENTH HUNDRED

company	factories	truck	chance	France
radio	settled	fair	born	repeated
we'll	yellow	printed	level	column
action	isn't	wouldn't	triangle	western
capital	southern	ahead	molecules	church

sister	shoes	stretched	difficult	corn
oxygen	actually	experience	match	substances
plural	nose	rose	win	smell
various	afraid	allow	doesn't	tools
agreed	dead	fear	steel	conditions
opposite	sugar	workers	total	cows
wrong	adjective	Washington	deal	track
chart	fig	Greek	determine	arrived
prepared	office	women	evening	located
pretty	huge	bought	nor	sir
solution	gun	led	rope	seat
fresh	similar	march	cotton	division
shop	death	northern	apple	effect
suffix	score	create	details	underline
especially	forward	British	entire	view

Dolch Basic Sight Vocabulary

a	clean	green	many	run	together
about	cold	grow	may	said	too
after	come	had	me	saw	try
again	could	has	much	say	two
all	cut	have	must	see	under
always	did	he	my	seven	up
am	do	help	myself	shall	upon
an	does	her	never	she	us
and	done	here	new	show	use
any	don't	him	no	sing	very
are	down	his	not	sit	walk
around	draw	hold	now	six	want
as	drink	hot	of	sleep	warm
ask	eat	how	off	small	was
at	eight	hurt	old	so	wash
ate	every	I	on	some	we
away	fall	if	once	soon	well
be	far	in	one	start	went
because	fast	into	only	stop	were
been	find	is	open	take	what
before	first	it	or	tell	when
best	five	its	our	ten	where
better	fly	jump	out	thank	which
big	for	just	over	that	white
black	found	keep	own	the	who
blue	four	kind	pick	their	why
both	from	know	play	them	will
bring	full	laugh	please	then	wish
brown	funny	let	pretty	there	with
but	gave	light	pull	these	work
buy	get	like	put	they	would
by	give	little	ran	think	write
call	go	live	read	this	yellow
came	goes	long	red	those	yes
can	going	look	ride	three	you
carry	good	made	right	to	your
	got	make	round	today	

Common Phonics Generalizations

Clymer (1963) looked at phonics rules to determine how often the rule stood and how often there was an exception to the rule. Most of the rules had exceptions. What follows are the rules Clymer examined, an example of the rule, and when needed, an exception to the rule.

Consonant Generalizations	Example	Exception
1. When two of the same consonants appear side by side in a word, only one is heard.	berry	suggest
2. When the letter *c* is followed by the letter *o* or *a*, the *c* makes the /k/ sound.	cat	
3. The digraph *ch* is usually pronounced /ch/ as in *chair.*	each	chef
4. When the letters *c* and *h* appear next to each other in a word, they stand for only one sound.	rich	
5. The letter *g* often has a sound similar to that of the letter *j* in *jump* when it comes before the letter *i* or *e*.	ginger	give
6. When the letter *c* is followed by the letter *e* or *i*, the /s/ sound is likely to be heard.	cent	ocean
7. When a word ends in the letters *ck*, it has the /k/ sound as in *book.*	sick	
8. When the letters *ght* appear together in a word, the letters *gh* are silent.	fight	
9. When a word begins with the letters *kn*, the letter *k* is silent.	know	
10. When a word begins with the letters *wr*, the letter *w* is silent.	write	

Vowel Generalizations	Example	Exception
11. If there is one vowel letter in an accented syllable, it has a short sound.	city	lady
12. When a word has only one vowel letter, the vowel is likely to be short.	lid	mind
13. When two vowels appear together in a word, the long sound of the first one is heard and the second is usually silent.	seat	chief
14. When a vowel is in the middle of a one-syllable word, the vowel is short.	best	gold
15. The letter *r* gives the preceding vowel a sound that is neither long nor short.	torn	fire
16. When there are two vowels, one of which is final *e*, the first vowel is long and the *e* is silent.	hope	come
17. The first vowel is usually long and the second silent in the digraphs *ai, ea, oa,* and *ui.*	nail bead boat suit	said head board build
18. When words end with silent *e*, the preceding *a* or *i* is long.	bake	have
19. When the letter *y* is the final letter in a word, it usually has a vowel sound.	dry	tray
20. When the letter *y* is used as a vowel in words, it sometimes has the sound of long *i*.	fly	funny
21. When *y* or *ey* appears in the last syllable that is not accented, the long *e* is heard.	monkey	

Vowel Generalizations (*continued*)	Example	Exception
22. The letter *a* has the same sound as /ô/ when followed by *l, w,* and *u*.	fall	canal
23. The letter *w* is sometimes a vowel and follows the vowel digraph rule.	snow	few
24. When there is one *e* in a word that ends in a consonant, the *e* usually has a short sound.	pet	flew
25. In many two- and three-syllable words, the final *e* lengthens the vowel in the last syllable.	invite	gasoline
26. Words having double *e* usually have the long *e* sound.	feet	been
27. The letters *ow* stand for the long o sound.	own	town
28. When the letter *a* follows the letter *w* in a word it usually has the sound that *a* stands for as in *was*.	watch	swam
29. In the vowel spelling *ie*, the letter *i* is silent and the letter *e* has the long vowel sound.	field	friend
30. In *ay* the *y* is silent and gives *a* its long sound.	play	bayou
31. If the only vowel letter is at the end of the word, the letter usually stands for a long sound.	me	do
32. When the letter *e* is followed by the letter *w* the sound is the same as represented by *oo* /o͞o/.	blew	sew
33. When the letter *a* is followed by the letter *r* and final *e*, we expect to hear the sound heard in *care*.	dare	are
34. When the letter *i* is followed by the letters *gh*, the letter *i* usually stands for its long sound and the *gh* is silent.	high	neighbor

Syllable Generalizations	Example	Exception
35. If the first vowel sound in a word is followed by two consonants, the first syllable usually ends with the first of the two consonants.	bullet	singer
36. If the first vowel sound in a word is followed by a single consonant, that consonant usually begins the second syllable.	over	oven
37. In a word of more than one syllable, the letter *v* usually goes with the preceding vowel to form a syllable.	cover	clover
38. If the last syllable of a word ends in *le*, the consonant preceding the *le* usually begins the last syllable.	tumble	buckle
39. When the first vowel in a word is followed by *th, ch, wh*, or *sh*, these consonant teams are not broken when the word is divided into syllables, and they may go with either the first or second syllable.	dishes	
40. In most two-syllable words, the first syllable is accented.	famous	polite
41. When the last syllable is the sound /r/, it is unaccented.	butter	appear
42. In most two-syllable words that end in a consonant followed by *y*, the first syllable is accented and the last is unaccented.	baby	supply
43. If *a, in, re, ex, de*, or *be* is the first syllable in a word, it is usually unaccented.	above	insect
44. When *tion* is the final syllable in a word, it is unaccented.	nation	
45. When *ture* is the final syllable in a word, it is unaccented.	picture	

175 Most Common Syllables in the 5,000 Most Frequent English Words

1. ing	26. ti	51. po	76. tle	101. fac	126. li
2. er	27. ri	52. sion	77. day	102. fer	127. lo
3. a	28. be	53. vi	78. ny	103. gen	128. men
4. ly	29. per	54. el	79. pen	104. ic	129. min
5. ed	30. to	55. est	80. pre	105. land	130. mon
6. i	31. pro	56. la	81. tive	106. light	131. op
7. es	32. ac	57. lar	82. car	107. ob	132. out
8. re	33. ad	58. pa	83. ci	108. of	133. rec
9. tion	34. ar	59. ture	84. mo	109. pos	134. ro
10. in	35. ers	60. for	85. an	110. tain	135. sen
11. e	36. ment	61. is	86. aus	111. den	136. side
12. con	37. or	62. mer	87. pi	112. ings	137. tal
13. y	38. tions	63. pe	88. se	113. mag	138. tic
14. ter	39. ble	64. ra	89. ten	114. ments	139. ties
15. ex	40. der	65. so	90. tor	115. set	140. ward
16. al	41. ma	66. ta	91. ver	116. some	141. age
17. de	42. na	67. as	92. ber	117. sub	142. ba
18. com	43. si	68. col	93. can	118. sur	143. but
19. o	44. un	69. fi	94. dy	119. ters	144. cit
20. di	45. at	70. ful	95. et	120. tu	145. cle
21. en	46. dis	71. get	96. it	121. af	146. co
22. an	47. ca	72. low	97. mu	122. au	147. cov
23. ty	48. cal	73. ni	98. no	123. cy	148. da
24. ry	49. man	74. par	99. ple	124. fa	149. dif
25. u	50. ap	75. son	100. cu	125. im	150. ence

151. ern
152. eve
153. hap
154. ies
155. ket
156. lec
157. main
158. mar
159. mis
160. my
161. nal
162. ness
163. ning
164. n't
165. nu
166. oc
167. pres
168. sup
169. te
170. ted
171. tem
172. tin
173. tri
174. tro
175. up

Source:. For a longer list of common syllables, see Blevins, W. (2001). *Teaching Phonics and Word Study in the Intermediate Grades.* New York: Scholastic, p. 196.

J

Interesting Sorts

Directions: For each sort, put one word on an index card. Do not keep words separated as they are here. Give students the words and ask them to sort to figure out what the rule is that would help them understand whatever is the target of that sort. As students figure out rules for sorts, they should be able to state that rule. Have them look through books for other words that would either confirm the rule they've generated or be an exception to the rule. You can also do this with the whole class by writing each word on a transparency, cutting out the words, and sorting on the overhead projector. Finally, put the rules on large pieces of chart paper with the words underneath. As students find additional words that fit the rule or don't, they should add those words to the chart paper.

For Plurals of Words Ending in *y*

babies	boys
ponies	toys
carries	monkeys
funnies	keys
tummies	enjoys
lobbies	days
flies	plays

Sort Rule: When the word ends in a *y* that is immediately preceded by a consonant, change the *y* to *i* and add *es*. When it ends in a *y* that is immediately preceded by a vowel, just add *s*.

For Adding -ing

running	riding	boating
hopping	hiding	floating
sitting	biking	sweeping
batting	faking	fighting
swapping	poking	painting
tanning	making	doing
tapping	smiling	treating
bragging	shaving	docking

Sort Rule: When the word ends in the VC pattern and the vowel makes its short sound, double the final consonant before adding -ing. This keeps the vowel sound short. If the word ends in a VCe pattern, drop the *e* and add -ing. This preserves the VCV pattern that makes the vowel long. If the word ends in a VVC pattern or just a V, just add *-ing*.

For Choosing Between *ch* and *tch* at the End of a Word

				exceptions
each	fetch	bench	couch	
bleach	witch	wench	pouch	rich
coach	patch	clench	vouch	which
peach	pitch	trench	crouch	such
screech	sketch	French	grouch	much
speech	hitch	drench	slouch	
roach	switch	quench		

Sort Rule: If the vowel sound in the word is long, as in *each,* is followed by the letter *n* as in *bench,* or makes the sound as in *cow,* just add *ch.* If the vowel sound is short but not followed by the letter *n,* add *tch.* Exceptions to this include *rich, which, such, much.*

For Adding -tion Versus -sion

selection	profession
extinction	procession
subtraction	discussion
prediction	succession
traction	depression
contraction	repression

Sort Rule: If the base word ends in *ct*, add *-ion*. If the base word ends in *ss*, add *-ion*.

creation   repulsion
imitation   convulsion
congratulation   expulsion
reproduction
introduction
seduction
deduction

Sort Rule: If the base word ends in *te*, drop the *e* and add *-ion*. If the base word ends in *se*, drop the *e* and add *-ion*. If the base word ends in *ce*, drop the *e*, change the *c* to *t* and add *-ion*.

transmission   omission
permission   emission
commission

Sort Rule: If the base word ends in Vt, change the *t* to *s* and add *-sion*.

explosion   inclusion
conclusion   persuasion
erosion

Sort Rule: If the base word ends in *de*, drop the *e* and change the *d* to *s*, then add *-ion*.

For Adding *-able* Versus *-ible*

dependable	horrible	usable	changeable	amicable
breakable	visible	desirable	manageable	applicable
agreeable	terrible	excusable	noticeable	despicable
profitable	legible	lovable	peaceable	impeccable
remarkable	possible	comparable	serviceable	
doable	feasible	trainable		

Sort Rule: If the base word can stand alone, add *-able*. If the base word cannot stand alone, add *-ible*. If the base word can stand alone but ends in *e*, drop the *e* and then add *-able*. If the base word ends in *ce* or *ge* and the *c* or the *g* makes its soft sound, then add *-able*. If the *c* makes its hard sound, add *-able*.

Easily Confused Words

Not quite homophones, these words sound so much alike that students often confuse them. When a student uses one of these words incorrectly, spend some time asking the student what word he thought he was using to determine if he knows the correct word or not.

accede (v.)—to agree
exceed (v.)—to go beyond

accent (n.)—pronunciation
ascent (n.)—climb
assent (v., n.)—agree

accept (v.)—agree to, believe
except (prep.)—not including

access (n.)—way in, admission
excess (n., adj.)—extra, more than what's needed

adapt (v.)—to become adjusted to
adept (adj.)—skillful
adopt (v.)—to accept

adverse (adj.)—unfavorable
averse (adj.)—reluctant

affect (v.)—to influence
affect (n.)—feeling
effect (n.)—result of a cause
effect (v.)—to make happen

alley (n.)—narrow street
ally (n.)—supporter

all ready (adj.)—completely ready
already (adv.)—even now or by this time

all together (pron., adj.)—everyone in one place
altogether (adv.)—total, completely

anecdote (n.)—a short story
antidote (n.)—cure

angel (n.)—heavenly body
angle (n.)—space between where two rays intersect at a point; slant

annul (v.)—to cancel
annual (adj.)—yearly

ante—prefix meaning before
anti—prefix meaning against

any way (n.)—however you want
anyway (adv.)—nonetheless

area (n.)—region, surface
aria (n.)—melody

biannual (adj.)—twice per year
biennial (adj.)—every other year

bizarre (adj.)—strange
bazaar (n.)—market

breadth (n.)—width
breath (n.)—amount of air taken in
breathe (v.)—to inhale and exhale

calendar (n.)—almanac, a chart of days and months
colander (n.)—a strainer

casual (adj.)—informal
causal (adj.)—relating to cause

cease (v.)—to stop
seize (v.)—to grab

click (n.)—snap, short sound
clique (n.)—small group

collision (n.)—accident
collusion (n.)—conspiracy

coma (n.)—unconsciousness
comma (n.)—a punctuation mark

command (n., v.)—an order, to order
commend (v.)—to praise, to entrust

comprehensible (adj.)—understandable
comprehensive (adj.)—extensive

confidant (n.)—best friend, one you turn to for advice
confident (adj.)—certain

confidentially (adv.)—privately
confidently (adv.)—certainly

conscience (n.)—sense of right and wrong
conscious (adj.)—mindful, aware

costume (n.)—attire
custom (n.)—usual practice of habit

credible (adj.)—believable
creditable (adj.)—worthy

deceased (adj.)—dead
diseased (adj.)—ill

decent (adj.)—proper
descent (n.)—way down
dissent (n., v.)—disagreement, to disagree

deference (n.)—high esteem
difference (n.)—not similar

depraved (adj.)—immoral
deprived (adj.)—disadvantaged

desert (n., v.)—arid land, to leave
dessert (n.)—course served at the end of a meal

detract (v.)—to take away from
distract (v.)—sidetrack

device (n.)—machine, gadgit
devise (v.)—to plan

disapprove (v.)—to condemn
disprove (v.)—refute

disassemble (v.)—to take apart
dissemble (v.)—to evade

disburse (v.)—to pay out
disperse (v.)—disband, scatter

disinterested (adj.)—impartial
uninterested (adj.)—indifferent

elicit (v.)—to draw out
illicit (adj.)—unlawful

elusive (adj.)—hard to pin down
illusive (adj.)—deceptive

emerge (v.)—appear
immerge (v.)—plunge into

emigrate (v.)—to leave your country
immigrate (v.)—to move to another country

eminent (adj.)—well known
imminent (adj.)—about to happen

envelop (v.)—to enclose
envelope (n.)—a wrapper for a letter

expand (v.)—get bigger
expend (v.)—to use, to spend

farther (adj.)—beyond
further (adj.)—additional, more

finale (n.)—the end
finally (adj.)—at the end

fiscal (adj.)—economic
physical (adj.)—relating to the body

formally (adv.)—officially
formerly (adv.)—previously

human (adj.)—relating to mankind
humane (adv.)—caring

imitate (v.)—to copy
intimate (v.)—personal; familiar

incredible (adj.)—hard to believe

incredulous (adj.)—doubtful, skeptical

indigenous (adj.)—native

indigent (adj.)—poor

indignant (adj.)—angry

ingenious (adj.)—clever

ingenuous (adj.)—honest

later (adj.)—to be very late

latter (adj.)—second in a series of two

lay (v.)—to set something down

lie (v.)—to recline

loose (adj.)—not tight

lose (v.)—not win, misplace

message (n.)—communication

massage (v.)—rub

moral (adj.)—ethical

morale (n.)—confidence

morality (n.)—virtue

mortality (n.)—being mortal

of (prep.)—having to do with; indicating possession

off (adv.)—not on

official (adj., n.)—approved; person with authority

officious (adj.)—offering services where they are neither wanted nor needed

oral (adj.)—verbal

aural (adj.)—having to do with listening, hearing

pasture (n.)—grassy field

pastor (n.)—preacher

perpetrate (v.)—to be guilty of; to commit

perpetuate (v.)—to make perpetual

persecute (v.)—to harass

prosecute (n.)—to take legal action against

personal (adj.)—private

personnel (n.)—a body of people, usually employed in some organization

peruse (v.)—to read thoroughly

pursue (v.)—to chase

picture (n.)—drawing

pitcher (n.)—container for liquid; baseball player

precede (v.)—to come first

proceed (v.)—continue

preposition (n.)—a part of speech

proposition (n.)—a proposal or suggestion

pretend (v.)—to make up

portend (v.)—foreshadow

quiet (adj.)—calm

quite (adv.)—very

recent (adj.)—current

resent (v.)—dislike

than (conj.)—used in comparison

then (adv.)—next

through (prep.)—finished, during

thorough (adj.)—methodical, complete

use (v.)—employ something

used (adj.)—secondhand

Source for many of these words: Fry, E. B., Kress, J., and Fountoukidis, D. L. (1993). *The Reading Teacher's Book of Lists,* 3rd edition. Englewood Cliffs, NJ: Prentice Hall.

Common Spelling Rules

1. Rules for Adding Prefixes

  a. When a prefix is added to a word, do not drop a letter from either the prefix or the base word (*dis-* + *approve* = *disapprove; ir-* + *regular* = *irregular, mis-* + *spell* = *misspell, il-* + *legal* = *illegal*).

  b. The exception to the prefix rule is for *ad-, com-,* and *in-*, which can be "absorbed" by the base word so that the last letter in the prefix changes to match the beginning consonant of the base word. This is done to make the word easier to say. For example, instead of *inlegal* (meaning not legal), we write *illegal*. Instead of *adsemble* (meaning toward moving together), we write *assemble*. Instead of *conmit* (meaning to send together), we write *commit*. Other examples of words with absorbed prefixes include *allot, affair, arrange, acclaim, colleague, correlate, irresponsible, immature, irrational, immortal.*

2. Rules for Plurals

NOUNS

  a. For most nouns, add *s* (*boy/boys, table/tables*).
  b. For nouns ending in *s, x, z, ch,* or *sh,* add *es* (*glasses, foxes, arches, wishes*).
  c. For nouns ending in *y* when the *y* is preceded by a vowel, add *s* (*turkeys, attorneys*).
  d. For nouns ending in *y* when the *y* is preceded by a consonant, change the *y* to *i* and then add *es* (*cities, spies*).
  e. For some nouns ending in *f* or *fe,* add *s*; others change the *f* or *fe* to *v* and add *es* (*roofs, beliefs, scarves, leaves*).
  f. For nouns ending in *o* when the *o* is preceded by a consonant, add *es* (*tomatoes, heroes*).
  g. For nouns ending in *o* when the *o* is preceded by a vowel, add *s* (*patios, rodeos*).

h. For some nouns that end in *o* when the *o* is preceded by a vowel, just add an *s*. This is particularly true of words that are connected to music (*solos, altos, sopranos*).

i. For some nouns, the plural form is a new word: *teeth, mice, oxen*.

VERBS

a. While verbs are not plural like nouns, they take the plural form to be in agreement with the subject: He *does*; They *do*. Verbs that end in *o*, add *es*; verbs that end in a consonant, add *s* (*go/goes; win/wins*).

3. Rules for Suffixes

a. If adding the suffix *-ly* or *-ness*, do not change the spelling of the base word unless the base word ends in *y* (*careful/carefully; usual/usually; fond/fondness; happy/happily*).

Rules for adding a suffix to words that end in silent e

a. If adding a suffix that begins with a vowel to a word that ends in a silent *e*, drop the final silent *e* (*give/giving; safe/safest; take/taking; admire/admirable, create/creative*).

b. If adding a suffix that begins with the letter *a* or *o* to a word that ends in *ce* or *ge*, keep the final *e* (*manage/manageable; notice/noticeable; outrage/outrageous*).[1]

c. If adding a suffix that begins with a consonant to a word that ends with a silent *e*, keep the silent *e* (*measure/measurement; use/useful; creative/creatively*).

Rules for adding a suffix to words that end in y

a. If adding a suffix to a word that ends in *y* when the *y* is preceded by a consonant, change the *y* to *i* to add any suffix that does not begin with *i* (*cry/cried/crying; terrify/terrified/terrifying*).

b. If adding a suffix to a word that ends in *y* when the *y* is preceded by a vowel, do not change the *y* to *i*; instead, just add the suffix (*annoy/annoyed; delay/delayed/delaying*). Exceptions include *say/said, pay/paid, lay/laid.*

Rules for doubling the final consonant in a word before adding the suffix

a. If the word is a one-syllable word that has only one vowel and only one consonant after the vowel, then double the final consonant before adding a suffix that begins with a vowel (*sit/sitting; run/running;*

---

[1] The *e* must be kept at the ends of the words to keep the *c* and *g* making their "soft" sounds of /s/ and /j/. Usually *c* makes the /k/ sound except when followed by the letters *e, i,* and *y*. *G* usually makes the /g/ sound except when followed by *e, i,* and *y*.

pit/pitted; wrap/wrapper). This is sometimes called the 1-1-1 Doubling Rule (one syllable-one vowel-one consonant after the vowel).

b. If the word has two or more syllables and the last syllable is a CVC pattern (consonant-vowel-consonant) and is the accented syllable, then follow the 1-1-1 Doubling Rule (*permit/permitted; refer/referring; forbid/forbidden; occur/occurred; forget/forgetting*).

c. If the word has two or more syllables and the last syllable follows the CVC pattern but is unaccented, do not double the last consonant (*barrel/barreling; gallop/galloping; blanket/blanketing; trumpet/trumpeting*).

Rules for adding the suffixes -ible or -able

a. If the root is not a complete word (technically called a *bound morpheme*), add *-ible*. Examples: *visible, horrible, terrible, possible, edible, eligible, incredible, permissible, suitable, invisible, illegible*.

b. If the root is a complete word without the suffix (technically called an *unbound morpheme*), then add *-able*. Examples: *fashionable, laughable, suitable, dependable, comfortable*.

c. If the root is a complete word that ends in silent *e*, drop the silent *e* and then add *-able*. Examples: *excuse/excusable, advise/advisable, desire/desirable, value/valuable, debate/debatable*.

d. Exceptions to the *-ible/-able* rule occur when the final sound is the hard *g* or hard *c* sound; then the suffix is *-able*: *navigable, applicable*. Other exceptions include *digestible, contemptible, inevitable, flexible, responsible, irritable*.

Rules for adding -ion

a. If the root ends in *ct*, add *-ion* (*selects/election; subtract/subtraction*).

b. If the root ends in *ss*, add *-ion* (*discuss/discussion; impress/impression*).

c. If the root ends in *te*, drop the *e* and add *-ion* (*educate/education; create/creation*).

d. If the root ends in *it*, change the *t* to *s* and add *-sion* (*permit/permission; omit/omission*).

e. If the root ends Vde (vowel, letter *d*, letter *e*), drop the *e*, change the *d* to *s* and add *-ion* (*explode/explosion; persuade/persuasion*).

f. If the root ends in Vre, Vne, or Vze, drop the *e* and add *-ation* (*declare/declaration; combine/combination; organize/organization*).

4. Other Helpful Rules

a. Use the word *a* before words that begin with a consonant sound; use *an* before words that begin with a vowel sound (*a car; an apple; an hour*—the *h* is silent; *a one-dollar bill*—the *o* makes a /w/ sound).

b. Use an apostrophe to take the place of omitted letters in contractions. Examples: *let's, that's, don't, doesn't, it's, can't, won't, wouldn't, shouldn't, couldn't, I'm, I've, I'd, I'll, they're, they've, they'd, they'll, you're, you've, you'd, you'll, we're, we'll, we've, we'd, she'd, she'll, could've, would've, should've.*

c. Long vowel sounds will not precede a doubled consonant. Exceptions include *toll, roll, droll,* and *troll*.

d. Do not end words in the letter *v* or *z*. Add a silent *e* to words that end in those sounds (*give*, not *giv*; *breeze*, not *breez*; *have*, not *hav*; *love*, not *lov*; *snooze*, not *snooz*; *above*, not *abov*).

e. Only one English word ends in *-sede*: *supersede*. Three words end in *-ceed*: *exceed, proceed,* and *succeed*; all other verbs ending in the /sed/ sound are spelled with *-cede*: *intercede, precede; concede*.

f. Spelling the wrong word the correct way is still a spelling error. So, using *right* for *write* isn't right. Help students to spell homophones correctly by making sure they know the meaning of each word.

Booklists

As you look through these booklists, you'll find more than five hundred titles of books that have been divided into the following categories:

♦ Biography, Autobiography, and Historical Fiction
♦ Fantasy and Science Fiction
♦ Humor and Laughter
♦ Informational Books
♦ Mysteries
♦ Poetry
♦ Realistic Fiction
♦ Short Story Collections
♦ Sports and Sports Stories
♦ Stories Told in Picture Book Format

Many thanks go to Jeanette Choy and Erica Quintella, students at the University of Houston during this writing, who worked for months on these lists. More thanks must go to Teri Lesesne, young adult book review column editor for the NCTE journal *Voices from the Middle,* for her many suggestions to these lists. These three people helped immensely in creating these lists. While I borrowed their ideas without shame, I must claim sole responsibility for any mistakes made in these lists.

I've included young adult titles, fiction and nonfiction, that engage our reluctant readers. While the list leans toward the newer books, some older titles are so popular with reluctant readers that I simply could not omit them. If your favorite title doesn't appear in this list, then simply pencil it in. You, of course, need to be the final judge for whether or not a particular book is right for a particular student.

Biography, Autobiography, and Historical Fiction

Anderson, Laurie Halse. *Fever 1793*.

Beals, Melba Patillo. *Warriors Don't Cry*.

Bitton-Jackson, Livia. *I Have Lived a Thousand Years: Growing Up in the Holocaust*.

Blackwood, Gary. *The Shakespeare Stealer*.

Bruchac, Joseph. *Sacagawea: The Story of Bird Woman and the Lewis and Clark Expedition*.

Cadnum, Michael. *The Book of the Lion*.

Campbell, Patty. *Presenting Robert Cormier*.

Chang, Pang-Mei Natasha. *Bound Feet and Western Dress*.

Cormier, Robert. *Heroes*.

Cox, Clinton. *Buffalo Soldiers*.

Crowe, Chris. *Presenting Mildred Taylor*.

Curtis, Christopher Paul. *Watsons Go to Birmingham, 1963; Bud, Not Buddy*.

Cushman, Karen. *Catherine Called Birdy; The Midwife's Apprentice; The Ballad of Lucy Whipple*.

Denenberg, Barry. *Voices from Vietnam*.

Dorris, Michael. *Morning Girl*.

Dyer, Daniel. *Jack London: A Biography*.

Elders, Joycelyn, and Chanoff, David. *Joycelyn Elders, M.D.: From Sharecropper's Daughter to Surgeon General of the United States of America*.

Erdich, Louise. *The Birchbark Home*.

Feelings, Tom. *The Middle Passage: White Ships/Black Cargo*.

Fleischman, Paul. *Dateline: Troy; Bull Run*.

Fox, Paula. *Slave Dancer*.

Fradin, Dennis Brindell, and Judith Bloom Fradin. *Ida B. Wells: Mother of the Civil Rights Movement*.

Freedman, Russell. *Martha Graham: A Dancer's Life; Babe Didrickson Zaharias; Lincoln: A Photobiography; The Life and Death of Crazy Horse*.

Fritz, Jean. *Bully for You, Teddy Roosevelt*.

Gantos, Jack. *Hole in My Life*.

Garden, Nancy. *Dove and Sword: A Novel of Joan of Arc*.

Garland, Sherry. *Indio*.

Giblin, James Cross. *Charles A. Lindbergh: A Human Hero.*

Giff, Patricia Reilly. *Lily's Crossing; Nory Ryan's Song.*

Gottlieb, Lori. *Stick Figure: A Diary of My Former Self.*

Hansen, Joyce. *The Captive.*

Haskins, Jim. *Black Eagles.*

Hesse, Karen. *Out of the Dust; Witness.*

Hickam, Homer H. *Rocket Boys: A Memoir.*

Hite, Sid. *Stick and Whittle.*

Hobbler, Dorothy, and Hobbler, Thomas. *The Ghost in the Tokaido Inn; Demon in the Teahouse.*

Holm, Jennifer. *Our Only May Amelia.*

Hoose, Philip. *It's Our World, Too! Young People Who Make a Difference.*

Hopkins, Lee Bennett. *Pauses: Autobiographical Reflections of 101 Creators of Children's Books.*

Ingold, Jeanette. *The Window.*

Jiang, Ji-Li. *Red Scarf Girl: A Memoir of the Cultural Revolution.*

Kerr, M. E. *Blood on the Forehead.*

Krull, Kathleen. *Lives of the Presidents; Presenting Paula Danziger.*

Lanier, Shannon, and Feldman, Jane. *Jefferson's Children: The story of One American Family.*

Lasky, Kathryn. *Beyond the Burning Time; Beyond the Divide.*

Lawlor, Laurie. *Helen Keller: Rebellious Spirit.*

Lee, Bruce; selected and edited by John Little. *Bruce Lee: The Celebrated Life of the Golden Dragon.*

Lester, Julius. *Pharaoh's Daughter: A Novel of Ancient Egypt.*

Levine, Ellen. *A Fence Away from Freedom; Freedom's Children.*

Lipsyte, Robert. *Arnold Schwarzenegger; Jim Thorpe.*

Lobel, Anita. *No Pretty Pictures: A Child of War.*

Lowry, Lois. *Number the Stars.*

Mah, Adeline Yen. *Chinese Cinderella: The True Story of an Unwanted Daughter.*

Marrin, Albert. *Commander-in-Chief.*

Matas, Carol. *The Burning Time.*

Mazer, Norma Fox. *Good Night, Maman.*

McKissack, Patricia. *Young, Black, and Determined: A Biography.*

Morris, Gerald. *Parsifal's Page.*

Murphy, Jim. *Blizzard: the Storm That Changed America.*

Myers, Walter Dean. *Bad Boy: A Memoir; The Greatest: Muhammad Ali; At Her Majesty's Request.*

Na, An. *A Step from Heaven.*

Napoli, Donna Jo. *Song of the Magdalene.*

Nelson, Marilyn. *Carver: A Life in Poems.*

Orgill, Roxane. *Shout, Sister, Shout! Ten Girl Singers Who Shaped a Century.*

Park, Linda Sue. *A Single Shard.*

Paterson, Katherine. *Lyddie; Jip, His Story.*

Paulsen, Gary. *Nightjohn; Sarney; Soldier's Heart.*

Peck, Richard. *A Long Way from Chicago; A Year Down Yonder; Fair Weather.*

Rinaldi, Ann. *A Stitch in Time; Hang a Thousand Trees with Ribbons: The Story of Phillis Wheatley.*

Robinet, Harriette. *Forty Acres and a Mule.*

Ryan, Pam Munoz. *Esperanza Rising.*

Salisbury, Graham. *Under the Blood Red Sun.*

Spinelli, Jerry. *Knots in My Yo-Yo String.*

Taylor, Theodore. *The Bomb.*

Temple, Frances. *The Ramsey Scallop.*

Thomas, Jane Resh. *Behind the Mask; The Life of Queen Elizabeth I.*

Tillage, Leon Walter. *Leon's Story.*

Winnick, Judd. *Pedro and Me.*

Wolff, Virginia Euwer. *Bat 6.*

Yolen, Jane. *Devil's Arithmetic.*

Fantasy and Science Fiction

Atwater-Rhodes, Amelia. *In the Forest of the Night.*

Barron, T. A. *Tree Girl; The Lost Years of Merlin; The Ancient One.*

Card, Orson Scott. *Ender's Game; Ender's Shadow; Shadow of the Hegemon.*

Dickinson, Peter. *Eva.*

Gilmore, Kate. *The Exchange Student.*

Haddix, Margaret Peterson. *Among the Hidden; Among the Impostors.*

Hautman, Pete. *Mr. Was; Hole in the Sky.*

Hesse, Karen. *The Music of Dolphins.*

Kindl, Patrice. *Goose Chase.*

Klause, Annette Curtis. *Blood and Chocolate.*

Levine, Gail Carson. *Ella Enchanted.*

Logue, Mary. *Dancing with an Alien.*

Lowry, Lois. *The Giver; Gathering Blue.*

McKinley, Robin. *Rose Daughter.*

Napoli, Donna Jo. *Sirena; Crazy Jack; Spinners; Zel.*

Naylor, Phyllis Reynolds. *Jade Green.*

Nix, Garth. *Sabriel.*

Pullman, Philip. *The Golden Compass; Amber Spyglass; Subtle Knife; I Was a Rat.*

Rowling, J. K. *Harry Potter and the Sorcerer's Stone; Harry Potter and the Chamber of Secrets; Harry Potter and the Goblet of Fire; Harry Potter and the Prisoner of Azkaban.*

Shusterman, Neal. *Downsiders.*

Skurzynski, Gloria. *Virtual War.*

Sleator, William. *Boxes; Interstellar Pig; Others See Us; Rewind; The Duplicate.*

Tolan, Stephanie. *Welcome to the Ark.*

Vande Velde, Vivian. *Never Trust a Dead Man.*

Wrede, Patricia. *Dealing with Dragons.*

Humor and Laughter

Bauer, Joan. *Squashed; Thwonk; Hope Was Here; Rules of the Road.*

Cabot, Meg. *The Princess Diaries; Princess in the Spotlight; Princess in Love.*

Chbosky, Stephen. *The Perks of Being a Wallflower.*

Conford, Ellen. *A Royal Pain.*

Coville, Bruce. *Odder Than Ever.*

Curtis, Christopher Paul. *Bud, Not Buddy; The Watsons Go to Birmingham, 1963.*

Danziger, Paula. *The United Tates of America; This Place Has No Atmosphere.*

Eberhardt, Thomas. *Rat Boys: Dating Experiment.*

Hite, Sid. *Stick and Whittle; Cecil in Space.*

Horvath, Polly. *Everything on a Waffle.*

Howe, Norma. *The Adventures of the Blue Avenger.*

Gantos, Jack. *Joey Pigza Swallowed the Key; Joey Pigza Loses Control; Jack's Black Book.*

Groening, Matt. *Simpsons Comics Royale.*

Korman, Gordon. *No More Dead Dogs.*

Lynch, Chris. *Slot Machine; Extreme Elvin.*

Paulsen, Gary. *The Schernoff Discoveries.*

Pilkey, Dav. *Captain Underpants and the Wrath of the Wicked Wedgie Woman; Ricky Ricotta's Mighty Robot vs. the Mecha-Monkeys from Mars.*

Pinkwater, Daniel. *Fat Camp Commandos.*

Rennison, Louise. *Angus, Thongs, and Full Frontal Snogging; On the Bright Side, I'm Now the Girlfriend of a Sex Goddess.*

Sciezska, Jon. *Squids Will Be Squids; True Story of the Three Little Pigs; Tut Tut; See You Later, Gladiator.*

Snicket, Lemony. *The Bad Beginning.*

Townsend, Sue. *The Adrian Mole Diaries.*

Informational Books

Alexander, Caroline. *The Endurance: Shackleton's Legendary Antarctic Expedition.*

Allison, Anthony. *Hear These Voices: Youth at the Edge of the Millennium.*

Armstrong, Jennifer. *Shipwreck at the Bottom of the World: The Extraordinary True Story of Shackleton and the Endurance.*

Ash, Russell. *Top Ten of Everything.*

Atkin, S. Beth. *Voices from the Streets: Young Former Gang Members Tell Their Stories.*

Bachrach, Susan D. *The Nazi Olympics: Berlin 1936.*

Bartoletti, Susan Campbell. *Kids on Strike.*

Bode, Janet, and Mack, Stan. *Hard Time: A Real Life Look at Juvenile Crime.*

Branzei, Sylvia. *Grossology: The Science of Really Gross Things!*

Calabro, Marian. *The Perilous Journey of the Donner Party.*

Colman, Penny. *Corpses, Coffins and Crypts; Toilets, Bathtubs, Sinks and Sewers: A History of the Bathroom.*

Cooper, Michael. *Fighting for Honor: Japanese Americans and World War II.*

Csillag, Andre. *Backstreet Boys: The Official Book.*

Dominick, Andie. *Needles.*

Dougall, Alastair. *James Bond: The Secret World of 007.*

Farrell, Jeanett. *Invisible Enemies: Stories of Infectious Diseases.*

Fishbein, Amy. *The Truth About Girlfriends.*

Fradin, Dennis Brindell. *Bound for the North Star: True Stories of Fugitive Slaves.*

Freedman, Russell. *Give Me Liberty! The Story of the Declaration of Independence.*

Friedman, Linda, and White, Dana, editors. *Teen People: Real Life Diaries: Inspiring True Stories from Celebrities and Real Teens.*

Garner, Eleanor Ramrath. *Eleanor's Story: An American Girl in Hitler's Germany.*

Gaskins, Pearl, editor. *What Are You? Voices of Mixed-Race Young People.*

Glover, Savion, and Weber, Bruce. *Savion: My Life in Tap.*

Gourley, Catherine. *Good Girl Work: Factories, Sweatshops, and How Women Changed Their Role in the Workforce.*

Gravelle, Karen. *5 Ways to Know About You.*

Greenberg, Gary. *Pop-Up Book of Phobias.*

Greenberg, Jan, and Jordan, Sandra. *Vincent Van Gogh: Portrait of an Artist.*

Groening, Matt. *Simpson's Comics A-Go-Go.*

Guinness Book of World Records.

Hart, Christopher. *Manga Mania: How to Draw Japanese Comics.*

Hoose, Phillip. *We Were There, Too! Young People in U.S. History.*

Jennings, Peter, and Brewster, Todd. *The Century for Young People.*

Johns, Michael-Anne. *Cool in School: What the Stars Were Like When They Went to School.*

Kalergis, Mary Motley. *Seen and Heard: Teenagers Talk About Their Lives.*

Katz, Jon. *Geeks: How Two Lost Boys Rode the Internet Out of Idaho.*

Keenan, Sheila. *Scholastic Encyclopedia of Women in the United States.*

Kendall, Martha. *Failure Is Impossible: The History of American Women's Rights.*

Ketchum, Liza. *Into the New Country: Eight Remarkable Women of the West.*

Kirberger, Kimberly. *Teen Love: On Relationships, a Book for Teenagers.*

Krizmanic, Judy. *Teen's Vegetarian Cookbook*.

Kuhn, Betsy. *Angels of Mercy: The Army Nurses of World War II*.

Larson, Gary. *There's a Hair in My Dirt: A Worm's Story*.

Levine, Ellen. *Darkness over Denmark: The Danish Resistance and the Rescue of the Jews*.

Levinson, Nancy Smiler. *She's Been Working on the Railroad*.

Macauley, David. *The Way Things Work*.

Macy, Sue. *Winning Ways: A Photohistory of American Women in Sports*.

Mannarino, Melanie. *The Boyfriend Clinic: The Final Word on Flirting, Dating, Guys and Love*.

Marrin, Albert. *Terror of the Spanish Main*.

Masoff, Joy. *Oh, Yuck! The Encyclopedia of Everything Nasty*.

Mattison, Chris. *Snake*.

McFarlane, Evelyn, and Saywell, James. *If . . . Questions for Teens*.

McKee, Tim, and Blackshaw, Anne. *No More Strangers Now*.

McKissack, Patricia C., and McKissack, Fredrick L. *Rebels Against Slavery: American Slave Revolts*.

Mitton, Jacqueline, and Mitton, Simon. *Scholastic Encyclopedia of Space*.

Murphy, Jim. *Blizzard: The Storm That Changed America*.

Myers, Walter Dean. *One More River to Cross: An African American Photograph Album*.

O'Donnell, Kerri. *Inhalants and Your Nasal Passages: The Incredibly Disgusting Story*.

Okutoro, Lydia Omolola. *Quiet Storm: Voices of Young Black Poets*.

Opdyke, Irene Gut. *In My Hands: Memories of a Holocaust Rescuer*.

Orgill, Roxane. *Shout, Sister, Shout! Ten Girl Singers Who Shaped a Century*.

Owen, David. *Hidden Evidence: Forty True Crimes and How Forensic Science Helped Solve Them*.

Paulsen, Gary. *Puppies, Dogs, and Blue Northers: Reflections on Being Raised by a Pack of Sled Dogs; Guts*.

Piven, Joshua, and Borgenicht, David. *The Worst-Case Scenario Survival Handbook*.

Sandler, Martin W. *Inventors*.

Schwager, Tina, and Schuerger, Michele. *Gutsy Girls: Young Women Who Dare*.

Seckel, Al. *The Art of Optical Illusions*.

Shaw, Tucker. *Dreams: Explore the You That You Can't Control.*

Shaw, Tucker, and Gibb, Fiona. *. . . Any Advice?*

Stine, Megan. *Seventeen Trauma-Rama: Life's Most Embarrassing Moments . . . and How to Deal.*

Ung, Loung. *First They Killed My Father: A Daughter of Cambodia.*

Wilcox, Charlotte. *Mummies, Bones, and Body Parts.*

Winick, Judd. *Pedro and Me.*

Mystery

Almond, David. *Skellig.*

Atkins, Catherine. *When Jeff Comes Home.*

Avi. *Wolf Rider; The Man Who Was Poe; Midnight Magic.*

Cooney, Caroline. *The Face on the Milk Carton; Whatever Happened to Janie?; The Voice on the Radio; Fatality.*

Cormier, Robert. *In the Middle of the Night.*

Cross, Gillian. *Tightrope.*

Duncan, Lois. *Don't Look Behind You; Stranger with My Face; The Third Eye; Gallow's Hill.*

Gilmore, Kate. *The Exchange Student.*

Glen, Mel. *Who Killed Mr. Chippendale?; The Taking of Room 114; Foreign Exchange.*

Hobbs, Will. *Ghost Canoe.*

Konigsberg, E. L. *Silent to the Bone.*

Levin, Betty. *Shadow-Catcher.*

MacGregor, Rob. *Prophecy Rock; Hawk Moon.*

McDonald, Joyce. *Swallowing Stones.*

Myers, Walter Dean. *Monster.*

Nixon, Joan Lowery. *Nobody Was There; Secret, Silent Screams; The Dark and Deadly Pool; Playing for Keeps; The Other Side of Dark; The Haunting; Who Are You?*

Plum-Ucci, Carol. *The Body of Christopher Creed.*

Qualey, Marsha. *Close to a Killer.*

Roberts, Willo Davis. *Twisted Summer; Pawns.*

Ryan, Mary Elizabeth. *Alias.*

Sachar, Louis. *Holes.*

Springer, Nancy. *Secret Star; Sky Rider.*

Sweeney, Joyce. *Shadow.*

Sykes, Shelley. *For Mike.*

Van Draanen, Wendelin. *Sammy Keyes and the Hollywood Mummy.*

Vande Velde, Vivian. *Never Trust a Dead Man.*

Werlin, Nancy. *The Killer's Cousin; Black Mirror; Locked Inside.*

White, Robb. *Deathwatch.*

Authors of Adult Mysteries Teens Often Enjoy

Baldacci, David.

Brown, Sandra.

Clark, Mary Higgins.

Cook, Robin.

Cornwell, Patricia.

Grafton, Sue.

Grisham, John.

Kellerman, Jonathan.

King, Stephen.

Koontz, Dean.

Poetry

Alarcon, Francisco. *From the Bellybutton of the Moon and Other Summer Poems; Laughing Tomatoes and Other Spring Poems.*

Carlson, Lori M. *Cool Salsa: Bilingual Poems on Growing Up Latino in the United States.*

Cotner, June. *Teen Sunshine Reflections: Words for the Heart and Soul.*

Dakos, Kalli. *If You're Not Here, Raise Your Hand: Poems About School.*

Fletcher, Ralph. *Buried Alive: The Elements of Love.*

Franco, Betsy, editor. *You Hear Me? Poems and Writings by Teenage Boys; Things I Have to Tell You: Poems and Writings by Teenage Girls.*

Glenn, Mel. *Class Dismissed; Class Dismissed II.*

Gordon, Ruth. *Pierced by a Ray of Sun: Poems About the Times We Feel Alone.*

Greenberg, Jan. *Heart to Heart.*

Herrera, Juan Felipe. *Laughing Out Loud, I Fly.*

Hopkins, Lee Bennett. *Opening Days: Sports Poems.*

Hughes, Langston. *The Block.*

Janeczko, Paul, editor. *Seeing the Blue Between; Poetspeak; The Place My Words Are Looking For.*

Janeczko, Paul, and Nye, Naomi Shihab. *I Feel a Little Jumpy Around You.*

Johnson, Dave, editor. *Movin': Teen Poets Take Voice.*

Korman, Gordon. *The D- Poems of Jeremy Bloom; The Last Place Sports Poems of Jeremy Bloom.*

Mora, Pat. *My Own True Name.*

Nye, Naomi Shihab. *This Same Sky; The Space Between Our Footsteps; What Have You Lost?*

Smith, Charles R., Jr. *Short Takes.*

Soto, Gary. *Baseball in April and Other Poems.*

Straus, Gwen. *Trail of Stones.*

Turner, Ann. *A Lion's Hunger: Poems of First Love.*

Von Ziegesar, Cecily. *SLAM.*

Wong, Janet S. *Behind the Wheel: Poems About Driving.*

Realistic Fiction

Anderson, Laurie Halse. *Speak.*

Atkins, Catherine. *When Jeff Came Home.*

Avi. *Nothing But the Truth.*

Bauer, Cat. *Harley: Like a Person.*

Bauer, Joan. *Hope Was Here; Rules of the Road.*

Bauer, Marion Dane. *A Question of Trust.*

Bennett, Cherie. *Life in the Fat Lane; Love Him Forever.*

Bloor, Edward. *Tangerine.*

Blume, Judy. *Here's to You, Rachel Robinson.*

Brashares, Ann. *Sisterhood of the Traveling Pants.*

Burgess, Melvin. *Smack.*

Cabot, Meg. *The Princess Diaries; Princess in the Spotlight; Princess in Love.*

Cart, Michael. *My Father's Scar.*

Carter, Alden R. *Bull Catcher.*

Coman, Carolyn. *Many Stones*.

Conford, Ellen. *I Love You. I Hate You, Get Lost!; Crush*

Conly, Jane Leslie. *Crazy Lady!*

Cooney, Caroline. *Driver's Ed; Fatality; Fire; The Terrorist*.

Cormier, Robert. *Tenderness*.

Couloumbis, Audrey. *Say Yes*.

Creech, Sharon. *Chasing Redbird*.

Crutcher, Chris. *Whale Talk*.

Danziger, Paula, and Martin, Ann. *P. S. Longer Letter Later; Snail Mail No More*.

Davis, Jenny. *Sex Education*.

DeVries, Anke. *Bruises*.

Di Camillo, Kate. *Because of Winn Dixie*.

Dorris, Michael. *The Window*.

Draper, Sharon M. *Forged by Fire; Tears of a Tiger; Romiette and Julio*.

Ferris, Jean. *Of Sound Mind; Love Among the Walnuts*.

Fine, Ann. *Flour Babies*.

Fleischman, Paul. *Whirligig*.

Flinn, Alex. *Breathing Underwater; Breaking Point*.

Frank, E. R. *Life Is Funny; America*.

Giff, Patricia Reilly. *Pictures of Hollis Woods*.

Griffin, Adele. *Amandine*.

Giles, Gail. *Shattering Glass*.

Haddix, Margaret Peterson. *Don't You Dare Read This, Mrs. Dunphrey; Leaving Fishers*.

Heneghan, James. *Flood*.

Hesser, Terry. *Spencer Kissing Doorknob*.

Hobbs, Will. *Downriver; The Maze*.

Holt, Kimberly Willis. *When Zachary Beaver Came to Town*.

Howe, James. *The Misfits*.

Herrera, Juan Felipe. *Crashboomlove: A Novel in Verse*.

Johnson, Angela. *Toning the Sweep; Heaven*.

Klass, David. *You Don't Know Me*.

Koertge, Ron. *The Brimstone Journals*.

Lasky, Kathryn. *Memoirs of a Bookbat*.

Mack, Tracy. *Drawing Lessons*.

Mackler, Carolyn. *Love and Other Four Letter Words*.

Martinez, Victor. *Parrot in the Oven: Mi Vida*.

McCormick, Patricia. *Cut*.

McDonald, Janet. *Spellbound*.

Moore, Martha. *Matchit*.

Myers, Walter Dean. *Monster*.

Naylor, Phyllis Reynolds. *Outrageously Alice*.

Oates, Joyce Carol. *Big Mouth and Ugly Girl*.

Rennison, Louise. *Angus Thongs and Full Frontal Snogging*.

Salisbury, Graham. *Lord of the Deep*.

Sebestyen, Ouida. *Out of Nowhere*.

Snyder, Zilpha Keatley. *Cat Running*.

Sones, Sonya. *What My Mother Doesn't Know*.

Soto, Gary. *Local News*.

Spinelli, Jerry. *Maniac Magee; Crash; Stargirl*.

Strasser, Todd. *Give a Boy a Gun*.

Tashjian, Janet. *The Gospel According to Larry*.

Thomas, Rob. *Doing Time: Notes from the Undergrad*.

Trueman, Terry. *Stuck in Neutral*.

Walter, Virginia. *Making Up Megaboy*.

White, Ruth. *Belle Prater's Boy*.

Williams, Carol Lynch. *A Mother to Embarrass Me; My Angelica*.

Williams, Lori Aurelia. *When Kambia Elaine Flew in from Neptune*.

Wittlinger, Ellen. *Razzle*.

Wolff, Virginia Euwer. *Probably Still Nick Swanson; Make Lemonade; True Believer*.

Woodson, Jacqueline. *If You Come Softly*.

Yolen, Jane, and Coville, Bruce. *Armageddon Summer*.

Short Story Collections

Appelt, Kathi. *Kissing Tennessee and Other Stories from the Stardust Dance*.

Bauer, Marion Dane. *Am I Blue? Coming Out from the Silence*.

Blume, Judy. *Places I Never Meant to Be*.

Book, Rick. *Necking with Louise*.

Canfield, Jack, Hansen, Mark, and Kirberger, Kimberly, compilers. *Chicken Soup for the Teenage Soul II: 101 More Stories of Life, Love, and Learning*.

Carlson, Lori, editor. *American Eyes: New Asian-American Short Stories for Young Adults.*

Cart, Michael, editor. *Love and Sex: Ten Stories of Truth; Tomorrowland: 10 Stories About the Future.*

Cofer, Judith Ortiz. *An Island Like You: Stories of the Barrio.*

Conford, Ellen. *Crush.*

Cormier, Robert. *8 Plus 1.*

Coville, Bruce. *Odder Than Ever.*

Crowe, Chris, editor. *From the Outside Looking In: Short Stories for LDS Teenagers.*

Crutcher, Chris. *Athletic Shorts.*

Dines, Carol. *Talk to Me.*

Duncan, Lois, editor. *Night Terror: Stories of Shadow and Substance.*

Gallo, Donald R., editor. *On the Fringe; No Easy Answers: Short Stories About Teenagers Making Tough Choices; Sixteen; Visions; Connections; Join In; Ultimate Sports.*

Galloway, Priscilla. *Truly Grimm Tales.*

Hughes, Monica, selector. *What If . . . ? Amazing Stories.*

Lynch, Chris. *All the Old Haunts.*

Mazer, Anne, editor. *Working Days: Short Stories About Teenagers at Work.*

Mazer, Harry, editor. *Twelve Shots: Outstanding Short Stories.*

Myers, Walter Dean. *145th Street Short Stories.*

Nixon, Joan Lowery. *Ghost Town.*

Rochman, Hazel, and McCampbell, Darlene. *Leaving Home.*

Shusterman, Neal. *Mindstorms: Stories to Blow Your Mind.*

Silvey, Anita, selector. *Help Wanted: Short Stories of Young People at Work.*

Stearns, Michael. *A Wizard's Dozen.*

Vande Velde, Vivian. *The Rumplestiltskin Problem.*

Wiess, Jerry, and Weiss, Helen. *From One Experience to Another: Award-Winning Authors Sharing Real-Life Experiences Through Fiction.*

Yolen, Jane. *Twelve Impossible Things Before Breakfast: Stories.*

Sports and Sports Stories

Anderson, Dave. *The Story of Basketball; The Story of Football; The Story of the Olympics.*

Anderson, Joan. *Rookie: Tamika Whitmore's First Year in the WNBA.*

Barnidge, Tom. *Best Shots: The Greatest NFL Photography of the Century.*

Breashears, David, Salkeld Audrey, and Mallory, John. *Last Climb: The Legendary Everest Expeditions of George Mallory.*

Cadnum, Michael. *Redhanded.*

Carter, Alden. *Bull Catcher.*

Christopher, Matt. *Cool as Ice; On the Course with Tiger Woods.*

Crutcher, Chris. *Athletic Shorts; Ironman; Running Loose; Stotan!; Whale Talk.*

Deuker, Carl. *On the Devil's Court; Night Hoops.*

Draper, Sharon. *Tears of a Tiger.*

Dygard, Thomas J. *Second Stringer.*

Ferris, Jean. *Eight Seconds.*

Freedman, Russell. *Babe Didrikson Zaharias: The Making of a Champion.*

Genet, Robert. *Funny Cars; Lowriders.*

Glenn, Mel. *Jump Ball: A Basketball Season in Poems.*

Gottesman, Jane. *Game Face: What Does a Female Athlete Look Like?*

Guinness Book of World Records, 2001.

Hayhurst, Chris. *Bicycle Stunt Riding: Catch Air!*

Hawk, Tony, and Mortimer, Sean. *Hawk: Occupation Skateboarder.*

Jenkins, A. M. *Damage.*

Jeter, Derek. *Game Day: My Life On and Off the Field.*

Johnson, Scott. *Safe at Second.*

Junger, Sebastian. *The Perfect Storm: A True Story of Men Against the Sea.*

Klass, David. *Danger Zone.*

Krull, Kathleen. *Lives of Athletes: Thrills, Spills (and What the Neighbors Thought).*

Lee, Marie. *Necessary Roughness.*

Lewin, Ted. *I Was a Teenage Professional Wrestler.*

Lewman, David. *When I Was Your Age: Remarkable Achievements of Famous Athletes at Every Age from 1 to 100.*

Lipsyte, Robert. *The Contender; Shadow Boxer.*

Lynch, Chris. *Gold Dust.*

Macy, Sue, and Gottesman, Jane, editors. *Play Like a Girl: A Celebration of Women in Sports; A Whole New Ball Game: The Story of the All-American Girls Professional Baseball League.*

Marshall, Kirk. *Fast Breaks.*

Myers, T. Nelson. *My Life as a Beat-Up Basketball Backboard.*

Myers, Walter Dean. *Slam!; Hoops; The Greatest: Muhammad Ali.*

Rappoport, Ken. *Sports Great Wayne Gretzky.*

Ritter, John. *Choosing Up Sides; Over the Wall.*

Roberts, Jeremy. *Rock and Ice Climbing: Top the Tower!*

Rock with Joe Layden. *The Rock Says.*

Ryder, Bob, and Scherer, Dave. *WCW: The Ultimate Guide.*

Schwarzenegger, Arnold. *The New Encyclopedia of Modern Bodybuilding.*

Service, Pamela. *Vision Quest.*

Slote, Henry. *Finding Buck McHenry.*

Smith, Charles R. *Tall Tales: Six Amazing Basketball Dreams.*

Spinelli, Jerry. *There's a Girl in My Hammerlock.*

Wallace, Rich. *Wrestling Sturbridge; Shots on Goal; Playing Without the Ball.*

Weaver, Will. *Hard Ball; Striking Out; Farm Team.*

Wolff, Virginia Euwer. *Bat 6.*

Zusak, Markus. *Fighting Ruben Wolfe.*

Easy Reading Sports Series

The #1 Sports Series for Kids, published by Little, Brown and Company.

NFL Today Series, published by Creative Education.

Race Car Legends Series, published by Chelsea House.

Hoops series, published by Ballantine.

Scrappers series, published by Aladdin.

Girls Only (GO!) series, published by Bethany House.

Sports Great series, published by Enslow.

Pro Wrestling Legends series, published by Chelsea House.

Stories Told in Picture Book Format

Ada, Alma Flor. *With Love, Little Red Hen.*

Beneduce, Ann Keay, reteller. *Jack and the Beanstalk.*

Bridges, Ruby. *Through My Eyes.*

Colville, Bruce. *Macbeth.*

Curlee, Lynn. *Brooklyn Bridge.*

Fanelli, Sara. *My Map Book.*

Frasier, Debra. *Miss Alaneius: A Vocabulary Disaster.*

Garland, Sherry. *You Don't Know Me.*

Innocenti, Roberto. *Rose Blanche.*

Janeczko, Paul. *A Poke in the "I."*

Leedy, Loreen. *Mapping Penny's World.*

Lester, Julius. *From Slave Ship to Freedom Road.*

Lewis, J. Patrick. *Doodle Dandies.*

Locker, Thomas. *Sky Tree.*

Miller, William. *Tituba.*

Muth, Jon. *The Three Questions.*

Myers, Christopher. *Wings.*

Myers, Walter Dean. *Malcolm X: A Fire Burning Brightly.*

Polacco, Patricia. *Pink and Say.*

Prelutsky, Jack. *Awful Ogre's Awful Day.*

Rappaport, Doreen. *Martin's Big Words.*

San Souci, Robert. *Cinderella Skeleton.*

Scieszka, Jon, and Smith, Lane. *Math Curse; The True Story of the Three Little Pigs; The Stinky Cheese Man.*

Sierra, Judy. *Monster Goose.*

Solheim, James. *It's Disgusting and We Ate It! True Food Facts from Around the World and Throughout History.*

St. George, Judith. *So You Want to Be President?*

Stanley, Diane. *Good Queen Bess, The Story of Elizabeth I of England; Shaka: King of the Zulus; Bard of Avon: The Story of William Shakespeare; Charles Dickens: The Man Who Had Great Expectations; Michelangelo; Peter the Great; Leonardo da Vinci; Cleopatra; Rumpelstilskin's Daughter; Saving Sweetness.*

Thomas, Velma Maia. *Lest We Forget: The Passage from Africa to Slavery and Emancipation.*

Tsuchiyz, Yukio. *Faithful Elephants.*

Van Allsburg, Chris. *The Mysteries of Harris Burdick.*

Weitzman, Jacqueline Preiss. *You Can't Take a Balloon into the Metropolitan Museum.*

Wiesner, David. *Three Little Pigs.*

Wild, Margaret. *Let the Celebrations Begin.*

Poem for Tea Party

GRANDMOTHER GRACE

I didn't give her a good-bye kiss
as I went off in the bus for the last time,
away from her house in Williamsburg, Iowa,
away from her empty house with Jesus
on all of the walls, with clawfoot tub and sink
with the angular rooms that trapped all my summers.

I remember going there every summer—
every day beginning with that lavender kiss,
that face sprayed and powdered at the upstairs sink,
then mornings of fragile teacups and old times,
afternoons of spit-moistened hankies and Jesus,
keeping me clean in Williamsburg, Iowa.

Cast off, abandoned, in Williamsburg, Iowa,
I sat in that angular house with summer
dragging me onward, hearing how Jesus
loved Judas despite his last kiss,
how he turned his other cheek time after time,
how God wouldn't let the good person sink.

Months later, at Christmas, my heart would sink
when that flowery letter from Williamsburg, Iowa,
arrived, insistent, always on time,
stiff and perfumed as summer.
She always sealed it with a kiss,
a taped-over dime, and the words of Jesus.

I could have done without the words of Jesus;
the dime was there to make the message sink
in, I thought; and the violet kiss,

quavering and frail, all the way from Williamsburg, Iowa,
sealed some agreement we had for the next summer
as certain and relentless as time.

I didn't know this would be the last time.
If I had, I might even have prayed to Jesus
to let me see her once again next summer.
But how could I know she would sink,
her feet fat boats of cancer, in Williamsburg, Iowa,
alone, forsaken, without my last kiss?

I was ten, Jesus, and the idea of a kiss
at that time made my young stomach sink.
Let it be summer. Let it be Williamsburg, Iowa.

—Ronald Wallace

References

Adams, D., and Cerqui, C. (1989). *Effective Vocabulary Instruction.* Kirkland, WA: Reading Resources.

Adams, M. J. (1990). *Beginning to Read.* Cambridge, MA: Harvard University Press.

Allen, J. (1999). *Words Words Words: Teaching Vocabulary in Grades 4–12.* York, ME: Stenhouse.

Allen, J. (2000). *Yellow Brick Roads: Shared and Guided Paths to Independent Reading.* York, ME: Stenhouse.

Allington, R. L. (2001). *What Really Matters for Struggling Readers: Designing Research-Based Programs.* New York, NY: Addison Wesley Longman.

Anders, P. L., and Levine, N. S. (1990). "Accomplishing Change in Reading Programs." In G. G. Duffy (ed.), *Reading in the Middle School* (pp. 157–170). Newark, DE: International Reading Association.

Anderson, R. C., and Freebody, P. (1981). "Vocabulary Knowledge." In J. T. Guthrie (ed.), *Comprehension and Teaching: Research Reviews* (pp. 77–117). Newark, DE: International Reading Association.

Anderson, R., Heibert, E., Scott, J., and Wilkinson, I. (1985). *Becoming a Nation of Readers: The Report of the Commission on Reading.* Champaign-Urbana, IL: Center for the Study of Reading.

Atwell, N. (1998). *In the Middle,* 2d edition. Portsmouth, NH: Boynton/Cook.

Baker, S. K., Simmons, D. C., and Kameenui, E. J. (1995). "Vocabulary Acquisition: Curricular and Instructional Implications for Diverse Learners" (Technical Report No. 13). Eugene, OR: University of Oregon, National Center to Improve the Tools for Educators.

Bannon, E., Fisher, P. J. L., Pozzi, L., and Wessel, D. (1990). "Effective Definitions for Word Learning." *Journal of Reading,* 34, pp. 301–302.

Baroody, W. (1984). Foreword. In N. Thimmesch (ed.), "Aliteracy: People Who Can But Won't." A conference sponsored by the American Enterprise Institute for Public Policy Research, Washington, D.C. (ERIC Document Reproduction Service No. ED 240 543.)

Barr, R. Blachowicz, C., Katz, C., and Kaufman, B. (2001). *Reading Diagnosis for Teachers: An Instructional Approach.* Boston, MA: Allyn and Bacon.

Baumann, J. F., and Kameenui, E. J. (1991). "Research on Vocabulary Instruction: Ode to Voltaire." In J. Flood, J. M. Jensen, D. Lapp, and J. R. Squire (eds.), *Handbook on Teaching the English Language Arts* (pp. 604–632). Newark, DE, and Urbana, IL: International Reading Association and the National Council of Teachers of English.

Bear, D., Invernizzi, M., Johnston, F., and Templeton, S. (2000). *Words Their Way: Word Study for Phonics, Vocabulary, and Spelling Instruction,* 2d edition. Englewood Cliffs, NJ: Prentice-Hall.

Beck, I. L., Perfetti, C. A., and McKeown, M. G. (1982). "Effects of Long-Term Vocabulary Instruction on Lexical Access and Reading Comprehension." *Journal of Educational Psychology,* 74, pp. 506–521.

Becker, W., Dixon, R. C., and Inman-Anderson, L. (1980). *Morphographic and Root Word Analysis of 26,000 High-Frequency Words.* Eugene, OR: College of Education, University of Oregon.

Beers, J. (1980). "Developmental Strategies of Spelling Competence in Primary School Children." In E. H. Henderson and J. W. Beers (eds.), *Cognitive and Developmental Aspects of Learning to Spell: A Reflection of Word Knowledge.* Newark, DE: International Reading Association.

Beers, J., and Henderson, E. (1977). "A Study of Developing Orthographic Concepts Among First Graders." *Research in the Teaching of English,* 2, pp. 133–148.

Beers, K. (1990). "Choosing Not to Read: An Ethnographic Study of Seventh-Grade Aliterate Students." Unpublished doctoral dissertation, University of Houston.

Beers, K. (1996a). "No Time! No Interest! No Way! The Three Voices of Aliteracy, Part I." *School Library Journal,* 42(2), pp. 30–33.

Beers, K. (1996b). "No Time! No Interest! No Way! The Three Voices of Aliteracy, Part II." *School Library Journal,* 42(3), pp. 110–113.

Beers, K. (1999). "Literature: Our Way In." *Voices from the Middle,* 7(1), pp. 9–15.

Beers, K. (2001). *Reading Strategies Handbook*. Austin, TX: Holt, Rinehart and Winston.

Beers, K., and Probst, R. (1998). "Classroom Talk About Literature: The Social Dimensions of a Solitary Act." *Voices from the Middle,* 5(2), pp. 16–20.

Blachowicz, C. L. Z. (1986). "Making Connections: Alternatives to the Vocabulary Notebook." *Journal of Reading,* 20, pp. 643–649.

Blachowicz, C. L. Z. (1987). "Vocabulary Instruction: What Goes on in the Classroom?" *Reading Teacher,* 41, pp. 132–137.

Blachowicz, C. L. Z., and Fisher, P. (2000). "Vocabulary Instruction." In M. L. Kamil, P. B. Mosenthal, P. D. Pearson, and R. Barr (eds.), *Handbook of Reading Research* (Vol. 3, pp. 503–524). White Plains, NY: Longman.

Blau, S. (1992). "The Writing Process and the Teaching of Literature." Keynote address given at the annual meeting of the Greater Dallas Council of Teachers of English, February 15, Fort Worth, TX.

Bleich, D. (1975). *Reading and Feelings: An Introduction to Subjective Criticism*. Urbana, IL: National Council of Teachers of English.

Blevins, W. (2001). *Teaching Phonics and Word Study in the Intermediate Grades*. New York: Scholastic.

Brown, H., and Cambourne, B. (1990). *Read and Retell*. Portsmouth, NH: Heinemann.

Brown, R., Pressley, M., Van Meter, P., and Schuder, T. (1996). "A Quasi-Experimental Validation of Transactional Strategies Instruction with Low-Achieving Second Grade Readers." *Journal of Educational Psychology,* 88, pp. 18–37.

Brown, R., and Coy-Ogan, L. (1993). "The Evolution of Transactional Strategies Instruction in One Teacher's Classroom." *Elementary School Journal,* 94, pp. 221–233.

Carlsen, G. R. (1954). "Deep Down Beneath, Where I Live." *English Journal,* 43(5), pp. 235–239.

Carroll, J. B., Davies, P., and Richman, B. (1971). *Word Frequency Book*. Boston, MA: Houghton Mifflin.

Carroll, L. (1961 reprint, originally published in 1865). *Alice in Wonderland*. New York, NY: Holt, Rinehart and Winston.

Carter, B., and Abrahamson, R. (1990). *Nonfiction for Young Adults: From Delight to Wisdom*. Phoenix, AZ: Oryx Press.

Cazden, C. (1986). "Classroom Discourse." In M. Wittrock (ed.), *Handbook of Research on Teaching* (3d edition, pp. 432–462). New York, NY: Macmillan.

Chall, J. S., and Popp, H. (1996). *Teaching and Assessing Phonics: Why, What, When, How.* Cambridge, MA: Educators Publishing Service, Inc.

Clay, M. M., and Imlach, R. H. (1971). "Juncture, Pitch, and Stress as Reading Behavior Variables." *Journal of Verbal Learning and Verbal Behavior,* 10, pp. 133–139.

Clymer, T. (1963). "Utility of Phonics Generalizations in the Primary Grades." *The Reading Teacher,* 16, pp. 252–258.

Collins, C. (1991). "Reading Instruction That Increases Thinking Abilities." *Journal of Reading,* 34, pp. 510–516.

Collins, C., and Pressley, M. (2002). *Comprehension Instruction: Research-Based Best Practices.* New York, NY: The Guilford Press.

Cunningham, P. (1995). *Phonics They Use: Words for Reading and Writing.* New York, NY: HarperCollins.

Daniels, H. (2002). *Literature Circles: Voice and Choice in Book Clubs and Reading Groups.* York, ME: Stenhouse.

Davey, B. (1983). "Think-Aloud: Modeling the Cognitive Processes of Reading Comprehension." *Journal of Reading,* 27, pp. 44–47.

Decker, B. (1985). "Aliteracy: What Teachers Can Do to Keep Johnny Reading." Paper presented at the Southeastern Regional Conference of the International Reading Association, Nashville, TN. (ERIC Document Reproduction Service No ED 265 528.)

Dole, J., Brown, K., and Trathen, W. (1996). "The Effects of Strategy Instruction on the Comprehension Performance of At-Risk Students." *Reading Research Quarterly,* 31, pp. 62–89.

Duffy, G. (1991). "What Counts in Teacher Education? Dilemmas in Empowering Teachers." In J. Zutell and C. McCormick (eds.), *Learning Factors/Teacher Factors: Literacy Research and Instruction 40th Yearbook of the National Reading Conference* (pp. 1–18). Chicago, IL: National Reading Conference.

Duffy, G. (1992). "Let's Free Teachers to Be Inspired." *Phi Delta Kappan,* 73, pp. 442–446.

Duffy, G. (2002). "Direct Explanations of Strategies." In C. Block and M. Pressley (eds.), *Comprehension Instruction: Research-Based Best Practices* (pp. 28–41). New York, NY: The Guilford Press.

Durkin, D. (1993). *Teaching Them to Read,* 6th edition. Boston, MA: Allyn and Bacon.

Early, M. (1960). "Stages of Growth in Literary Appreciation." *English Journal,* 49(3), pp. 161–167.

Ehri, L. (1980). "The Development of Orthographic Images." In U. Frith (ed.), *Cognitive Process in Spelling* (pp. 311–338). New York, NY: Academic Press.

Ehri, L. (1997). "Learning to Read and Learning to Spell Are One and the Same, Almost." In C. Perfetti, L. Rieben, and M. Fayol (eds.), *Learning to Spell: Research Theory and Practice Across Languages* (pp. 237–269). Mahwah, NJ: Erlbaum.

Ehri, L., Nuves, S., Stahl, S., and Willows, D. (2001). "Systematic Phonics Instruction Helps Students to Read: Evidence from the National Reading Panel's Meta-Analysis." *Review of Education Research,* (71)3, pp. 393–447.

Ehri, L., and Stahn, S. (2001). "Beyond Smoke and Mirrors: Putting Out the Fire." *Phi Delta Kappan,* 83 (1), pp. 17–20.

Engelmann, S., and Bruner, E. (1995). *Reading Mastery I Presentation Book A.* Worthington, OH: SRA, Macmillan/McGraw-Hill.

Feathers, K. (1993). *Infotext.* Portsmouth, NH: Heinemann Publishers.

Fischer, P. (1993). *The Sounds and Spelling Patterns of English: Phonics for Teachers and Parents.* Morrill, ME: Oxton House Publishers.

Fountas, I., and Pinnell, G. (1996). *Guided Reading: Good First Teaching for All Children.* Portsmouth, NH: Heinemann.

Fox, B. (1996). *Strategies for Word Identification: Phonics from a New Perspective.* Englewood Cliffs, NJ: Prentice Hall.

Fry, E. B., Kress, J., and Fountoukidis, D. L. (1993). *The Reading Teacher's Book of Lists,* 3d edition. Englewood Cliffs, NJ: Prentice Hall.

Galda, L. (1988). "A Response-Based View of Literature in the Classroom." *The New Advocate,* 1(2), pp. 92–102.

Ganske, K. (2000). *Word Journeys: Assessment-Guided Phonics, Spelling, and Vocabulary Instruction.* New York, NY: The Guilford Press.

Garan, E. (2001a). "Beyond Smoke and Mirrors: A Critique of the National Reading Panel Report on Phonics." *Phi Delta Kappan,* 82(7), pp. 500–506.

Garan, E. (2001b). "More Smoking Guns: A Response to Linnea Ehri and Steven Stahl." *Phi Delta Kappan,* 83(1), pp. 21–24.

Garan, E. (2001c). "What Does the Report of the National Reading Panel Really Tell Us About Teaching Phonics?" *Language Arts,* 79(1), pp. 61–70.

Gaskins, I., and Elliot, T. T. (1991). *The Benchmark Model for Teaching Thinking Strategies: A Manual for Teachers.* Cambridge, MA: Brookline Books.

Gough, P. B., and Tunmer, W. E. (1986). "Decoding, Reading, and Reading Disability." *Remedial and Special Education,* 7, pp. 6–10.

Harris, A. J., and Sipay, E. R. (1990). *How to Increase Reading Ability: A Guide to Developmental and Remedial Methods,* 8th edition. White Plains, NY: Longman.

Harste, J. C., Short, K. C., and Burke, C. (1988). *Creating Classrooms for Authors: The Reading-Writing Connection.* Portsmouth, NH: Heinemann Publishers.

Hart, B., and Risley, T. (1996). *Meaningful Differences in the Everyday Experience of Young American Children.* Baltimore, MD: Brookes Publishing.

Harvey, S., and Goudvis, A. (2000). *Strategies That Work: Teaching Comprehension to Enhance Understanding.* York, ME: Stenhouse Publishers.

Hayes, D., and Athens, M. (1988). "Vocabulary Simplification for Children: A Special Case for 'Motherese.'" *Journal of Child Language,* 15, pp. 395–410.

Henderson, E. (1990). *Teaching Spelling,* revised edition. Boston, MA: Houghton Mifflin.

Hill, P. (1998). "Reaching Struggling Readers." In K. Beers and B. Samuels (eds.), *Into Focus: Understanding and Creating Middle School Readers* (pp. 81–104). Norwood, MA: Christopher-Gordon.

Hipple, T., editor. (1996). *Writers for Young Adults.* New York, NY: Charles Scribner's Sons.

Huey, E. (1908). *The Psychology and Pedagogy of Reading.* New York, NY: Macmillan.

Hughes, M., and Searle, D. (1997). *The Violent E and Other Tricky Sounds.* York, ME: Stenhouse.

Invernizzi, M. A. (1992). "The Vowel and What Follows: A Phonological Frame of Orthographic Analysis." In S. Templeton and D. Bear (eds.), *Development of Orthographic Knowledge and the Foundations of Literacy* (pp. 105–136). Hillsdale, NJ: Erlbaum.

Johns, J. L. (1980). "First Graders' Concepts About Print." *Reading Research Quarterly,* 15.

Juel, C. (1988). "Learning to Read and Write: A Longitudinal Study of Fifty-Four Children from First Through Fourth Grade." *Journal of Educational Psychology,* 80, pp. 437–447.

Keene, E. O., and Zimmermann, S. (1997). *Mosaic of Thought: Teaching Comprehension in a Reader's Workshop.* Portsmouth, NH: Heinemann.

LaBerge, D., and Samuels, S. J. (1974). "Toward a Theory of Automatic Information Processing in Reading." *Cognitive Psychology,* 6, pp. 293–323.

Langenberg, D. N., Correro, G., Ehri, L., Ferguson, G., Garza, N., Kamil, M., Marret, C., Samuels, S., Shanahan, T., Shaywitz, S., Trabasso, T., Williams, J., Willows, D., and Yatvin, J. (2000). "Report of the National Reading Panel: Teaching Children to Read." Washington, D.C.: National Institute of Health, National Institute of Child Health and Human Development.

Lesesne, T. (1998). "Reading Aloud to Build Success in Reading." In K. Beers and B. Samuels (eds.), *Into Focus: Understanding and Creating Middle School Readers* (pp. 245–260). Norwood, MA: Christopher-Gordon.

Livaudais, M. (1985). "A Survey of Secondary Students' Attitudes Toward Reading Motivational Activities." Unpublished doctoral dissertation, University of Houston.

MacOn, J., Bewell, D., and Vogt, M. (1991). *Responses to Literature.* Newark, DE: International Reading Association.

Martinez, M., and Roser, N. (1985). "Read It Again: The Value of Repeated Readings During Storytime." *The Reading Teacher,* 38, pp. 782–786.

McKeown, M. G., Beck, I. L., Omanson, R. C., and Perfetti, C. A. (1983). "The Effects of Long-Term Vocabulary Instruction on Reading Comprehension: A Replication." *Journal of Reading Behavior,* 15(1), pp. 3–18.

McKeown, M. G., Beck, I. L., Omanson, R. C., and Pople, M. T. (1985). "Some Effects of the Nature and Frequency of Vocabulary Instruction on the Knowledge and Use of Words." *Reading Research Quarterly,* 20, pp. 522–535.

Metsala, J., and Ehri, L. (eds.). (1998). *Word Recognition in Beginning Reading.* Mahwah, NJ: Erlbaum.

Mikulecky, L. (1978, May). "Aliteracy and a Changing View of Reading Goals." Paper presented at the annual meeting of the International Reading Association, Houston, TX. (ERIC Document Reproduction Service No. ED 157 052.)

Moffett, J. (1968). *A Student-Centered Language Arts Curriculum, K–13.* Boston, MA: Houghton Mifflin.

Nagy, W. (1988). *Teaching Vocabulary to Improve Reading Comprehension.* Newark, DE: International Reading Association.

Nagy, W. E., Herman, P. A., and Anderson, R. C. (Winter, 1995). "Learning Words from Context." *Reading Research Quarterly,* 20, pp. 233–253.

Ogle, D. (1986). "K-W-L: A Teaching Model That Develops Active Reading of Expository Text." *The Reading Teacher,* 39, pp. 564–570.

Olshavsky, J. E. (1976–77). "Reading as Problem-Solving: An Investigation of Strategies." *Reading Research Quarterly,* 12, pp. 654–674.

Pilgreen, J., and Krashen, S. (1993). "Sustained Silent Reading with English as a Second Language High School Students: Impact on Reading Comprehension, Reading Frequency, and Reading Enjoyment." *School Library Media Quarterly,* 22, pp. 21–23.

Pressley, M. (2000). "What Should Comprehension Instruction Be the Instruction Of?" In M. L. Kamil, P. B. Mosenthal, P. D. Pearson, and R. Barr (eds.), *Handbook of Reading Research* (Vol. III, pp. 546–561). Mahwah, NJ: Erlbaum.

Pressley, M., El-Dinary P. B., Stein, S., Marks, M. B., and Brown, R. (1992). "Good Strategy Instruction Is Motivating and Interesting." In A. Renninger, S. Hidi, and A. Krapp (eds.), *The Role of Interest in Learning and Development* (pp. 333–358). Hillsdale, NJ: Erlbaum.

Probst, R. (1987). "Adolescent Literature and the English Curriculum." *English Journal,* 3, pp. 26–30.

Probst, R. (1988). *Response and Analysis: Teaching Literature in Junior and Senior High School.* Portsmouth, NH: Boynton/Cook.

Purves, A. C., Rogers, T., and Soter, A. O. (1990). *How Porcupines Make Love II: Teaching a Response-Centered Literature Curriculum.* New York, NY: Longman.

Raphael, T. (1982). "Question-Answering Strategies for Children." *The Reading Teacher,* 36, pp. 186–190.

Reed, C. (1971). "Pre-school Children's Knowledge of English Phonology." *Harvard Educational Review,* 41 (1), pp. 150–179.

Richards, J. (2002). "Taking the Guesswork Out of Spelling." *Voices from the Middle,* 9 (3), pp. 15–18.

Rosenblatt, L. M. (1938/1983). *Literature as Exploration.* New York, NY: Modern Language Association.

Rosenblatt, L. M. (1978). *The Reader, the Text, the Poem: The Transactional Theory of the Literary Work.* Carbondale, IL: Southern Illinois University Press.

Samuels, J. J. (1979). "The Method of Repeated Readings." *The Reading Teacher,* 32, pp. 403–408.

Samuels, J. J., Shermer, N., and Reinking, D. (1992). "Reading Fluency: Techniques for Making Decoding Automatic." In J. Samuels and A. Farstrup (eds.), *What Research Has to Say About Reading Instruction.* Newark, DE: International Reading Association.

Schlagal, R. (1989). "Constancy and Change in Spelling Development." *Reading Psychology,* 10(3), pp. 207–229.

Schoenbach, R., Greenleaf, C., Cziko, C., and Hurwitz, L. (1999). *Reading for Understanding: A Guide to Improving Reading in Middle and High School Classrooms.* San Francisco, CA: Jossey-Bass Inc., Publishers.

Shanahan, T. (2001). "Response to Elaine Garan." *Language Arts,* 79(1), pp. 70–71.

Sherrill, A., and Ley, T. (eds.). (1994). *Literature Is . . . : Collected Essays by G. Robert Carlsen.* Johnson City, TN: Sabre. p. 53.

Short, K., Harste, J., and Burke, C. (1996). *Creating Classrooms for Authors and Inquirers,* 2d edition. Portsmouth, NH: Heinemann Publishers.

Simmons, R. (2002). *Odd Girl Out: The Hidden Culture of Aggression in Girls.* New York, NY: Harcourt Brace.

Smith, D. D. (1979). "The Improvement of Children's Oral Reading Through the Use of Teacher Modeling." *Journal of Learning Disabilities,* 12, pp. 39–42.

Smith, F. (1988). *Understanding Reading: A Psycholinguistic Analysis of Reading and Learning to Read.* Hillsdale, NJ: Lawrence Erlbaum.

Snow, C. E., Burns, M. S., and Griffin, P. (1998). *Preventing Reading Difficulties in Young Children.* Washington, D.C.: National Academy Press.

Stahl, S. (1997). "Teaching Children with Reading Problems to Recognize Words." In L. Putnam (ed.), *Reading Son Language and Literacy: Essays in Honor of Jeanne S. Chall.* Cambridge, MA: Brookline Books.

Templeton, S. (1983). "Using the Spelling/Meaning Connection to Develop Word Knowledge in Older Students." *Journal of Reading,* 27, pp. 8–14.

Templeton, S. (2002). "Effective Spelling Instruction in the Middle Grades: It's a Lot More Than Memorization." *Voices from the Middle,* 9(3), pp. 8–14.

Tierney, R., and Cunningham, J. (1984). "Research on Teaching Reading Comprehension." In P. D. Pearson, R. Barr, M. Kamil, and P. Mosenthal (eds.), *Handbook of Reading Research* (pp. 609–656). New York, NY: Longman.

Tierney, R. J., Readence, J. E., and Dishner, E. K. (1995). *Reading Strategies and Practices: A Compendium,* 4th edition. Boston, MA: Allyn and Bacon.

Tovani, C. (2000). *I Read It But I Don't Get It.* York, ME: Stenhouse.

Trelease, J. (2001). *The Read-Aloud Handbook.* New York, NY: Penguin.

Wallis, J. (1998). "Strategies: What Connects Readers to Meaning." In K. Beers and B. J. Samuels (eds.), *Into Focus: Understanding and Creating Middle School Readers* (pp. 225–244). Norwood, MA: Christopher-Gordon Publishers.

Weaver, C. (1994). *Reading Process and Practice: From Socio-Psycholinguistics to Whole Language,* 2d edition. Portsmouth, NH: Heinemann Publishers.

Wiley, R., and Durrell, D. (1970). "Teaching Vowels Through Phonograms." *Elementary Education,* 47.

Wilhelm, J. (2001). *Improving Comprehension with Think-Aloud Strategies.* New York, NY: Scholastic Professional Books.

Wilhelm. J., Baker, T., and Dube, J. (2001). *Strategic Reading: Guiding Students to Lifelong Literacy.* Portsmouth, NH: Heinemann Publishers.

Wilson, R. M. (1981). "Anyway You Read It, Illiteracy Is a Problem." *Presstime,* 3(9), pp. 4–8.

Wood, K. (1984). "Probable Passages: A Writing Strategy." *The Reading Teacher,* 37, pp. 496–499.

Vacca, J., Vacca, R., and Gove, M. (2000). *Reading and Learning to Read,* 4th edition. New York, NY: Longman.

Vygotsky, L. (1934/1986). *Thought and Language,* translated by A. Kozulin. Cambridge, MA: Harvard University Press.

Acknowledgments

If I have seen farther,
It is by standing on the shoulders of giants.

—Isaac Newton

Until two years ago, my family and I lived within minutes of downtown Houston. We loved living in the heartbeat of one of the largest cities in the United States, and yet both Brad and I missed what we grew up with: the simpler life of a small town. Unwilling to leave our Houston ties yet wanting a different lifestyle, we sold our home, built a new one, and moved about thirty miles out of Houston to a much smaller community called The Woodlands. Though we've now become part of the commuting masses, we love our new surroundings and marvel at this place we now call home. The name fits the location, as homes and shops are hidden behind 75-foot pines, 60-foot red oaks, and 45-foot cypress. You'd better love trees if you live in The Woodlands, for in this community they are protected with a fierceness that still astounds me.

Two roads take you into The Woodlands; each takes you past an amazing sculpture. One is a group of life-sized deer that appear to be running out from the trees, jumping up and over the tall pampas grass that grows between the trees and the road's edge. The first time you see this dozen or so deer you'll almost stop, sure that Bambi and family are about to run into the street. The other sculpture is a larger-than-life man holding a laughing child on his shoulders. The child has his arms flung high above his head, laughing at a moment that only the two of them share. At the base of that sculpture are words that I read every time I pass by it, the same words that open this acknowledgment: "If I have seen farther, it is by standing on the shoulders of giants."

With much admiration, I now acknowledge those giants who have helped me see farther than I ever thought possible. Without their guidance, I fear how diminished my teaching, and at times, my life, would have been. To each of them who I am about to name, my thanks for offering strong shoulders time and time again.

To begin, I must thank the students who appear on the pages of this book. Their willingness to talk with me, to share their concerns, their questions, their fears, and their hopes always impressed me. Their powerful words are the strength of this book. Their honesty, tenacity, and humor offer lessons for us all.

Likewise, I want to thank the many teachers from across this country who have shared their classrooms with me, let me teach their students, tried strategies I have suggested, and provided detailed comments on what worked and what didn't. In particular, many of the teachers at Lanier Middle School in the Houston Independent School District have been a part of my professional life for more than three years. As we've worked together, their conversations, questions, comments, suggestions, and insights have directed my thinking in more ways than they've ever imagined. I owe tremendous thanks to each of them: Kenan Rote, Ann Crowley, Linda Cooper, Jenny Freytag, LeeAnn Dilabio, Tracy Thibodeaux, Mary Ellen Wolf, Betty Fotinberry, and Amy Taylor. Additionally, teachers in the Aldine Independent School District (Aldine, Texas), Katy Independent School District (Katy, Texas), as well as participants of the South Carolina Summer Reading Institute and the South Coast Writing Project at the University of California Santa Barbara have been a part of multiple-year projects that have allowed me to work with them and to visit their districts and schools repeatedly. These dedicated teachers generously shared their time and expertise with me. Finally, I'm very grateful to some special teachers who offered valuable comments and suggestions about working with struggling readers: Sandy Robertson, Mary Santerre, Shawn Bird, and Kenan Rote. Each of these teachers shared his or her expertise with me not only during the school day but also during late-night phone calls, summer retreats, and weekend meetings.

A special thanks to colleagues across the country who have influenced my thinking and volunteered to read and critique parts of this manuscript: Richard Abrahamson, Hal Foster, Robert Probst, Deborah Appleman, and Margaret Hill.

Dick Abrahamson not only offered very helpful comments about key parts of the manuscript, but he introduced me to the work of Margaret Early, Robert Carlson, Louise Rosenblatt, and Robert Probst more than fifteen years ago. He said he wanted us, his graduate students, to read the scholarly works of the giants in young adult literature. In short time, we realized that we were studying with a giant. He has been both mentor and friend; for both I am very grateful.

Robert Probst and Hal Foster have shared their time with me generously over the past several years. We've talk again (and again) about ways to connect reluctant and struggling readers to literature. Bob's seminal work in literary response and analysis has shaped much of my thinking; Hal's keen ability to contextualize conversations against the backdrop of the inner-city classroom kept me grounded in the practical.

Deb Appleman proved herself not only an incredible scholar but also a valued friend; she always seemed to know when it was time to say "enough talk about reading" and steer me into talking about something else. Even now, those "something else" conversations make me smile. Peggy Hill began many of our discussions this past year with, "But don't forget . . . ," as she'd remind me of yet another piece of research or tell me about another struggling reader. Her incredible memory for detail was very helpful at critical times this past year. Thanks to each of you for sharing your time and wisdom with me throughout this project.

Many conversations with Jeff Wilhelm, Harvey Daniels, Richard Vacca, Linda Rief, Cyndy Greenleaf, Christine Cziko, and Donald Graves have challenged my understanding about reading, writing, and teaching. All of these people, through their books, their workshops, and the time they freely shared with me, have influenced what I understand about how children learn. Each has contributed significantly to the national conversations about reading, writing, and learning. They have proven themselves to be giants in education, willing to help us all see more.

I owe a special word of thanks to Teri Lesesne. I so appreciate how generously she shared her knowledge of children's and young adult literature with me as we debated books for the booklists. Her willingness to help me create the booklists for this book went far beyond the bounds of friendship.

Without the support of colleagues at the University of Houston, this book would still be a thought. In particular, Linda Ellis co-taught a class with me during the spring semester so I could disappear in March and April and do nothing but write; Will Weber, then the department chair, understood when I needed to miss yet another meeting; Richard Abrahamson answered my doctoral students' questions as they attempted to avoid interrupting me, though he doesn't even know I know he did that. Thanks, Dick. Two of my students at UH, Jeanette Choy and Erica Quintella, added my request that they help me with the booklists for this book to their already demanding schedules. My thanks to both of them for their thorough work.

Most special thanks must be given to Carol Schanche, the production editor for the NCTE journal *Voices from the Middle*. Carol helped me juggle being editor of that national journal while I was writing this book. In the short two years we've worked together on *Voices from the Middle*, I've come to value not only her keen writing and editing ability but also her incredible sense of humor. In more ways than I care to recount, Carol got me through this book. She spent her time at home after work reviewing many of the chapters, offering suggestions, asking questions, pointing out parts that needed more attention. Thank you, Carol, for all your work on this project.

From the beginning, people at Heinemann Publishers embraced this book with a passion. Lisa Luedeke, my editor for this project, provided valuable support. She somehow knew when to leave me alone and when to not to. Lisa's careful reading and keen questions made the manuscript better. Lisa Fowler talked with me extensively about the cover and text design, always cheerful even when my response was "No, that's not quite it." Lesa Scott flew to Houston to have dinner with me to talk about this book as it began. I'll never forget her willingness to share her time with me that night. Her interest in the book underscored the commitment from others at Heinemann. All the others—Leigh Peake, Deb Burns, Susie Stroud, Abby Heim, Lynne Reed, and Eric Chalek—believed in this book long before it even began to look like a book. My heartfelt thanks to each of these folks.

Two specific children should be thanked for their contributions to this book: Baker, my eleven-year-old, and Meredith, my seventeen-year-old. Though some Baker and Meredith stories appear on these pages, those stories are not the contributions I have in mind. Their contribution to this project came in the form of their constant encouragement, the countless cups of coffee they brought to me, their understanding that dinnertime conversations were most likely going to focus on some sentence that I did or did not like, and their absolute faith that this book was important enough to keep mom busy "just one more minute." I adore these children and thank them for all they bring to my life.

Finally, I thank Brad, my husband. If I've ever accomplished anything at all, it's been with his assistance, encouragement, and guidance. If Newton had had Brad's shoulders to stand upon, there's no telling how far he would have seen.

Index

lack of, 259–60
power of, 258–60
reading problems and, 17–18
smart words, giving students, 276
social, building, 276, 277
SSR, providing time for, 196, 276, 278
using appropriate literature, 275
value of, 258–60
Conflicts, reluctant readers and easily defined, 288
Conford, Ellen, 286
Confusing words, 343–45
Connell, Richard, 160
Consonant blends, defined, 225–26, 228–29
Consonants
common syllables, teaching, 232–33, 339
defined, 225
Consonant teams, defined, 225
Constructing meaning. *See* During-reading strategies
Content, comprehension strategies and, 47–48
Context clues, learning words with, 183–87, 230–31
Contrast clues, 187
Contrasting and comparing with ABC boxes, 132–33
Cormier, Robert, 142, 282
Correcting, prompting versus, 217–18
Cumulative Tale Structure, 163
Curtis, Christopher Paul, 140, 296
Cziko, Christine, 300

D
"Daily," 114
Daniels, Harvey, 276
Danziger, Paula, 286
Death of a Salesman, 178
Decoding
automaticity and, 205–8
in comprehension, 13

defined, 223
problems in sample student profiles, 29–31
through prompting, 217–18
"Deep Down Beneath, Where I Live," 275
Definition clues, 186
Dependent readers, 15–16. *See also* Non-readers; Struggling readers
behaviors, dependent reading, 24–28
characteristics of, 17–18
defining "non-reader," 23–24
instructional beliefs and, 36–39
miscue analysis of, 211
moving, toward independent reading, 16–21
thinking like, 282–83
types, 17–18
Dependent readers, assessing needs of, 23–39
behaviors, dependent reading, 24–28
defining "non-reader," 23–24
If-Then chart, 27–28
sample student profiles, 29–34
Derivational constancy stage of spelling development, 248
Diary of Anne Frank, The, 32, 77, 256
Digraphs, 225, 226
Diphthongs, 225
Direct instruction, 44, 45
comprehension strategies, direct teaching of (*see* Comprehension)
Diversity in class, celebrating, 265–66
Dolch Basic Sight Vocabulary, 212–13, 334
Dorling Kindersley books, 288
Dormant readers, 279
Double-entry journals; as reading strategy, 127, 129
Dube, Julie, 105

Dunn, Stephen, 114
During-reading strategies, 102–37
ABC boxes, comparing and contrasting with, 132–33
bookmarks, 130–32, 309–14
character bulletin boards, 134
classroom talk during reading, 104–5
classroom teaching, examples of, 103–4, 105–6, 111–13, 119–22
double-entry journals, 127, 129
figuring it out as reading, 102–4, 113
logographic cues, 129–30
making reading make sense, 102–4, 113
Post-it Notes, 133–34
rereading, 110–19
Say Something, 105–10, 126–27
signal words, 136
Syntax Surgery, 135–36
Think-Aloud, 43, 119–27, 128, 307–8

E
Early, Margaret, 274
Echo reading, 215
Efferent stances toward reading, 269–73
"Eleven," 49
Embedded questions, 8–12, 22
Emergent stage of spelling development, 247
Emotional confidence, 17, 18
Encyclopedia Brown, 274
English Journal, 297
Esperanza Rising, 118
Even More Five-Minute Mysteries, 69
Expectations, maintaining high, 260–63
Explanation clues, 186
Explicit teaching of comprehension strategies. *See* Comprehension

Modeling *(continued)*
  scales, 143
  Somebody Wanted To But
    strategy, 149–51
  SSR, 199–200
  Think-Aloud, 123
Mora, Pat, 114
Mori, Kyoko, 282
Mosaic of Thought, 105
"Most Dangerous Game, The,"
  132, 160
Most Important Word, after-reading
  strategy, 173–75, 325
Mr. Tucket, 130
Mufaro's Beautiful Daughters, 78
My Antonia, 178
Myers, Walter Dean, 270, 282
Mysteries
  booklists, 358–59
  reluctant readers and, 286
Mystery Writers Organization, 298

N
Names, students knowing students',
  265
Napping House, The, 163
National Council of Teachers of
  English (NCTE), 62, 73, 183
  journals, 246, 297, 350
National Reading Panel
  Teaching Children to Read, 220–22
Native Son, 118
"Necklace, The," 144
Negative behavior, not tolerating,
  266–68
Nightjohn, 269
Nixon, Joan Lowry, 282
Nolen, Han, 282
Nonfiction
  booklists *(see* Booklists)
  features of, for reluctant readers,
    288–90
  SWBS with, 151
*Nonfiction for Young Adults: From
  Delight to Wisdom,* 296

Non-readers. *See also* Dependent
    readers; Struggling readers
  defining, 23–24
  thinking like, 282–83
*Norton Anthology of Short Stories,
  The,* 4
Notebooks, vocabulary, 178
Number the Stars, 152
Numeroff, Laura Joeffe, 162
Nye, Naomi Shihab, 114

O
Oats, Joyce Carol, 282
*Odd Girl Out: The Hidden Culture
  of Aggression in Girls,* 266
Oliver, Mary, 114
Oliver Twist, 178
One Bird, 282
One Fat Summer, 282
Onsets, defined, 227, 334
Open Court, 44
Oral reading
  cognitive benefits of, 196–200
  hearing fluent reading, strategies
    for, 215–16
  measuring fluency through oral
    reading rates, 208–11
  motivational benefits of, 290–91
  vocabulary instruction through,
    196–200
Oral thinking, 119
Othello, 282
Out of the Dust, 269, 282

P
Parent-teacher conferences, 4–5
Parrot in the Oven, 282
Participation, encouraging risk,
  263–68
Passive reading, dependent readers
  and, 73–74
Paterson, Katherine, 153
Paulsen, Gary, 130, 269, 286
Perona, Sue, 95
Personal response to text, 270, 271

Philbrick, Rodman, 149
Phonemes, defined, 224
Phonics, 59
  defined, 223–24, 230
  generalizations, common
    phonics, 335–38
  for middle and high school
    dependent readers, 221,
    242–43
  in National Reading Panel
    report, 220–22
  politics and, 220
  scripted programs, 44
  and word recognition, 221–22,
    230–31, 335–38
Phrasing, teaching, 216
Picture book format (list), stories
  told in, 365–66
Pigman, The, 137
Pilkey, Dav, 286
Plots
  reflection about plot,
    encouraging, 270–71
  reluctant readers and, 286
Poe, Edgar Allen, 114
Poetry, booklists, 359–60
Point of view, encouraging
  reflection about, 273
*Polar Bear, Polar Bear, What Do You
  Hear?,* 163
Post-it Notes, as reading strategy,
  133–34
Predicting, 45, 52
  Probable Passage prereading
    strategy, 87–94
  Tea Party prereading strategy,
    94–101
Prefixes
  common, 316
  teaching, 188, 241
Prereading strategies, 73–101
  anticipation guides, 74–80
  classroom teaching, examples of,
    75–77, 80–83, 84–85,
    88–91, 95–98

Words *(continued)*
sight, improving fluency through, 212–15
smart words, giving students, 276
vocabulary, teaching (*see* Vocabulary instruction)
Words Across Contexts activity, 191–92, 324
word study versus word memorization, 179–83

Words, Words, Words, 179, 193
Words Across Contexts activity, 191–92, 324
Words by Heart, 282
Words in Context, 193
Word sorts, spelling instruction with, 251–54, 340–42
Word Splash, 94
Words Their Way, 246
Word walls, 213–14, 255

Workshop approach, explicit teaching of strategies and, 58–59
Worthy, Jo, 300
Writers for Young Adults, 296
Wuthering Heights, 178

Z
Zero tolerance of disrespect, 266–68
Zimmerman, Susan, 105, 300